◆ NOBILITY LOST

NOBILITY LOST

FRENCH AND CANADIAN MARTIAL
CULTURES, INDIANS, AND
THE END OF NEW FRANCE

CHRISTIAN AYNE CROUCH

CORNELL UNIVERSITY PRESS
Ithaca and London

Copyright © 2014 by Cornell University

All rights reserved. Except for brief quotations in a review, this book, or parts thereof, must not be reproduced in any form without permission in writing from the publisher. For information, address Cornell University Press, Sage House, 512 East State Street, Ithaca, New York 14850.

First published 2014 by Cornell University Press
Printed in the United States of America

Library of Congress Cataloging-in-Publication Data

Crouch, Christian Ayne, 1977– author.
    Nobility lost : French and Canadian martial cultures, Indians, and the end of New France / Christian Ayne Crouch.
        pages cm
    Includes bibliographical references and index.
    ISBN 978-0-8014-5244-4 (cloth : alk. paper)
  1. Seven Years' War, 1756–1763—Campaigns—New France. 2. Anglo-French War, 1755–1763.
3. Canada—History—1755-1763. 4. France—History—Louis XV, 1715–1774. 5. Indians of North America—Wars—1750–1815. 6. War and society—New France—History—18th century. 7. War and society—France—History—18th century. I. Title.

    F1030.9.C76 2014
    940.2'534—dc23

                                              2013034197

Cloth printing   10 9 8 7 6 5 4 3 2 1

ISBN 978-1-5017-7897-1 (pbk.)

For Mom and Ababa

Contents

Acknowledgments ix

Introduction: Glory beyond the Water 1

1. Onontio's War, Louis XV's Peace 16
2. Interpreting Landscapes of Violence 38
3. Culture Wars in the Woods 65
4. Assigning a Value to Valor 95
5. The Losing Face of France 126
6. Paradise 153

Epilogue: *Mon Frère Sauvage* 178

Notes 191
Index 243

Acknowledgments

Writing a book can be excruciating but it is a pleasure to write acknowledgments. It is here that I can state clearly how fortunate I am to be part of a supportive and wonderful community and what I owe all these individuals, as well as many others who are here unmentioned, but to whom I also give thanks.

My greatest intellectual debt goes to my graduate advisor at New York University, Karen Ordahl Kupperman. She is both the most impressive and the most generous historian I have ever met. There is no way to better express what her support over these many years has meant to me other than to say, once more, that she is the historian I will always strive to be. I also wish to recognize the contributions made by each member of my dissertation committee, Lauren Benton, Manu Goswami, Walter Johnson, and John Shovlin. Their continued critiques and advice, in many cases years after I completed my dissertation, helped me to turn rough research into a book. Under the early tutelage of Cristina Mirkow, William A. P. Childs, and Andrew Isenberg, I learned to love bringing the past to life.

Leaving the tight-knit community of graduate school is a daunting prospect and I have been lucky to find mentors and intellectual guides in the years after NYU. I owe a special debt of thanks to James Merrell, who generously read and commented on a large portion of this manuscript. Sophie Lemercier Goddard provided a wonderful French perspective; Wayne Lee always encouraged further cultural studies of war. At a Harvard International Seminar on the History of the Atlantic World, organized by Bernard Bailyn and Patricia Denault, Fred Anderson offered a reading of my working paper that completely transformed chapter 4 and set me off in a fresh, productive direction. I would never have come to see geography and landscape in new ways had it not been for the work being done by Christine DeLucia and Cynthia Radding, who always made the time for great conversations.

Research is the lifeblood of the historian and I am immensely grateful to the institutions that have provided me with funds, access to their rich archives and resources, and have nurtured a welcoming community of librarians and scholars. The John Carter Brown Library, the William L. Clements Library, the Massachusetts Historical Society, and the Newberry Library offered both generous grants and essential workspaces; I owe the men and women at these institutions a great debt. Special thanks to Susan Danforth, Kimberly Nusco, Brian Dunnigan, Clayton Lewis, and Conrad Wright for going above and beyond the call of duty. The New York Public Library's Jay Barksdale oversees the Wertheim Study where I completed many of these revisions and kindly let me keep coming back. Andrew Lee provided essential research aid at Bobst Library when I was at NYU and then continued to do so for the duration of this work. The staff at the Library of Congress, the Archives nationales de France (Paris and Aix-en-Provence), the Archives départementales d'Indre-et-Loire, the Bibliothèque nationale de France, the Bibliothèque de l'Arsenal, and the Service Historique de la Défense helped in every way from arranging for document reproduction to seat reservations in the reading room on short notice. At Bard, the office of the Dean of the College provided invaluable aid in the continuation of my research at French archives and in securing image permissions. The librarians at Stevenson Library dealt with unceasing interlibrary loans and ConnectNY requests with tremendous grace. My colleagues in the Historical Studies program have given me a great intellectual home and the Bard History Colloquium was a wonderful place to present work in progress and keep me going. The interdisciplinarity of Bard College and its commitment to research excellence have made this a truly wonderful place to grow.

NYU's Atlantic History Workshop and the Columbia Seminar on Early American History have been wonderful intellectual forums from my time in graduate school onward and I thank all the participants of these seminars, faculty and graduate students alike, for their feedback on my work over the years and for fostering such convivial and thought-provoking spaces. Conferences cosponsored by the British Group in Early American History, the European Early American Studies Association, the French Atlantic History Group, the Harvard International Seminar on the History of the Atlantic World, the McNeil Center for Early American Studies, the Omohundro Institute for Early American istory and Culture, and the Society of Early Americanists, as well as sessions at individual archives and a workshop at the University of New Mexico's history department, offered many opportunities to test out ideas and I am grateful to the individuals at these forums for their suggestions and critiques over these years. Numerous friends and colleagues have been sounding boards for ideas and arguments informally as

ACKNOWLEDGMENTS

well at conferences, workshops, and working groups. Others made my continued revisions possible through the gift of their friendship and support. Thanks especially to: Jennifer Anderson, Zara Anishanslin, Ralph Bauer, Florian Becker, Lauren Benton, Christopher Bilodeau, Kristen Block, Ken Buhler, Kerry Bystrom, Cathleen Cahill, Nicole Caso, Maria Cecire, Noah Chasin, Greg Childs, Karoline Cook, Andrea Robertson Cremer, Robert Culp, Laurie Dahlberg, Christine DeLucia, Catherine Desbarats, Michèle Dominy, Alexandre Dubé, Robert Englebert, Nicole Eustace, Tabetha Ewing, Eliza Ferguson, Charlie Foy, François Furstenberg, Alison Games, Noah Gelfand, Sophie Lemercier Goddard, Evan Haefeli, Eric Hinderaker, Christopher Hodson, Karl Jacoby, Heather Kopelson, Michael Lacombe, Wayne Lee, Ann Little, Jean-François Lozier, Mark Lytle, Michael McDonnell, James Merrell, Susan Merriam, Kate Mulry, John Murrin, Cynthia Radding, Dina Ramadan, Daniel Richter, Gabriel Rocha, Jonathan Rosenberg, Marie-Jeanne Rossignol, Brett Rushforth, John Ryle, Geoffrey Sanborn, Andrew Sandoval-Strausz, Elena Schneider, Jenny Shaw, Anelise Shrout, Alice Stroup, William Tatum III, Frederika Teute, Eric Trudel, Samuel Truett, Thomas Truxes, Jerusha Westbury, Edward Widmer, Sophie White, and Marina van Zuylen. I also owe a special debt of gratitude to the incredible students I have had the privilege of teaching over the years at Bard, many of whom have encouraged and inspired me. Special thanks to Blake Grindon, Joshua Kopin, and Irina Rogova for reading and commenting on pieces of this work.

At Cornell University Press, I have been fortunate to work with Michael J. McGandy. His careful and unflinching readings of this entire manuscript have made me a better writer. He is everything I ever hoped for in an editor. Sarah Grossman kept everything running smoothly; Carol Hoke and Pamela Nelson were an expert copyediting and production team; Annelieke Vries-Baaijens is the talented mapmaker with whom it has been a pleasure to work. Two anonymous readers gave me valuable input on this manuscript; it is all the better for their suggestions.

A few individuals—Jenny Shaw, Sarah Cornell, and Karen Kupperman—have bravely read this manuscript repeatedly over the years and have given me invaluable advice, insights, suggestions, and questions that pushed me further. They are extraordinary thinkers and this book would never have been possible without their efforts. Lengthy conversations over archival finds, very incomplete works-in-progress, and the state of the field with Elena Schneider, Jenny Shaw, and with my fellow francophile and powerhouse on early modern France, Tabetha Ewing, have enriched my work. All have been amazing friends along this path. And a heartfelt *merci* goes to my *bonne fées*, Anne-Claire Faucquez, Élodie Peyrol, Audrey Bonnet, and Marion Godfroy-Tayart de Borms, my friends and scholars who gave me warm welcomes on numerous trips to France and provided invaluable research advice over the years.

I could never have done this without a lifetime of love, support, advice, and reality checks given to me without question or hesitation by my parents, Sarah and Miller Crouch. This book is for you both, the greatest independent scholars and bravest people I know. Three very special women, Dorothy Ruth Miller Crouch, Belainesh Bedilu, and Edna McNabney, gifted me with stamina and brought the past to life through their wonderful tales. Bill Crouch Jr. and Dorothy Ruth Crouch kept up a steady stream of history books and R&R breaks, respectively. Megan Mackenzie and Ben Dickman welcomed me into their Michigan home on very short notice. Mary Welch and Paden Reich have kept me standing longer than I can count. To all my family, you have helped me to see this through to conclusion and I could not have done it without you. My husband, Chris Bertholf, shuttled the infamous "Research," a hefty collection of papers stuffed into a noxiously red bag, for the better part of ten years around Manhattan, throughout Brooklyn, to Italy, Arizona, Kansas, and back, as well as to upstate New York more times than I can remember; thankfully, I finished writing *before* Iceland. When I needed a lifeline, he was there. When I needed a push, he became my coach. When I just wanted a hug, he gave me a hundred. I can only imagine the toll this type of work takes on the person who has to live with you—and I cannot thank him enough for sticking with me through it all and for believing in me, every step of the way.

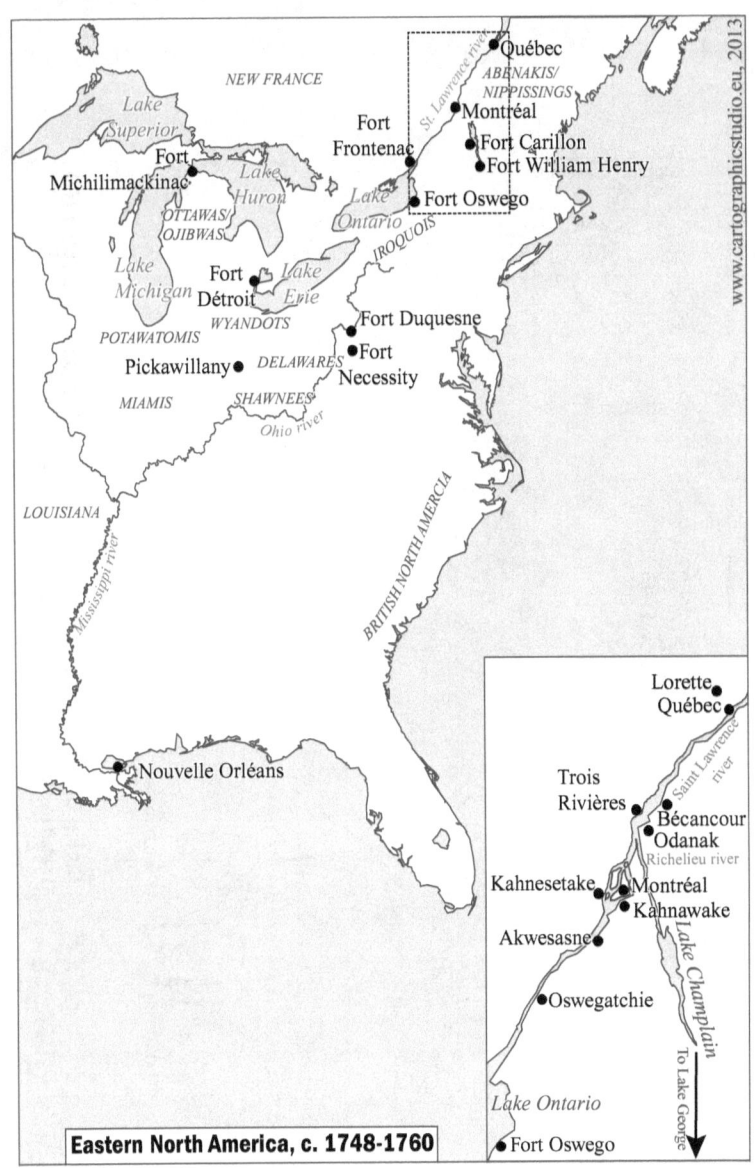

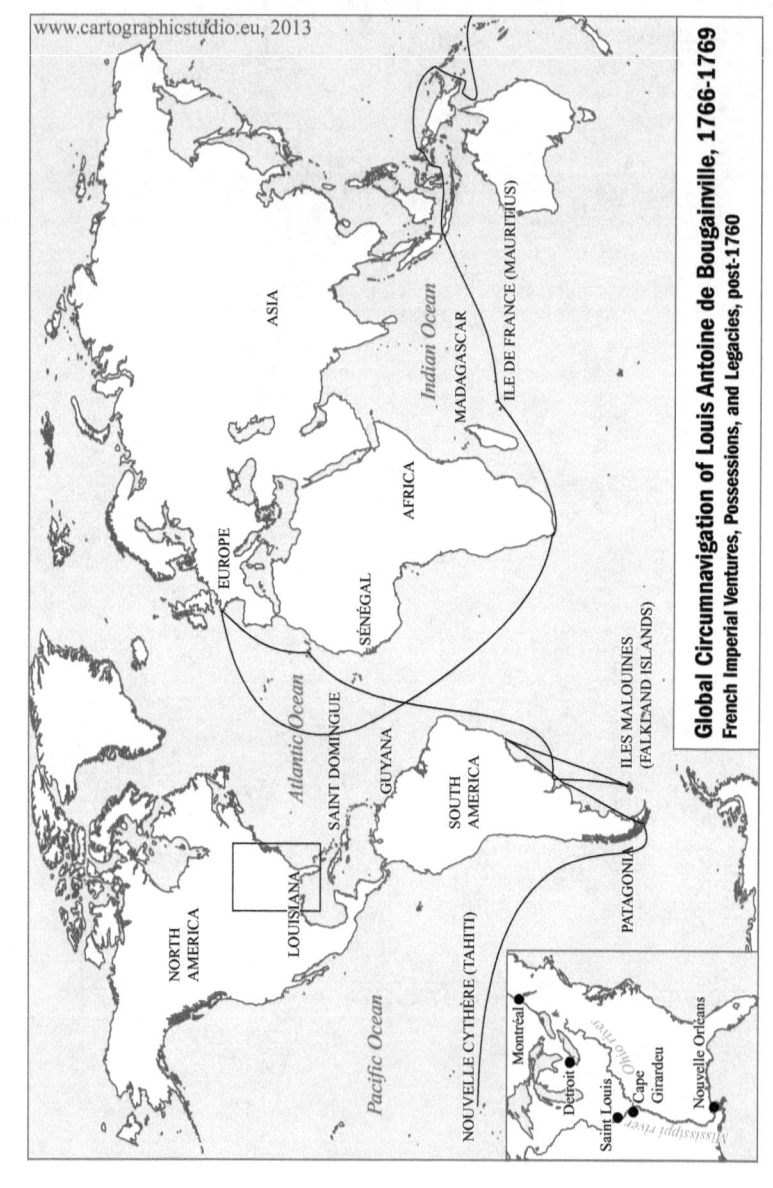

Introduction
Glory beyond the Water

> Rage—Goddess, sing of the rage of Peleus'
>   son Achilles,
> Murderous, doomed, that cost the Achaeans countless
>   losses,
> Hurling down to the House of Death so many sturdy
>   souls,
> Great fighters' souls, but made their bodies carrion,
> Feasts for the dogs and birds . . .
>
> —*Iliad*, I: 1–3

Clad in local and imported finery, a diverse crowd assembled at Montreal in 1756 to see, welcome, and interact with the newly arrived French army commanders in North America. After two years of unofficial war in the Ohio River Valley fought by New France (Canada), the river region's Native inhabitants, and Britain's colonies, troops from the metropole—mainland France—had finally arrived to assist in the conflict. The French regulars' canvas tents and white flags emblazoned with the royal gold fleur de lys began dotting some of the fields on the outskirts of Montreal; other pastoral spaces on the southern shores of the Saint Lawrence allowed large delegations of Native and colonial notables, with their retinues of clerks, warriors, and translators, to gather face to face for discussions and feasts. Smaller meetings could have been held in Montreal inside the private Ville-Marie homes of prominent marines, like the mansion of the Vaudreuil family, or in the longhouses of Native settlements found fifteen and thirty miles southwest of Montreal. For almost a month, both indigenous North American and European dignitaries and leaders listened to hours of speeches, punctuating their statements with purple and white wampum belts and strings, sitting on mats until their legs grew numb, due to the need to translate these words into several Native languages as well as French and possibly English. Gift exchanges and testaments of friendship opened the potential for alliances in the imminent war.

These formal introductions brought together the French leaders in North America, the army's new commander, Louis-Joseph de Saint Véran, Marquis de Montcalm-Gozon, who arrived in Montreal on May 22, and Pierre-Joseph, Marquis de Vaudreuil-Cavagnal, governor general of New France, along with prominent indigenous representatives visiting the city. Many interactions took place outdoors, allowing dozens of onlookers to quench their curiosity and to form their own impressions of the guests, new and old, North American and metropolitan French. Respected Indian matrons, Canadian and Indian children, hardened officers of the *troupes franches de la marine* (colonial regulars), the *troupes de terre* (French army), and New France's militia all mingled alongside distinguished Indian warriors, Catholic priests and nuns, elite colonial ladies, and the *habitants* of Montreal. Over the course of these few weeks, senior French officers would continue to meet their marine counterparts as well as valued Native allies: the Iroquois, Abenakis, Hurons, and Nipissings from the Saint Lawrence Valley *réserves* (mission communities) at Sault Saint-Louis (Kahnawake), Lac des Deux Montagnes (Kanesatake), Saint François (Odanak), and La Présentation (Oswegatchie), who lived closest to Montreal. As the summer wore on, more distant guests—the Ottawas, Ojibwas, and Menominees from the *pays d'en haut* (the Great Lakes region)—traveled the five hundred miles or more to Montreal to see these new French for themselves and participate in their own ceremonies of arrival.

Indians came and went at will during the councils, which began in the final week of May and continued well into the third week of June. These ceremonies of introduction presumed the North American habits of material diplomacy, involving wampum belts, feasts, pelts, and a few commodities that would stun the new French arrivals. Heading home after raiding in the vicinity of Saratoga, a group of Nipissings neared Montreal and learned of the arrival of their new French partners in war. As a gesture of goodwill and in a demonstration of their own protocol of politeness, the group traveled to pay their respects, meeting the Marquis de Montcalm on June 18. Machiqua, the Nipissing chief, commemorated the solemn occasion by presenting an English woman from a captured family to Montcalm. She was a grand gift and represented the affirmation of relationships between the allies. How fortuitous, the Nipissings may have thought, that they had procured an offering worthy of Montcalm's stated rank—a prize that honored both the French and the Nipissings' own cultural norms. The shocked French general discovered that, "so as not to displease these gentlemen, I had to accept their gift, give them the expected price [of the captive] of forty *écus* and provide an additional bonus, for having honored the general of His Majesty's troops with such an extravagant present."[1]

Like the living gift, the Indians' dress, body art, altered European clothes, and trade metal worked into fine jewelry made strong impressions on the recently arrived French army officers. But Native sartorial expression paled in comparison to their experiences with the councils themselves. The metropolitan army officers imagined that the colonial authorities summoned the Indians at will in Canada and dictated the terms of interaction. What they encountered in the diverse, autonomous encampments surrounding Montreal and later at the French forts throughout New France resembled the assemblage of the many Greek armies joining to attack Troy, as recounted in Homer's *Iliad*. Identical to the careful diplomacy required to bind those fractious, mythical Illyrian armies, the French officers discovered they, too, had to work hard to encourage cooperation. The war began with diplomacy and "nothing but visits, harangues, and deputations from these gentlemen," Montcalm wrote to his mother, and the French officers' onerous duty of having to return such favors, often by traveling to the Native centers at Kahnawake or Kanesatake.[2] Each nation had the right to speak, François Gaston de Lévis, the army's second-in-command, learned when Abenakis, Nipissings, and Mississaugas met with him to present the three strings of wampum as proof they would "do [Lévis's] will." At the end of that day's exchanges, Lévis gave these Native representatives a wampum belt made of two thousand beads and food enough for a feast.[3] His diary left no record of who counseled him to make his gift, and Lévis drew no parallels between these deputations and the formal French court presentations at Versailles or the ostentatious noble martial masculinity with which he and his colleagues were familiar, though the similarities in these performances of power to our modern eyes is inescapable. Although individual relationships remained critical to these Algonquians, an Indian agreement to "do his will" did not indicate medieval fealty in a European sense. Rather, it confirmed both parties to be equals undertaking a collaborative project of violence against a common British enemy.

The celebratory welcome of 1756 was intended to reinforce the accepted tenets of diplomacy and war that had been discussed for more than a century between Native peoples and the French domiciled in North America. The fluidity and repetition of councils signaled the continual nature of indigenous diplomacy and war preparations and revealed, though not to the new French arrivals, the strict protocols to which most Native peoples expected their counterparts to adhere. In the short term, and from the varying perspectives of the Indians, marines, and colonial officials, this goal seemed accomplished. The status of the French in North America rested on magnanimity and the maintenance (at French expense) of open spaces for trade and discussion—these ceremonies achieved just this.[4] The diverse participants came away believing that they were on the same side of the struggle to hold back British forces. In a moment of crisis for New France, Canadians and Indians alike expected that the resilience of inherited models of diplomacy and war in North America, now bolstered by reinforcements from the metropole, would again suffice. However, the transformation of a North American conflict into a transatlantic one and the insertion of French troops, elite officers, and modern French war making into North America changed everything.

This book explains the conflict between France and New France by exploring the meanings of violence and empire during the 1750s. It offers new insights into the French imperial experience and the legacy of the Seven Years' War. At the heart of my narrative are the events that informed and followed the multiple meetings from May through June 1756, events that reveal the profound ramifications of the encounter between the Canadian, Indian, and French cultures of war. The struggle to defend New France from British expansion between 1756 and 1760 challenged and reshaped metropolitan French ideas about what methods were legitimate in defense of the empire's borders and eventually raised queries about the meaning of empire altogether. Elite soldiers in both North America and Europe engaged in the traditional martial business of French aristocrats in order to defend the monarch's honor and claims. All of these officers understood themselves to be working on behalf of France but discovered over time that they defined their actions from radically different perspectives. Ultimately, their interpretations clashed in such a way as to render impossible the continuation of the colonial project in New France. When the 1763 Treaty of Paris restored sugar-rich Guadeloupe and Martinique to France in exchange for New France's cession to Britain, the terms appeared to confirm Voltaire's 1759 description of New France in *Candide* as the little valued "few meters of snow." I argue that the causes of this cession require an investigation beyond Voltaire's pithy but poorly informed opinion because the decision to forgo France's extensive territorial claims in North America went hand in hand with a reevaluation of the purpose of the empire and a decision to alter metropolitan expectations of the French Atlantic world. Carefully considering the broad picture of both war and loss through this study exposes the transformative nature of this mid-eighteenth-century conflict.[5]

In this book I offer a fresh look at the French Seven Years' War by juxtaposing the experiences of the remarkably diverse individuals who fought in it and by examining the elite combatants' perceptions of it. The Seven Years' War overturned centuries of tradition by canceling the "no peace beyond the line" premise, which had governed European attitudes toward the Americas. Interpreting the western Atlantic as a place of permanent potential conflict, where Europeans could not exert complete control, monarchies and republics implicitly agreed to the principle that war in North America or the Caribbean could not spark outright violence in Europe. In 1756 the Western Hemisphere achieved new prominence because the conflict began in North America and, within two years, dragged Europe into it. As a result, I argue in this book that it is impossible to consider the war in France or that in Canada without connecting the two.

Multiple ethnicities and cultural traditions collided during the conflict, with Indians, Europeans, and creoles interpreting and misinterpreting each others' actions. The core of this book attends to French military disputes, foregrounding the place of military authority in making decisions within the French empire and illuminating the new thresholds of violence participants crossed during the war. To more accurately portray a time of decisive transformation of these communities, I utilize European, Native, and colonial perspectives and argue that we need to give greater weight to the relationship between colony and metropole by analyzing these belligerents side by side and teasing out the contexts in which they came together.[6] Equally critical is the consideration of the circumstances informing French and Canadian elites immediately preceding, during, and after the war and of the expansion of the temporal boundaries of the war's legacy to recover critical but little-studied postwar events. The return of Canadian veterans to France after the surrender of Montreal in 1760, the metropolitan corruption trial called *l'affaire du Canada* (1761–1763), which ran concurrently with the peace negotiations, and new attempts in the 1760s to claim empire in the Atlantic and the Pacific all highlight the impact of the decisions made in North America and show a different facet of a crisis in elite French leadership at midcentury. If events in North America helped to shape the outcomes of the war and peace, the surviving individuals in Europe and the Americas also had to make sense of the war's aftermath. Tracing their experiences, as I demonstrate, is essential to our understanding of how the memory of New France continued to be relevant in the framing of French imperial goals.

The end of New France appears deceptively simple: starved of resources, exhausted by the final four years of war, surrounded and outnumbered four to one by thousands of British troops, Canada surrendered in 1760. However, the loss of New France after 150 years cannot be only about expedience justified by cold weather and expense, which were constants. This story is more complicated, a fact suggested simply by the many names that describe the war in the 1750s. The Francophone Canadian term *la guerre de la Conquête* (the War of Conquest) and Quebec's provincial motto, *Je me souviens* (I remember), instituted in 1883, echo the trauma and loss of a war that reduced New France to British-possessed Canada. Across Canada's southern border, U.S. tradition promotes the "French and Indian War," foregrounding the place of Native peoples in the violence and defining both French and Indian as outside the anachronistically imagined boundaries of the United States, then British North America. If "the War of Conquest" erases actors through title, "French and Indian War" attempts to make no distinction between French Canadian and metropolitan French and obscures the many indigenous nations allied to their own interests, to Britain, or to France by using the catch-all term "Indian." Both Québecois and U.S. visions place this conflict exclusively in North America, unmooring it from any European tradition. Yet neither takes into consideration what Native peoples may have called this conflict at the time or how descendants in these communities today refer to the war.[7] "Seven Years' War," the preferred neutral phrase now in use by scholars, appears more inclusive by neither limiting violence to the Americas nor defining the actors who engaged in the war. Though seemingly prosaic, this term, too, is restrictive. The reality was much more fluid for the participants. The war's duration shifted from place to place—nine years in French North America, two years in Spanish Cuba, seven years in Europe, and potentially twelve years in British North America if one includes the Anglo-Indian conflict popularly remembered as "Pontiac's War."

If "Seven Years' War" rankles by its vagueness, it also invites consideration of how the War of Austrian Succession (1744–1748), for Indians and marines and for French army officers, inflected the attitudes that would be borne out from 1755 on. Louise Dechêne elegantly paves the way for such breadth by calling the *guerre de la Conquête* a "sixteen-year war" for the people of New France. Using her terminology as a starting point, I recover the antecedents of the differing *mentalités de guerre* on either side of the Atlantic, so crucial to the clash between marines, Indians, and army. I also use the expanded chronology identified by Dechêne and emphasized by François Furstenberg's term, "the Long War for the West," to unearth the implications of a similar timeline for France's empire.[8]

As a cultural history of war, this book places the military struggle for New France in dialogue with metropolitan French history in order to demonstrate that the marines and the army officers, at least, understood themselves to be working in an international and comparative arena. The most recent work in borderlands history has encouraged looking for "entangled" histories and posited that revealing such narratives requires a careful evaluation of the familiar historical touchstones and the contexts in which we place them. Undertaking such work demands a "different way of conceptualizing turning points . . . and plotting change differently."[9] Moreover, just as Samuel Truett and Pekka Hämäläinen posit that it is more fruitful to consider borderlands changing, as opposed to borderlands disappearing, this approach is most useful when considering France's North American empire. Rather than seeing New France as a loss, I consider how the war and its aftermath profoundly shaped the imperial French world by "revealing continuities and persisting legacies."[10] My approach to the French experience in this conflict entailed reframing events to better explain the causes of the conflict, particularly foregrounding the search for martial glory and advancement that influenced French actions in Europe and North America, as well as tracing the outcomes of the war to uncover how North American narratives helped reenvisage France's imperial engagements—and how indigenous Americans' influence extended well beyond their own continent.

In North America, the first half of the eighteenth century did not look quite the same as in Europe: away from mainland France the stakes of empire and violence had different valances. Between 1689 and 1756 France and Britain (joined on occasion by Spain, Russia, and Habsburg Austria) went to war approximately every other decade over continental rights of succession and changing constellations of alliance. Costly and often resolving little, these violent episodes acted as proving grounds for armies and new forms of military infrastructure and served the cause of maintaining royal prestige. New France and the British North American colonies found themselves dragged into these major wars—the War of the League of Augsburg, the War of Spanish Succession, the War of Austrian Succession (tellingly renamed by English colonists King William's War), Queen Anne's War, King George's War—analogous to their European counterparts. These conflicts defined the reverse to the "no peace beyond the line" principle; people living beyond "the line" in the Americas had to fight every time the metropole instigated hostilities. These wars disrupted trade, the lifeblood of New France, and threatened the security of the *habitants*, the *marchands*, and land-holding officers of the *compagnies franches de la marine* (marines) alike.

Allowed favorable tax exemptions that were bound to Atlantic and long-distance domestic trade and completely dependent on the monarch's continued interest, Canadian *habitants* and elites had a far greater investment in empire and in the defense of their North American homes than did Europeans. War caused trouble in tenuous Indian alliances, and peace in Europe seemed to conclude more swiftly and with fewer grudges than in North America. Moreover, unlike their French army counterparts, official war was not the sole route for marines' advancement. This militarized colony embraced its soldier elite, placing these officers in the top social echelons. These roles provided opportunities for astute marines to exploit their official work regulating the king's trade so as to distribute all manner of gratuities to assuage Indian allies and, at the same time, enrich themselves.

Distinct in administration and governance from these marines, the *troupes de terre*, or French regulars, imported their own continental culture of combat to North America, thereby bringing a third tradition of war that existed alongside that of Native peoples and the elite marines. In New France's last struggle for survival, each martial community's definition of appropriate war violence (Indian, Canadian marine, or French army) constituted a category that by the 1750s had assumed the characteristics of a sacred affiliation. As Susan Juster suggests, "what seems to distinguish sacred violence from other acts of aggression is not its form but its intensity," arguing that there is utility in exploring "how, and where, the thresholds of legitimacy come to be established in different cultures."[11] Although Juster is reflecting on religious violence, the idea also carries weight with regard to the highly ritualized and critical role that war violence played for Native and French societies. Indigenous Americans in the northeast woodlands and Great Lakes believed that violence in war restored community balance and reinforced their sovereignty in the face of constantly growing imperial pressures.[12] Noble officers of the *troupes de terre* saw war as the ultimate expression of virtuous honor (monarch and nation above self), which they considered characteristic of their aristocratic *race* (blood lineage), justifying both their natural right to lead society and their special status over that of wealthy but common-born men. Marines in New France saw less virtue in the bald exercise of violence than they did in the efficacy of combat in ensuring the results the king expected of them. They were charged with holding down the boundaries of empire to favor the benefits of trade for the king and for themselves. Established to defend a militarized, royal colony in 1683, the officers of the *compagnies franches de la marine* in New France understood that war provided for their special, exalted position in society. Their honors and advancements depended on their ability to defend and expand the king's claims in North America. The parallels between French cultures and Indian cultures should have—and in a different context might have—formed a basis for greater sensitivity and connection between actors. Instead, French officers remained blind to commonalities in behavior and thought. Conditioned by social expectations and willfully eschewing shared affinities with people they may not have seen as equals, French army officers annihilated any possibilities for a reconstructed and redefined common ground.

Many works that look broadly at ideas of empire and the institutions formed while administering Atlantic colonies, both in the French context and beyond, have been an inspiration for this book.[13] Case studies from the French Caribbean and Louisiana have provided excellent models for how to bring colonial experiences alongside metropolitan ones and thereby generate new questions and conversation about lived experience.[14] French military elites from both sides of the Atlantic came together in North America, carrying with them their own imaginaries of a greater France and how their actions contributed to defining the empire's mores and practices of violence. Colonial and metropolitan interactions with Native Americans also show the tremendous influence of New France's Indian alliances in shaping the physical and cultural boundaries of the French empire. Tracking the elite actors who moved through this world extends the boundaries and spaces of battle, offers new insight into French imperial goals and failures, and brings an elusive empire into focus through its residents. By studying the physical space and effects of the war, one also comes to understand how violence can become a text to be read, recorded, and remembered by European and Native actors alike.

Reinstating New France into dialogue with the eighteenth-century trajectory of French history places this book in conversation with works on colonial and metropolitan relationships.[15] New France (especially given Voltaire's assessment) appeared tangential to the Hexagon (continental France), although no one disputes that colonial affairs were shaped by and reacted to metropolitan events. Starting in 1755, the physical presence of French officers and the active maintenance of communication with France throughout the war point to an Atlantic exchange that necessarily shaped more than just Canada. The army officers' efforts to exert control over practices of war in North America show how internal French debates over noble martial masculinity and access to power inserted themselves into local colonial affairs. Montreal's 1760 capitulation terms, for instance, reveal the level of conflict between marines and metropolitans over French imperial goals. Governor

Vaudreuil and his council sought to safeguard the rights to property and to Roman Catholic worship of both Indian converts and *habitants*; General Lévis preferred to let the colony burn if this would better preserve the honor of the king's army. When the fighting ended in 1760 and the army and many marine officers returned to France, the "peripheral" members of the French empire literally came home, blurring definitions of what constituted the edges or the heart of the realm. The exposure of the divergent martial cultures in Canada shaped the reception of veterans in France as well as the French government's perspectives on who best represented royal imperial interests after 1763. Finally, the legacy of the French conduct of the North American war continued to affect the lives of both French and Indians remaining on that continent, adding more nuance and complexity to this history of violence.

Narratives about war run the danger of becoming overwhelmed by their subject matter, which suffocates by either macabre fascination and the allure of romantic conflict or by the sheer horror and magnitude of pain and suffering. Like Ian K. Steele or Karl Jacoby, I am wary of the drama of a "massacre" and give such events a thorough, sympathetic, and yet critical treatment.[16] Throughout this book, instead of focusing exclusively on the battle narratives of the Seven Years' War, I investigate the meanings imbedded in the performances of civility or martial prowess during and after campaigns that informed the better-known military engagements like the sieges of Oswego or Fort William Henry. The myriad battles helped to organize the narrative flow, but I limit these descriptions as a way of minimizing the distortions caused by focusing exclusively on marches, campaigns, and strategic schemes, maximizing instead the interpretations of how these events occurred. Privileging the reconstruction of the context of military camps (as opposed to battles) in the winter quarters of New France's cities (as opposed to those in besieged forts) and of the interactions of Native peoples and Europeans throughout the North American landscapes, which included the expectations, triumphs, and failures of actors on all sides (as opposed to delving into simple scenes of conflict), is critical.[17] The multiple readings of the victories and losses that involved diverse participants are accessible only if we attend to the cultural context from which the belligerents derived these individuals' motivations and values.

Reconstructing this special war experience—a "combatant's-eye view" that included audiences, expectations, and networks on both sides of the Atlantic (and beyond)—required me to focus on French imperial and military elites who produced the official and private correspondence and memoirs examined here. In order to tease out the breakdown of authority within a world of equals, I followed the transatlantic elites from *la marine*, like Joseph Marin de La Malgue, the naval and war ministries, and army officers such as Louis-Antoine de Bougainville. These actors moved back and forth across the ocean during and after the war, had real access to networks of power, and, by virtue of their position, understood themselves to have a vital stake in a French imperial project. Inhabiting a tight, privileged world, this small group of elite French men and their imperial handlers enables me to reconstruct a lively transatlantic dialogue between Canada and France, where victories in North America could turn French officers into hometown heroes in regional magnets like Candiac and Grenoble.

Although this book focuses predominantly on French elites, French war, and French empire, I cannot tell this narrative accurately without also paying attention to the indigenous North Americans and their dialogic role in the arguments over legitimate violence and imperial aims.[18] To fight in North America—to defend a French empire—necessarily meant fighting in Native America, the homeland of Native peoples. French and Canadian soldiers and officers traversed the forests and rivers of the North American interior where allied, or antagonistic, Native states held the balance of power. Canadian marines remained as aware of indigenous opinions of France in the Great Lakes as they did of battlefield honors in Europe. "European" victories and defeats engendered bargaining over power, prestige, and strategy between colonial authorities and Ottawas, Nipissings, Abenakis, or Mohawks just as much as they did with French ministers or officers. Furthermore, these Native Americans understood how information was conveyed through imperial channels—presenting what appeared to be subordinate actions (such as the Ottawa support for the raid on Pickawillany) in terms that New France's administrators read as submission while using these occasions to pursue purely indigenous aims. Indians are elusive in the archival sources, though a few prominent persons occasionally break through European-dominated accounts and are identified by both name and nationality, thus affording access to some individual experiences. In most cases, I read multiple French accounts and triangulated among French, Canadian, and British sources to obtain a variety of perspectives on indigenous experiences and opinions. Indians critically shaped the terms of legitimate war in the Americas as important actors and spectators of this internal French dissention. When the war concluded, Native peoples remained independent and challenged the Europeans' imperial aspirations and legacies.[19]

Manuscripts and printed French sources, as well as a few British materials, helped me to reconstitute the mid-1750s' world of French army and marine officers, colonial and imperial administrators, and indigenous North

American allies and foes with whom the French engaged. I located the original editions of existing copies of works from the eighteenth century, such as Pierre Pouchot's *Histoire de la guerre* or the numerous printed depositions from officers in *l'affaire du Canada*, and in a few cases managed to obtain the copies that actually belonged to the actors in this narrative. Nineteenth-century transcriptions of French manuscripts and twentieth-century editions and translations filled in lacunae in the record and are interwoven throughout. Whenever possible, I read the original French and, rarer still, the manuscript text because I found that considering these materials in their original language and doing my own translations forced me to think differently about the work (other translators are explicitly noted). In particular, I grappled with troublesome period terms such as *sauvage*, the common name used by French individuals to refer to indigenous peoples in the Americas and elsewhere. Although few today would unquestioningly translate *sauvage* as "savage" since many French Canadian and even French sources interpreted *sauvage* as "Indian" or "wild" (as in the medieval European tradition of "wild men"), we cannot forget that some French officers and administrators intended a derogatory meaning.[20] I generally render *sauvage* as "Indian," but I also try to make the author's viewpoint clear so as to allow readers to imagine for themselves how the word was meant.

Indigenous individuals appear using the names found in my sources, with as much precision as is possible for these men and women and cognizant of some French interpretive misunderstandings in their written renditions. Some tribal affiliations and names have changed in the intervening three centuries, and I have opted to use the contemporary terms, such as Menominee and Delaware (or Lenape) in lieu of Folles Avoines or Loups. At times, the broad linguistic categories "Iroquoian" and "Algonquian" serve to distinguish actors when further information is not available. "Iroquois" presents some confusion. By the mid-eighteenth century, the Iroquois Confederacy comprised the Mohawks, Oneidas, Onondagas, Cayugas, Senecas, and Tuscaroras. However, Francophone sources continued to routinely refer to *les Cinq Nations* (Five Nations), and members of all these communities had kin in Native settlements in New France. The Seven Nations of Canada eventually arose from the confederation of these *réserves*, or mission communities, established at Bécancour, Lac des Deux Montagnes, Lorette, Saint François, Saint Régis, Sault-Saint-Louis, and La Présentation. For these locations claimed and identified by Natives and French, such as La Présentation (Oswegatchie), I use both names, employing an indigenous appellation (to showcase Native perspectives) or a French one when describing a European context: Sault Saint Louis (Kahnawake), Saint François

(Odanak), Saint Régis (Akwesasne), Lac des Deux Montagnes (Kanesatake), Lorette (Wendake), and La Présentation (Oswegatchie). Some of these villages, like Kahnawake or Odanak, had majority populations of Mohawks and Abenakis, respectively. But all of these communities were heterogeneous, and French sources lumped them together under the term *sauvages domiciliés* (domiciled Indians). In this book, *réserves* and "domiciled Indians" are my general terms to represent peoples of Mohawk, Onondaga, Huron, Abenaki, Algonquin, and Nipissing descent who hailed from these villages. I distinguish as well between Iroquois of the Six Nations and Iroquois living in New France. Overall, my translations and word choices employ vocabulary that reflects the attitude of my sources at the time, the terms that were used and thus represent language that presents their reality rather than our hindsight.

"Canada," a term in use by the seventeenth century, indicates the territory of New France, encompassing the Saint Lawrence River Valley, Great Lakes region (*pays d'en haut*), and the contested Ohio River Valley. All other French American territory fell under the jurisdiction of la Louisiane, administered from New Orleans by its own governor. "Canadians" were New France's creole (American-born) French population but no less French in the eyes of the law than other subjects of the French king. Although the *Encyclopédie* (1751) identified the inhabitants of Canada as *sauvages* (Indians), it never once called them *Canadiens*, and the ministerial correspondence and French army letters from the 1750s reinforce this fact by distinguishing between French Canadian *habitants* and Native peoples.

The military culture of the French Atlantic world appeared to be uniform at midcentury, framed by the goal of maintaining and augmenting France's preeminence as a European power. In the colonies, the *compagnies franches de la marine*, also known as *troupes franches de la marine* or *la marine* and who reported to the Ministère de la Marine (Naval Ministry), defended the Bourbon claims to global prestige. Marines served long terms as colonial regular troops overseas, not on naval vessels, and should not be confused with sailors or naval officers. Under the Ministère de la Guerre (Ministry of War), the *troupes de terre*, or army regulars, engaged in the same pursuits in Europe. Chapters 1 and 2 outline the various interpretations of legitimate violence in the French Atlantic world and describe the stakes that induced European and indigenous men to conduct campaigns or undertake violent actions in the years between 1748 and 1756. The War of Austrian Succession (1744–1748) never really concluded at the peace of Aix-la-Chapelle for Indians and French colonists in North America. Those years destabilized

Franco-Indian relationships, led to the ascendency of certain Native groups (especially Miamis, Ottawas and other Anishinaabeg, and Kahnawakes), and weakened France's grasp in the West, forcing *troupes franches de la marine* to work harder to maintain old alliances and ways of doing business. Chapter 1 also provides an overview of the different goals and concerns that military elites in France drew from their prior war experience, thereby providing insight into how multiple noble, martial masculinities could coexist in the French Atlantic empire so long as they did not come into direct contact. Together, chapters 1 and 2 demonstrate worlds of violence, alliance, and practice on either side of the Atlantic that seemed to be set in stone but that, in reality, would change dramatically after 1756.

Focused on the years of officially declared war, chapters 3 and 4 outline the expectations of French officers for their American service, how they anticipated their allies would act, and the role the metropolitans envisioned for themselves in framing the conflict's violence before contrasting these with the reality of events in North America. These chapters study the Franco-Indian alliances and show how a putative "middle ground" quickly soured by suggesting the reasons that all sides (Indian, French, and Canadian) grew increasingly dissatisfied with each other. Focused less on the battles and skirmishes that usually dominate the narrative of this period and more on an interpretation of how French and Indian fighters "read" one another, we discover how all sides drew increasingly unfavorable conclusions that in turn corrupted New France's ability to win, or at least to stalemate, the war.

Chapters 5 and 6 narrate various experiences at the conclusion of the Seven Years' War in order to demonstrate what may be gained by following the veterans beyond the battlefield. In chapter 5, the homecoming of military veterans of New France from both the marine service and the army tells us much about how the French Crown interpreted and dealt with its reversal of war fortune and about how New France proved to have been a colony worth giving up and erasing from the nation's memory. The sacrifice of 150 years of North American colonization, chapter 6 argues, was assuaged by colonial experiments in the 1760s and the hope for a more positive experience that would reinforce, rather than challenge, the *mission civilisatrice*. Finally, in the Epilogue we return to North America to touch on two moments, one in the late eighteenth century, the other in the early nineteenth century. Rather than ending the Seven Years' War with a piece of paper on a table in Paris in 1763 or foregrounding the roots of the American and French Revolutions, the epilogue reflects on how narratives both change and present new questions if the legacy of the French Atlantic empire and the late war are considered from the perspective of Native peoples living at midcontinent.

Montcalm, his officers, and even some of the marines received an education that valued the contributions of the classical world. For the arriving French nobles in 1755 and 1756, the *Iliad*, the *Odyssey*, and the *Aeneid* provided a lens through which to view and understand their new assignments overseas. Classical allusions littered their writings, official and unofficial, and mirror the heroic roles these men envisioned for themselves. The French army was to save the Bourbon expedition of conquest and bring low a hated British rival. The opening ceremonies of late spring 1756 showed the initial observations these allies made of one another—a moment ripe with possibility when it appeared that old, familiar models could build new working relationships. Like Achilles and his crack Myrmidons in Homer's *Iliad*, Montcalm and his thousands of French troops—competent and prideful, guarantors of future victory—found themselves caught up in a destructive quarrel no one had foreseen—a quarrel not over the rules governing the spoils of war but over the rules governing war itself. This inner conflict between canny warriors would ultimately undo the unified effort required of France to maintain its North American empire. Underneath the politeness expressed on all sides in spring 1756, opinions about the others swiftly formed: a culture war had begun in earnest.

Chapter 1

Onontio's War, Louis XV's Peace

Joseph Marin de La Malgue's service report filed with the Naval Ministry recorded him as being in Acadia (Nova Scotia) in 1748. It was there, ranging the territory contested by France and Britain, that the marine captain learned of the ending of the War of Austrian Succession; New France's governor general, Roland-Michel Barrin, Marquis de La Galissonière, ordered Marin to "cease all acts of hostility and come back," which he did.[1] The terms of peace returned Cape Breton and its fortress of Louisbourg, captured by New England militia in 1746, to New France, but they also upheld the 1713 cession of Acadia to the English Crown. As British officers moved to reassert their empire's claims to "Nova Scotia" and with borderland politics remade once more, Marin headed back west to receive new instructions from La Galissonière at Quebec.

Wars shape both civilians and soldiers, and hostilities rarely conclude in the minutes it takes the ink to dry on the treaties that signal their end. Europe returned to peace in name on October 18, 1748, but at least six weeks passed before news of the Treaty of Aix-la-Chapelle crossed the Atlantic to reach French and British colonies in North America. Though European monarchs and politicians could demand that their colonial subjects cease hostilities, their orders mattered little to the sovereign indigenous peoples of North America. Turning off the enmities among Native peoples, European migrants, or rival colonies in North America proved to be challenging. Enforcing a *status quo ante bellum* displeased almost all of the belligerents. New Englanders feared continued French threats to their safety after the return of Louisbourg, popularly nicknamed the "key to the Saint Lawrence." A cessation of conflict meant that the French court expected New France's governor to order his Native allies to agree to Europe's terms. A recent arrival in the colony, Roland-Michel Barrin de La Galissonière failed to grasp the intricacies of the task before him. He had to repair Franco-Indian alliances made fragile by four years of war and by four years of diminished supplies and diplomatic gifts. Convinced of the correctness of his ideas and eager to seize this moment to demonstrate French supremacy in North America, La Galissonière's demands changed the terms of French and Indian interaction from one of equals to one in which Algonquians would be treated "as subjects or, in Algonquian terms, as slaves." In so doing, the governor general thrust the *pays d'en haut* (the Great Lakes region) into turbulence.[2] Where persuasion was needed, La Galissonière ordered; the Indians were not impressed. Colonists and Indians may have thought that affairs seemed simpler on the other side of the ocean. They were not.

To the French public, Louis XV's actions at the treaty table appeared incomprehensible. When the smoke cleared from the fields of conflict in 1748, France controlled much of the Netherlands and went into negotiations from a position of strength. But in the terms agreed upon that October, Louis XV withdrew royal troops from territory conquered in Europe and overseas, returning the Low Countries to the Dutch Republic and handing Madras back to Britain. He recognized Prussia's claim to Silesia and even arrested and, at Britain's request, cast out of France Charles Edward Stuart, "Bonnie Prince Charlie," the Catholic claimant to the British throne. Such choices, in the eyes of French critics, diminished the greatness of their country's battlefield victories like those at Fontenoy and at Maastricht in the Austrian Netherlands.[3] These successful feats of arms had thrilled the nation and unified it behind a vigorous, formidable king. Martial success in 1745 had enabled Louis XV to overcome, or at least neutralize, a serious crisis to his reputation; now the monarch's acceptance of this weak peace dealt a fresh blow to his name. It suggested that the king's behavior had changed little; scorn for the royal person—and his court—resumed.

Understanding the later dissention between French elites in the army (*armée de terre* or line infantry) and the marine (*compagnies franches de la marine* or colonial regulars) in New France is considerably more challenging if not placed in the context of the aftermath of the War of Austrian Succession. Separated from the Seven Years' War by only by eight years, according to official European dates, almost all of the elites who served in the first war found themselves recalled to duty in the second. As a result, the experience of the 1740s framed the expectations and outlooks of the actors on whom the defense of Canada rested in the 1750s. The year 1748 brought about different results for martial elites in both France and New France. Louis XV's peace in Europe returned French military nobles to a world of anxiety over their future position, status, and opportunity. New France, on the other hand, experienced no peace at all, making a sixteen-year war in North America, not a seven-year war.[4] Conflict among Native nations, British colonies, and the French regime in Canada carried on after the Treaty of Aix-la-Chapelle went into effect and flowed seamlessly into the "new war" in 1756. Onontio, the indigenous name for both the governors of New France and the king of France, remained at war, continuing a pattern of borderlands conflict more than a half century old. On the eastern side of the Atlantic, calm borders belied animosity within the French aristocracy; the recent war compounded a debate over unequal access to honors and promotion among French nobles that expanded in the early 1750s.

⚔ Unhappy Nobles

The French soldiers and officers who had fought during the War of Austrian Succession were the successors of the standing army model perfected by Louis XIV. Aristocratic military service derived from the ancient wartime services that had once been the exclusive purview of the *noblesse d'épée* (nobility of the sword). As France's Second Estate grew larger in the Renaissance and Baroque eras, ever more noblemen from the various tiers of the aristocracy—the ultraelite *noblesse de cour* (court nobles), the growing *noblesse de robe* (administrative nobles), and often-impoverished but ancient provincial members of the *noblesse d'épée*—sought to make their fortunes and reputations in the army. All of these men saw themselves as the guardians of France's honor and chivalry and claimed they acted accordingly in the field. While the army adapted to its growing numbers and the changing social opportunities of its leadership, it also accommodated the transformations in the practices and rules of war. Reforms after the Thirty Years' War had made certain modes of violence that had been widespread in the early seventeenth century (such as raiding and razing towns and villages) relatively rare by 1700, and the perception of what violence was permissible on military campaigns in the eighteenth century came from innovations such as academies to train officers, improved troop discipline, regular pay, and the army's increased sense of loyalty to the nation.[5] Still, brutal battles and sieges like the French attack at Bergen-op-zoom (1747) or the British suppression of the Scottish Highlanders (1745–1746) proved that purposely brutal acts of targeted tactical violence, as opposed to the collateral effects of loose troop discipline, could and did still occur.[6] Such excessive cruelty made a point to the enemy, especially as the number of armies living purely off the land diminished during eighteenth-century campaigns. The continuation of episodic total war despite the more desired, restrained combat endowed officers with the ability to select the parameters of destruction—and made these choices both potent and perilous.[7] Improved projectile technologies along with the standardization and professionalization of war made military engagements ever more complex; formal training for engineers and officers became essential.[8] Military academies qualified their graduates as experts who could identify what constituted legitimate war and pursue it as efficiently as possible, replacing the tradition of warrior-nobles, mercenaries, and feudal armies. As these schools developed in the mid-eighteenth century, run for and by professional officers, they defined appropriate, legitimate modes of violence through their curricula and publications, which often adopted the preference of the great Maurice de Saxe, maréchal de France, for "scientific" sieges that yielded tangible gains rather than battles.[9]

In France, the École militaire, founded in 1751, served an additional purpose. Established under the patronage of the minister of war, Marc Voyer Paulmy d'Argenson, and Louis XV's *maîtresse en titre* (official mistress), the Marquise de Pompadour, the admissions policy of the École militaire addressed the questions of professionalization and the discontent of poor nobles. This was no *académie* or *collège*, institutions focused on classical education or chivalrous graces. Instead, the school pledged to provide a meritocratic route to position and advancement by enabling the poorer sons of proven nobles to gain access to the resources needed for a successful military career. It trained boys in mathematics, history, modern languages, and militarized discipline in order to give them the best possible start and helped them bypass the traditional system of promotion by proprietary patronage. The meritocratic impulse nevertheless remained limited. Though many other royal academies encouraged talented youth from a broad spectrum of backgrounds, the applicants to the École militaire had to be not only impoverished but also able to incontrovertibly prove noble birth.[10]

Whether poor or rich, French nobles spoke a language of honor and appropriate conduct in war, in which their peers decided—based on mutual respect for their professional and class qualifications—the humane and honorable course of action for victors and losers. Modern war allegedly minimized brutalities, and doing so required including an elaborate system of conduct that governed everything from life in camp to surrenders and prisoner exchange, all the way down to the etiquette of firing first on the field. In this top-down hierarchy, nobles set, and ideally enforced, the rules of engagement by constraining and outlining the actions of the entire army from foot soldiers to generals. Officers and leaders could utilize violence to enforce the responsibilities of their subordinates and the rank and file. To discipline and motivate their peers, aristocrats could bring to bear extreme social pressure and reputation to constrain and shape their behaviors. The result of these carefully drawn rules and formational institutions was to encourage the aristocratic officers in Europe's armies to feel a greater commonality with enemy officers, fellow aristocrats of courage, courtesy, and custom, than with the lowborn men in their own ranks.

Celebrating the idea that Europe had achieved a "good war" (which it had not) required a denial of the violence taking place in theaters of war beyond Europe's borders. That noble standards of war might be unrecognizable or unacceptable for non-European situations or actors mattered little.[11] Elaborate performances refined and ritualized violence with "the assurance that faith would be mutually kept, and rules of war provided a comprehensive, contractual etiquette of conduct between enemies whose personal and professional honor was impugned by any accusation of breach of their rules."[12] If war could not be restrained, it could at least be reshaped by military codes and rules of conduct. Hammered out in dialogues between noble officers and military academies, rules defined what was deemed legitimate or illegal, civilized or barbaric and became accepted practice when successful experience showed that restriction in war benefited everyone.[13]

Public opinion in Paris, the epicenter of intellectual and public life in France, sought a return to the strength and magnificence of the age of Louis XIV or even of Henry IV. Noble officers, especially those who sought advancement from middle commands to high-status positions through their service in the War of Austrian Succession, agreed with the public on this matter. As France returned to peace, many noble officers found that court luxury, court vice, and court impropriety placed their class under the disapproving gaze of the nation. Most galling was that even if they wanted to behave like the court and run the risk of disapproval by some individuals, few provincial male nobles could follow the example of the king's actions with women, appointments, patronage, or games of chance because they lacked the necessary funds. If these nobles could not break into the sought-after circles at Versailles, they could nonetheless contribute to the critique of court behavior and valorize themselves.[14]

French women of good birth also bristled at court politics and the diminished access available to their men to forge sterling reputations in war or peace. The rise of foreign-born generals limited the advancement of native French noblemen, while the rise of scandalous royal mistresses (especially the *anoblis* Marquise de Pompadour) impugned the reputation of noblewomen. *Gloire*, achieved through bravery and daring on the field of battle, was the quality on which French noblemen's reputation rested: it was an essential part of aristocratic masculinity. In the late seventeenth century, Madame de Sevigné made clear the vital connection between elite women and noblemen in the realm of masculine martial virtue: "Since one constantly tells men that they are only worthy of esteem to the extent that they love *gloire*, they devote all their thoughts to it; and this shapes all French bravery."[15] Feminine delicacy translated into physical weakness, but a true aristocratic woman pushed her noblemen to be just that: men. Gender politics increased the seriousness of the declining spiral of nobility for aristocrats: the king's social failings and the French army's troubled performance suggested a feminization, through luxury and martial failure, of noblemen. The rise of unsuitable women at Versailles, particularly royal mistresses, who in turn shaped court culture based on female sins (vanity, lust, greed), diminished the honor of legitimate noble mothers, wives, and sisters—the traditional individuals who encouraged men to seek *gloire*.

France's noblesse spent much of the seventeenth and eighteenth century elaborating and refining the meanings and performances of noble honor as a means to set apart true aristocrats from recently ennobled rich commoners.[16] Inasmuch as the nobleman was born with a tendency toward virtue, only breeding and service cultivated this natural aptitude in him and realized his honorable potential. Through his own choice of conduct, a nobleman could develop and reinforce the positive inclinations of both his bloodline and his education. Sin and laziness remained areas of particular concern, and only conscious adherence to daily reinforcements of virtuous intellectual or physical work countered the deleterious effects of these vices that depleted "natural" honor. Although a nobleman could deviate from honorable behavior by pursuing a dubious lifestyle, a *roturier* (commoner), being of a different *race* (bloodline), could never hope to attain noble honor. That was the birthright of the true aristocracy. Within the army, "the presumption of the nobility's hereditary predisposition to military service was rarely articulated in terms of blood, race, or innate characteristics."[17] More than anything else in the eighteenth century, noble army officers believed their families and their rearing conditioned them to be uniquely suited to lead. The best officers came from families, titled, of course, that had produced exemplary servants of the Crown in the past. They had paid the "blood tax" in service to the state that had entitled aristocrats to their position for centuries.[18]

A Canadian source affords a glimpse into this anxiety about bloodlines at the conclusion of the Austrian war. Marie-Isabelle-Élisabeth Rocbert de La Morandière, daughter of Montreal merchants, married the chevalier Charles-Michel Bégon, the scion of a French noble family with Atlantic interests, over the strenuous objections of both families. Elite Canadian society soon forgave the fuss and accepted the young couple; the Bégons became a leading political household in Montreal. Upon her husband's death and her migration to France in 1749 Madame Bégon discovered a different, harsher world. In Blois, Bégon's in-laws remained cold toward her, notably reminding the widow that she "did not know how to live and was only an *Iroquoise*."[19] The French Bégons faulted their widowed daughter-in-law for her common roots, going so far as to imply Indian *métissage* with that term's attendant connotations of savagery, avarice, apostasy, and skewed gender roles. Ultimately, Élisabeth's unsuitability rested on her *roturier* birth. Her proximity to Indians as a colonial subject served to damn her further.

Élisabeth Bégon's letters to her son-in-law, Michel de Villebois, an administrator in Louisiana, illuminated the culture of French middling nobles in the mid-eighteenth century. The unhappy woman compared her misery in French society unfavorably to her former, warm life in Canada. "This country is pleasant only in climate. In all else it is worse than Canada for glory, envy, jealousy and all that is least good in society. Only money and the wealthy are beloved; those who are not [wealthy] curse the others."[20] Even if Bégon's criticism rang true, her in-laws would have been appalled by such a frank admission of the sorry affairs of the Second Estate. Because she had not been brought up in France, Élisabeth Bégon palpably felt the tension in her relationship with the elites with whom she interacted. And while her overall experience may have been excessively framed by her difficult interactions with her in-laws, her ability to so easily read the anxieties of nobles and their obsession with wealth and position tells us how visible the aristocracy's concerns were in the 1750s.

Aristocrats had to police the perimeters of their position when the hoi polloi, especially those who had great wealth, challenged the "essence" of nobility in order to overturn their exclusion from privilege. Poor or rural nobles serving in the army saw the answer in securing their preeminence in the hereditary martial values that had created the very idea of nobility in the early medieval period.[21] Any commoner of means could purchase fine goods, hire servants, and, for a very fortunate few, even buy a title to enter the junior ranks of the administrative elite. Wealth in particular enabled a usurpation of nobility, "that is, to pass off an aristocratic lifestyle as the natural product of birth," for being a noble was an elusive category that shifted and changed in response to social practices and legal categories.[22] However, those who considered themselves to be true aristocrats eschewed mixing honor with the pursuit of financial gain, unlike their social subordinates, from lowly shopkeepers all the way up to lofty financiers. Involvement with trade was the antithesis of nobility itself, and any aristocrats directly caught engaging in commercial pursuits faced the possibility of being stripped of their elite status.[23] The preservation and definition of martial honor as a commodity available exclusively to the noblesse allowed even the poorest, most geographically marginalized or ill-educated aristocrats to retain their preeminence over the wealthiest but nonennobled subjects. Social conventions on the battlefield, in military academies, and among commanders produced ever more rarified and contorted forms of martial honor. The more complicated the form, the more securely the aristocrats who encouraged and practiced such behaviors were able to make themselves the arbiters of who were or were not permitted to be truly noble. Despite the carnage of the battlefield, war was also to be a "school of elegant behavior" that emulated the manners and practices of court even though it did not ignore the primal task of killing one's opponent.[24] Every moment of military life afforded a noble officer an opportunity to display his natural right to lead.

⚜ A Dishonored King

In the 1740s, the upper echelons of French society found themselves under attack from a wide variety of critics such as philosophers, scientists, Jansenist reformers, and upwardly mobile bourgeois. The general indictment made by these disparate groups revolved around what they perceived as weakness, effeminacy, and moral corruption in France's political, cultural, and military institutions.[25] Louis XV was supposed to play the role of the "first gentleman" in a hierarchy of aristocratic equals, but at the court in Versailles the rift between the middling nobles and the most privileged aristocrats grew wider. The blows to Louis XV's reputation as monarch and general during the War of Austrian Succession exacerbated this situation. Scandals surrounding the king tainted the French nobility by association, as in the "affair of the three sisters."[26] From 1738 to 1744, several royal mistresses came from the Mailly-Nesle family. Louise-Julie, Comtesse de Mailly, Pauline-Félicité,

CHAPTER 1

Marquise de Vintimille, and Marie-Anne, Duchesse de Châteauroux, each occupied the royal bed in turn, an action that rendered the king susceptible to charges of adultery and incest. In some sense, nobility was governed by custom, and this made the public assertion and confirmation of virtue, masculinity, martial honor, *noblesse de race* (ancient bloodline) for every noble—from the poorest all the way up to the king—essential behaviors to be practiced. It was especially important for Louis XV, who, as monarch, retained the royal privilege to rule on the legal nobility of all of his subordinates. The controversial affairs involving these sisters, as well as the ensuing publicity surrounding them, jeopardized the king's ability to be seen as a worthy royal by the public and his Second Estate.[27]

An epicurean delighted by the company of beautiful and intelligent women, Louis XV brought several noble mistresses on campaign after war officially began in 1744. Bullets and swords proved a lesser threat to the king's body and martial reputation than camp sickness or the warm arms of his mistresses. At Metz in August 1744, an illness nearly cost the king his life, and the experience terrified him sufficiently to publicly repudiate his sins and renounce his mistress Marie-Anne, Duchesse de Châteauroux (the third sister), at the order of his confessors. Recovery brought about a change of heart, and, to the public's dismay, the king attempted to reconcile with his dismissed lover. Reunion was not to be, however—the lady died unexpectedly in December 1744—but the damage to the king's name was done. Inviting mistresses to a military operation and then allowing them to delay bellicosity or royal entrance onto a battlefield constituted troubling behavior in a monarch. These liaisons did not demonstrate the link between virility and aggression but rather suggested that Louis XV did not take the business of war seriously. No king could lead by example if he allowed himself to be distracted by his lover. Worse still, the scandal and irresponsibility made France a laughingstock before its enemies. Nobles and bourgeois alike linked together the repudiation of the Duchesse de Châteauroux, the miraculous royal recovery, and the victory at Fontenoy in spring 1745.[28] Replacing the royal mistress in 1745 with Jeanne Antoinette Poisson, elevated to Marquise de Pompadour, ended Louis XV's association with the "three sisters." But the new favorite, Madame de Pompadour, also raised eyebrows, and that reaction laid the groundwork for future criticism of royal honor. Lurid affairs contrary to God's law desacralized the royal body, ending the crucial social service kings provided to mediate between their subjects and the divine. Now, in the selection of his newest lover, the king "literally climbed in bed" with financial interests that served only a few subjects, greatly compounding noble concerns about money overtaking virtue at court.²⁹ War was supposed to be a masculine pursuit, the battlefield a masculine space. The king of France, however, appeared to spend as much time sorting out his romantic life as he did considering tactics and strategy. If the ordering of the king's priorities had not been questioned, Louis XV's attention to women might not have been so damaging. After all, royal romance (and illegitimate royal offspring) proved a monarch's virility—a desirable male trait. Nonetheless, the Mailly-Nesle sisters and Pompadour made Louis XV appear to eschew duty in favor of pleasure. Even after the French victory at Fontenoy restored Louis XV's martial reputation, the public continued to read war fortunes in the context of God's judgment on royal behavior. The loss of Cape Breton and the capture of Louisbourg in Canada a month after Fontenoy, for instance, devastated Parisians.³⁰ Nobles, as much as the king, needed to continually provide proof to the nation of their aggression, their virility, their very "maleness" as the conflict continued.

Unlike the king he served, France's leading general during the war, Maurice de Saxe, emerged from the conflict with a reputation that lauded him as a great martial hero. German born and illegitimate (albeit of royal stock), Maurice de Saxe and his protégés led France to victory at Fontenoy (1745), Rocoux (1746), Bergen-op-zoom and Lawfeld (or Lauffeldt) (1747), and Maastricht (1748), earning Saxe the coveted position of maréchal de France (commander of all French armies) in 1747. Saxe's triumph at Fontenoy in 1745 typified the mode of elaborate, absurd "courtesy" between belligerents, which took officers' minds off of the butchery around them and showed the general's fluency in acceptable modes of war. But Saxe could also subordinate social expectations to his ends. In 1747 his adjutant, Ulrich Frédéric Woldemar, Comte de Lowendal, presided over the brutal sack of Bergen-op-zoom, earning the two men a decisive victory—and a reputation for unnecessary ferocity. Even if certain French critics despised Saxe for such actions, aggressive campaigns bolstered his masculinity as much as his military genius. And off the battlefield, in affairs of the heart, Saxe could act in ways the French king could not. Unconstrained by divine right and already marginalized by his religion, Saxe could and did engage in lovers' trysts without sustaining the same damage to his name as the king did. For better or worse, these foreign generals in the service of Louis XV reaped victories for France, and in doing so they, not French generals, claimed praise for distinguished leadership and the honors of war. Saxe's Protestantism made the situation for poor, ambitious French nobles all the more intolerable.³¹

French noble officers worried that they suffered by comparison with these non-French rivals, and the record between 1741 and 1748 appears to bear out their fears.³² In 1742 one of France's famous native-born generals,

Charles-Louis-Auguste, Duc de Belle-Isle, retreated from an untenable position in the besieged city of Prague. His maneuver saved the army, and though he later managed to obtain an honorable surrender, the French public ridiculed the entire affair. Worse still, the British captured Belle-Isle in Hanover in December 1743 and kept him prisoner for almost a year.[33] In July 1747 the battle of Assietta claimed the life of the general's younger brother, Chevalier Louis Charles Armand de Belle-Isle, widely considered a future military star. The Chevalier de Belle-Isle's gallant but foolhardy actions in Italy followed both the norms of continental war and the desire to prove his noble martial masculinity. In the one brother's failure to achieve success and in the other brother's capture, the Belle-Isles' example raised questions about French inferiority for ambitious nobles of the French army. The defeats—one killed, the other captured—of the sterling-reputed Belle-Isle brothers succeeded only in demonstrating why the king needed to depend so heavily on foreign generals.

The conclusion of this war led to questions about the future of nobles' military careers. If financiers and a "cabal" of courtiers dominated the king's council, then impoverished nobles could find no means in peacetime by which to advance. Active duty provided income, essential to the ambition of all nobles, though uncomfortable as a topic of conversation. Shifting back to peace placed hundreds of French nobles in a tight spot, bereft of the camaraderie of war, reduced to half pay, and returned to less desirable living situations. These circumstances were worsened by the resentment many of these veterans felt as the king created ever-more promotions and positions to honor his favorites. For long-serving nobles in the military, this practice had "cheapened the value of [their own] military grades and dignities," especially at a time when the army was seen to be the last refuge of the nobility.[34] War carried the threat of death, but it also offered glory, the ability to pursue the true *métier* of the aristocratic man, and the chance that a nobleman of limited means might be able to transcend his lot in life. Valor, bravery, and title could compensate for meager funds, but foreign competitors, like Saxe and Lowendal, appeared to bar that avenue as well. Saxe died in 1750, but plenty of Irish, Jacobite Scots, Swiss, and Germans still populated the ranks of the French army while ultrawealthy *roturiers*, hoping to advance from the Third Estate to the Second, and by this transition from bourgeois status to the aristocracy, added to the clamoring throng.[35] The French Crown limped forward, weighed down by personal scandal, while these issues festered in the ranks of France's military nobility.

↩ *La Marine*

Since the late seventeenth century the *compagnies franches de la marine* (also called *troupes franches de la marine* and *troupes de la colonie*) had served throughout New France and on Cape Breton at the Louisbourg fortress. They formed the elite core of the colony's defense. The *troupes franches* originated in the early seventeenth century as an innovation of Jean-Armand, Cardinal-Duc de Richelieu, in 1622. Reformed by Jean-Baptiste Colbert in 1674, after New France became a royal colony as *troupes de la marine* and again in 1690 as *compagnies franches de la marine* by Louis Phélypeaux, Comte de Pontchartrain, these soldiers served overseas exclusively under the French navy. At the end of the seventeenth century, the troops formed the only standing army in French North America—a situation that remained unaltered until 1755.[36] The importance of their military mission in New France continued from the late seventeenth century to the colony's final years. In 1665 one-quarter of New France's population was professional military, and one-tenth remained active in that role in 1760.[37]

Like their counterparts in the French army of the *ancien régime*, elite colonists with landed estates constituted the majority of the officers who defended New France. Although most of the initial officers leading the *compagnies franches* had been born and raised in France, by the eighteenth century, this trend began to reverse in Canada. New France's farms and domains expanded along both shores of the Saint Lawrence River and developed a hierarchical society as a result of a system of land tenure and government modeled after the absolute monarchy of France. Land *en roture* (small rented plots) appeared soon after New France was founded, quickly settling families on homesteads and bringing arable soils into production. The colony's elite arose from the residents with seigneurial holdings and from French migrants drawn from the ranks of the petty and provincial *noblesse d'épée* and *noblesse de robe* in France.[38] *Seigneuries*, income-providing land grants from the king to prominent colonists, undergirded New France and its social system, forming a breeding ground of the militarized colonial elite. The Crown chose soldiers and officers from among the seigneurs on the grounds that landholding "interested the officer and the foot soldier in the conservation of the country [Canada] as much as that of his own heritage."[39] Although seigneurs ascended to New France's dominant social class through the prestige conferred by being landed squires and later marine officers, neither occupation was particularly lucrative. As time wore on, seigneurs intermarried their heirs with the children of wealthy Montreal and Quebec merchants to improve their material circumstances and build family alliances.[40]

All colonial men had to serve in the militia (created in 1669 by order of Louis XIV), but as time passed, men of the seigneurial class showed a particular predilection for the officer corps first in the militia and then in *la marine*, where their worth as prominent landholders was reinforced by the noble profession of arms. This combination of blood service and elite background enabled marine officers to be regarded by their contemporaries as "indisputably members of the French [imperial] noblesse."[41] Entry into the ranks required the support of New France's civilian and military administrators, the intendant and the governor general, along with their recommendation for acceptance to the minister of the navy. Final decisions remained the king's prerogative.[42] Seigneurs and their male offspring began to dominate the military elite of the colony in the first third of the eighteenth century: by 1722 more than half of the officers of *la marine* in New France were creole. And by the 1750s, many of the junior positions in the *compagnies franches* were reserved for the sons and grandsons of serving officers, further cementing these trends.[43]

French army officers in the late seventeenth and eighteenth centuries used their birth, social rank, and wealth for advancement, but the officers in New France's *compagnies franches de la marine* additionally required arduous training before they were permitted to receive commissions and move up through the ranks.[44] A candidate's background and social connections facilitated obtaining a spot in the marines, but promotions depended on merit. Entering as cadets, marine officers had to demonstrate familiarity with and expertise in enticing and trading with Indian allies, as well as undertaking raids against Indian or English settlements (forms of engagement unknown to metropolitan French soldiers until the Seven Years' War). Such accommodations became routine by the era of the War of Austrian Succession in North America. Rather than carry out the punitive action recommended by New France's government, Paul le Moyne de Longueuil, commanding at Detroit in the 1740s, undertook conciliatory actions toward the Hurons and Algonquians of the region when informed of anti-French Indian conspiracies. His decisions drew on his twenty years of diplomatic and war experience, and he successfully quieted the unrest in the upper Great Lakes.[45] Many other young or midcareer marines spent the war years in the 1740s maintaining French defensive positions in the Great Lakes, like Longueuil, or on the long border between New France and New York colony on Lac Saint-Sacrement (now called Lake George) and Lake Champlain.

Describing his service during a raid along the Lake George frontier in late spring 1747, Ensign Luc de La Corne, also called La Corne St. Luc, wrote that, lacking wampum, he had promised his own gun to any Indian ally who brought him a British prisoner. Later on during this campaign, La Corne also chronicled his negotiating tactics with the Abenakis who were among his party, acceding to changes these Indians requested so as to minimize unnecessary exposure to danger.[46] The ensign's account showed resourcefulness when he lacked the necessary items to inspire the loyalty, confidence, and action of his indigenous allies. Moreover, if the Catholic Iroquois, Hurons, or Nippissings accompanying him to Lake George held him in high esteem, La Corne's gun may have been all the more valuable. Besides its utility, exchanging such a weapon conveyed an impression of courage or panache from one owner to the next, perhaps making La Corne's rifle a particularly desirable prize. Either interpretation demonstrated La Corne's conscious awareness of the role he was supposed to play for both a French and an Indian audience. Completing missions for the "good of the king's service," a phrase commonly used at the time, proved La Corne's worth as a French military figure. Nonetheless, in order to achieve French aims, La Corne had to respond to Indian expectations, illuminating the very different experience of war in North America, where the centrality of Native peoples shaped the conduct and practice of violence. This reality was reflected as well in La Corne's taking seriously Abenaki concerns, whether he did so of his own volition or because he knew these Indians had an independent authority and influence and that he must accommodate their expectations. Through the expression of their willingness or reluctance to follow plans, these Indians influenced the very process of campaigning.

The precautions and actions taken by the officer achieved success—La Corne's party claimed forty-seven prisoners and twenty-eight scalps. His brother, Louis La Corne, had achieved even greater victory earlier that same year leading an attack on Grand Pré in Acadia. The triumph enabled this marine captain to request, in September 1747, a recommendation for the coveted *croix de Saint Louis* from the Marquis de La Galissonière.[47] All of these marines, and in fact all of the elites in France's armed services, sought recognition for their bravery through membership in the order of Saint Louis, a military society created by Louis XIV to reward exceptional valor. Each grade—*chevalier*, *commandeur*, and *Grand-Croix*—carried a pension, an honorific decoration, and the title of chevalier, or knight, which could become hereditary after three generations.

Interpreting Captain La Corne's request in the light of both European and indigenous North American tradition provides a deeper insight into the entangled martial world of marines and the indigenous peoples of North America. When he proposed himself for the *croix* after his actions at Grand Pré, La Corne signaled that he saw his defense of France's imperial border as an essential service to his king that was in no way different from what was expected of an officer on the field at Fontenoy. The captain received this tribute in October 1749 and enjoyed both an increased salary and an actual decoration, an enamel and gilt-embellished cross bearing the image of Saint Louis, which hung from a red taffeta ribbon to be worn on his left breast. Portraits of military men of the eighteenth century show that Canadian soldiers and officers in Europe alike sported this symbol of royal approval.[48] Although it was unlikely that a recipient would wear such an embellishment into battle, the *croix* would have lent its owner an air of distinction at symbolic events. Indigenous leaders who received ceremonial medals from French and English regimes and who both wore and bore physical displays of their prowess and status as warriors may have viewed the *croix de Saint Louis* as fulfilling a function similar to that of their own adornments and body markings. Indians recognized the significance of the *croix*, but this appreciation did not imbue marines with a chief's status in Native eyes.[49] Still, the honor allowed La Corne to enhance his *crédit* among Native allies—particularly Catholic-converted Kahnawake Mohawks, Abenakis of Odanak, Akwesasne Iroquois and Nippissings, as well as Oswegatchie Onondagas and Mi'kmaqs in Acadia—by trotting out this proof of Onontio's trust in his military prowess. The Indian recipients of these badges of fidelity, called "medal chiefs" by the Europeans, at times passed down their prized symbols of authority to future generations; honored marines did so, too, creating a martial lexicon that each side could understand and appreciate.

Older marines or those descended from generations of Canadian-born officers could more fully appreciate the complicated reality of borderlands interactions and thus stood better chances of success in Indian affairs—a formula true for New France's governors as well. Resolving the conflict spreading throughout the Great Lakes in the late 1740s fell partly on the commanders of French posts in the region. Marin, La Corne, or their colleague on the Ohio River marches, Joseph Boucher de Niverville, might succeed by using correct protocol, preventive gift giving, or a formulaic threat where a more inexperienced commander or even a governor general, improvising, would err.[50] A year after he was recalled from Acadia at the news of peace, Joseph Marin de La Malgue marched west to Chagouamigon, an Indian post on the southwestern shores of Lake Superior, to fulfill La Galissonière's desire that he "bring peace and tranquility between the nations at war against one another and even at war against the French." Marin believed that his mission ended in success. He had spent sixteen years in the marine service and was in this territory because his father had served there, providing Marin *fils* trade and even linguistic links to Native peoples in the region. The process of traveling westward, gaining access to tribal notables, making himself appear credible and a figure of authority, and negotiating to further French aims took Marin two years.[51] Even those Frenchmen bred and raised for a career in the borderlands had to take their time, given the highly individualized nature of Franco-Indian relationships and the mutability of the process. New actors, new locations of interaction, and new economic conditions caused constant change on the frontier.

While thousands of French nobles galloped back across Europe in 1748 to return to their estates, colonial military elites in New France plunged further into borderlands diplomacy and uncertain violence. Joseph Boucher de Niverville, another officer, had spent the last war years raiding in the vicinity of Boston and Albany, noting with some pride his capture of "two enemy Mohawks." Peacetime found him, along with his brother, Pierre-Louis Boucher de Niverville Montizambert, in the Ohio River Valley, where they intended "to hold councils with different Indian nations who occupy this continent" on the orders of the new governor, Jacques Taffanel, Marquis de La Jonquière. His aim was "to implore them [Indians] to remain in the king's interest."[52] Niverville's encounters with Shawnees, Delawares, Mingos, and members of the Iroquois Confederacy during Céloron de Blainville's 1749 journey down the Ohio River meant that he was interacting with nations familiar with French and British struggles. Similarly, these indigenous groups were well aware of what they could request or demand of the representatives of New France. For these Native nations to even consider remaining loyal "in the king's interest" required the colonists to provide them with goods such as gunpowder, strouds, silk ribbon, brandy, or sugar. Marin, heading farther west, leaned even more on indigenous guides and translators as well as his own hard-earned experience to establish credibility among unknown nations. Both examples are representative of the type of work the marine officers engaged in during the late 1740s and early 1750s. The effort made to secure New France continued under one governor, then another, regardless of the social crisis unfolding in the metropole.

⚜ Dissension in the Marine Ranks

Jean-Frédéric Phélypeaux, Comte de Maurepas and long-serving minister of the navy, had been delighted when Canadian governors and intendants successfully reduced the costs of running New France in the 1740s, beginning what Maurepas hoped would be a balance between royal expenditure in the colony and New France's profitability. As New France's postwar governors and military personnel serving in the Great Lakes, *pays d'en haut*, Illinois Country, and Ohio River region learned, though, those cost-cutting decisions had come at a price. Only the restoration of plentiful gifts, the reinstitution of royally controlled trading posts, and the attempts made by individual marine commanders to mend relations among Native peoples began to calm the unrest along the western frontier.[53] The fragile French resurgence faced failure when Versailles again ordered austerity measures—defined as reducing colonial frontier expenditures—in the early 1750s. As Maurepas's successor, Antoine Louis Rouillé, Comte de Jouy, explained in 1754, "All resources are so depleted that if things cannot be put back into the condition they were in before the advent of these immense fiscal excesses, which we have been experiencing for some years, we shall be strongly compelled to abandon the colony."[54] Historians have been too quick to assume that phrases like Rouillé's "we shall be strongly compelled to abandon the colony" implied an imminent threat. New France was costly and certainly a source of frustration for bureaucrats at the naval ministry, an agency that seemed to be perpetually underfunded by comparison to its counterpart, the war ministry.[55] But fur and cod remained important resources for France. During the War of Austrian Succession, *gazettes* confiscated by the Paris police indicated the public's anger at the capture of Louisbourg because it diminished this Roman Catholic realm's steady supply of fish for Friday meals.[56] Neither Rouillé nor Louis XV wished to revisit the endangerment of French fisheries. However, in order to protect his own reputation from charges of reckless spending, Rouillé also had to document his disapproval of the expenditures lavished on fort building, Indian councils, and gifts made to encourage Indian trade and alliance with New France. The recipient of this letter was New France's newest governor, Ange Duquesne de Menneville, Marquis de Duquesne, who faced the unenviable task of pursuing both an aggressive policy to defend New France's borders and frugality.

Looking past this bureaucratic haggling, one notes dissension among the ranks of marines that eerily mirrored the debates taking place among French nobles in the metropole. In 1753, the same year that Rouillé demanded fiscal responsibility, Capt. Charles de Raymond, a French-born officer in the colonial regulars who had been serving in Canada since 1722, wrote a *dénobrement de tout les postes du Canada* (enumeration of all of the Canadian positions) to complain about his thwarted career ambitions. Although he had spent most of his career at Fort Niagara, he had not accumulated wealth from the fur trade, and bitterness fed his antipathy to Canadian marines who had done better, in some cases making fortunes.[57] The report provided a detailed look at France's North American forts. It described the negotiations and trade that marines engaged in at those garrisons, outlined the strategic advantages of English and French interests in North America, and, above all, listed fiscal abuses and corruption by New France's civilian and military elite. The report intended to expose colonial corruption to the naval minister and, in doing so, to place Raymond in the minister's good graces.[58]

Raymond's work attacked the reputations of numerous elite Canadian officers, including the sieurs Marin de La Malgue and La Corne St. Luc, in addition to many other colleagues and compatriots who had served with distinction during the War of Austrian Succession and who would acquire further renown in the upcoming conflict, such as Céloron de Blainville, Daniel Liénard de Beaujeu, and Claude de Ramezay.[59] All of these individuals spent at least some portion of their careers engaging in trade, war, and diplomacy with various Indian nations—an activity vital to the survival of New France but one that could also be greatly remunerative. So long as their primary actions forwarded royal interest, little attention fell on the individual economic interests of the military personnel. Raymond argued that just the opposite occurred: marines displayed an interest in acquiring their own wealth, engaging in Indian trade to this end, and subverted peacemaking so as to satisfy their own needs. This accusation was a serious charge in 1754, for Raymond claimed that these officers abused the king's trust in their martial abilities in order to enrich themselves. Worse still, the *dénombrement* linked the Crown's expenditures on its alliances with indigenous nations, so necessary during times of peace and war, solely to marine profiteering. Acting as if war had ended in 1748, although Raymond well knew this was not true in Canada, he located "peacetime" as a moment that facilitated abuses in the borderlands. His decision to adopt this strategy enabled him to present the diplomatic actions of *la Marine* in New France as "corrupt" rather than as important inducements designed to enlist the aid of allies during conflict and minimize the indigenous peoples' objections to French interests.

Like the middling aristocracy and the sons of French nobles who could not hope for army promotion without money to grease the wheels of advancement, Raymond vented his frustration about his better-connected peers. As a marine officer born in France, Raymond represented a minority among New France's officer class. His cousin, Jean-Louis, Comte de Raymond, served as a commander at Louisbourg, but Raymond appeared to have no ties to the seigneurial elite of the Laurentian Valley. He never used the word "inequality," but the *dénombrement* registered his anger at being unable to achieve wealth, promotion, or esteem among colonists and Indians.

By placing himself in a position of moral authority as France's provincial nobles had and praising himself for never having defrauded the Crown in Indian affairs, Raymond thwarted his own chance to profit by being an administratively lax fort commander in the future. His treatise gives no clues as to his interactions with indigenous groups, or their opinions of him, but his stalled advancement in a merit-driven system that tacitly took their perspectives into account suggests that he fared poorly in this crucial area of expertise.

Raymond sent his treatise to a well-placed contact in the French army, Col. Michel Le Courtois de Surlaville, who knew the Comte de Raymond and probably Captain Raymond as well. By passing his *dénombrement* to an army officer, Raymond increased the likelihood that others outside the ministry of the navy would see the work. Captain Raymond may have hoped to trigger Surlaville's sympathy on issues of honor, especially given the context of French midcentury military culture. After all, the moment in which Raymond composed his critique coincided with reassessments of European continental martial practice and adjustments to the nobility's relationship to military affairs and martial honor. Thus Raymond's voice joined the growing French criticism of the shape and efficiency of its own military system.[60]

Opportunistic corruption could and would become a central issue in New France when declarations of war in 1756 brought metropolitan officers of the *armée de terre* into contact with the Canadian and few French officers of the *compagnies franches de la marine*. During the Seven Years' War, Raymond's complaints about the economic and military entanglement between marines and Native peoples would be transformed from an expression of one man's bitterness over his stunted career opportunities to an indictment of an entire military elite by its metropolitan counterparts.

⚜ Valorizing the Empire

In 1749 and 1750 two French individuals at Versailles produced remarkable *mémoires* describing New France's utility to France's imperial goals. Adrien Maurice, Maréchal-Duc de Noailles and a powerful member of the *noblesse de cour*, and Roland Michel Barrin de La Galissonière, former governor of New France, placed Canada in a geopolitical perspective by subordinating actions on the ground to larger French strategy. Noailles's treatise, *Mémoire du maréchal de Noailles sur les colonies d'Amérique*, warned of Britain's "jealousy" over France's American colonies. Inaction in Atlantic affairs, Noailles feared, would adversely affect the French navy and trade. As a remedy, he suggested sending troops from France to aid in colonial defense rather than relying solely on the French colonists' innate, bellicose nature.[61] The aggression Noailles counted on from Canadians fit in completely with a French nobleman's interpretations of blood, service, honor, and descent. Louis XIV had dispatched the famous Carignan-Sallières regiment to defend New France from Indians in 1663 and then to populate the land; many influential seigneurs claimed descent from that regiment's officer corps. Military predilection and abilities passed from man to man, father to son. Noailles's desire to send thousands of troops from France to North America—a well-intentioned but impractical idea in 1749—shows that at least one notable aristocrat and former army officer began incorporating New France into a holistic view of France's future.[62] It opened up the possibility of considering what contributions the army could make to colonial policy beyond what the naval ministry was doing.

La Galissonière's *mémoire* showed a difference in perspective acquired as a result of his experience in colonial administration. He considered the positives and negatives of New France, balancing colonial expense with geopolitical need. His viewpoint boiled down to a critical argument: France required an empire in the Americas to combat British supremacy in Europe.[63] Drawing a relationship between North America (*l'Amérique septentrionale*) and the Caribbean (*l'Amérique tropicale*), the *mémoire* explained that Canada and Louisiana provided ports, vast stretches of land, and such an expansive shared border with the English colonies that the cost of defending them all could ruin Britain. A French American empire contributed honor and glory, expanded the reach of Roman Catholicism, and greatly advanced the monarch's name, but the *mémoire* added that the existence of New France and Louisiana also hampered Britain's capacity to challenge France in the Caribbean and in Europe.[64] La Galissonière pleaded for increased interest in the navy: "If there is anything destructive to France's superiority in Europe it is the English naval forces: they alone upheld [the Austrian Habsburgs] at the start of the War of Spanish Succession, just as they have cost France the fruits of her conquest in the Austrian Netherlands at the end of the last war."[65] Unlike Noailles's writings, La Galisonnière's work stressed what he had learned in New France: that both the Franco-Indian alliance and self-defense remained critical components of success and that funds that flowed through and enabled the expansion of the naval ministry's responsibilities were essential to French defense.

Between 1748 and 1755 the governors general of New France—La Galissonière, Jacques Taffanel de La Jonquière, and Ange de Duquesne—attempted to expand France's reach and influence in the western part of North America and hold off British trade and military infiltrations along the Ohio Valley. To do so meant sending out marine officers to engage in the work that they had performed for the better part of fifty years: cajoling and threatening indigenous peoples to form alliances, making strategic retreats as needed, finding new potential sites for forts, negotiating the creation of middle grounds, and, above all, spending, spending, spending along the frontier. These policies reinforced the reality that a successful marine officer was one who had *crédit* among Native peoples: he used both his martial prowess and his ability to distribute the desired goods. Above all, a marine officer served with valor in the name of the king and aspired to reap rewards like the *croix de Saint Louis*. Through the creation of military "dynasties" formed by the sons of seigneurs dominating the officer corps, the Canadian military elite sought to replicate the values of noble French army officers of a "hereditary reputation, a capital of honor passed down to the sons" who would emulate past success.[66]

In France, middling aristocrats in the French army faced formidable challenges at the end of the 1740s and into the 1750s. On the one hand, the nobility began to see the strains and stresses of financial inequality realized on a large scale. Attitudes toward consumption, luxury, and economy played a central role in the definition and critique of society, including aristocratic behaviors.[67] Consumerism caused particular discomfort. Not only was the purchase of offices—or even of tasteful, fashionable dress—unavailable to poorer elites, but such expenditure was also a feminized vice.[68] Tying the masculine virtues of war to a woman's sins by having to submit to the need to look like an officer as much as perform as one frustrated young nobles in the extreme. The importance of mistresses, not wives, and of conspicuous displays of wealth at court suggested a distortion of power, where restraint and virtue mattered little.[69]

In a world of peace and war, elite marines and noble army officers believed themselves to be defending France—and Louis XV—most effectively. Each group saw its particular construction of noble martial masculinity as respectful of and descended from true French tradition. Marines recalled that their primary duty, bestowed on their ancestors by Louis XIV, was to protect royal territory at all costs and by all means necessary. Marginalized French nobles in the army (and elsewhere) sought to save the Second Estate, France's bastion, from degenerate aesthetes drunk with luxury and fallen from their natural virtue. Moreover, they sought to stem the corrosive influence of wealthy parvenus in the future. Great anxiety reigned among noble army officers that rich commoners, whose wealth had obtained for them positions that character could not, had infiltrated their ranks.[70] Members of the army's noble officer corps would soon add to this list of unsavories the elite marines they were about to meet in Canada, men who claimed an officer's nobility for themselves but whose display of martial virtues reeked of bear grease and who proffered scalps to "savages" and made commerce honor's bedfellow.

CHAPTER 2

Interpreting Landscapes of Violence

In the early 1750s the Ohio Country erupted in violence as indigenous peoples, French, and English all attempted to impose their authority there. Though ownership of this region had long been disputed, this renewal of conflict resulted directly from the incomplete conclusion to the War of Austrian Succession in 1748. The European struggle to determine the Habsburg succession had promoted the long territorial dispute between British New England and New France's claims to the north and west. The peace treaty of Aix-la-Chapelle did not resolve European sovereignty over the Ohio River lands, nor did it take into consideration indigenous Americans' perspectives as the peace was hashed out. Instead, the treaty restored colonial boundaries to their 1744 limits. With the return of the Louisbourg fortress in Cape Breton to Quebec, the treaty of Aix reversed Britain's most significant gain in North America. New France once more seemed to be as strong and threatening to Britain's North American interests as before 1748. However, appearance belied reality. Losing Louisbourg during the war undermined Canadian confidence, and four years of interrupted trade and privation caused by the British naval blockade had complicated New France's ability to foil Britain's efforts to expand its influence through the Indian trade in both the Ohio River country and the northeast. English traders took advantage of the falling off of French trade goods beginning in 1744 and continued to do so after the 1748 treaty, moving to attract Miamis, Wyandots, Shawnees, and other nations to Pennsylvania's trade circuit.[1]

Now, with the European war concluded, the French Crown in 1748 and 1749 ordered the colonial government of New France to force the English off land claimed by Louis XV and to return the Indians of the region, forcibly if necessary, to French trading orbits. Drawing the Native peoples from the Great Lakes, Illinois Country, and Ohio Country back into alliance with France was a challenging goal that required significant expenditures. The process began with a diplomatic mission cum show of force in the Ohio region to resolve French claims. French marine captain Pierre-Joseph Céloron de Blainville set out in the summer of 1749 to enforce French rights to North American soil by delivering messages showing French strength to the Iroquoians, Delawares, and Miamis situated along and near the Ohio River. Céloron's diplomacy carried a visual element designed to dominate the landscape both physically and metaphorically. As his expedition sailed down the Ohio River, his men plunged lead plaques inscribed to Louis XV into the riverbanks and nailed similar items to trees. Céloron claimed that French intentions were less intrusive to Native Americans than those of the British, but English traders and Native interpreters translated the territorial claims evidenced by the plaques to Native communities. Incensed, the indigenous residents of the "Beautiful River," as they called the Ohio, rebuffed Céloron. The French mission could neither force British traders to leave nor impose French trading rules on Native leaders like Memeskia, the Miami chief at Pickawillany, or Scarouady, an Oneida of influence in Loggs Town.[2]

Besides threatening Native sovereignty, Céloron's intentional symbolism of imposing Louis XV's name onto the North American landscape spoke to the visual culture of power and war in the late 1740s and early 1750s. French administrators interpreted their river plates and tree tags as marking this space as their king's own. But in the eyes of the indigenous residents, the lead plaques buried Louis XV, the Great Onontio, in the mud, and from that place he offered his children no gifts and no strength. Such markers were without significance to them. Worse still, gender divisions among many Algonquian and Iroquoian communities placed agriculture and the soil under the care of women. Céloron's gesture may have also been understood as an emasculation of French power. It was hardly a valid way for men to claim this land. For two years after Céloron's mission, relations continued to deteriorate between the French and the Ohio Natives over the activity of English merchants in the west.[3] As New France came to accept the failure of Céloron's mission, the French colonial government resorted to new, more concrete efforts to stake its claims. Between 1750 and 1756 the French erected or rebuilt seven forts in the western borderlands from the Great Lakes to the Ohio River at the extraordinary cost of thirty million *livres*.[4] This display was designed to impress indigenous peoples and Europeans alike and to strengthen the connections between New France and Louisiana. Each structure spoke to French ambition and French power, whether a hastily constructed, fortified trading post, such as the Portage du Niagara, or an imposing military installation like Fort Duquesne. On the cleared landscape approaching a fort, its garrison and livestock, the smoke from the cooking fires, and flags whipping in the wind could be seen for miles. These structures also served as attractions to encourage travelers and nearby residents to seek trade, refuge, companionship, and news. With few Canadian colonists willing to resettle permanently in the Ohio and Illinois Country, the fort-building campaign helped to carve France's presence into the borderland.

France was not alone in its desire to show strength and claim supremacy in the contested West. Many indigenous nations inhabited this space or had designs on it, and Native ambitions also marked the land. European encroachments made the "colonial corners of the woods" frightening for the indigenous peoples, and many hoped to restore safety of life and travel in these regions.[5] In 1751 New France's governor general, Jacques-Pierre de Taffanel, Marquis de la Jonquière, recognized the Iroquois Confederacy's claims to the Ohio Country and promised the Onondagas that no French subjects would enter the region without permission. The governor hoped that his gesture of goodwill would counter the attractiveness of cheaper, higher-quality, and plentiful English trade goods. When La Jonquière died suddenly in office, this tone of conciliation passed with him. Naval minister Antoine-Louis Rouillé, Comte de Jouy, ordered the new governor, the Marquis de Duquesne, to drive home the point that France, not the Onondagas or other Indians, owned the West—peacefully (and cheaply) if possible but using force if necessary.[6]

The actions undertaken by Céloron, the fort-building campaign, and Rouillé's directives underscore France's preoccupation with making this landscape carry the imprint of their power. Indians also manipulated the landscape they built their homes on, raised crops on, hunted on, and held by birthright or war. The landscape of the Ohio Country was a book still being written, one that each contending nation meant to be read according to its own interpretations.[7] Each attempt by France to exert its power over this region and thereby to seize control of the Ohio Country, and Native reactions to this, altered the physical space with demonstrations of imperial authority. Lead plaques and repaired imperial trade depots, coercive actions like fort building and the burning of homes all courted upheaval along the trade routes. These actions helped New France regain some of its lost diplomatic and territorial influence and created a vivid impression of renewed French strength. They also made violence the preferred instrument of influence for both Europeans and Indians in the borderland in peacetime.

Later events previously seen as the classic European or Atlantic turning points of the "French and Indian War," such as Washington's ignominious surrender in 1754 or Dieskau's defeat in 1755, would be interpreted very differently in indigenous settlements, by colonial authorities, and by European officers. For Native communities in particular, these moments did not necessarily constitute the key turning points at all. There was no shared understanding between Europeans and Indians or even among Indian communities about how to limit the growing recourse to violence or to control its terms. As a result, the escalation of violence in the borderlands from 1750 to 1755 and the proliferation of actors in these situations would reshape what constituted order and disorder in war as well as its purpose.

⚜ Two Deaths in a Borderland

Reconsidering the Ohio borderlands in the early 1750s demonstrates how quickly modes of violence overlapped and how many different ways struggles for dominance could be interpreted. Quebec's demands that the Miamis, in particular, return to an alliance with New France continued to meet with little success three years after Céloron's 1749 voyage. After Governor La Jonquière's diplomatic overtures, entreaties, and gifts failed, French frustration turned to rage. The focus of this anger was Pickawillany, a trading town on the Miami River inhabited by Miamis, Piankashaws, some Iroquois, and, most recently, English traders like George Croghan, who threatened France's tenuous grasp in the disputed Ohio Valley. The disaffected Miamis, irritated by both the increasingly domineering policies of New France's government and the collapse of an independent negotiating space, had tried to find their own path to political and cultural survival in this region. Memeskia, Pickawillany's leader, had firmly refused Céloron back in 1749; by 1751 authorities in New France recognized that French intimidation was achieving no results and that only action would resolve this resistance to French authority. Plans began for a military expedition against the Miamis, and with great pains and over many months the French colonial regime courted the residents of the *pays d'en haut*, encouraging them to come into the Ohio Country to punish these renegade members of the French alliance.[8]

In the fall of 1752 Governor Ange-Menville, Marquis de Duquesne, reported good news to Versailles—the complete victory of a French military force over Memeskia (known as La Demoiselle or "Old Briton" to the French and British, respectively) and his English allies. Marine cadet Charles-Michel Mouet de Langlade had left the French post at Michilimackinac in late spring 1752 with about two hundred Ottawas and Ojibwas, adding to his numbers with French soldiers from Detroit. They had traveled about four hundred miles in order to reach Pickawillany to show definitively the fate of those who reneged on alliances with New France and to send a warning to English traders to stay away from the frontier. Langlade's force destroyed the town early on the morning of June 21, killing a number of individuals, including Memeskia and an Englishman, taking five more English merchants captive, raiding the town's warehouses, setting the settlement's storehouses (some of the largest west of the Appalachians) ablaze, and hoisting a French flag. When the British failed to support any indigenous rebellion after this French demonstration of coercive power, the Miamis unwillingly returned to the putative "middle ground."[9]

Memeskia's demise proved the most arresting moment of the violence. Surrounded and outnumbered, the old man finally succumbed, after which the Ottawas boiled and consumed him in front of the Miami chief's terrified followers. Feasting was not limited to indigenous flesh. "One of the white men that was wounded in the belly, as soon as they got him, they stabbed and scalped, and took out his heart and eat it."[10] Historians have read a great deal into this haunting moment of frontier violence and used it to propose a variety of meanings that include the consumption of Memeskia as a literal reabsorbing of the Miamis into the French alliance.[11] Rarely, though, is the violence at Pickawillany considered from the perspective of Versailles. The actions undertaken and the rewards given out by the Crown demonstrate how little the French government concerned itself in the early 1750s with the forms of violence being practiced by the colonial soldiers and Indian allies of New France. Gubernatorial letters to the Naval Ministry highlighted how the Pickawillany raid succeeded in defending the colony's borders and strengthening Native alliances. Rouillé had issued a directive to defend western land claims, and there was no reprimand of Cadet Langlade from the court after the raid he led ended with death and ritual cannibalization.[12]

The expedition leader's journal, including a complete account of the campaign, was forwarded to France for royal review. To honor the accomplishment, Governor Duquesne also requested a pension of two hundred *livres* for Cadet Langlade, who had demonstrated bravery, applied himself to the royal mission with zeal, and motivated Indian nations in support of France.[13] Minister Rouillé denied Langlade the pension, but this decision reflected a desire to curb expenditures rather than a reproof of the violence used. The high cost of maintaining Indian alliances had to be balanced in the royal treasury against the debts still outstanding from the War of Austrian Succession. Duquesne persisted in his efforts, offering proof to the minister in 1753 of the good effect wrought by the mission; the letter appended the transcript of an Indian council in which the Miamis asked for French pardon.[14] Two years after Pickawillany, Duquesne again appealed on Langlade's behalf, this time to Rouillé's replacement, Machault d'Arnouville: "Since by your silence I have inferred that you do not wish to accord him this favor [the pension], and since he is a person to humor from the power he has on the minds of the Indians, let me, I beg of you, ask for him a commission as ensign *en second*, half pay; this will suffice to arouse his zeal when he is needed."[15] In March 1755 Duquesne's glowing reports and three years of French ascendance in the Ohio Country convinced the ministry to grant Langlade a commission as a full ensign.[16] Four months later, in July 1755, the young officer confirmed the faith bestowed on him. Langlade participated prominently at the battle of the Monongahela, a conflict largely fought and won by France's indigenous allies against Gen. Edward Braddock's English troops.

The official colony-ministry correspondence conveys the expectations placed on individuals like Langlade, who could attract and sustain Franco-Indian alliances in the Great Lakes and *pays d'en haut* for the colonial government's benefit.[17] This was a role that Langlade performed quite effectively as he was the ideal representative to prove the legitimacy of the French land claim. In his very self, Langlade embodied France's aspirations to naturalize its rights to North America. Langlade was *métis*, as well as an officer in the *troupes franches de la marine* at Michilimackinac. Son of the prominent merchant Augustin de Langlade and his Ottawa wife, Domitilde, Charles was, on his mother's side, the nephew of the respected Ottawa leader Nissowaquet (called "La Fourche") and had participated since childhood in military campaigns with his Ottawa relatives.[18] This man who led the Ottawas' excursion against Pickawillany had proven his worth to both French and Indian observers through his successful imperial service at the trading post village of Michilimackinac and his maintenance of Native community ties. Langlade's credit among indigenous peoples at Michilimackinac arose from both his war prowess and his access to French goods, which could be distributed among local populations to further the French Crown's—and his family's—interests.[19] New France's ability to plan and execute the attack on Pickawillany stemmed from the administration's knowledgeable reliance on Langlade's personal intervention in these affairs, using his family connection.[20] The victory achieved by Ottawas and Ojibwas in destroying the most significant trading post west of the Appalachians reinforced France's need for these allies; Langlade's burning of Pickawillany and the ritual cannibalization of Memeskia enacted a frontier diplomacy that creatively and equally responded to Ottawa, *métis*, and French martial traditions.

The methods Langlade employed to achieve French imperial objectives in North America showed the flexible parameters of what constituted legitimate violence in the Ohio River Valley and Great Lakes interior. The composition of the force going to Pickawillany also signaled elasticity in who could suggest, participate in, and control these acts of violence. As an officer, Langlade was especially versatile. Although French bureaucrats or certain Canadian elites may have brushed off *métis* individuals as corrupted by blood, Langlade's status as a cadet and his later commission as an ensign proved he was conversant in French norms of war, was considered a loyal soldier, and was understood by the Crown to be a French officer.[21] When Commander Jacques Legardeur de Saint Pierre sent George Washington, the envoy of Governor Dinwiddie of Virginia, back to Williamsburg in 1753, refuting British claims to the Ohio region, Saint Pierre's note stated the following: "I paid special attention to receiving Monsieur Washington [the envoy] with the distinction worthy of your Grace, his quality, and his great merit. I hope he will do me the same courtesy with you. . . ."[22] Officers had to be equally able to engage in this level of European courtliness and to be responsive to the sophisticated diplomatic rituals of the Abenakis, Ottawas, or Oneidas.

Langlade would not have achieved his position without demonstrating a talent for the demands of cross-cultural etiquette. But, unlike most marine officers, his *métissage* and consistent connection to his mother's family gave the Ottawas a direct voice in official French imperial military action not only by sustaining French territorial claims but also by determining the parameters of acceptable conduct by the colonial military elite. Langlade was not alone—the Chabert de Joncaire family, composed of merchants, interpreter-envoys, and marine officers, had spent several generations cultivating diplomatic and kinship ties with the Senecas. With a father and a brother who each had a Seneca wife, Capt. Daniel-Marie Chabert de Joncaire (and his translator brother, Philippe) enabled the Senecas to assume a privileged voice in marine affairs as well.[23]

Langlade's actions combined his awareness of French aims and his understanding of his Ottawa relatives' own motivations. The war party had traveled almost four hundred miles to make this assault on the Miami village. To the French this was a French raid because it was led by a marine officer, and its goal was to reassert Louis XV's ownership of the Ohio River basin and its tributaries. To the Ottawas, however, this was a vital demonstration of Ottawa power, which, through their French alliance, extended even into the Ohio Country. By French standards, Langlade achieved a complete success: he attained his objective (subjugating the town), he neutralized the Crown's enemy (executing Memeskia), and he returned France to a position of relative influence (forcing the Miamis back into the alliance, as proven by the 1753 council at Montreal). These successes formed the basic narrative forwarded by the governors of New France to the French Crown.

However, there were also indigenous aims that Langlade and his forces realized at Pickawillany. The Ottawas' violence suited their own interests first—not simply the purposes of France—and enabled them to assimilate diverse peoples, goods, and influence flowing from the Atlantic world into their own autonomous, Native society.[24] In the ritual cannibalization of Memeskia and the English trader, the warriors claimed the spiritual power of these enemies for their own people. If the French were so threatened by English traders in this town that they required the destruction of Pickawillany, then here the Ottawas proclaimed their strength and took the trade goods for themselves, not France. The Ottawas came from a trading nation, their very name, "Odawa," means "trader," and their language, Central Algonquian, was the mercantile lingua franca of the Great Lakes.[25] The acquired property profited Langlade's community at Michilimackinac by bringing that population items to bolster, through trade and gifts, the regional prestige of the Ottawas and the Ojibwas.

The Ottawas also left a statement burned into the landscape when they destroyed the Miami town, one to be read in much the same way as the building of a fort or the founding of a village. Killing and eating Memeskia marked the individuals who participated in this action directly, either as consumers or as spectators. When Miami and English survivors spread the news of the Ottawas' violence back east, the war party accrued a greater reputation for itself. However, events at Pickawillany communicated to a wider audience for a much longer period of time as well. Many Algonquians and Iroquoians celebrated victory by altering the physical space of their travels to and from battle. After defeating enemies, Anishinaabeg (Ottawas, Ojibwas, Potowatomis) of the *pays d'en haut* often stripped bark from trees along their route home, writing an account of their deeds so "that travelers

CHAPTER 2

that way may know they have been there, recording also in their way, the number of scalps or prisoners they have taken" on these prepared surfaces in a mixture of coal (from burned bark) and fat or oil, which could last for more than a decade. Any individual who walked past the charred remains of the formerly thriving trading post would know the terror of Ottawa wrath and the helplessness of the Miamis and their English allies. Metropolitan French officials noticed none of these visual markers, no doubt because they considered the Ottawas to be located on the periphery of Native America. Given this attitude, the French rendered themselves culturally illiterate in reading the borderlands. If Canadian colonial agents did pay attention, they made no mention of it. But Langlade and Native peoples understood the power of the ruins. The devastation spoke clearly to a resurgence of the Anishinaabeg and a claim to the opportunistic expansion of their influence in this time of violence. The actions of these individuals from the upper Great Lakes circulated a message to indigenous peoples throughout the Ohio Country and colonists on the frontier that paid only secondary attention to the interests of the French ministry and colonial government.[26]

A year after Pickawillany, Governor Duquesne moved more officers into the Ohio Country to build on Langlade's success and to firm up French claims, sending Capt. Paul Marin de La Malgue out with an army in 1753 to dominate the region. Marin counted many nations among his military contingent, including Kahnawake Mohawks from the Saint Lawrence Valley, as well as some Ottawas. These forces crossed Seneca territory with little difficulty after an embassy of Seneca matrons met with Marin and determined French intentions to their own satisfaction; the rumors spawned and the detritus from Langlade's raid had made Ohioan Indians skittish, and the northern Indians moving with Marin unnerved these nations further.[27] To officers like Marin or his subordinate, Legardeur de Saint Pierre, the mission to the Ohio Country was on behalf of France, and its success rested on the recruitment of Indian allies. Although the two members of the colonial regulars had decades of borderlands experience, they were used to employing Indians as auxiliary French troops, mercenaries who received their pay in kind through elaborate gift-giving conventions. Their French martial logic did not encompass accommodating the aims of indigenous kin the way that Langlade's approach did. Two years after the raid, Pickawillany spoke separately to French, English, and indigenous audiences, with each side finding its own meaning in the violence that had occurred. An incident in a woodland glen offered further demonstration of how differently metropolitans, colonials, and Indians construed the violence that dogged peaceful commerce in the Ohio borderland.

Like Memeskia, Ensign Joseph Coulon de Jumonville answered to someone's policy requirement that he die a violent and well-remembered death in the Ohio Country. The manner of his demise and the violence that immediately followed affected everyone, becoming part of the Ohio landscape to be read in different ways by Europeans and indigenous nations. In May 1754 Jumonville ventured out from Fort Duquesne to reply to the chosen representative of Virginia's Ohio land claims, George Washington, who was heading west to announce Britain's intentions. The French and English parties finally met in a forested glade under a flag of truce on May 28 to discuss each empire's claims. Brief negotiations uncontrollably turned into a firefight that did not end well for Jumonville and his men. Witnesses left confused accounts as to whether Virginians or Indians sparked the violence, and at least one account reported a scandalous demise for the French envoy. The Iroquois "half king," Tanaghrisson, accompanying Washington, motivated by his own interests and deeply frustrated by English inaction against the reemergence of French interests in the Ohio Country, allegedly dispatched a wounded Jumonville after saying to him, "tu n'est pas encore mort, Mon Père [you are not yet dead, My Father]."[28] As soon as word of the disastrous end of the mission, which the French had conceived as diplomatic, not military, reached Fort Duquesne, Louis Coulon, sieur de Villiers, begged to be dispatched to avenge his dead brother. Villiers left Fort Duquesne with a French and Indian force composed, on the indigenous side, of Iroquois from Sault-Saint-Louis (Kahnawake) and La Présentation (Oswegatchie), Huron-Wendats, Abenakis likely from Saint François (Odanak), Nipissings, Ottawas, Delawares, and at least one *panis* (enslaved Indian) of undetermined nation. Acting according to their own political and economic motivations, these Indians offered their support by responding to appeals they understood in indigenous terms: respect for the mission leader, reciprocal obligation, and negotiations cemented by gifts of tomahawks, wampum belts and strings, wine, and shoes.[29] In his journal, Villiers recorded regularly consulting his Indian troops about strategy and at times relying on them for more. At least once during the month-long pursuit of Washington's retreating force, when things went amiss, Villiers depended on Iroquois influence with recalcitrant Nipissings to proceed with the campaign.[30] As he himself noted during the journey, "he would do nothing without consulting the Indians." Villier's ability to successfully engage with his allies demonstrated the officer had a more than passable understanding of indigenous motivations.

Washington retreated toward Virginia for more than a month, correctly fearing swift reprisal by the French. Finally, Villiers caught up with Washington and defeated him where the Virginians had hastily constructed a rough fort, aptly named Fort Necessity, at the Great Meadows, east of the Monongahela River. Handed a barely legible, poorly translated French document, Washington accepted, along with capitulation, the responsibility for *l'assasinat*, or murder, of Ensign Jumonville. He also acknowledged that Jumonville represented France's claims to Ohioan land. With his signature on this document, young Washington sparked an international incident and gave France a legitimate justification for war.[31] French propagandists seized on Jumonville's decent service record and death in the line of duty to make him the center of a French publicity campaign. Cast as plain, simple, and brave in life, Ensign Jumonville, dead, became a rallying point for the new ideals of *la patrie* and *la nation* because he was murdered under a white flag of truce. His sacrificed youth symbolized devotion to the nation in both France and Canada.[32] Moreover, in dying a hero and a patriot to the French, Jumonville did not benefit French nationalism alone. Metropolitan polemicists cared about Villiers's mission because of England's responsibility for events, confirmed by the capitulation terms and dramatized further by the poetic justice of a brother avenging a brother, a point Villiers emphasized in his own expedition record.[33] *L'affaire Jumonville* attests to the information the literate French publics had access to regarding colonial affairs generally and North American events specifically, suggesting the need to consider metropolitan and colonial affairs together. Moreover, the campaign record reveals more clues about the forms, sense of place, and language of violence that marines and Indians shared, fought over, and together shaped on the 1750s' frontier. Villiers's mission to avenge Jumonville's death enables a deeper consideration of how the French authorities, marine officers, and Indians understood—in this situation—the purpose of organized violence.

Edited, printed French reproductions of Villiers's journal that circulated in 1756 show the elements of borderlands violence the metropole was aware of. The record published in Jacob-Nicolas Moreau's *Mémoire contenant le précis des faits, avec leur pièces justificatives* (along with Washington's captured campaign journal) omitted most of the details regarding Villiers's councils with his indigenous allies; it does describe the gifts given for the mission, however. This version honed in on the tragedy of Jumonville's death, the stop made at "the place where my brother was murdered, where I saw bodies still," and the terms exacted from Washington.[34] It emphasized that Villiers had prevented cruelties and pillage by his Indian allies, in contradistinction to Washington's ineffectiveness at "Jumonville Glen."[35] The journal described the British need to surrender as "we told them since it was *peacetime*, we wished to spare them the cruelties of the Indians that would result from a more lively defense . . . we offered clemency, having come only to avenge my brother's murder, which violated *the most Sacred Laws* and to force them off the King's lands."[36] As a dedicated officer, Villiers may truly have weighed the legality of his actions when considering his presentation of the events. His account had to explain the taking of prisoners of war during peacetime: neither Villiers nor the journal's editor, Moreau, wanted decisions made by a French officer to cause scandal as Washington's had.[37] Through the journal, this marine was successful in his projection of himself as an officer worthy of serving Louis XV and France, a man who respected the limits of violence during peacetime. This approach contrasted favorably with Washington's (and Britain's) dishonorable actions. The propaganda battle waged between British and French colonies and metropoles caused most of the textual focus naturally to follow the motivations and actions of each empire's European representatives in the Ohio Country, glossing over the actions of North American Native participants during the *affaire Jumonville* and the Villiers mission.

However, few, if any, indigenous peoples who followed Villiers did so in order to simply bolster French prestige and claims to the Ohio. From an Iroquoian or Algonquian perspective, Villiers had an understandable unique grievance: the solemn right of the brother to decide to pursue, capture, kill, or spare those responsible for his sibling's murder. The concept of avenging a death, or covering a death, existed in both French and Indian societies.[38] Villiers himself stated that his aim was to punish his brother's murderers, and his superior, Capt. Claude Pecaudy de Contrecoeur, explicitly told Native Americans who were being invited to go on this mission that it was to avenge the death of Villiers's brother.[39] Contrecoeur used a politic rationale with these indigenous allies, one that avoided asserting French ownership of the Ohio, the claim that Céloron back in 1749 had discovered most of the region's Indians disputed. Villiers and Contrecoeur may well have succeeded, especially among the Iroquoians, because Tanaghrisson, Jumonville's killer, was supposed to be a representative (along with the Oneida leader Scarouady) of the Six Nations' interests in the Ohio. For the Laurentian Iroquois accompanying Villiers, their presence in the French contingent atoned for the rebellious and dangerous factional self-interest of Tanaghrisson's actions. That Iroquoian purposes dovetailed with French goals was then a serendipitous coincidence; there is no reason to believe that the Indians in Villiers's force supported the imperial goals of the mission.[40]

The Ottawas could harbor their own reasons for aiding the French in the assault on Pickawillany and the killing of Memeskia and left their own record of that violence on trees in the woods and in the village clearing, now growing over, as well as in the long memory of the Miamis. Similarly, the avenging of Jumonville indicated more to the Indians of the Ohio Country than French accounts recognized. By killing Jumonville, Tanaghrisson rejected the French claims to the Ohio that had been forcefully made at Pickawillany, but the French came back, forcing Washington first to retreat, then to surrender at Fort Necessity. Washington's military failure left the Ohio Indians with no alternative but to try to mollify the French for Tanaghrisson's bad behavior without, however, acknowledging France's territorial claims. As the British at Fort Necessity came to realize with horror, Villiers's indigenous allies comprised "*our own . . . Shawnesses* [sic], *Delawares, and Mingos.*"[41] Aiding Villiers allowed these individuals to cover the French dead (by attacking Washington and letting Villiers allocate some of the spoils). More important, this action insulated Ohio Indians from a dangerous escalation of border tensions, the brunt of which would inevitably be borne by their communities in the region, not by British squatters to the east. New France's administration portrayed and metropolitan France read these Indians' actions as subordination, though they were not. The most rational explanation for Villiers's "restraint" of his allies was not his French superiority. It was that, following the protocols of revenge or mourning war, as the wronged relative, Villiers could claim the right to decide the fate of his captives. To his Native allies and enemies, Villiers's personal actions appeared reasonable in terms of their own rules of war; to them, the participation against Washington did not signify support for a permanent, militarized French presence in the Ohio Country with its fort-building project.

Pickawillany and the Jumonville affair pointed to complicated, persistently changing interplays of martial practice and legitimate violence on the western frontier after 1750. In the *troupes franches* alone there were "multiple faces of France" among the elite officers representing Louis XV. Charles de Langlade, Joseph Coulon de Jumonville, and Louis Coulon de Villiers were all equally but differently authorized conveyors of imperial authority and French interest in the way that they individually expressed the indigenous nations' interests. Their common task was to fulfill the Naval Ministry's directive to aggressively protect western land claims by assisting imperial expansion as agents of the borderland's defense. Ottawas at Pickawillany and Kahnawakes at Great Meadows were easily taken to also represent the face of France whenever their actions coincided with French interest. It seemed so to a French metropolitan audience, somewhat less so in the French colonial context, where administrators and marines spent a great deal of time and money managing indigenous relationships, and not so from a Native perspective, where each community was concerned primarily with its own prospects, not the French king's.

The actions taken by the colonial regulars and the indigenous allies at Pickawillany and at Fort Necessity could be read in multiple ways by those involved in the battle over the Ohio Valley. Langlade was especially well placed to interpret violence and its aftermath in both North American and European contexts, given his cross-cultural fluency. Other military personnel, like Villiers, understood the importance of recognizing the contributions and necessity of indigenous allies even if he might have missed or misconstrued the broader implications of certain rituals and engagements. Meanwhile, Ottawas, Kahnawakes, and other Native Americans on the borderlands used the landscape of conflict to mark their own victories and fit the outcome of battles into their conceptions of honor, retribution, and legitimate forms of violence. If events had continued without interference from the French metropolitans, perhaps both sides would have found new methods of communicating, peacefully or aggressively. The biggest obstacle to the different protagonists acquiring the capacity to interpret one another's statements, actions, and physical markers was, however, that the players in the borderlands changed in 1755.

⚜ Borderlands Trampled into Battlegrounds

This was the precarious situation on the ground and in the minds of protagonists, when the appearance of newcomers in the borderlands, thousands of soldiers and hundreds of officers arriving from the eastern Atlantic, raised expectations on all sides. In 1755 a British army sent from Europe descended on the Ohio Country to resolve the region's future; later in the year a French army struck for the same purpose farther to the north and east on the Lake George frontier. At first it seemed that the new arrivals would be absorbed right into the practices of war in North America, for better or worse. Instead, the violence of 1755 would bring major new consequences for French and British imperialist aspirations. Both Gen. Edward Braddock, the British commander who set out to attack Fort Duquesne in the summer of 1755, and Jean Erdman, Baron de Dieskau, the French commander whose orders were to push the British out of the Lake George area in September 1755, inaugurated changes in the conduct of their campaigns that would bring new scrutiny to the practices of war. These men and the officers they commanded asserted their authority over martial practice, albeit in a North American landscape, in which they were untried. Their battles did not go as planned but instead produced an explosive mix of incomparable European and North American customs competing with one another in real time on battlefield after battlefield, subjecting previously unquestioned forms of violence to new interpretations and official scrutiny.

In the summer of 1755 Braddock marched more than twenty-one hundred regular British troops and provincials into the Ohio Country to capture the French Fort Duquesne, located at the strategic river forks of the Ohio and the Monongahela Rivers, and thus end, once and for all, France's western claims. Things did not go as planned. A grueling march from Virginia to the Monongahela drained Braddock's army, and the general badly mismanaged Native allies. The English general informed the prominent Delaware, Shingas, and other important Ohioan leaders that the English would not return the Ohio Valley to its Indian inhabitants.[42] This statement led to the subsequent withdrawal of most of the Iroquois, Delawares, and Shawnees, who were disgusted by such treatment, and meant that Braddock proceeded with only eight Indians accompanying him, badly damaging the army's ability to scout and acquire information. As a result, when the English army was two days' march away from Fort Duquesne, Indians, Canadian marines, and militia lured the English troops into a disadvantageous ravine and ambushed them there. The British advance guard sustained devastating casualties; Braddock himself died in the engagement.

An official French pamphlet on the battle, published by the royal press in Paris as the *Relation de ce qui s'est passé en Canada, 1755*, related details of interest to a European audience, such as the magnitude of English casualties despite the numeric superiority of British forces and the prominent roles played by European officers.[43] The *Relation* did not mention how tumultuous the frontier violence seemed to the British survivors, preferring to emphasize marine officers' control and direction of the battle along European lines despite the Indian presence. Indians, in fact, played little role at all in this Parisian publication. But it was more than six hundred Indians allied with New France, including Ottawas, Potowatomis, and Wyandots, who formed the majority of the force that awaited Braddock in the woods that July day. They had descended to the rivers' confluence from the northern Great Lakes, lured by prestige goods to be captured and reputations to be made, in some cases due to the personal relationships between Canadian officers and their Native communities. Charles de Langlade returned from Michilimackinac, for example, accompanied once more by his Ottawa kinsmen. French marines understood that at the heart of Native motivation was their standing with their own societies. Success in war meant prizes, so much so that the commander at Fort Duquesne, Captain de Contrecoeur, plainly stated that it would be impossible to force the Indians to stay once they claimed their rewards.[44] The war parties left shortly after the engagement to return home, laden with goods, unconcerned with a possible British counterattack on the fort. It was not their cause to defend a fixed installation, especially after the spoils of victory they needed to share with their communities had been distributed.[45]

For the English, the battle served as a fearsome introduction to a new mode of war that seemed without order or boundary and one in which they sensed a disadvantage in controlling how events that transpired would be interpreted afterward. French field correspondence corroborated English accounts of disorder; beyond Indians claiming their rightful share of prizes, more than a few Canadian veterans had pillaged the fallen instead of pursuing the retreating English. Not only did surviving British officers and soldiers register the shock of unfamiliar war practices, but they also even had to improvise Braddock's burial to preserve the fallen commander from unimaginable but anticipated mutilation—they placed the general in the road and marched over his grave to preserve its anonymity.[46] Just as capturing Braddock's papers on the field of battle yielded a tactical and a psychological advantage to the French, surviving Anglo-Americans and British soldiers alike feared the level of humiliation that would be added to their defeat if Braddock's body fell into Indian hands.[47]

Almost two months to the day after the Native and French Canadian victory on the Monongahela, on September 8, 1755, the Baron de Dieskau's army of French regulars, marines, Canadian militia, and Indians lost to Col. William Johnson and his colonials along the southern shores of Lake George. Jean Erdman, Baron de Dieskau, resembled Braddock in that he was a European commander, but he proved more open to suggestion than the English general had been. Dieskau courted Native Americans, encouraged to do so by the current Canadian-born governor, Pierre de Rigaud, Marquis de Vaudreuil, who worked hard to maintain Franco-Indian alliances. Dieskau was also willing to adapt to North American conditions, using irregular forces to pursue his tactical objectives, following Canadian traditions and inspired by the French successes at Pickawillany, at Great Meadows, and most recently on the Monongahela. Indeed, the official French report describing the Lake George battle commented on the multinational character of the army and noted the prominent Indian and Canadian roles in tactical discussions.[48] Even after Dieskau's defeat, Intendant François Bigot, Canada's senior civil administrator, had reported to Naval Minister Rouillé that the general was "well suited to war in this country, being loved and respected by Canadians, Indians, and French troops."[49] Confident in his own command and the efficacy of his troops, Dieskau fought Johnson mostly with Canadians, a few Indians, and only two hundred regular grenadiers. Earlier in his career in Europe, Dieskau had a positive experience deploying irregulars. But this was not Flanders, Hungary, or Italy, and it was Dieskau's mismanagement of these alliances that resulted in the French defeat.

First, local Abenakis and Iroquois from the Laurentian Valley and the Adirondacks, who accompanied Dieskau to Lake George, resisted Dieskau's orders that they assault a fortified position. The Nipissings spoke plainly with their marine commander, Legardeur de Saint Pierre, stating they would not attack the fort and predicting that Dieskau would lose the forthcoming battle. Next, on the morning of Dieskau's attack, a scouting party led by Col. Ephraim Williams from Massachusetts and the elderly Mohawk King Hendrick (Theyanoguin), ran into a successful French ambush. Williams and Hendrick did not survive. Worse yet, unhorsed, King Hendrick was slain after he fell into a group of armed Kahnawake Mohawk women—and his body, when discovered, was found to have been "amateurishly scalped"—an act that enraged and appalled his supporters and relations.[50] After the "Bloody Morning Scout," Kahnawake Mohawks did not want to attack the English camp, in which they likely had kin, and certainly did not want to suffer more losses. Finally, the Abenakis would go nowhere without the Mohawks, and once indigenous aid was withdrawn, the Canadians agreed with the indigenous advice to avoid attacking the fort.[51] Unaware of or unconcerned about the complexities so apparent to his Indian allies, and especially with Mohawks serving on both sides, Dieskau's inattention to the motivations of his Native allies cost him any advantage. Counting on only his regulars now, Dieskau led his grenadiers forward across the open in fine, French continental style and produced a disastrous defeat.

Europeans and elite colonists in 1755 chose to understand the losses at the Monongahela and at Lake George as the result of the troops' failure, not the inadequacies of the commanders or their unsuitability to the Americas. Braddock could not explain himself, but George Washington, in defense of Braddock, noted that if only the British regulars had shown more discipline and had better training in North America, things would have turned out differently.[52] In his explanations of his loss, Dieskau upset Governor Vaudreuil by placing the blame squarely on the Canadians and Indians, claiming that they had shown no discipline or bravery and had disregarded his orders. How to discipline and control troops on campaign and in battle would lead to much conflict among French and Canadian officers after 1756. The contest to decide this dispute would form some of the most crucial issues for France's North American war effort. What stands out in Dieskau's reporting is that, despite his shameful defeat and humiliating capture, he did not criticize how the Indians made war. He only faulted them for running away before and during his assault at Lake George. Perhaps his stoicism came from his familiarity with *la petite guerre* (guerrilla or irregular war), the category into which he placed Indian warfare. A protégé of the legendary Maurice Auguste, Maréchal de Saxe (a fellow Saxon), Dieskau had served with that general during the War of Austrian Succession, a war in which the French army used irregular troops and engaged in *la petite guerre* on the Austro-Hungarian frontier.[53]

Braddock's and Dieskau's defeats proved that the ingredients for military success were more elusive than either adopting or rejecting North American modes of warfare. Embracing North American methods of violence did not necessarily guarantee victory—for there was no single "North American" way of war despite eighteenth-century accounts that made such suggestions.[54] Braddock rejected Indian assistance and irregular warfare, whereas Dieskau accepted both, demonstrating that following regional practices did not guarantee victory. Yet even though Dieskau was willing to take Indian advice up to a point, he never grasped the precise nature of alliances and how they could affect certain events. Understanding the reasons behind local means of war influenced military outcomes more than tactics. Governor Vaudreuil reported that the Monongahela victory rested on captains Jean-Daniel Dumas and François-Marchand de Ligneris, who encouraged the troops after the death of the commanding officer, Daniel Liénard de Beaujeu, by fighting alongside Indians and the militia and prevailing.[55] These officers attempted to meet indigenous allies on the latter's terms—in doing so, they succeeding in obtaining their allegiance at critical moments. But no officer, not even Charles de Langlade, could have forced the Indians to come and fight by the mere fact of their military rank—this the marines well knew, even if their metropolitan superiors did not.

To their detriment, the European generals both misinterpreted and dismissed Indian concerns. It was not only because each behaved as a superior dealing with inferiors. It was also because they could neither access nor understand the meaning to the Indians of the landscape they had known before lead plaques, French forts, and Braddock's corduroy road changed its contours. What Dieskau and Braddock saw as the borderlands, Indians saw as the center. Even the images produced to illustrate troop movements and battles reflected the different ways in which indigenous and European audiences visualized territory, violence, and the coming of war, as shown in figures 1, 2, and 3.

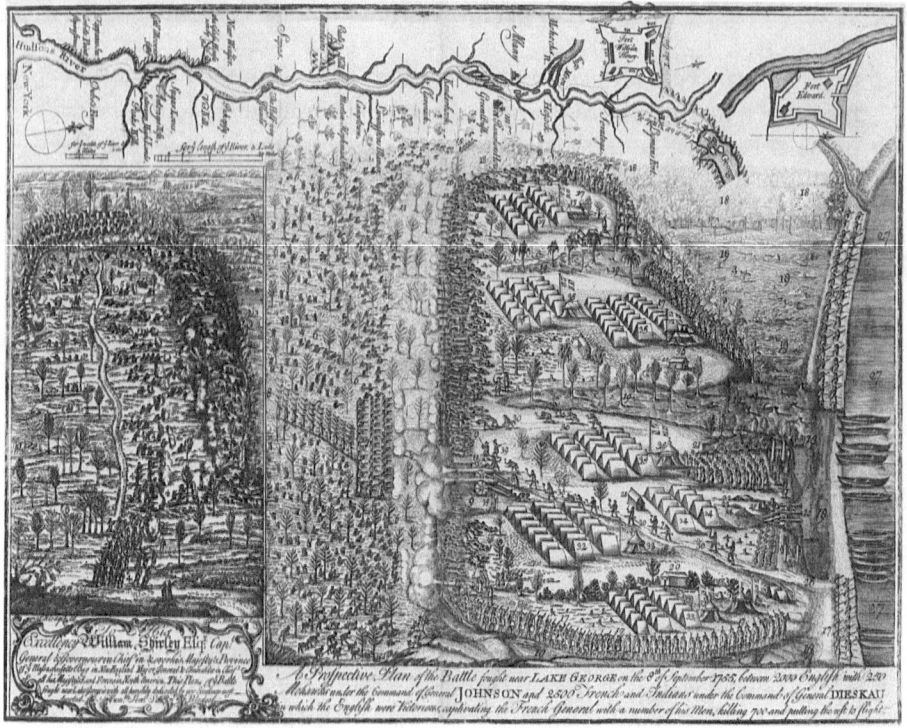

FIGURE 1. Samuel Blodget, *A Prospective View of the Battle fought near Lake George, on the 8th of Sepr. 1755*, printed in Boston, 1755. Courtesy of the John Carter Brown Library at Brown University.

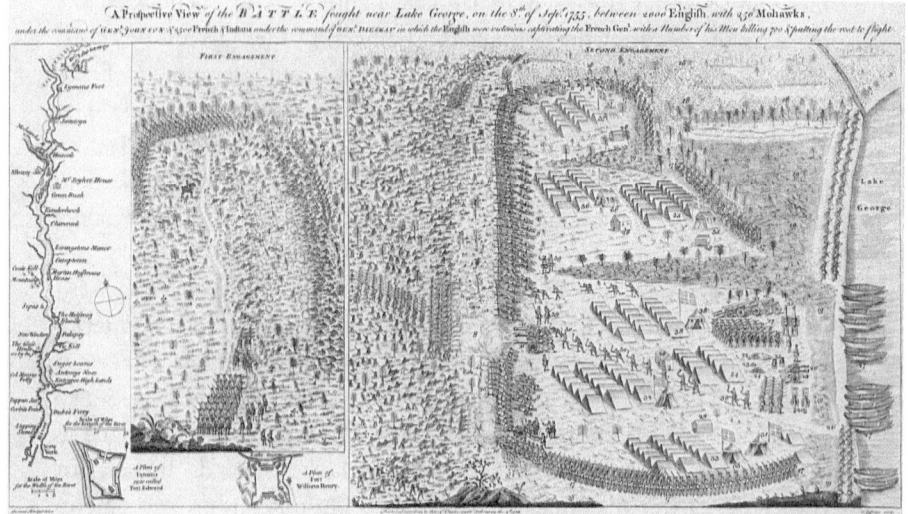

FIGURE 2. *A Prospective View of the Battle fought near Lake George, on the 8th of Sepr. 1755*, printed in London by Thomas Jefferys, 1756. Courtesy of the John Carter Brown Library at Brown University.

These changes to the land made by peripheral metropolitans scarred what the Indians regarded as their own spaces, symbolized by the signs with which they continued to mark forest trees. The senior European officers' indifference, in spite of colonial and Native counsel, caused trouble.[56] Braddock's high-handed response to Delaware and Iroquois concerns cost him his allies, confirming Ohio Indians' suspicions of British perfidy. The withdrawal of an Indian presence on the English side ensured that, in the battle, most of the indigenous participants were those from the *pays d'en haut* who had fought on the French side. Although the physical presence of Anishinaabeg and Hurons on Delaware and Mingo land presented to those Indians a challenge to their Ohioan sovereignty, it proved temporary. Moreover, abandoning Braddock insulated English-inclined Indians from experiencing casualties on July 9, a lack of deaths that in turn prevented blood feuds between English-allied Indians and those fighting with the French. Braddock's misreading of Native peoples allowed Mingos, Delawares, and Shawnees to avoid both the French and British expeditions and to pursue their own agenda of Native disengagement, eschewing the unpleasant situation of an intraindigenous conflict.

But other violence left an imprint in the summer of 1755 and demonstrated how Indians read narratives of violence involving Europeans and Indians on the eve of the official commencement of war on both sides of the Atlantic. One of the few Indians on campaign with Braddock, the leader Scarouady, lost his son while marching to Duquesne and was inconsolable. What "Old Monacatothé [Scarouady's Lenape name]," wrote a British officer, "regretted most was his [son] being killed by our own people." The incident brought home the danger of colonial warfare for Native communities even when Indians were not the direct target of an army.[57] The Mohawk

---

Samuel Blodget's 1755 print, *A Prospective Plan of the Battle of Lake George* (figure 1), suggests how a North American battlefield might have been interpreted by Anglo-American, British, and perhaps even certain French audiences. The print translates both Blodget's eyewitness view and testimony that "the battle was now carried on in the *Indian* way by the whole *French* army, *regulars* as well as *irregulars*, some fighting behind trees, and stumps, and others squatting" (Charles Chauncy, *A Second Letter to a Friend; Giving a more particular Narrative of the Defeat of the French Army at Lake-George, by the New-England Troops, than has yet been published* [September 29, 1755] [Boston: Edes and Gill, 1755], 8). The print's collapse of the morning and afternoon engagements obscures how Dieskau's grenadiers attacked alone, in a more formal, European style. The print's heavy lines and tight planes reflect the chaos and terror experienced by not only New England militias but also the provincials, French marines and grenadiers, Canadians, and Indians fighting each other in close quarters. The Boston map contrasts with a 1756 reworking of the original engraving, produced by Thomas Jefferys in London (figure 2). In Jefferys' image, made for a European market, the London printer favored an evenly spaced war, reflecting a greater European concern with depicting actors, orderly encampment, and the hierarchy of command.

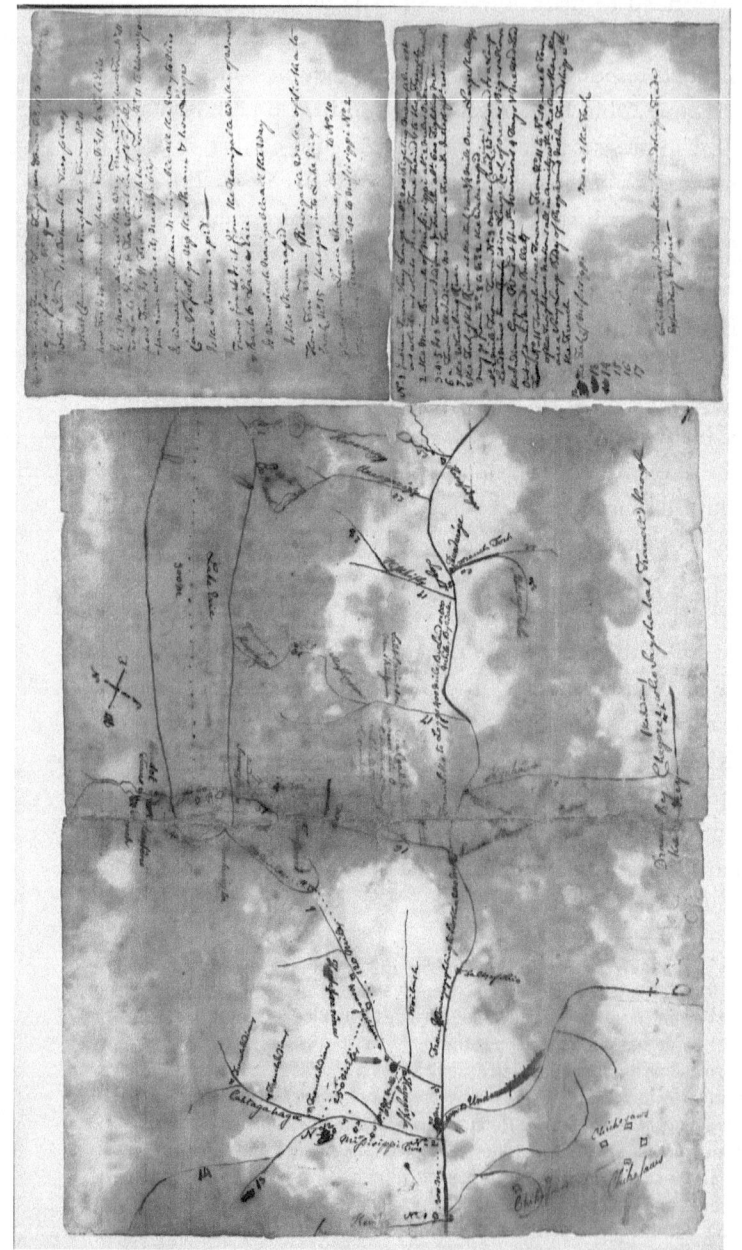

FIGURE 3. *Map of the country about the Mississippi. Drawn by Chegeree (the Indian) who says he has travelled through the country*, circa 1755. The manuscript map drawing by "Chegeree," an Indian of the Ohio Country, depicting the territory from Lake Erie to the mouth of the Ohio River, contrasts with figures 1 and 2 in its representation of land claims and spatiality. Chegeree foregrounds Indians' movement across the landscape, noting appearances of "French and Indians" along river ways as opposed to indicating a single battle line. European actors are minimized in favor of the intimate relationships between the observer on the ground (Chegeree), local Native information networks, distances, and water routes. Courtesy of the Library of Congress.

Hendrick's death spoke to other ominous realities—unlike Pickawillany, Jumonville Glen, Fort Necessity, and the Monongahela battle, the "Bloody Morning Scout" at Lake George had pitted Mohawks against Mohawks—threatening the long-held policy of neutrality between relatives who leaned toward France and those who favored alliance with Britain. For Kahnawake Mohawks, and women at that, to have taken a trophy such as Hendrick's scalp meant that a social boundary had been crossed.[58] However, the death of the Anglophilic Hendrick enabled the Iroquois Confederacy to return to neutrality without further dissension, and, although tragic, this act supported a renewal of cooperation around broad Iroquois interests instead of those of a few individuals.[59] Women were crucial to Iroquois decision making, especially as it pertained to war, peace, and the fulfillment of community needs. When Hendrick stumbled into the women's ranks, a few matriarchs may have chosen to kill him in order to prevent further intra-Iroquois bloodshed. However, the demise of the old "king" on the field of battle, with no formal council discussions, demonstrated the inversion of the world. Here civilians ritually unprepared for the violence of battle seem to have committed an act unthinkable to the community. If this was the case, it was an unsettling vision of the future for the Iroquois.

One final engagement illuminates Native perspectives on European war in 1755. Most accounts of the North American Seven Years' War focus on the interplay among Europeans, Indians, and colonists in battle, as at the Monongahela or Lake George. But in the early years of the war, one battle involved "white-on-white" frontier violence—the March 27, 1756, attack on the English Fort Bull. Canadian marine engineer Gaspard Chaussegros de Léry had trekked from Montreal to the western New York frontier with more than three hundred soldiers, Canadians, Iroquois, Algonquins, Nipissings, and metropolitan French regulars to attack this fort on the Oneida Carry, which threatened French interests on Lake Ontario and in the Indian trade. After the English defenders refused to surrender in exchange for protection, Léry and his troops charged, fired through the holes in the fort's poorly built walls, and then broke down the door. They killed almost everyone they encountered, and "very few escaped, among them a woman," before the entire structure exploded from burning gunpowder.[60] But with the exception of a few individual guides, Léry's "miserable" Indian allies "waited at a distance . . . when they understood the fort was to be attacked." It was the French regulars, marines, and Canadian militia who undertook the attack, afterward dubbed a "massacre" by the English.[61] Despite this victory, Léry had to return to Canada after assaulting the fort rather than proceeding to the next British post, Fort Williams, because the Indians with him informed him that they would not support such an action. Instructed that he could not stay in this region without his Native allies, Léry had no choice but to turn north.[62] The calculation behind the Kahnawakes' ultimatum to Léry included securing their share of the spoils and keeping Léry from either overextending himself and thus endangering their gains or dealing too great a blow to the British trade, on which their Iroquois kin in the area depended to make it through the rest of winter.

The indigenous nations disliked assaulting fortified positions, which would inevitably result in a greater risk of death for individual warriors. Destroying a trading post that granted access to cheaper, higher-quality English goods was mostly in the French, not the indigenous, interest. Furthermore, the Iroquois and the Algonquians possibly reasoned it was best to let the competing Europeans kill each other rather than risk their own lives (and English revenge). Tensions had heightened between the Mohawks in New York and in New France after the disaster of the "Bloody Morning Scout." Fort Bull was in the Six Nations' territory, and that may have made some Kahnawake Mohawks unwilling to further provoke their relations and the Iroquois League. From the Kahnawake perspective, allowing the Six Nations to decide how they wanted to address this type of physical obstruction on their land may have been preferable to actively helping the French decide the matter for all of the Iroquois.[63] Shattered as a result of the explosion, the remains of Fort Bull left a dramatic mark near the southern shore of Lake Ontario at Wills Creek. Taken together, the destruction of the fort, its garrison, and its stores showed what the French regulars, alongside Canadians, were willing to do to other Europeans to further the interests of their king. It was an act of explicitly performative violence as much as what had happened at Pickawillany, but at Fort Bull the Indians themselves were the observers of the violence and its results, not its authors. As they returned home, *réserve* Indians may have reflected on the lack of restraint these Europeans showed toward each other.

The participation of metropolitan Europeans and colonials, professional soldiers and volunteers, and diverse Indian nations in these battles guaranteed that violence, loss, and martial practice would be defined in a variety of ways. Some constants transcended culture—all violence threatened the lives of participants and destabilized homes, families, and modes of authority. However, a principal failure of the metropolitan generals who managed the battles of 1755 and their European handlers was to have assumed that only one scenario counted—the one they sought to enact. Meanwhile, sovereign indigenous nations, Indian refugee communities, and lone individuals in the borderlands persisted in viewing themselves as independent actors and followed their own national or factional interests as circumstances permitted.

Like Braddock, Dieskau demonstrated the failure of metropolitan plans and metropolitan officers on the ground to take into account the specificities of local practice needed to achieve victory. Even though the new European arrivals in the borderlands saw the residue of violence left on the landscape, they missed the multiple meanings of the acts of violence in which they participated and misinterpreted the significance of past battles and raids. Some new features of the Ohio Country were the physical reminders of conflict, left in the wake of defeat or in the face of desperation: in his journal Coulon de Villiers mentioned passing by the bodies of his brother's men along the path to the Great Meadows. English troops marching with Braddock toward Fort Duquesne saw the "many human bones all around ye spott" of Fort Necessity, the testament to Washington's dead companions.[64] Other physical evidence was deliberately placed in order to create a dialogue with passersby. When Braddock's army stumbled across the remains of a French and Indian camp, they saw "drawn many odd figures on ye trees expressing with red paint, ye scalps and Prisoners they had taken with them; there were three french Names wrote there, Rochefort, Chauraudray, & Picauday."[65] The French names—denoting prisoners or warriors—in this otherwise Native record of deeds suggest this particular spot was meant for viewing by Braddock's troops, the newest European and colonial audience.

But just as the British officer recording this sign failed to connect to it any obvious meaning, the significance of these signs clearly also evaded the Native participants. Indians cared little about the meaning and propaganda effect of English battle plans discovered by the French at the Monongahela or the importance for the British of hiding Braddock's body underneath the road, though to the English, the experience they were trying to avoid was akin to what the Mohawks experienced when they discovered Hendrick's mutilated body. Even those whose homeland this was were now passing through a landscape in which their interpretations of legitimate violence were increasingly incomplete. The violent future of this place would not be determined by either Indians or Europeans according to anyone's plans but rather as the outcome of escalating misunderstandings of the others' intentions.

⁕ Before the Storm

No Miamis returned to the charred remains of Pickawillany, formerly a thriving trading town—its shell stood witness to France's aggressive pursuit of its former allies and to the possibilities open to other Indian nations if the Ohio Country continued to roil with violence. Memories endured long after the event as well; thirteen years later the Miamis explained their decision to support the Anishinaabeg war in 1765 against the British by referencing their last defiance of the Ottawas, in 1752.[66] The forts constructed or strengthened by New France between 1750 and 1756 marred the horizon and reminded everyone passing by of the imminent threat and claims of Louis XV. Pickawillany was a place that attested to the blood price of the extension of power. Marine lieutenant Joseph Marin de La Malgue, who thought about the French forts in the Ohio Country, would have read a similar message. His father, Captain Paul Marin de La Malgue, had spent the early 1750s overseeing the construction of Forts Presqu'isle, Le Boeuf, and Machault and had undertaken a show of force in 1753. Exhausted by these efforts in the service of empire, the elder Marin had expired on October 29, 1753, at Fort Le Boeuf.[67]

The voluminous correspondence among marine commanders at these western forts and between these forts and Quebec relied on the presence of Indian runners who crisscrossed the North American interior bearing dispatches, orders, and the latest news. As they traveled over the trails that ran past the sites of violence—Pickawillany, Jumonville Glen, the battles at the Monongahela and Lake George, even Fort Bull—they reconciled what their eyes saw with the information they carried. Upon arriving at their destinations, these bearers of dispatches engaged directly with the military culture, delivering messages, exchanging impressions, and talking with the marines and colonial leadership, and they must have been aware of how the conflict taking place in their homelands had escalated by the end of 1755.

The couriers could not have guessed, however, when they engaged with the marine officers of New France whom they knew, that the conflict about to be officially declared was also to become a contest to see what it meant to be a French nobleman and a soldier and who could be the face, the voice, and the hand of the French empire at war; it would also reveal how central their own indigenous communities would be to the thinking of the contestants, especially since, from many Natives' perspectives, this determination had already been made. After the battle of Lake George, several communities had told Governor General Vaudreuil that they would no longer serve under metropolitan officers.[68] Vaudreuil himself knew that Dieskau's capture and the imminent outbreak of formal European declarations of war guaranteed that a new commander from France would arrive sooner or later.

The governor's fury with Dieskau for letting himself be captured partly stemmed from a suspicion that his differences over tactics with a foreign-born general would be minimal compared to having to negotiate issues of strategy and legitimate martial practice with a fellow French nobleman, one who would necessarily conduct himself and lead his troops according to his own sense of class and regard for national honor.

Many marines and Vaudreuil believed that New France's ability to prevail absolutely required sustaining a winning martial reputation among the Indians in the Ohio Country and the northeast.[69] The Shawnees, Mingos, Delawares, and Miamis of the Ohio region reluctantly sided with France because of repeated British inability to defend or protect Indian land and settlements and because the new British policy, which they had heard with their own ears from Braddock, explicitly claimed their land.[70] At least the French were not numerous enough to flood them with squatters and speculators. Although Langlade could draw on his influence with the Ottawas, and officer-diplomats like Daniel-Marie and Philippe Chabert de Joncaire had strong family and diplomatic connections to the Senecas, these personal relationships could not guarantee Indian participation in subsequent violent encounters. Every planned engagement had to be negotiated anew with Indian allies. The French had won at Pickawillany and at the Monongahela in the Ohio, then lost in the northeast at Lake George, but won at Fort Bull. None of these actions had reduced the ongoing expenses of New France's frontier diplomacy; instead, they augmented the pull on the imperial purse.[71]

Repeated appeals from the Naval Ministry to reduce expenses in Canada were not met, but even though financing the colony's escalating military needs strained relations between metropole and colony before the official outbreak of war in 1756, they did not rupture them. Only when French noble officers arrived in North America and attempted to wrest control of the colonial struggle to make it resemble a continental war did unity waver. Until then different methods could be and were used to pursue the defense of French honor in war, the choice seeming to depend on whether one was a rural or a wealthy French noble or a Canadian or a *métis* elite. Acts of violence were constantly changing; no one attempted to or could pin down what exactly was "legitimate" or "standard." Acting in accordance with definitions of masculinity and war that ran along a spectrum of Native to European traditions, all of these men had in common that they believed themselves to be defending France's empire most effectively. French Canadians recalled their injunction from Louis XIV to protect royal territory at all costs and drew strength from it. After 1756, French military elites from both sides of the Atlantic found themselves under arms together. They angled for advantage regarding their roles in determining how to defend the empire, and eventually they argued over the larger question of what that empire represented. Indigenous martial practices and Indian soldiers themselves (particularly those who straddled contested and changing French and Native traditions) came to dominate this quarrel between military elites, influencing the colonial understanding of war and empire and sharpening metropolitan notions of civility and martial honor by providing a counterpoint to both.[72]

← CHAPTER 3

Culture Wars in the Woods

As icy winds howled across snowbanks, the government of New France planned for the upcoming 1756 campaign season and the new troubles it would have to face. The roiling North Atlantic ruptured communication lines between Canada and Versailles, leaving Governor Pierre de Rigaud, Marquis de Vaudreuil-Cavagnal, to imagine what difficulties English designs, a new French commander, and French reinforcement troops might bring in May. Without an official declaration of war, the governor's planning had to follow the policies of his predecessors, the Marquis de Duquesne, the Marquis de Jonquière, and the Marquis de La Gallisonière. All three men had expanded French fortifications along the Ohio River, in the western Great Lakes, and on Britain's New York/Pennsylvania border with New France, consistently repelling English mercantile and military incursions into French territory. Throughout the winter, Governor Vaudreuil made diplomatic overtures to encourage the Indians of the Great Lakes and along the Ohio River to provide more military support for New France, and he attempted to sway the Iroquois Confederacy to side with France. Defensive warfare, heavily reliant on Native participation, was a method familiar to the new governor. The son of a long-serving previous governor general, he had been born in Canada, grown up there, and participated in numerous fur-trading missions in the Indian countries as a young man.

Knowing that imperial war loomed, Vaudreuil had already written to Versailles requesting military reinforcements. He hoped that their command would be given exclusively to him. After all, as New France's governor he both embodied the person of the king and was officially the sole leader of military affairs in the colony.[1] Vaudreuil's request was unrealistic, however. Patronage, an indispensible component of the ancien régime, achieved new heights at the court ruled by Louis XV and his favorite, the Marquise de Pompadour. War led to the astronomical expansion of military positions. Multiple theaters of conflict meant that the interests of many Crown clients and patrons could be advanced. The French nobility, already the largest in Europe, funneled its young men into the army's officer corps, a vestige of Louis XIV's policy to keep his male aristocrats occupied while he consolidated royal power. Louis XV had continued this tradition—but did so now as a calculated measure to reassure aristocrats of their preeminent position in society. Prestige, rather than royal necessity, kept the army officer corps under the purview of the Second Estate. War for the first time since 1748 meant potential for advancement, and French nobles, young and old, swelled the army's officer ranks. A generalship in New France could be used by the Crown to forward the king's policy by rewarding yet another faithful aristocrat.[2] To send French metropolitan officered reinforcements to North America, though, ran the risk of causing friction with the militarized elites of New France, who derived their own position from defending the colony's boundaries, not least among them Governor General Vaudreuil himself.

← Imperial War

While Vaudreuil planned the raid of the English Fort Bull (near Lake Ontario) in the early spring of 1756, fêted Indian embassies at Montreal, and assessed frontier strengths, assignments were drafted at the Ministry of War for Louis-Joseph de St. Véran, Marquis de Montcalm. Aiding the newly appointed general were François Gaston de Lévis and François Charles de Bourlamaque, along with staff aides, including the young Louis-Antoine de Bougainville. The embarkation of the army to New France was complete by mid-March 1756, but it was late May before the three thousand *troupes de terre* (army regulars) arrived there with Montcalm. Delighted though he was to have fresh troops, it was his reunion on June 12, 1756, with his fellow marine and trusted younger brother, François Pierre de Rigaud, who had been an English captive for a year, that pleased Governor Vaudreuil the most.³

New France's colonial leadership presided over numerous Franco-Indian festivities celebrating the arrival of new French troops and Native leaders, warriors, and their families in Montreal during the late spring and early summer of 1756. These were the diplomacies necessary to bind indigenous alliances before war. During this period, French officers observed and interacted with Iroquois, Abenakis, Nipissings, and Algonquins in a variety of ways: in embassies, at councils, as trading partners, and by observing Indians who were servants or slaves in colonial households. Kahnawake Iroquois arrived in early June "with their council women to compliment [senior French officers]," bearing wampum belts and congratulations for "Father Onontio (this is what they call the governor general)" and for "King Onontio Goa [Louis XV]." This delegation must have been pleased to receive Montcalm's assurance "that I would come to them and visit."⁴ Such interactions repeated themselves to the point of fatigue for both hosts and guests. "There have been nothing but visits, harangues, and deputations from these gentlemen [Indians], ever since I came here," Montcalm wrote to his mother in mid-June.⁵ The tone of these earliest encounters suggested the fruitful possibilities of concerted efforts between Indians, French, and Canadians in the upcoming campaign. However, these meetings also created important expectations and misconceptions that would haunt the interactions of colonial officers, Indians, and French nobles for the rest of the war.

At Montreal, Native peoples and colonists saw the new troops for themselves and caught up on war news brought by the recent arrivals from Europe. Montcalm, Lévis, and Bourlamaque presented their orders to Canada's leadership, along with correspondence describing British preparations for war and outlining the chain of command between colonial and metropolitan troops. Vaudreuil received word from Machault d'Arnouville, naval minister, that John Campbell, Earl of Loudoun, was replacing the dead Edward Braddock.⁶ This development meant that war would continue and was now in earnest even if the declarations of hostilities between George II and Louis XV had not yet reached Canada.

Amid routine memoranda, orders, and appointments was a letter hinting at an issue that would become critical in shaping New France's later war effort. Dated February 20, 1756, Machault's missive warned Vaudreuil of His Most Christian Majesty's displeasure at the 1755 loss of the Acadian Fort Beauséjour due to an inadequate defense. Both king and minister desired that such an event never recur; Vaudreuil even received a rare note from

Louis XV himself, demanding the court martial of the responsible officers, the Canadian sieurs Vergor and Villereau. The royal reaction to this surrender made it evident that the king of France jealously guarded the glory of his arms and the honor of his troops wherever they were.[7] The governor was not alone in being reminded of the importance of victory and military honor. The new senior French officers sent to New France (Montcalm, Lévis, and their staffs) were very aware that they were replacing two disgraced former commanders, Dieskau and his second-in-command, the chevalier de Rostaing, now captives of the English.[8] These French nobles had no intention of letting down their monarch. Dieskau was a foreigner, but Montcalm was a true French aristocrat. He had to uphold a higher standard.

The faith of metropolitan officers like Montcalm in their own values sprang from their aristocratic lineage and military training. Montcalm's officers perceived their martial responsibilities through a lens of chivalry, honor, and etiquette. They therefore interpreted this new war, like all wars, as a defense of the kingdom's honor. Every action they took in New France to protect French claims necessarily reflected their personal values and virtue. Battles would showcase their noble bravery, devotion to the monarch and the realm, and the French nation's civility. Montcalm and his officers were ambitious to add to the glory of the king, his arms, and their own noble class. Their obligation to meet these goals never left their minds during their North American service. They were unaware that the war practices they brought with them had little to do with the conflict that had been waged in North America for almost a decade.[9]

The royal council wished to avoid any disagreements over strategy, so even though Vaudreuil and Montcalm held equivalent military ranks (as a full captain in the navy, who held the same grade as a brigadier general), the two men would not have had the same status in the execution of war. Vaudreuil was to serve as chief strategist, while Montcalm as his subordinate would oversee all matters pertaining to his army and its discipline. In order for Montcalm to execute Vaudreuil's vision on the battlefield, the colonial and army leadership would have to work together in a partnership that the ministry hoped would showcase both colonial and army expertise.[10]

Even at an institutional level, the French army and the French navy were completely distinct services. Each had its own ministers, each of whom was appointed by the king and had his own enormous staff, so large that both bureaus began constructing their own ministerial office wings at Versailles in the 1750s. The army was the older and more prestigious of the two services, dating back to the beginnings of the French monarchy. The navy, which oversaw the Ponant and the Levant fleets, all French colonies and their colonial troops, and the *compagnies franches de la marine*, dated only to the late seventeenth century.[11] Although the Naval Ministry had an infrastructure for dealing with colonial affairs, relying by 1748 on eight expert *premiers commis* (chief clerks) and more than sixty *commis* (subclerks), the army had no such framework until 1755. Nonetheless, the Ministry of War had its own advantages in addition to prestige—abundant financing and institutional stability. Marc-Pierre Voyer de Paulmy, Comte d'Argenson, had been secretary of state for war since 1743.[12] By contrast, engulfed in scandal in the late 1740s, the Naval Ministry passed through the hands of three ministers between 1746 and 1756 (and would go through four more by 1763).

Separate ministries meant separate career networks, separate routes to power, and separate patrons. Competition between *compagnies franches* marines and army officers who sought honors and position on the same campaigns in North America ignited bureaucratic and interservice rivalries. Each side appealed to its respective ministry as its source of patronage and to air grievances. The situation was exacerbated by the fact that New France's politics followed the same patronage dynamics as Versailles, just on a smaller, local scale. Vaudreuil, Montcalm, their senior officers, and Canadian administrators all rewarded personal loyalty. In their Atlantic correspondence they praised favored troops and officers—almost always exclusively from their own services—often at the expense of the other's clients. Jealously protective of their spheres of influence, the leaders of the war effort, Vaudreuil and Montcalm, were soon at odds. In mid-June, Vaudreuil wrote to Machault, complaining about the transfer of the militia and some *troupes de la marine* to Montcalm's command. Meanwhile, the Comte d'Argenson, minister of war, was told not only that the governor was showing extravagant courtesy to Montcalm but also that Vaudreuil was "slow and indecisive" and trusted no one from old France.[13] If French divisions in the organization of the martial services challenged a coherent war effort, however, it was the presence and engagement of Indians that decisively shaped discussion over how to wage this war.

✦ American Encounters

Jesuit letters from the seventeenth century had formed basic French knowledge of Indians and Canadians; by the early eighteenth century, later travel narratives, part of a growing canon describing French colonial ventures worldwide, supplanted the Jesuit accounts.[14] Louis Lom d'Arce Lahontan's *New Voyages to North America* (1703), Claude Charles Le Roy Bacqueville de La Potherie's *History of North America* (1722), and the Jesuit priest Pierre F. X. Charlevoix's *History and Descriptions of New France* (1744) presented more or less accurate accounts of the exotic flora, fauna, and peoples of Canada in volumes rich with detailed illustrations and maps. Denis Diderot and Jean Le Rond d'Alembert's *Encyclopédie* (1751) drew heavily on Lahontan's works as its source of information, with the explicit intention of correcting errors and myths such as the misconception of "Indian hairiness." The most contemporary report on New France in circulation at the time war was declared was *Travels into North America*, by naturalist Per Kalm. With its publication starting in 1753 and continuing until 1761, Kalm described his firsthand experiences with New France's creole and colonial populations. But it was Charlevoix's 1744 work that was the preferred reading choice of the elite French officers assigned to New France. Soon after arriving in Canada, Montcalm wrote home to tell his mother to read volumes five and six of Charlevoix's account to learn about Indians, for "as a rule, all that he says is true."[15] *History and Descriptions* would be the reference against which the Montcalm ladies and many other metropolitan audiences could place the private letters and public relations accounts that arrived from Canada. Still, it was one thing to discuss or read about North America in the abstract; a soldier's vocation was active duty, and these troops looked forward to going into the field. For the French officers, learning about Native methods of war through hearsay or secondhand reports could not compare with working with these new allies themselves.

Many of the letters sent home by the officers who arrived with the massive French reinforcements of 1756 mimicked travel literature. For the first time in seventy years metropolitan soldiers could measure their imagined perceptions of Indians against flesh-and-blood interactions. Personal diaries or letters to family members and friends described Canada, its cities, its population, and the Indians encountered (including their dress, customs, games, foods, and martial habits). These writings responded to the understandable curiosity of the newly arrived French with regard to North America's indigenous peoples and Canadian colonists. Montreal, with an impressive diversity of Native individuals, hosted the first sustained interactions between colonists, Indians, and curious metropolitans. The city was a cosmopolitan center surrounded by thriving indigenous communities, a place where Mohawk women traveled "to visit French chapels, Nipissing men brought deer meat to the market square, Oneida families visited French friends, enslaved Apache girls carried water to the garden." Important meetings, such as the many councils and speeches held to welcome the French army to North America, could temporarily enlarge Montreal's Native population to almost equal the number of French residents.[16]

In their initial interactions with Abenakis, Mohawks, Nippissings, Hurons, Oneidas, and Anishinaabeg of the *pays d'en haut*, French officers had to reconcile whatever book knowledge of Indians they had, if any, with what they saw in front of them. "The Savages of Canada are very different from the idea commonly held of them in France," Jean Baptiste d'Aleyrac wrote in his journal. "Far from being hairy, as is believed, they are much less covered with hair than we are."[17] This young officer, not having consulted the most current travel literature, had transposed the idea of the European wild man living in a state of nature onto indigenous North Americans. The chevalier Le Duchat, a junior officer in the Languedoc regiment, referenced a different metropolitan perception when he told his father in July 1756 that the Indians lived up to every violent image he had imagined. Their cruelties in this war were without bounds, he said, and the practice of scalping, which he described in detail, was particularly revolting.[18]

Not all of the metropolitan assessments were negative or fantastical, however. The French officers had not anticipated the formal etiquette of Native culture—the councils, the speeches—which they saw and recorded. French sources repeatedly identified respected leaders and orators like the Lac des Deux Montagnes Nipissing chief Kinsenik or Pennahouel, an Ottawa chief, in their letters and memoirs. Le Duchat, d'Aleyrac, and other officers also noted their admiration of Native athleticism, attributing the Indians' endurance to their "constant exercise of hunting, fishing, dancing, and lacrosse" and added that the Indians were "tireless, hardened to pain" and could face heat and cold with little difficulty.[19] The Comte de Malartic, in the Béarn regiment, made a comment that was frequently repeated by French observers that Indians were "large and well-made," adding that only sunburn separated Indians from Frenchmen in color.[20] Few sources, however, took the time to distinguish between mission Indians of the *réserves*, nations of the *pays d'en haut*, Native enemies of France (although not necessarily British-allied peoples), and *panis* (Indian slaves).

The French officers looked at the Canadians, too. Though Indians and French colonists never fell into the same category, many French officers drew some parallels between these two populations. Canadians showed "particular skill with a rifle and hatchet" and were tireless and hardy, "especially on campaign."[21] Through their close attention to physicality, customs, and carriage, French officers began to form their own opinions of Native and Canadian characters. Some said of Indians that "in no other nation does one hold himself so tall as with the Indians who always walk with their heads high up."[22] Others faulted the "robust" Canadians for remaining "quite ignorant, having no concept of sciences and interested only in trade" and the Indians for their "natural cunning" and lack of refined culture.[23]

French preconceptions of Indians as "savages" explains why so many metropolitan officers expressed shock at English prisoners being offered as diplomatic "gifts" or traded as slaves at meetings in Montreal in the early summer of 1756. Prisoners, scalps, and other trophies of war witnessed by the French continued to be subjects of epistolary fascination during that summer's marches to Fort Carillon and Fort Oswego.[24] However, in May, June, and July 1756 more positive evaluations of Indians appeared alongside these harsh statements. Many French officers believed that the French expeditionary army's task was to save Canada, so they expected and sought expressions of the indigenous nations' gratitude. Thus, Montcalm could both describe Indians as "an ugly crowd" with whom one needed "an angel's patience" and also proudly report in almost the same breath that "the Iroquois ladies, who always have a share in their government . . . did me the honour to bring me necklaces."[25] After two months in New France, the general wrote the following to his wife, his mother, and his sister-in-law to tell them about the Indians' and the Canadians' desire to serve under him: "I have got on well, so far, with the Canadians and the Indians; they worship me . . . I spend whole days with them, holding councils of war."[26]

In their detailed reports about New France's climate, peoples, and current affairs, French officers sought to understand the dynamics around them and to prove to those at home how well prepared they were for service in North America. But their close observations also revealed how thoroughly they misunderstood the key element of Canadian-Indian relations—the reciprocity, exchange, and trade that made diplomacy and alliance possible. François Gaston de Lévis, Montcalm's second-in-command, understood that by giving the Nipissings, Mississaugas, Abenakis, and Algonquins elaborate wampum belts and materials for a feast, he was committing them to a sacred compact to aid Canada in the upcoming French summer campaign.[27] However, his diary never mentioned that, for the Indians, this compact went both ways—Lévis was also undertaking, wittingly or not, obligations to his new companions. Moreover, these ritualized forms of diplomacy demonstrated indigenous respect but never adulation for the leadership and status Lévis and Montcalm were described as holding among the French. Native overtures saluted the office, not the man.

French officers thought of war, campaigns, and diplomacy as a masculine space, but in their first few months in Canada they learned that things were rather different in North America. Montcalm discovered in June 1756 that he was actually, not metaphorically, expected to visit the Kahnawake matrons who had "honored" him with necklaces and was also expected to "sing war songs with them." Months later at Niagara, Capt. Pierre Pouchot received his first female ambassador, the mother of the Mississauga chief Techicabavoui, who met with him to discuss issues of war.[28] The degree to which women in North America played an active role in war startled these metropolitan officers—nothing had prepared them for either the intersections of matrilineal authority and martial spheres of influence or the willingness of marine officers to work around or through these mediators. Canadian officials recognized the importance of pleasing Native women and offered large quantities of gifts to them at the Franco-Indian councils in June and July 1756. Many of the items responded to the specific compensation Native women requested in exchange for their men's hunting, military assistance, and farming labor—doeskins, coverlets, kettles, hatchets, and flints, among other items—the very materials elite French soldiers used on their own campaigns and items of no little value.[29]

Even Canadian women in Montreal and the other communities of New France played roles unfamiliar to the French. Many colonial women (except those of the very highest status or in religious orders) dressed in short skirts, which enabled greater freedom of movement in a style popularly called "*à la sauvagesse.*" With their men serving in the militia or the marines, urban Canadiennes relied in part on the labor of captive New England men (virtual slaves) or *panis* (Indian) slaves.[30] These practices were a far cry from metropolitan French practice and gender divisions. Although aristocratic women in France held a significant position in politics and social life, serving as the arbiters of social mores, their relationship to war and authority differed from that of Native and colonial women. Louis-Antoine de Bougainville's most important private correspondent besides his brother was Madame Marie-Hélène Hérault de Séchelles, his elite Parisian patroness, who advanced his career. Respectable women, like Madame de Séchelles, and even mistresses, like the Marquise de Pompadour, derived their power to influence war and policy by their proximity to powerful men and exerted influence through indirect channels. By contrast, Native American women held power in their own right, and the active role they played in the affairs and economy of war in North America gave French officers pause. Years of service in North America did little to change most of these French officers. Near the end of the war, the chevalier de Lévis had enough experience to express less astonishment when he encountered a delegation of Onondaga women in his camp. He referred to the spokeswoman as a "Sybille," however, suggesting that even after almost four years in North America, he associated indigenous female power at most with pagan prophetesses living in the woods—a religious influence rather than a political or military one.[31] Despite continuing examples of female authority that suggested French officers should attend more closely to Native women of status, the metropolitans failed to do so.

The campaigns from June through September 1756 introduced French officers newly arrived in Canada to a conception and performance of warfare radically different from what they had known in Europe and set the boundaries of cooperation between metropolitan and colonial military elites. Vaudreuil planned to target a key British supply station, Oswego, whose removal would keep the frontier unstable and prevent Britain from gaining traction among Indians in the west. This English fort, built on Iroquois land, threatened New France's settlements, fur trade, and supply lines to the Great Lakes. French officers and Montcalm expected that the Oswego venture would provide them with a realistic assessment of the marines and the Canadian militia; they would learn to work with Indian soldiers and could evaluate British strength. A successful campaign would prove the army's "zeal to the king" and their ability to work with Canadians and would demonstrate the senior officers' tactical talents. Victory might even suggest to the Ministry of War that they should be recalled from service on the edge of the empire to aid the (more important) European front.[32] Unfortunately for the hopes of these ambitious French officers, the Oswego campaign was to become the first blow to the French war effort. It revealed splits in expectations, strategic planning, and concepts of victory.

➳ Unruly Marches and Camps

For French troops the Oswego campaign began with a journey through unfamiliar and rough terrain, where the principal landmarks were the remnants of battles and forts along the way. To participating marines, Iroquoians and Algonquians from Kahnawake, Kanesatake, or Odanak, and even some Canadian militia, however, the Saint Lawrence corridor and the Ohio region was hunting territory in the neighborhood of relatives' homes, trading locales, and places of war and peace they already knew. Indigenous peoples who came from farther west—the Great Lakes and the Ohio River Valley—carefully surveyed the landscape they now traversed for messages left by spirit and human intervention because it was less familiar to them. Waterways facilitated travel, but when moving by land, people (disproportionately the Canadian militia) pushed ordnance, hoisted packs, and dragged recalcitrant goats and cattle and also the officers' trunks.[33] Scouts moved around and among the troops, at times disappearing and returning with captives or food, at other times leaving and not returning at all. Marching changed soldiers' relationship to the foreign setting—only on campaign did Anne Maurès de Malartic begin "the native diet of deer" after Indians sold the men of his encampment "venison for bread, powder, and shot."[34] At forts, on scouts, and in camp, *troupes de terre*, marines, and Indians now fell into regular and often unsupervised contact, exchanging supplies and local products and always studying one another.

Throughout the Seven Years' War in North America, formal military campaign seasons ran from early summer to midautumn and involved the movement of significant numbers of regulars, marines, militias, and indigenous peoples to various theaters of combat. It was on these movements that French assessments began to crystallize; marching and camp life thrust many actors into close contact under difficult conditions and with uncontrollable variables. Although many participants might have considered going to war to be a familiar and natural masculine occupation, strategists and officers held that careful planning and discipline, not innate sensibility, were the keys to successful operations. Generals could not influence the terrain, the weather, or the enemy, but they could try to manage their troops and life in camp to promote a fiction of elite control. For the European officers, good army camps were those that replicated and upheld social hierarchy through disciplined behavior and that showcased the hierarchy of command and authority.[35] In the summer of 1756, metropolitan officers began to discover that indigenous peoples behaved in a manner radically different from what they had expected on marches, in battle, and in camp. These allies appeared to upset the ordered campaigning that the upper echelon of French officers relied on. Any action deemed undisciplined by Indians (and to an extent by Canadians) became a focus of particular concern. The first major challenge the army encountered as it set off for Oswego concerned the consumption of alcohol.

Drinking before battle was a common European phenomenon. Taking spirits on campaign assuaged the hardships and boredom the troops experienced, and fine liquors demonstrated the officers' prestige as well.[36] Alcohol-fueled violence occurred throughout Europe's taverns; in some cases lower-class men claimed brawling was in defense of their honor, a *roturier* pastiche of dueling etiquette among nobles that suggested that some poor men aspired to parity with elites. For their part, aristocrats interpreted brawling as proof of low birth and associated commoners, their drunkenness, and their fighting with a destabilized social hierarchy.[37] Indian consumption of liquor and the types of violent acts it produced greatly upset French officers. During the Oswego campaign Malartic chronicled the following in his diary: "The 21.st. The Indians got drunk and acted like Devils and killed the officers' sheep."[38] Even if exaggerated in the record, it is clear that drunkenness—whether Indian, colonial, or French—was troublesome, as the numerous studies recording the detrimental social effects of inebriation have shown.[39] Numerous French officers described scenes similar to that recorded by Malartic. "Having seen the disastrous effects and several in this state," Le Duchat wrote of Indians accompanying the French forces, "once they are drunk on this they become enraged, capable of doing anything."[40]

Focused on the effects of disruptions to their orderly campaigns, metropolitan officers remained blind to the religious or social motivations for indigenous drinking, and many paid scant attention to interethnic rivalries that could potentially spark violence (despite the diversity of nations thrust together on a single campaign). Iroquois, Abenakis, Nipissings, Ottawas, and other Indians in camp had to make efforts to prevent disputes from turning deadly—fatalities would require gifts to aggrieved kin to "cover the dead" or risk sparking revenge feuds.[41] A few French observers, like Jean Baptiste d'Aleyrac, did notice that Indians policed the boundaries of their own behavior, noting that "as soon as they [Indians] perceive someone to be drunk, those who are sober take his weapons, bind him . . . so that he may only roll" but failed to interpret these acts as community-imposed discipline.[42]

As early as summer 1756, French officers interpreted Native alcohol consumption as indicative of degeneracy. When a Nipissing Indian named Hotchig killed the French engineer Descombles in August 1756 on the eve of the Oswego battle, Descombles's replacement, Jean Nicolas Désandrouins, wrote to the Comte d'Argenson that "I will not talk to you about the cruelties and horrors of the Indians. The image of this that is in France is quite accurate." The only explanation Désandrouins offered for the engineer's murder was that "it is unfortunate to have to make war with such people, especially when they are drunk, a case in which nothing will stop their fury."[43] A French observer at the Ministry of War might well have asked how such violence could have occurred in a French military camp—Désandrouins ignored the lack of French control by suggesting that unregulated Indian violence stemmed from unbridled savage passion.[44] Although the chevalier de Lévis posited that Descombles had been murdered due to Native contempt, he made sure to record his thoughts in his private journal, not in a letter to his minister, which might raise questions about the efficacy of the army's high command.[45]

Subsequent campaigns reinforced and extended the threat posed by Indian volatility to established French hierarchies.[46] Most of the French public shared a low opinion of common soldiers. Maintaining order on campaigns was deemed critical. Any infraction could threaten authority, explaining Louis-Antoine de Bougainville's nervous assessment that "The troops have too much cash. A soldier of Languedoc yesterday lost 100 *louis* gambling." The unfamiliar North American environment and interaction with Indians, French colonists, or even Britons might inspire more mischief, and Bougainville added that "This country is dangerous for discipline."[47] However, if French soldiers, Canadian marines, and militias became disorderly, they could, in theory, be punished. An officer's authority and the discipline of the army relied on a system in which the violation of rules and insubordination carried severe penalties. Public reprimand of offenders further helped to maintain the general order of the rest of the soldiers. To their dismay, noble officers discovered as early as the summer 1756 campaign that Indians believed that a drunk man could not be held accountable for his actions because "a man in this state has lost his spirit" and that inebriation was a different state of being, one that required forgiveness.[48] If the French could not enforce consequences on Indians who were disruptive or committed unauthorized violence on the campaign, they feared such "contagious examples" might corrupt the discipline of their own common soldiers, the backbone of the entire army; preventing this demanded the "complete attention of senior staff officers."[49]

More generally, Indians stubbornly refused to behave in predictable ways. Indians—even some Canadians—could not be drilled, punished, or coerced into regular behavior on marches or in camp, limiting the French officers' authority in ways that vexed them to no end.[50] Writing to François-Charles de Bourlamaque a year later, in spring 1757, Montcalm offered the colonel advice on planning the upcoming campaign. While on the topic of obtaining the greatest use of Indians, the general warned, "based on my experience . . . even the officers in whom the Indians show the greatest trust are often embarrassed." A few months afterward, Bourlamaque and Montcalm discussed the court case of an Ottawa who had brained a French soldier in Montreal. "Indians here have the privileges of old Frenchmen," said Montcalm, frustrated since 1756 by his inability to directly punish such an egregious breach of standards.[51]

The marines appeared less concerned with the behaviors that metropolitan officers deemed outrageous. Governor Vaudreuil complimented his brother that the Indians behaved far better once Rigaud arrived at Oswego in mid-August 1756, neither deserting nor getting drunk. The governor's comment showed that such behavior by Indians was expected. Elite marines assured their French counterparts that *les troupes franches de la marine* had the skills to influence Native peoples. Canadian leaders hoped that camp violence could be lessened by providing marine officers whom Indians respected as campaign leaders or who could mediate fights through discussion, persuasion, and, of course, gift giving.[52]

Still, the army officers could not comprehend why their colonial counterparts, as fellow officers and as civilized compatriots, chose to adopt non-European modes of behavior. At times the senior staff of the *compagnies franches de la marine* appeared wholly officer-like to army eyes. They followed a chain of command, wore French service uniforms, and engaged in the traditional behaviors of officers (inviting surrendered enemies to lunch, penning gallant courtesies to one another, taking servants to war). On campaign, though, the nobles of the *troupes de terre* saw the marines put unfamiliar practices into play. They bargained for Indian aid with gifts and promises. They seemed resigned to Native peoples wandering in and out of camp, meeting up with relatives (even relatives who were serving the British), and "borrowing" freely from the supply trains or, as one marine put it after a successful capture of an English convoy, "helping themselves" to these goods and the marines' own food.[53] The *compagnies franches* even sang war songs in Native languages with Indians in front of the governor and presented scalps as tokens of alliance.[54] Even militias in Canada appeared to have learned from the Indian example, withholding their "good guns" upon conscription in favor of being armed at the king's expense.[55] This manner of camp life challenged the noble French officers at every turn.

Unwilling to admit that they had no power to stop such behavior, French officers sublimated their command weakness into cultural superiority. By tying Indian violence to alcohol, they linked what was also a common problem in European armies exclusively to Indians (and later to their enemies, the British). Calling Indians "savages" and "devils" kept the army elites from delving further into why these episodes occurred and focused them and their home audience on a different problem: the threat to their own honor by association with Indian ways. Most officers wanted to avoid the types of accommodations the marines made on campaigns. Violence was both legitimized and limited by the exercise of honorable norms that they, as officers, controlled. How to assert their control over violence would preoccupy the French officers as the war dragged on and grew into an obsession as French military honor became more and more subject to the behavior of their allies and French war fortunes declined.

↝ Cultural Clashes

Despite an irritating march in an unfamiliar climate through immense forests filled with unknown flora with allies they perceived as ill behaved, the French army and its leadership looked forward to the engagement at Oswego. The first French forces reached the British depots on August 9, and the main body of the army laid siege on August 11, 1756. British capitulation on August 14 delighted Montcalm and his staff and added to their self-confidence. The march had proven harder to control than the blockade, where success had been accomplished by an application of classic European siege warfare. The primary concession to war in North America made by these French forces had been to trust in the Indians' and Canadians' contempt for Anglo-American provincials and British troops. "The nature of the country, the weakness of the English troops, the fear they have of the Indians assured me [of victory]," Montcalm wrote, because "the transplanted English are not the same as those in Europe."[56]

Savoring his win at Oswego, Montcalm derided English plans for a simple invasion of Canada and congratulated himself on having ensured the safety of all of New France. The general credited the work of the Canadian expeditions against the New York frontier in March and July, which had preceded his own—but only insofar as they had set the stage for his complete success. Moreover, he set himself apart from his unfortunate Saxon predecessor because, unlike "the M. Dieskau," who had "listened too much to the confidence of the Canadians, who believe themselves to be the first nation in the world," Montcalm had trusted his aristocratic French martial instincts and training and so had achieved victory.[57] The official published *Relation* described how this victory reaffirmed Canadians' devotion to their monarch and to his victorious representatives, the army officers who had produced this achievement.[58] Although the publication shared credit between the French army, Montcalm, Governor Vaudreuil, and the marines, Montcalm's private letters to the Marquise de Montcalm and Marquise de Boulay, his wife and his sister-in-law, almost exclusively credited the army's actions: "I cannot too highly praise the zeal shewn by all the troops."[59] The public face of the victory claimed the triumph for the combined colonial and metropolitan military forces, with no mention of the tensions over discipline that had arisen on campaign, and this presentation of a united front greatly pleased the Crown.[60]

But despite the appearance of harmony in the afterglow of conquest, Oswego opened fissures among the military commanders of Canada because in victory Montcalm had denied his Indian allies what they saw as their due:

goods and captives. Vaudreuil began complaining that Montcalm had moved slowly on campaign and that the regulars had prevented both Canadians and Indians from partaking in the division of the spoils after the fort fell into French hands.[61] Captured goods served as an important inducement for the Indians' participation, and Vaudreuil tried to highlight the seriousness of Montcalm's error in his letter to Naval Minister Machault. After Oswego's surrender, Montcalm and his troops assumed responsibility for (and control of) its garrison and vast storehouses. However, French claims to all of the British prisoners, ostensibly to protect them from Indian fury, denied some of France's Native allies access to captives, scalps, and trade goods. Montcalm planned to take captives and materiel back to the Laurentian valley and from there conduct detainee exchanges or send British and North American provincials as hostages back to France.[62] In the cases in which French officers ransomed English prisoners already in Indian hands, they reinforced indigenous associations of captive English bodies as commodities for commerce, not just martial prestige. Indians connected prisoners with material goods—an economy of slaves.[63] For the Abenakis and Oswegatchie Iroquois, who had taken no British prisoners, Montcalm's bid for jurisdiction over British bodies and goods and his refusal to allow scouting parties to claim more prisoners registered as the general selfishly enriching himself through their efforts and risks. The disgruntled Indians returned to Montreal, protesting Montcalm's "high-handed treatment of them" directly to Vaudreuil. They added that they would go anywhere the governor sent them "provided they were not under the orders of M. de Montcalm." An exasperated Vaudreuil concluded that, "in the next campaign, I will have to ensure the Indians and Canadians are treated in a manner worthy of their zeal and value."[64] For now, he felt required to appease his Native allies for both their loss and the insult to their honor with a costly outlay of gifts.

Vaudreuil's comment provides an important insight that was lost on the French officers of the Oswego campaign: Native peoples used war as an opportunity to evaluate the French as much as they were themselves being scrutinized. At Oswego, the indigenous participation came mostly from the Catholic mission communities, the *réserves* around Montreal—traditionally the staunchest allies of New France. Furthermore, the conclusions these Indians reached about their partners in war were not flattering. Oswego had proven French behavior appalling; Indians from La Baye "returned to their villages without having been able to take a single thing" despite the fort's prodigious supplies of "sugar, coffee, chocolate, and . . . even money."[65] By withholding captives and goods and sending in the Guyenne grenadiers "to secure the [spoils]," the French failed to honor the "sacred bond" of alliance cemented in the gifts Lévis had mentioned back in June. At one of those June meetings, the leader Machiqua had generously offered on behalf of his group of Nipissings a valuable captive to Montcalm to establish goodwill and draw the Frenchman into the world of Nipissing protocol. The general had accepted her, giving forty *écus* in return, which in Machiqua's eyes indicated Montcalm's willingness to operate on Nipissing terms.[66] If Machiqua had been among the 260 Abenakis, Nipissings, or Iroquois with the French troops at Oswego and found grenadiers blocking his path to similar spoils of war, he would have considered such treatment a serious breach of established relationships. Ian Steele correctly labeled French-Indian engagements "betrayals" when studying the 1757 Fort William Henry campaign; the roots of misrepresentation, for the mission communities, began at Oswego.[67] Some senior French officers had already devalued themselves in Native eyes by early fall 1756.

Most important, these negative indigenous perceptions would come to tarnish their view of Canadian soldiers as well. Men like Governor Vaudreuil or his brother Rigaud or even intercultural officers like Daniel-Marie Chabert de Joncaire often presented themselves in indigenous terms—they were "fathers" because they provided gifts to their "children"; they were "men" because they fought and provided for their dependents.[68] However, in the negotiation between Canadian and French elites, the marines of New France undermined their own position in Native eyes. Discussing French tactics after William Johnson's provincials had mowed down Dieskau's elite grenadiers at Lake George and roundly defeated the French in September 1755, an Oswegatchie Onondaga chief informed Lt. Gaspard-Joseph Chaussegros de Léry that "The time of Lake George [the battle of Lake George] still weighed on them [and] their augurers considered the long sword I have, similar in resemblance to that of M. the Baron de Dieskau, as a bad omen."[69] Why, these Onondagas wondered, would a man like marine officer Léry listen to or work with the French army officers, who so clearly were dangerous to everyone who understood how to make war in the woods? The inappropriate use of tactics, the inflexible demands, and the ungenerous natures of the French officers threatened compacts of alliance in part because putting up with these situations undermined the marines' standing in indigenous eyes.

The army had its own complaints about the August campaign. Bougainville's journal tone soured after Oswego:

> The Indians have seventeen prisoners; they have already knocked several of them on the head. A detachment of a lieutenant and thirty men [were] ordered to bury the two dead. The cruelties and the insolence of the barbarians is horrible, their souls are as black as pitch. It is an abominable way to make war; the retaliation is frightening, and the air one breathes here is contagious of making one accustomed to callousness.[70]

He, like all the other officers, had already witnessed scalping and the brisk slave trade in captives in Montreal and Quebec. But these actions seemed to take a different cast after the battle. They had besieged a fort with a proper garrison, not attacked some frontier farm. Such acts of violence after the fort's surrender continued the pattern in which Canadian marines and Native peoples seemed unimpressed by French army leadership and the demands of hierarchy, and they let it show by their behavior. Chevalier de La Pause wrote of the Indians that "they found all the alcohol" at the fort, which in turn led them to disregard French orders; of Indians and the Canadian militia he added that their bad example had encouraged all of the soldiers to "pillage, as the others did."[71] All of this convinced Bougainville that it was the very nature of the country that caused such outrageous behavior. Only the "contagious" air might explain how colonists became accustomed to such illegitimate means of war.[72] A number of British prisoners at Oswego had recognized the protection offered by French troops; a New Hampshire carpenter noted that "all those who obeyed the orders and crossed the river to the French army [after surrender] was [sic] very well used." But when illicitly acquired rum reached the prisoners, they "got intoxicated and soon began to fight with one another, while others [were] singing, dancing, hallowing and cahoosing. That it appeared more like bedlam than a prison."[73] If the elite French officers needed confirmation of what they perceived as the degeneracy of war in North America, it was evident on all sides, even among the British prisoners.[74]

The reliance on *la petite guerre* (loosely translated as frontier or guerilla fighting) in North America gave the metropolitans further reasons to be unhappy. Numerous men of the Béarn, Guyenne, La Reine, La Sarre, Languedoc, and Royal Roussillon regiments could claim a familiarity with the practices employed in conducting irregular combat, such as reconnaissance and supply raids, given their former experience in the War of Austrian Succession, which had ended in 1748. About 30 percent of the *troupes de terre* in New France had served in the army for at least a decade; more than 50 percent had been soldiers since 1750. But exposure to *la petite guerre* and the light infantries trained to conduct it in the 1740s did not mean that the officers embraced this method of war. Much of the idea of guerrilla combat affronted the noblemen of the French army. Successful scouting and screening of troop movements (two of the signal characteristics of *la petite guerre*) required choosing men for important missions on merit rather than by seniority or rank. For French officers already nervous about their social and military positions, such breaches of hierarchy were unacceptable.[75]

With British North America nursing yet another defeat at French hands at Oswego as 1756 drew to a close, campaigning lulled, and attention shifted to the business of the harvest and of garrisoning New France's forts and cities. The North American experience, from climate to lifestyle to warfare, convinced many ambitious French officers that service in Canada meant being exiled from what they perceived to be the real war, which was being conducted in Europe. Autumn brought more leisure, and many officers took the opportunity to share their thoughts with their superiors. Several grumbled about being unable to leave New France. The Chevalier Lemercier, an artillery officer, went so far as to formally request his recall to France as early as October 30, adding that most of the army was irritated about not being in Europe. Keeping Minister of War Argenson apprised of morale, Montcalm reported that his third-in-command, Bourlamaque, hoped to soon be recalled home to France "for health reasons."[76] Bourlamaque's sanitary concerns accorded with the corrupting nature of North America's climate as Bougainville depicted it. The desire to leave Canada demonstrated how little French officers and troops understood the conflict. Having arrived at the start of summer, the army had expected a quick and successful battle, achieved it at Oswego, and now looked forward to being rewarded by returning to France. But despite their victory, they remained in North America, which would soon be in the grip of winter.

When the weather allowed during those five long winter months, the Canadian government encouraged raids against the English to destabilize the enemy, gather intelligence from captives, maintain military preparedness, and occupy regulars, colonial militias, and marines while leaders planned the upcoming summer campaigns. North American weather tested the endurance of the regulars, who faced "marching and sleeping almost daily on snow or ice" or temporary snow blindness from blustery winds, experiences that compared unfavorably even to the worst European conditions.[77] Still, experienced officers made North American geographic and climatic conditions seem more familiar by comparing New France to terrain they had experienced in their most recent past war. For instance, Montcalm evaluated Canada's terrain in relation to that of the Bohemian campaigns of the

1740s and found it not much different. The parallel made everything more understandable and allowed the general to assume that at least the French veterans of the War of Austrian Succession could serve on equal footing with the Canadians.[78] New France's most significant winter expedition took place in March 1757, when fifteen hundred *compagnies franches*, Canadian militia, volunteers from the regulars, and Indians departed from New France to weaken British Fort William Henry, at the southern tip of Lake George, in anticipation of the formal siege planned for that summer.

Although Montcalm, Bourlamaque, and Lévis found the March expedition to Fort William Henry of less value than a proper siege of the fort itself, they expected to be awarded command of the mission, and the junior officers, like young Malartic, also actively sought to be included. But the honor of command went instead to marine officer François de Rigaud de Vaudreuil, the governor's brother, over the objections of several senior French officers who insinuated favoritism even if some later praised Rigaud's success after the fact.[79]

Patronage and a marine's acclimation to winter conditions on the trail only partially explain why Vaudreuil was unwilling to entrust this risky, high-value raid on Fort William Henry to anyone besides his brother or another veteran marine officer. The governor's letters to Versailles that spring focused on indigenous relations and aid: the ongoing Ohio River Valley attacks, the meetings with disaffected Indian groups of the region, the March mission to Lake George. A creole commander would be less likely to further upset Indian alliances. French claims about their experience were limited to the one victory at Oswego, and this was insufficient to convince Canadians that the March mission should or could be led by a Frenchman with less than a year's service in New France and no North American winter campaigning experience. Rigaud's raid modestly succeeded in hampering the English at Fort William Henry. Unfortunately, it better served to broaden the wedge between Canadians and the regulars before the summer 1757 campaigns began.

Complications mounted in late spring 1757, when news of yet another bureaucratic change at the Naval Ministry arrived from France. François Marie Peyrenc de Moras had replaced Machault d'Arnouville and stepped into the demanding position of minister.[80] Since Oswego, the officers of the *troupes de terre* and senior *troupes de la marine* had been struggling for preeminence and had forwarded their complaints to the Ministry of War and the Naval Ministry. When Moras took office, he faced innumerable responsibilities, which included resolving the tensions between regulars, Indians, and Canadians. The specialized *commis* (clerks), who received the thousands of pages of colonial correspondence and drafted responses had, in some cases, decades of experience with complaints about the difficulties of Indian diplomacy and helped to frame the prescient advice Moras penned to Vaudreuil in May 1757 in answer to a letter from the Canadian governor describing Franco-Indian tensions:

> [It] would not be surprising that he [Montcalm] mistakenly caused them to experience some moments of excitement, especially the Indians. One cannot immediately grow accustomed to their characters and qualities, and one must learn these well in order to lead them successfully. But experience will soon teach M. de Montcalm, who [has] always shown good intentions and talents, and it will not be long before he understands that kindness, patience, and moderation are often the keys to success with these people.[81]

Clearly French missteps flowed from the army's recent introduction to American diplomacy—Montcalm's troops had been in New France barely a year.

While acknowledging Vaudreuil's frustrations, Moras expressed no doubt that the officer corps would be able to get results once given time to adapt. Then, writing separately to Montcalm, Moras encouraged the French aristocrat's interest in disciplining and controlling Indian and Canadian minds and bodies:

> The last campaign must have shown you how useful Canadians and Indians can be for the assignments that need to be undertaken. One may count on the bravery of the Canadians as well as on their zeal and goodwill when they are treated in a manner that is not insulting . . . As for the Indians, you will have learned that it is best not to inflate their egos, especially concerning the help they provide us with, but it is just as important to indulge the pretensions that motivate them. It requires much patience to *use them* successfully.[82] (emphasis mine)

Inflated "egos" and "indulging" Indian pretensions infantilized both Indians and Canadians. Moras suggested that both Canadians and Indians had to be managed if one were to be able to "use" these individuals effectively, implying their status as tools to be improved rather than as autonomous actors. The minister's sympathy for Montcalm, who had to justify his right to command, was very real. It arose from being an aristocrat who could well imagine Montcalm's frustration at having to negotiate constantly to maintain his status in a hierarchy—something Moras experienced daily at court. In addition, he showed his implicit support for Montcalm's actions by awarding the *cordon rouge* (a coveted military honor) to the general as a token both of the minister's understanding of the situation and the king's continuing favor to his army and its commander.[83]

During his tenure as naval minister, Moras altered the interservice rivalry that had previously netted the marines' greater regard in their own home ministry than their army rivals enjoyed. After about a month in office, Moras initiated a dialogue directly with the elite staff of the French army, writing to Montcalm that in order "to obtain a more intimate and secret correspondence with you" he was sending "a code for your use when you need to communicate something important regarding operations or secret administrative affairs." Furthermore, the naval minister assured Montcalm he could "count as much on my discretion as my confidence."[84] This private cipher and privileged correspondence may have resulted from a social connection between the naval minister and a member of Montcalm's staff. Peyrenc de Moras was the brother-in-law of Madame Marie-Hélène Hérault de Séchelles, the patroness of Louis-Antoine de Bougainville, and this relationship was exploited by Bougainville, Montcalm, and the lady herself.[85] The army's direct access to Moras emboldened these officers to make grand claims to the head of the French Navy. With Moras backing them, they envisioned a quick victory in North America and their return to the main front in Europe. It did not matter that Moras had no experience in Canada. Too much experience in Canada was part of the problem, as they saw it.

Fort William Henry

Taking Fort William Henry was the major French objective as the campaign of summer 1757 got under way. More than a thousand indigenous men from many different nations joined the French army, marines, and Canadian militia on an arduous two-month march by land and by canoe from New France south to Lake George. As the senior French commanders feared, the march was replete with disorders alleviated only when the army laid siege to the fort on August 3, 1757. After resisting for a week, the English capitulated. Montcalm granted Col. George Monro an honorable surrender on August 10, and the English began preparations to withdraw to Fort Edward, sixteen miles farther south. However, events quickly got out of hand. On the evening of August 11, French officers explained the terms of the capitulation to the Indians, specifying that the English were free to leave, unmolested, with their personal effects.[86] The next day, when the British marched out of Fort William Henry in good order, heading with their baggage for Fort Edward, the Indians attacked them. Chaos ensued until French soldiers intervened to protect the English, ending what the British and Anglo-Americans called the "Fort William Henry massacre." How this event was used and portrayed within a French Atlantic context shaped the future of New France's war.

At Fort William Henry, Native peoples aiding the French campaign, especially Anishinaabeg of the Great Lakes and the Iroquois, Abenakis, Nipissings, and Hurons of the Saint Lawrence *réserves*, felt betrayed by Montcalm's generous European terms of surrender. Displeased because this arrangement denied them the captives, commodities, and scalps that constituted the trophies of Native victory and unwilling to return home without these items, they attacked the English troops the day after the battle. The French were horrified by the Indians' attack; the Native peoples were attempting to force the fulfillment of the promise made to them in return for their assistance with the French campaign. Believing that Montcalm's terms of surrender should have kept their soldiers safe from harm, the English officers became convinced that Montcalm's French troops had behaved perfidiously by willfully turning over the soldiers who had surrendered to France's indigenous allies.[87]

The description of the Fort William Henry campaign varied among official French sources, but certain elements remained constant. Vaudreuil's initial letter to Moras on August 18 blamed the English for the horrific turn of events and pointedly highlighted the gifts of liquor made by some of the English to the Indians to buy favor as an explanation for the violence that followed. Lévis's and Bougainville's journals reiterated English culpability in giving brandy to indigenous allies, and Lévis added that the British did so "specifically against French advice."[88] In the months that followed, Vaudreuil and Montcalm both reinforced this explanation publicly, describing English attempts to escape by means of bribes of brandy and their hurried departure for Fort Edward as having aroused Native suspicions. Despite his frustration with the French army command, Vaudreuil endorsed the metropolitan officers' narrative of their humanitarian efforts to save English lives and property. In a communiqué to his English counterpart, Lord Loudon, Governor Vaudreuil emphasized his commitment to ransoming back the Indians' captives taken from Fort William Henry and also attempted to shed light on Native motivations, pointing out that an earlier English murder of Abenaki ambassadors, a breach of diplomacy in any civilized context, had created a powerful and understandable motive for revenge.[89]

Bougainville's diary (written with an eye to publication) and the memoirs of d'Aleyrac and Malartic privately described how aghast the regulars were at what had happened. D'Aleyrac drew on the language of "murder" and "barbarity" in his description of the *mêlée*, adding that such an atrocity would "inspire great compassion in European hearts . . . especially among the French, whose goodness, humanity, and generosity equal their valor."[90] Junior officers did not provide the text for the official *relation* of the battle, but their writings help uncover internal questions that had been raised by what they considered the degenerate behavior of the Indians and, for the first time, the poor behavior of the marines. Bougainville asked, "Will they in Europe believe that the Indians alone have been guilty of this horrible violation of the capitulation[?] . . . one today may see one of these leaders [a marine officer], unworthy of the name of officer and Frenchman, leading in his train a Negro kidnapped from the English commander under the pretext of appeasing the shades of a dead Indian. . . . *Heu fuge crudeles terras fuge littus iniquum.*"[91] The reference to Virgil's *Aeneid*, recounting the harsh, Mars-ruled land and greedy shore of Thrace, was deliberate. The killing fields of North America, like those of Thrace, voraciously consumed blood and brought disaster on all those born there.

The "leader" referenced by Bougainville likely was marine officer La Corne St. Luc. La Corne was an experienced soldier, fluent in multiple Native languages, and with enough credibility and respect among Indians to have led the *réserve* Nipissings during the siege. Therefore, he was well placed to negotiate for prisoner release (which he did), but as one of New France's preeminent slaveholders, he thought nothing of appropriating a British man of color for himself.[92] The marine officers' tacit acceptance of a virtual slave trade in captives with Native allies and their engagement (for their own material benefit) in an actual slave trade of African individuals made their French counterparts deeply uncomfortable. As Bougainville wrote to Madame de Séchelles, "Would you believe men who claim to be French were complicit in this abominable action? Their greed, the certainty of claiming the Indians' pillage at low cost, caused a nightmare that the English will long hold against us." He frankly repeated to his *chère maman* what he had told both her brother-in-law, Moras, and the Marquis de Paulmy.[93] This putative degeneracy of European men existed not only on the battlefield and was something that other officers commented on as well. In his study of New France, D'Aleyrac had noted that "Canadians do not perpetrate the same [Indian] cruelties on their prisoners, but they use them as slaves" and that "men are bought like cattle here."[94] The disparities involved in human existence in North America may also have upset metropolitan officers, proving a further inversion of the order of life. In the grand captive sales after the battle, French soldiers learned that, to indigenous and Canadian sellers and buyers, "blacks are sold for 600 to 1,500 francs, and whites for 120 to 200."⁹⁵ In the realm of war, where rules were supposed to curb the violence associated with unbridled passions, Captain La Corne's calculated and potentially barbarous choices seemed, to French observers, especially horrifying.

French officers may have flattered themselves into believing that they could control Indian actions; Montcalm tried to encourage Colonel Monro's early surrender by warning, "I have [it] yet in my power to restrain the savages." But the fact that French officers had to hold councils with Native peoples after the fort's surrender to make sure European terms were honored showed the fragility of this claim.⁹⁶ French and Canadian officers could not prevent the Indians' attack, but they had intervened by pulling captives out of Indian hands and putting their own lives on the line for honor. *Compagnies franches* and Jesuits had also tried to help, but they had interceded by using indigenous terms to buy or trade for captives, as Bougainville and other eyewitnesses recorded. In Montreal, Governor Vaudreuil redeemed captives in exchange for 130 *livres* of goods and thirty bottles of brandy—each.⁹⁷ At Oswego, even had they been aware that Montcalm himself had inadvertently strengthened in his Indian allies' minds the association between taking English prisoners and then forcing the French officers to buy them back for substantial ransoms, it would not have mattered to these French noblemen. Bougainville and d'Aleyrac, Malartic or Désandrouins did not save English lives for personal profit, but to them it appeared that the marines did. Here was incontrovertible proof of the corrupting nature of North American soil and North American war. And because they—the French officers—had been present, their own reputations were tainted.

The official French army correspondence from August 1757 first sought to downplay the aftermath of the siege, expressed most mildly as a "few infractions on the part of the Indians."⁹⁸ Within days a horrified Montcalm dispatched letters to Gen. Daniel Webb at Fort Edward, explaining what had occurred but nevertheless requesting that the terms of surrender be honored. Though the Indian attack on the British prisoners could not be concealed from a metropolitan French audience, its impact was minimized in the public retelling. Of the twelve pages that formed the official 1757 narrative pamphlet, only one line alluded to the actual fighting: despite the promises of Indian chiefs at the capitulation, "the Indians caused disorder in the English camp." The remainder of this paragraph excused the French troops from any direct involvement in the trouble and exonerated both Montcalm (who dispatched the troops to protect the English and force the Indians to return the prisoners) and Vaudreuil (who redeemed the prisoners taken to Canada).⁹⁹

CHAPTER 3

In private Vaudreuil intimated to Moras as early as mid-August that the whole debacle had resulted because Montcalm had taken so few precautions, granting little authority to Rigaud or to individual officers who had influence over the Indians and had accompanied their Native counterparts—men like La Corne St. Luc, the sieurs Longueuil, Langlade, and Lorimier, or even the missionaries who had accompanied the domiciled Natives.[100] The "special" correspondence and relationship between Moras and Montcalm and between Bougainville and Madame de Séchelles proved useful in undermining Vaudreuil's assignment of blame. Montcalm and Bougainville sent detailed reports directly to the Ministry of War and the Naval Ministry, accusing the English of bringing this on themselves, yes, but—through the details they provided—also tarnishing the reputations of the marines who were present.

Neither the French officers nor the Canadian administrative elite stopped to consider the effect that William Henry (and Oswego the previous summer) had on their own reputations in the eyes of Native Americans. In November 1757 Montcalm assured the Minister of War, the Marquis de Paulmy, that he had the respect of the marines and indigenous Americans (although his own actions showed the feelings were not mutual).[101] The French commissary general André Doreil, concerned about Vaudreuil's desire to please Indians, argued that the governor was being "duped by his overconfidence in them." According to Doreil, the Indians apparently played Vaudreuil (though of course not Montcalm) for a fool.[102] At least one Canadian bureaucrat offered a similarly harsh assessment, reinforcing the idea that the trouble stemmed from listening to Indian opinions:

> This action [Fort William Henry] was portrayed as terrible, and it is, but it should be blamed neither on M. de Montcalm nor on the other generals but instead on the lax discipline that M. de Vaudreuil encouraged among the Indians—a quality he inherited from his father, such as believing Indians to be essential; one saw them [Indians] running through Montréal, knife in hand, every one threatening and often making insults; when we complained, nothing was said; instead, after this *coup* [at Fort William Henry], instead of chastising them and making them undergo repercussions, he [Vaudreuil] showered them with gifts, believing that this would diminish their cruelty. . . .[103]

Although this harsh statement was not entered into the official correspondence, one has to assume that if Courville made a point of writing it down, then it was a topic of gossip in Montreal. A few strokes of the pen cast the blame for Fort William Henry entirely on Vaudreuil despite the fact that he was not present at the siege. His problem, according to Doreil and Courville, lay in worrying about what the Indians thought.

If French officers had considered Native opinions, they would have learned that their indigenous allies were swiftly reviewing their impressions following events at Fort William Henry. The French may have paid minimal attention to the distinctions between Ottawas, Ojibwas, and Detroit Hurons from the *pays d'en haut*, the Iowas from the Great Plains, the Iroquois of Kahnawake, Kanesatake, and Oswegatchie, and the Abenakis of Odanak. But the Indians were not so unsophisticated as to be incapable of differentiating between colonial and metropolitan Europeans.[104] Every battle appeared to provide an opportunity to distinguish the marines from the army officers. In August 1756 Rigaud de Vaudreuil "assembled the Indians to tell them how pleased he was with their good service" at Oswego, and it was also Rigaud, not Montcalm, whom eight Onondagas sought out to disclose that "their Chiefs would be leaving in two days" to meet with the Marquis de Vaudreuil (no doubt to complain about Montcalm's missteps in diplomacy).[105] Marine and army officers, in particular, were both French. They served royal ministries, they held equivalent elite status in the French empire, and their British enemies described them as "French" without distinction. Yet after a lengthy period of interaction between the "French" and the Indian peoples from the *réserves* and the borderlands of the Great Lakes, Ohio River, and Illinois, Native witnesses began to believe something was wrong with their European allies. They had ceased to behave as they should have. Gifts became contested, siege assaults were expected, and French military leaders interacted awkwardly with or neglected female delegates, young men, and orators. Even if Native peoples recognized the institutional differences between the French army and the French marines, they still might draw confusing and upsetting conclusions. Why would Onontio, who claimed to love his "brothers" and his "children," send these terrible representatives? Marines who sought indigenous respect, like Marin de La Malgue, Claude-Nicolas Lorimier, or Jean Baptiste, sieur de Langy Montegron, proved to the domiciled Iroquois and Abenakis to be men worthy of respect. Charles de Langlade, officer at Michilimackinac and son of an Ottawa mother, showed his fluency in Native terms of war, diplomacy, and hospitality. Some, if not most, of these men appeared reasonable and normal in indigenous eyes, but for these military men to obey Montcalm cast doubt on their intelligence.

⚔ Ignominious War

The siege of Fort William Henry had been the most concrete French attempt since 1755 to fit the performance of war into traditional European categories and to use practices with which European officers felt comfortable. The victory was meant to be representative of France's overall war effort (in Europe as well as North America) by being a disciplined battle in the imperial war, with regulars and predetermined rules. This engagement should have been entirely European in conduct and result—proving the efficacy of French army strategy, undermining Canadian authority to control the terms of violence, silencing Native peoples in any conversations about legitimate war, and proving the competence of French military nobles to defend and govern the empire. But these goals were predicated, of course, on everything going according to a metropolitan French plan. In addition, as Ian Steele writes, "Ultimately, terms derived from the latest European etiquette of war were only as meaningful as they were to an Ottawa or Potawatomi warrior."[106]

The actual breach of discipline, the Canadian response to engage Native peoples on indigenous cultural terms, and the hasty improvisations army officers had to make as the unthinkable occurred before their eyes spoiled the regulars' victory at Fort William Henry. The "massacre" impugned the personal honor of the senior French officers and, by extension, the honor of all French aristocrats who were serving in the French regulars and following the same rules of war. One officer recorded a frantic Montcalm facing the disorder after the British parole, screaming at the many Indians around him, "Come, barbarians, kill your father since you have broken your word and will no longer listen to his . . . !"[107] Regardless of whether this was heightened in its recounting, the description laid bare the general's—and his officers'—fears. In the wake of the Fort William Henry campaign, Bougainville wrote the following to his *chère maman*: "[I am] an ugly Iroquois of the Turtle clan."[108] Louis-Antoine, tainted by the massacre and by his association with Native peoples, portrayed himself as ugly. Perhaps what became most disturbing to the French officers was that the Indians' complaints and anger troubled Vaudreuil and the Canadians not at all.[109] With weary shrugs regarding Indian "betrayals," New France's elite paid the exorbitant ransoms demanded by the Indians for their captives, abetting this inversion of social and racial hierarchies.

In Europe, even if France managed to suppress or neutralize negative press about the battle, the French elite still had important questions about what had happened and why. English declamations of French savagery at

Fort William Henry renewed criticisms that the French army had heard during the War of Austrian Succession. There had been a widespread outcry after the French victories at Bergen-op-Zoom and Lawfeld because of the manner in which these successes had been achieved. The maréchal de Saxe and his second-in-command, Ulrich von Lowendal, had destroyed these towns and terrorized the civilian population for strategic advantage. The accusations of savage brutality and ferocity at these sieges was directed at these commanders but greatly upset the French nobles who served under them and were implicated by their own presence during these dishonorable assaults. To exonerate themselves, French nobles blamed the actions on the foreign-born (and Protestant) Saxe and Lowendal.[110] Montcalm, Lévis, and Bourlamaque had all served during the Austrian War. They had seen or heard of the dangers of battle honors being disqualified by disgraceful conduct. From their earliest arrival in New France, they had witnessed the actions of Native Americans—scalping, ritual torture, a virtual slave trade in captives. In North America, the specter of the 1740s and its negative impact on noble martial masculinity loomed again.

British charges impugning French honor began as a trickle from the Anglo-American colonies in autumn 1757 and steadily increased until the end of the war. In July 1758 the English openly issued statements that they would not honor a capitulation breached by the "murdering, pillaging, and captivating . . . of His Majesty's good subjects, in violation of the said capitulation, as well as of the law of nations."[111] Although France clearly sought to justify its behavior in a European court of opinion, British views mattered less than the metropolitan French officers' own burden of shame (at least until Jeffery Amherst denied the honors of war to the French army at the surrender of Montreal in 1760). The personal charge of dishonor against Montcalm and his officers called into question the glory of all the previous victories the French had achieved in North America.

Such problems could not have appeared at a more inauspicious moment in France: the king was increasingly seen by his elite subjects as effeminate and corrupt, the nobility as lazy and dissolute, the very culture of France as teetering on the brink of disaster. The most damaging blow to France of the "massacre" at Fort William Henry was that it occurred under the supervision of elite noblemen who were representing the honor of the king and the aristocracy. If French officers could not control the Indians, their putative subordinates and mere drunken savages, then the superiority of French culture and of its aristocracy was in jeopardy. North American war was being fought on the geographic periphery of the empire, but this issue of cultural supremacy was at the center of French national pride. French was the diplomatic language of Europe, and French notions of art and civility set the fashion across the continent. The refined sense of martial honor that French officers brought to war helped secure France's continuing international prestige. The weight of that prestige pulled at the metropolitan officers' sense that they had to remain strict in their ideas of legitimate warfare.

There is no guarantee that Montcalm's consistent complaints about Canadian and Indian behavior would have been as damning had it not been that the debacle after the Fort William Henry surrender made his case. The French war and naval ministries looked over the year's correspondence with fresh eyes. To win the culture wars, French nobles had to degrade both the modes of war (*la petite guerre*) and their practitioners (be they marines or indigenous allies). Some stated this explicitly to the minister of war. "I assure you, Milord," wrote the chevalier de La Pause, "that I will render myself worthy of the graces that it pleases you to grant me; I have everything to hope for under a minister who is as attentive to protecting nobility as he is to the merit of the army's officers."[112] The rationale behind dissociating European from North American modes of war rested on putting aside North American practices and their advocates. It was past time for the army and its aristocratic officers to have a greater say in colonial affairs.

Officially declaring war and then sending a metropolitan army to defend the empire truly put into play both who the authorized purveyors of imperial authority were and what acts constituted legitimate violence in defense of the North American empire. Colonial officers found themselves now having to negotiate a third tradition of violence, that of the French army, in addition to their own marine practices and those of diverse Native American nations. For their part, after 1755, Indians increasingly came to see that not all French elites in Canada could be relied upon to follow long-established norms of diplomacy, exchange, or war interaction. The events at Fort William Henry proved particularly instructive in illuminating for them the distinctions between French regulars with much experience in the borderlands and the French army. From this point forward, Native nations would need to consider the peculiarities of France's *troupes de terre* when weighing the benefits and risks of French alliance. Dieskau's defeat in 1755 had tarnished the reputation of French regulars and officers in the eyes of the indigenous peoples; the actions of Montcalm and most of his officers at Oswego in 1756 and Fort William Henry in 1757 did nothing to improve the situation, making Native peoples less eager to make any commitments to New France. Mistrust on all sides damaged the potential for alliances for the remainder of the war years.

← CHAPTER 4

Assigning a Value to Valor

After nine months of official war, violence visited the very seat of monarchical and imperial power in France on January 5, 1757. A disgruntled former servant and religious fanatic named Robert François Damiens was deeply frustrated with his monarch, "Louis le Bien Aimé," as Louis XV liked to think of himself. Armed with a modest penknife, Damiens stabbed the king at the Trianon as Louis XV walked through a covered passage toward a waiting carriage. The act shocked France, exposing the strained relationship between monarchical authority, the church, and the regional parliaments. Damiens, who had been a servant at a Jesuit institution, claimed to be motivated by the recent royal orders to deny extreme unction to Jansenists (a strict Catholic sect critical of the monarch).[1] Louis XV was not badly injured, but society remained stunned at the first attempted regicide since the assassination of Henri IV, the founder of the Bourbon dynasty, in 1610. A monarch who had once been called "the well loved" must have fallen far from the hearts of his people if a religious man like Damiens was willing to alter divine will by murdering the anointed king. The foiled assassination deeply depressed Louis XV. He withdrew further into his court, delegating ever more responsibility to his royal council and retainers to manage the war, unpopular because of its expenses and dubious success.[2] Almost four months after the attack, the culprit, who gladly confessed to his crime, received his brutal death sentence, carried out on March 28, 1757: Damiens was tortured, then drawn and quartered, the last person in France to receive this penalty.

Beyond traumatizing the royal state of mind, these events of early 1757 radically changed the composition of the royal council and the direction of the war in Europe and North America. Availing herself of an opportunity to dispatch political rivals, the mistress/advisor of Louis XV, the Marquise de Pompadour, orchestrated the downfall of both the naval minister and the war minister on February 1, 1757. Although this extended Pompadour's influence in national affairs and strengthened her circle at court, the shift in power excised two of the king's most experienced bureaucrats, Argenson and Machault. Intelligent and well connected, Marc Pierre de Voyer de Paulmy, Comte d'Argenson, had, both during and after the War of Austrian Succession, reformed France's armies and worked closely with France's greatest military hero, the maréchal de Saxe; in service since 1743, Argenson had been an energetic and creative minister of war.[3] Because of Argenson's long and successful tenure, his privileged position with the king had seemed unassailable, but after Damiens, the king took Madame de Pompadour's advice to remove Argenson rather than the comte's advice to drop her as a visible sign of renewal at the top.

The disgrace of Argenson was matched by an equally momentous shift at the rival Naval Ministry. The war effort suffered from Argenson's departure, but the fall of Jean-Baptiste de Machault d'Arnouville after almost three years in office thrust the ministry into a period of constant upheaval. The chief position changed four times in four and a half years, moving from Machault (July 1754 to February 1757) to François-Marie Peyrenc de Moras (February 1757 to May 1758) and from Claude-Louis d'Espinchal, Marquis de Massiac (May 1758 to October 1758), to Nicolas René Berryer (October 1758 to October 1761). The loss of tested men at the top of both the army and the navy was a disaster for France's war policy overall, and it created a vacuum of leadership that prevented the formulation of a coherent colonial policy.[4] Both ministries had extensive bureaucracies that could temporarily manage affairs, but the restructuring of the king's council altered the access of individuals in New France to royal authority. A month after assuming authority over the navy, Minister Moras, Madame de Séchelles brother-in-law, had not only written officially to Governor General Vaudreuil but also established a separate code in which to correspond privately with General Montcalm, who was the superior officer of Madame de Séchelles' protégé, Bougainville.

Dismissals and tension at court added to the Crown's military misfortunes in Europe in 1757 and 1758. Frederick II and a small Prussian army inflicted a humiliating defeat on the French at Rossbach (in Saxony) in November 1757, which placed France on the defensive and fueled public and court concerns about war strategy, alliances, and finance. This had become an unpopular war due to its cost: by continuing the conflict, the monarchy appeared even more out of touch with social, political, and economic criticisms.[5] Many French subjects also disdained the court's alliance with Austria (previously a traditional French enemy), cemented in May 1757, three months after the fall of Argenson, as proof of the Marquise de Pompadour's detrimental influence on the king. Prussia's sound defeat of Austria's army at Leuthen (one month after Rossbach, in December 1757) confirmed French public suspicions that the new Austrian alliance was a poor bargain.

Battlefield upsets in Europe also threatened to sap France's flexibility when the time came to negotiate a successful peace. Under Louis XIV, the French had effectively deployed captured enemy territory as diplomatic "bargaining chips" to exchange for captured French possessions. At the 1713 Treaty of Utrecht, Louis XIV bartered to keep France's fishing rights in Newfoundland and unrestricted Indian trade by ceding Acadia (Nova Scotia) and Hudson's Bay to Britain. The Sun King's great-grandson employed a similar treaty-making strategy more than forty years later. At the end of the War of Austrian Succession, Louis XV had regained the crucial Louisbourg citadel in Canada, captured by the Massachusetts militia, by ceding Madras to the English. That most recent war, however, also enabled Louis XV to add to France's international prestige by acting with unprecedented magnanimity. Because he abhorred comparison to a merchant haggling for advantage, as a matter of policy the king denied himself the territorial gains in Europe to which the success of French arms entitled him and which his enemies—and the French public—had expected him to take. His gesture was the talk of Europe. The Parisian public's opinion can be summed up by a popular phrase that developed soon afterward: "tu es bête comme la paix (you are as stupid as the peace)."[6]

It was unsurprising, then, that the king's ministers constantly referred to honor and zeal and sought positive examples of war to prove to the more pragmatically minded public that attention to the king's honor motivated the success of French arms. The French court made sure to monitor the international press for news in order to place any French success, wherever it occurred, in the service of propaganda.[7] By 1757 and 1758, most French victories were taking place overseas. In Canada the 1757 victory at Fort William Henry and that at Fort Carillon, which crowned the summer campaign of 1758, in particular, due to their importance and scale, provided much-needed good news for the monarchy. The Crown published accounts of both battles for dissemination throughout France.[8]

The slow nature of transatlantic communication, as well as an aggressive British navy, did not prevent officers in North America, just like the court and the public in France, from keeping abreast of affairs in order to be responsive to happenings within the empire. Events of national importance—whether they were the birth of another royal child, the celebration of a victory, or the observation of a fast day—had long taken place in a wider French community beyond the boundaries of continental France.[9] The army officers in New France circulated news through their own networks as well, thereby keeping themselves informed of the global context in which they were operating.[10] The Marquis de Montcalm, for instance, attempted to advance his son's European military career despite an oceanic divide. Closely following European war and power politics at court brought constant reminders that events in North America, as much as anywhere in the empire, could shape the entire family's future.[11]

War may have helped unify France into a "nation," but, when it did not go well, it also emphasized all the metropolitan social critiques that centered on Louis XV as an unsuitable martial chief.[12] The Damiens incident highlighted the Crown's lack of control and leadership in the midst of a war. Generally uninterested in battlefield glory (unlike his famously martial great-grandfather, Louis XIV), Louis XV had intensified public confusion by disappearing for a month after the stabbing despite the superficial nature of the wound. The sudden changes to the royal council, removing some of the most experienced and well-known royal advisors in favor of a mistress and her circle, exacerbated this blow to public confidence in him and suggested the king's virility had been weakened as much as his reputation.[13] The Marquise de Pompadour was neither a nobleman nor a legitimate wife, yet now her circle took the lead in making policy decisions. The Versailles Treaty of May 1757 confirmed the move toward an Austrian alliance and further diminished the king's standing. For the new ministers replacing Machault and Argenson, questioning the Crown's honor, masculine virtue, or legitimacy could no longer be tolerated. The war in Europe was going badly. The people's morale was shaken; so was the king's. The call to honor was at its most urgent.

↝ *Les Français, Sauvages et Polis*

The ripples of Damiens's heinous crime spread across the Atlantic, appearing in a letter between Montcalm and the *premier commis de guerre* (chief war department clerk) Monsieur de Fumeron in July 1757, less than a month before the capitulation of Fort William Henry. Addressing the "great respect" that Indians had for the king, Montcalm wrote, "[W]e have not told them about the horrible attempt on his sacred person. It made us shudder with horror and could have diminished the esteem in which these Barbarians, so ferocious in war and so compassionate in their huts would hold us, seeing that we are capable of producing such monsters [as Damiens]."[14] In this letter Montcalm and Fumeron provide a lens into a complicit clandestinity. It is embedded in the very choice of words, and it gives us rare insight into the world of French aristocrats. An attack on the king's "sacred person" was an unimaginable event, one so terrifying in its implication that it was uncomfortable to consider how others would receive this information. The unthinkable had occurred and therefore could not even be discussed openly lest the implications of the assassination attempt, even the very act itself, become real. Montcalm himself may have been envisioning monsters at work in French society, but he projected this onto the Indians in order to both share his own fear with Fumeron and mask his anxiety by assigning it to *les sauvages*. It is even possible that in Montcalm's focus on Indian reactions at home he signaled to Fumeron that they were really discussing the internal nature of this event with regard to France. If so, Montcalm and Fumeron comprehended that domestic problems should never be discussed with outsiders (non-French and nonnoble individuals), lest reputations be tarnished.[15]

News of the assassination attempt did not arrive in New France before May 1757, when the first dispatches from France landed; rumors may have filtered into the colony earlier through British colonial newspapers. A letter from Montcalm to Bourlamaque based on March dispatches from the Bureau of the Army discussed the change in minister and then noted that "the king received a minor knife wound; the killer admitted nothing."[16] When the news circulated by word of mouth or was passed by letter in Montreal in late May or early June, some Native peoples would have heard the tale. The domiciled Mohawks of Kahnawake and Kanesatake lived close to Montreal, and the Huron *réserve* of Lorette was near Quebec. It is hard to determine what or even whether the indigenous peoples thought of the affair, but their actual reactions appeared of less concern to the French than the French officers' expectation of what the Indians might think. Clearly, no Native individual would have disputed that Europeans were capable of "producing such monsters"—altercations ranging from the Cholula massacre to the Seven Years' War amply demonstrated European cruelty throughout the Americas. But in the eyes of these French nobles, Damiens was a blot on the national honor. Men like Montcalm or the young Comte de Malartic may have feared Damiens would make Frenchmen, especially metropolitan Frenchmen, appear irredeemably savage. Damiens had been neither drunk nor foreign born nor noble; the term by which at least one letter referred to him was "that fanatic" and compared Damiens to Ravaillac (Henri IV's murderer).[17] The affair called into question the tidy distinctions that French officers had been forming since the summers of 1755 and 1756 and that separated French civility from Native savagery.

Moreover, the manner of the assassin's execution placed French officers assigned to New France, and even Canadian elites, in a delicate position. While fully supporting the meting out of such justice in an attempted regicide, could Montcalm claim that the public ritual torture and execution of Damiens was civilized in some way that Ottawa or Mohawk practices were not? It is uncertain how a French lieutenant or a colonial bourgeois would have answered if questioned by an Oswegatchie Iroquois or an Abenaki from Odanak about Damiens's death. In France, the Damiens execution represented a judicial and political ritual in which the sovereign reasserted his right to control. The public and the accused himself had no access to the secret trial. This process was not about expiating community grief over their lost ones, as in the case of ritual, indigenous North American captive torture. Rather, to restore social order, the French example confirmed that lawful violence was the prerogative—even the responsibility—of the monarch.[18] This was a demand on Louis XV's honor; he could not refuse.

The assassination attempt exposed the lie in the controlling metaphor of French and Indian diplomatic relations: that these groups were equals and members of one family (reflected in the diplomatic language of French "fathers" and Native "children") and that respect circulated freely among them. Compassion manifested itself in Indian villages, where enemy prisoners could become beloved members of the victors' community. Even in death, sacrificial victims' contributions to assuaging family grief were formalized and recognized.[19] Montcalm understood that the French community, by contrast, would have appalled the Indians by harboring such "monsters" in its midst. What Montcalm missed was that many Algonquian and Iroquoian nations would find Damiens's execution completely understandable—and in fact maybe even a credit to French humanity. It would show a proper concern for expunging the community's grief. That should have been the public event's bloody intention. That neither army officers nor marines emphasized this point showed the sharp limitations on any shared language of violence.

In the months after Damiens, as France tried to cope with the political impact of the assassination attempt, troubling news came to the new naval minister concerning events in New France that had transpired in the early spring of 1757. Writing to Vaudreuil, Moras focused on the governor's use of his own unassailable position in colonial politics to General Montcalm's detriment:

> I imagine . . . you have, as you inform me, concealed the small reproaches that you think you must make publicly toward the commander, who is an officer of distinction. This is essential and it would be aggravating if it were known that there is anything less than perfect accord between you both. I have written to him on this subject and I believe he will attend to this matter so much so that you will see changes in his conduct toward you.[20]

The discord between Vaudreuil and Montcalm, once public, tarnished the complex etiquette of courtesy and grace of the French court and showed the cracks in an allegedly unified French front to their Indian allies and British enemies. Moras could not control the monarch's manners, but he did attempt to censure his own subordinates. So the minister focused on the open nature of Vaudreuil's disputes with Montcalm, which were based on differences in military strategy, personal rivalries, and frustration over the place of Native peoples in the war. At the moment that Moras wrote, in February 1757, the clashes between Montcalm and Vaudreuil primarily revolved around disgruntled Indians after Oswego and the credit given to marines and Canadians versus *troupes de terre* at that siege. Both senior Canadians and French officers reported to their subordinates the progress of competing requests for honors, suggesting that at least a certain circle of marines and army officers witnessed minor disputes between the two commanders. In addition, various Indian embassies came to Montreal between September and December 1756. As governor general, Vaudreuil, not his subordinate, General Montcalm, embodied the king's authority at these meetings. This public reflection of inferiority—to Indian dignitaries and elites no less—irked the French general and festered within him.[21]

The minister understood that the army general was contributing to the state of discord as much as the governor. In his advice to Montcalm, he focused on the connection between behavior and war. He doubted that Montcalm was working as closely with Vaudreuil as he could despite the general's claims of good communication between the two. Reminding Montcalm that, "for the good of the king's service," he needed to act in concert with the governor, Moras stressed that this was not the time to judge the qualities or talents of others. Both men were there to pursue "the glory of the king's arms and the colony's advantage."[22] Above all else, Moras appealed to each man to place duty above self-interest, in line with the eighteenth-century martial aristocratic ideal.[23] The minister's pointed rebukes suggested that their personal pride impeded military affairs and proved that, at least in this Naval Ministry, conduct counted as much as results.

Had Moras remained in office, his attempt to mediate between Vaudreuil and Montcalm might have resulted in a unified strategy that benefited colonial and Crown interests. The minister seemed to have a healthy dose of pragmatism in dealing with both commanders: he moderated Montcalm's focus on glory over colonial interests, and he certainly suspected that Vaudreuil actively needled his co-commander. Moras insisted on the subordination of their personal differences to the interest of the royal war effort, doubtless because he did not want to suffer the fate of his predecessor, Machault. Prudence dictated the need for surveillance of these royal servants to monitor their strategic choices and orchestration of violence. But Moras failed in this effort. He left office at the end of May 1758, and soon thereafter, in August 1758, Montcalm complained in a letter to Vaudreuil that "the semblance of [our] disunion [has] developed to the point . . . that an [account] was printed in a New York newspaper" and attached an extract from the offending publication to his note. Vaudreuil and Montcalm were imitating the behavior of court factions at Versailles, but making their animosity visible to North Americans was not French, and that made it shameful.[24] Although Moras, Vaudreuil, Montcalm, and any European observers understood the prevalence of such behavior in their own culture, no one considered how such behavior registered in Indian eyes. Iroquoian and Algonquian nations prized a lack of public disputes—harmony within a community was the ideal, and composure was paramount.[25] Montcalm might have been better advised to worry more about how the Kahnawakes rather than New York newspapers interpreted his distancing from Vaudreuil.

⚓ Assessing Victory at Carillon

By late spring of 1758, the British had gained little ground, had yet to invade New France, and had failed to unify their North American colonies in a war effort that successfully countered French and Indian raids. Undertaking a new summer campaign season meant more heated conflicts between the army and the marines; officers debated how to conduct future battles with honor and how to regulate camp behavior during military operations. Unable to change or govern indigenous tactics and stunned by Canadian refusal to exclusively rely on European modes of violence, Montcalm and his officers worked to amend the language and practices that constituted war in North America. The French general engaged in a correspondence with his new opponent, James Abercromby, who had replaced John Campbell, fourth Earl of Loudoun, as the British commander in chief. Montcalm was sensitive to the Briton's appeal: "Of the desire I feel that the war [ought to] be carried on with humanity and generosity as [it is] in Europe and as it ought to be everywhere."[26] The two officers' entente affirmed the effort that the French were making to save face after Gen. Edward Webb and Lord Loudon rejected Montcalm's terms of capitulation to Colonel Munro at Fort William Henry due to the "murdering, pillaging, and captivating . . . of His Majesty's good subjects."[27] Moreover, Montcalm's army officers knew that enforcing European practices of campaigning and modes of war undercut the marine officers' ability to determine military tactics and policy. And then, that summer, the French officers received an invaluable asset to advance their cause: the battle of Carillon, eleven months after the disgrace to France's honor at Fort William Henry.

The French fort at Carillon, erected in 1755 and known as Ticonderoga to Anglo-Americans, presided over the territory between Lac Saint Sacrement (Lake George) and Lake Champlain. The structure was important but poorly constructed, and if the British conquered the citadel, they would gain a direct route from which to advance on Montreal and New France. Despite the attack of a larger enemy army that outnumbered the defenders almost three to one, the French forces at Carillon achieved an upset victory on July 8, 1758, continuing two years of unbroken success against their British foes in North America. The triumph earned the troops the heartfelt congratulations of Louis XV and his newest naval minister, Claude-Louis d'Espinchal, Marquis de Massiac, who "had nothing more urgent than to take [Montcalm's] letters, and those of the Marquis de Vaudreuil, whose details recount an event most honorable for the King's army. His Majesty saw with greatest satisfaction your rebuff and defeat of an army of 25,000 men despite your inferior number of troops."[28] The official reports, both in New France and in the metropole, made the most of inflated British casualty rates to present this victory over Abercromby as all the more awe inspiring. Moreover, this accomplishment, Minister Massiac assured Montcalm, "can only be due to the valor of these troops," who had been nurtured by the foresight and devotion of their officers.[29] As the sound of the *Te Deum* faded from the battlefield, the officers of the French army indeed congratulated themselves on a battle so perfectly executed that it could have occurred in Europe. To its French participants, Carillon was as much a cultural victory as a military one because, in contrast to the prior battles waged by the *troupes de terre* in North America, the belligerents at Carillon were almost all European. This great victory clearly demonstrated that restoring the practice of war to a European orientation required more than the frontal assaults and cannon sieges in evidence at Carillon, as well as disciplined campaign life—it also required the removal of Native influence. Contemporary French accounts pointedly stated that it was the exclusive use of French regulars and European tactics that carried the day. Certainly the absence of Indian assistance allowed French nobles to claim all the glory of war for themselves—in the name of their king, of course.[30] However, from a strategic perspective and of great assistance to French officers in their campaign to determine what constituted legitimate violence in defense of New France, victory at Carillon provided a powerful answer to the question of whether France truly needed the ruinously expensive gift giving that Indian alliances demanded.

The winter before the siege of Fort William Henry in August 1757, France had spent heavily for Indian assistance, "paying in advance" in the eyes of French officers through feasts, councils, and gifts. During the extended December 1756 Montreal council to attract Native aid for the coming attack on the English fort, 180 deputies of the domiciled Iroquois, Nipissings, Abenakis, Potawatomis, and Weas had been hosted for close to a month with Vaudreuil promising to "take care of their needs" despite open knowledge that some of these nations had envoys among the English at Albany at the same time. Later Bougainville wrote that the Ottawas of Michilimackinac on the campaign to Fort William Henry spent the majority of their time "singing, dancing, drinking, and eating." Malartic observed more precisely that the Ottawas, in late June, killed all the available sheep, claiming rights to "all animals on earth," and then later demanded a council with Montcalm to request guns, equipment, and fresh meat. Montcalm reluctantly provided animals from his personal stock of ungulates, only to have Iroquois and Ottawas get drunk after the council and begin fighting.[31] French officers remembered the entire summer 1757 campaign, the march, the siege, and the aftermath of victory at Fort William Henry as one long trial. And then the French had paid more afterward, both in gifts to appease frustrated Native allies and in the heavy price the Indians exacted to redeem the British captives they took to Montreal to sell.[32] From the French officers' point of view, France's return on their investment in Indian allies had been minimal at best and would no longer be needed.

Now in a position to begin cleansing their martial honor from the stains of North American warfare, French officers moved to capitalize on what a French published account described as a "brilliant victory [that] infinitely honors all the French."[33] The unbroken success of the French army in North America after 1756, leading to up to the textbook victory at Carillon, made the goal of continuing their military careers in Europe, a cherished aspiration of most of the French officers, seem that much closer to reality.

Delight over the Carillon victory began fading within only three weeks after word arrived in Quebec that Louisbourg, the besieged stronghold on Île-Royale (Cape Breton), which guarded entry into the Saint Lawrence, had finally surrendered to an invading British navy on July 26. From a Canadian perspective, the fall of the fortress meant that New France's cities, Quebec, Montreal, and Trois-Rivières, along with all the Indian *réserves*, now risked exposure to British invasion. Moreover, from the perspective of the French army, this was not the only disaster. Leading Britain's forces, Gen. Jeffery Amherst specifically denied military honors to the surrendering Louisbourg garrison. This humiliation to France's honor could not be hidden from the French court. Before long an express sloop sent to Canada from France delivered a letter from the naval minister at Versailles to General Montcalm regarding the news from England of this "upsetting event."[34] The euphemism belied the extent of the psychological blow suffered at Louisbourg. Montcalm must have been mortified. General Amherst pointed to Montcalm's own broken promises, made a year earlier at the capitulation of Fort William Henry, as the reason for publicly stripping the defeated French army of its honor.

Amherst's retributive and sobering terms at Louisbourg galvanized senior French army officers in their efforts to reshape the modes of violence permissible in this war. Montcalm wrote the following to Vaudreuil in September 1758:

> This is no longer the time where a few scalps, a few burned huts, will be advantageous or even our object. Small means, small ideas, minute details are now dangerous, they drain materials and time. The circumstances demand measures that cleave, that decide. War is completely changed in this part of the world by the way that the English pursue it. It means no less than the complete and swift loss of the colony and it is based on this that we must act.[35]

Senior French officers comprehended that a proxy war using Indians on the western frontier forced British colonial militias to remain close to their home colonies for border defense. Men like Bourlamaque, Lévis, or Malartic refused, however, to jeopardize their *race* as nobles by bargaining for aid or further endangering their martial reputations with their British opponents. For their part, the British, from 1758 on, did come to use all that French officers sought to reject—Indian councils, North American rangers, Native auxiliaries. Nonetheless, commanders like Amherst deployed such measures as secondary, not primary, strategy. Moreover, it was the French, not the British, who had overseen the Fort William Henry capitulation and proven (in British eyes) unable to control the Indians. The only "massacre" Amherst permitted at Louisbourg was that of French honor.

From Vaudreuil's perspective, however, Native allies had "long contributed to the honor of [the king's] army and the safety of the colony."[36] For the colony's senior marine officer, Indians played as critical a role in advancing royal prestige and imperial aims and in providing a mantle of security to civilians (both European and indigenous) as any other soldiers. For these reasons Canadian administrators and marine officers endured the high expenditure of gift giving as the price of this policy. The bold nature of Vaudreuil's statement about Indian contributions to French claims so shocked and scandalized the metropolitan general that Montcalm pointedly recopied Vaudreuil's line into a letter to his patron, the minister of war. Who could better understand the need to suppress Indian agency in determining French honor than the most recently named minister of war (and distinguished veteran of the War of Austrian Succession), the same Duc de Belle-Isle, who had once been criticized for ordering a retreat that saved his troops? He was a man who had tasted the ashes of impugned honor and who also believed that the army officer corps should be limited to true nobles alone.[37] It was bad enough that the nobles of the French army suffered the presence of the wealthy sons of the bourgeoisie and foreign officers; to imagine that Kahnawakes, Ottawas, or Abenakis could equally serve the king and pass judgment on French military matters was intolerable.[38]

☙ Pleasures and Discontents in Winter

As happened every year in late fall, major campaigning came to an end in October 1758, and many French and Canadian troops, as well as Laurentian Indians, retreated to the three cities of New France: Montreal, Quebec, and Trois-Rivières and the nearby *réserves* of Odanak, Kahnawake, Kanesatake, and Bécancour. In these colonial urban centers, the military and civilian elites of New France engaged in their long-standing tradition of emulating the extravagance and brilliance of eighteenth-century French court culture despite strained Atlantic trade lines and a series of devastatingly cold winters and crop failures in Canada during the war years. French observers had been passing judgment on Canadian elites and Indians since their arrival, and many observations were made during the long winters of 1756, 1757, and 1758, when all of these individuals were billeted in close quarters. In the shadow of Amherst's victory and in urban areas that forced colonial, metropolitan, and Native communities into proximity with each other, antagonisms over strategy renewed and became the backdrop to other tensions among these groups.

In the eyes of aristocratic officers, the manifestation of noble virtue in battle and their eagerness to reject costly indigenous alliances had been rewarded by victory at Carillon. The Louisbourg surrender terms now reaffirmed in their minds the importance of practicing noble martial masculinity off the battlefield as much as on it. Bougainville and his colleagues dissociated themselves (at least in their letters) from the practices found in New France's cities that corrupted Canadians and made them callous (e.g., gambling and other dissolute pursuits) and instead cast themselves, in evident contrast to the marine officers, as soldiers who reflected decency and consideration. "What a country! What morals!" Bougainville wrote from his winter quarters in response to what he considered to be the Canadians' limited material aid and lack of compassion for refugee Acadians.[39] Wealthy Canadian civilians used revels and other entertainment to offset the dreariness of war despite royal edicts that not only disapproved of such displays of magnificence but also ordered a cessation of all gaming throughout the realm in winter 1757.[40] Montcalm smugly reported that "[Lévis and Bourlamaque] live modestly, something more indispensible in this colony than in France by comparison to the *troupes de la colonie* [marines]." Modesty played into the larger issue of honor. Although Argenson was no longer minister of war, letters to him that had impugned Vaudreuil's merits as a leader were read by his successor at the ministry, recounting the excessive and detrimental nature of the gambling that took place throughout the winters at the tables of civilian intendant François Bigot. The practice threatened to corrupt French officers, yet Vaudreuil refused to ban gaming.[41] Gambling, at least, could be understood as an emulation of French court culture (which embraced games of chance). However, French officers used New France's constant shortage of supplies to their epistolary advantage, undercutting Canadian imitation of metropolitan fashions with comments such as "There are times when magnificence is a crime against the state" and recalling the frugality that had favorably marked the 1746 Provence campaign, when officers ate a single course at their meals.[42] The sanctimoniousness of such statements, casting the colonial elite's embrace of the metropole as bordering on treacherous, is almost comical. Army officers participated in the social life of New France during the winter lulls just as their army colleagues in Bavaria attended and hosted banquets and balls because to do any less would have been a breach of gentlemanly *politesse*.[43] For officers, one's public behavior could either expose one's fraudulent claim to nobility or, handled appropriately (e.g., by displaying disinterested virtue), prove one's right to lead.

Montcalm maintained that respect for modesty had its limits: he could not be a noble general if he did not have the material objects required that showed his peers, troops, colonists, and British enemies that he was an aristocratic military leader. Atlantic patrols by the strong British navy during the war years made it challenging to send goods from France to North America. Yet between 1756 and 1759 the Marquise de Montcalm and the Marquise de Saint Véran, wife and mother, respectively, of the French general, sent thousands of *livres* worth of foodstuffs and luxury objects from the family seat at Candiac (in the Gard region of south-central France), from Montpellier, and from Bordeaux to Quebec. The cost of supplies rose astronomically, making the bountiful table that a leading commander expected to have whether in winter repose or on campaign much harder and far more expensive to provide. However, enough ships and cargoes evaded the British that Montcalm's table could boast of having "liqueurs, plums, Portmanteau, and [fine] wine."[44]

The French general's drive to cement his reputation was not unique; in Canada, army officers Bougainville or Pierre Pouchot, Governor Vaudreuil, and even marine lieutenant Chaussegros de Léry aspired to add to their prestige. They exercised their social responsibility to display an example of gracious living, in emulation of French continental practice. These practices were routine in Europe, and France exceeded all other powers in officer luxury. With French generals heading to battle with, among other essential items, provisions sufficient to host fourteen guests and tempt them with thirteen different dishes in two courses, Louis XV was forced to issue a sumptuary law in early March 1757 to govern the "magnificence" of the tables that officers laid on campaign.[45] North American agricultural products simply did not meet Montcalm's continental expectations with regard to the appearance and offerings of his dining table, that key component of an officer's social life. To satisfy his demands, he turned to home and requested the following:

200 lbs of preserves
200 bottles of muscatel wine,
300 bottles of liqueurs,
100 lbs of good figs,
30 lbs of semolina—"I omit the vermichelly and the macaroni"
2 barrels of anchovies,
2 barrels of olives,
1 barrel of capers,
50 sausages[46]

Year after year in North America, Montcalm continued his demands for all manner of exotic goods—Turkish raisins from Smyrna (far superior, he noted, to those of Marseille) or candied citrus peels. Inexperience evolved into studied insouciance.[47]

As commanding general and as a marquis, Montcalm in 1758 further reinforced his status by requesting that the dowager marquise send him not just fine bread but his own baker as well. Such extravagance is striking when one considers that, by this time, his own troops were subsisting on horseflesh, rationed beef and bread, and a little cod, and the Canadian peasantry lived on far less.[48] Montcalm's desire was dutifully filled from the home front. For Montcalm and his contemporaries, such requests were not luxuries—these were the bedrock of noble army life. In the context of war, the items requested (like capers) seem absurd, and it is tempting to see them only as evidence of a vain and demanding nature out of touch with reality. But one-third of every supply list the general dispatched to the Montcalm women included goods such as the following, which were not intended for Montcalm's personal consumption but rather for use by his retinue or as gifts to others:

Some gray cloth for making coats and breeches for six menservants; some scarlet cloth, idem; some small lace, with the usual border

Three cases, [with] the plainest possible sachet, 3 quilted pocketbooks, twelve ordinary scent bags containing lavender flour,

... Add a small case with a few pots of scented pomade in each; if only one reaches me, I will make a present of it, if three reach me, I shall have three [presents] to make. ... Even should peace be made, and my recall become certain, send the things asked for just the same.[49]

That the bolts of cloth and the trinkets needed to make the perilous journey across the ocean regardless of the circumstances tells us something of Montcalm's perspective. Fully expecting to return to France when war ended, Montcalm intended for his presents (given, one assumes, to favored subordinates or colonists) to perpetuate the refinement and generosity of his family name in New France. Following the tone set by his commander, as any ambitious and loyal junior officer would, Bougainville also sought to cut a generous figure. Pretty fans, Persian robes, and women's perfumes clearly intended as gifts shared space with practical woolens; wishing to fit in with fashionable Parisian intellectual circles when the war eventually would conclude and he would return home, Bougainville asked his brother, Jean-Pierre, to continue sending "interesting new books and plays that may have been published since my departure."[50] Every pastille consumed and lace collar knotted demonstrated the natural right of the French aristocrat to rule his world. In Candiac, those of inferior status knew who the Montcalms were. Through the consumption of these same items abroad, French nobles sought to announce to the world who they were and to instill reverence and awe in both Canadian officers, deemed to be of lesser status, and *les sauvages*. Montcalm's wife and mother would have expected no less.

Disagreements over military strategy in no way suggest that elite Canadian officers eschewed the living habits of their metropolitan counterparts. The town homes of the Canadian elite could run from tastefully furnished to spectacular mansions, with formal gardens and beautifully appointed rooms.[51] Vaudreuil and Bigot emulated Versailles for the same reasons that high-status European goods were attractive to marine officers at home on their seigneuries (if they could afford such expenditures). In his writings on Canadians, Jean Baptiste d'Aleyrac stated that "Canadians take luxury to the extreme. It is not above peasants to wear gowns and silk jackets, as well as lace collars and damask shoes . . . they call one another Sir and Madam . . . and they love to eat well."[52] He was not alone in his observation. "Peasants [in Canada]," Montcalm had noted in his diary in May 1756, lived "like little gentlemen in France."[53] But for the people of Canada, especially those in urban centers, circumstances and their access to fine goods had shifted visibly by 1758—and not for the better.

In the final two years of war, famine strained relations, and strife grew as the rural and urban populations of Canada dealt with scarce resources, while colonial and metropolitan elites accused each other of hoarding and excess. Riots over horsemeat plagued both civilians and military, forcing the chevalier de Lévis to intercede twice during the winter of 1757. He assuaged the women of Montreal by showing his solidarity with them, accepting horsemeat for his own table—or rather, ordering his servant to do so on his behalf—a classic performance of a noble leading by example. To handle discord among the troops, Lévis pointedly called on the soldiers of the Béarn regiment, who had accepted the reduced rations, to also "set the example," this time for the mutinous marines sharing their quarters. He also alternated threats with persuasion in order to enforce his will.[54] While Lévis received almost universal praise for his handling of urban tensions and made no attempts to assign blame for the situation, other French officers used their moral sobriety in this crisis as a means by which to contrast themselves with elite Canadians and marine officers.[55]

Despite the colony's diminishing circumstances, Vaudreuil (who ordered the reductions), Bigot, and others in their circle, like marine captain Michel Hugues Péan, continued to impress visitors with their well-appointed, open dining and gaming tables, while several French officers pleaded for financial relief from the Ministry of War.[56] Commissary Gen. André Doreil, Montcalm, and, at times, the chevalier de Lévis took to detailing myriad fiscal and moral abuses in the government of New France. The French engineer Pontleroy noted that corruption was rampant, especially as concerned royal war expenses.[57] While engaging in the responsible pursuit and display of luxury himself, Montcalm criticized his counterparts in the marines and colonial administration. Yes, a nobleman's honor, under early modern French definitions of nobility, revealed itself through martial courage and through bounty, generosity, and lavish living. But Bigot was not a noble, Vaudreuil was corrupt, and common *compagnies franches* troops caused disorder by refusing to accept the lower standard of rations.

The worst abuses appeared to be marine officers taking from the king's storehouses to supply and enrich themselves. Corruption did indeed exist in New France as a practice born of necessity when the poorly compensated *troupes de la marine* had to augment their salaries and equip themselves; certain western posts grew famously associated with graft.[58] However, perhaps most offensive and least comprehensible to French nobles in the army was the continuation of the marines' practice of lavishing funds and supplies, especially food, on Indians, particularly after Carillon indicated, certainly to French officers, that such allies were not essential. Officers and cultural brokers like Joncaire Chabert or Marin de La Malgue plummeted in the esteem of army officers on this point. Either Indians had deluded these men (confirming army suspicions of marine stupidity or credulity), or the officers were utterly corrupt.[59] Furthermore, nowhere did army officers have a better opportunity to confirm their worst suspicions than during winter quarters.

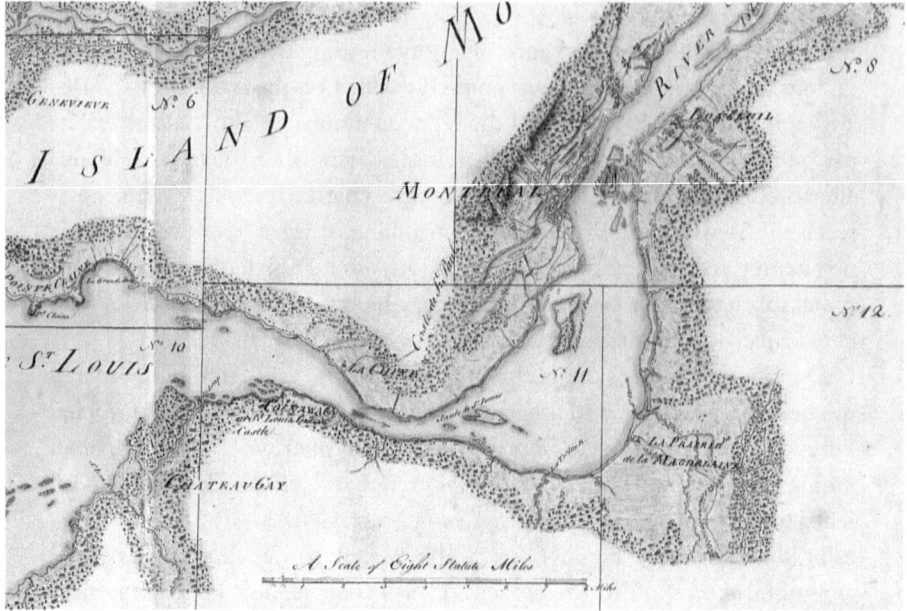

Figure 4. Detail of "Montreal" and "Counawaga" on a manuscript folio of the Murray Map of Canada, 1760–1761. James Murray commissioned surveys of the Saint Lawrence region, resulting in an enormous manuscript geographic depiction of the former New France. In this folio, the proximity of the French and Indian settlements of Montreal and Kahnawake (or Sault Saint Louis, and identified on the map as "Counawaga") speaks to the regular contact between Native peoples, *habitants*, and recent French (and later British) arrivals. Courtesy of the William L. Clements Library, University of Michigan.

The colonial government and the Indians, especially Iroquois and Algonquians of the *réserves*, also visiting delegations from throughout North America, came into more frequent contact from the fall to spring, as soldiers and warriors returned home, exchanged diplomatic envoys, and held councils to take stock of the previous years' campaigns. Certain indigenous centers, such as Kahnawake (or, Sault-Saint-Louis), were close to Montreal (see figure 4).

Despite leaving the "woods" for the city, the Indians, whom French officers hoped to avoid, still figured prominently. Often times, *compagnies franches* could be quartered in forts located within Native villages (as seen in figure 5) and, as the war dragged on, French officers of the *troupes de terre* could be placed in these installations as well. French and Indian interactions during winter campaign lulls were complicated. On the one hand, demonstrations of French superiority to Indians could be used to bolster the distinctions French officers sought to draw between themselves and the marines.

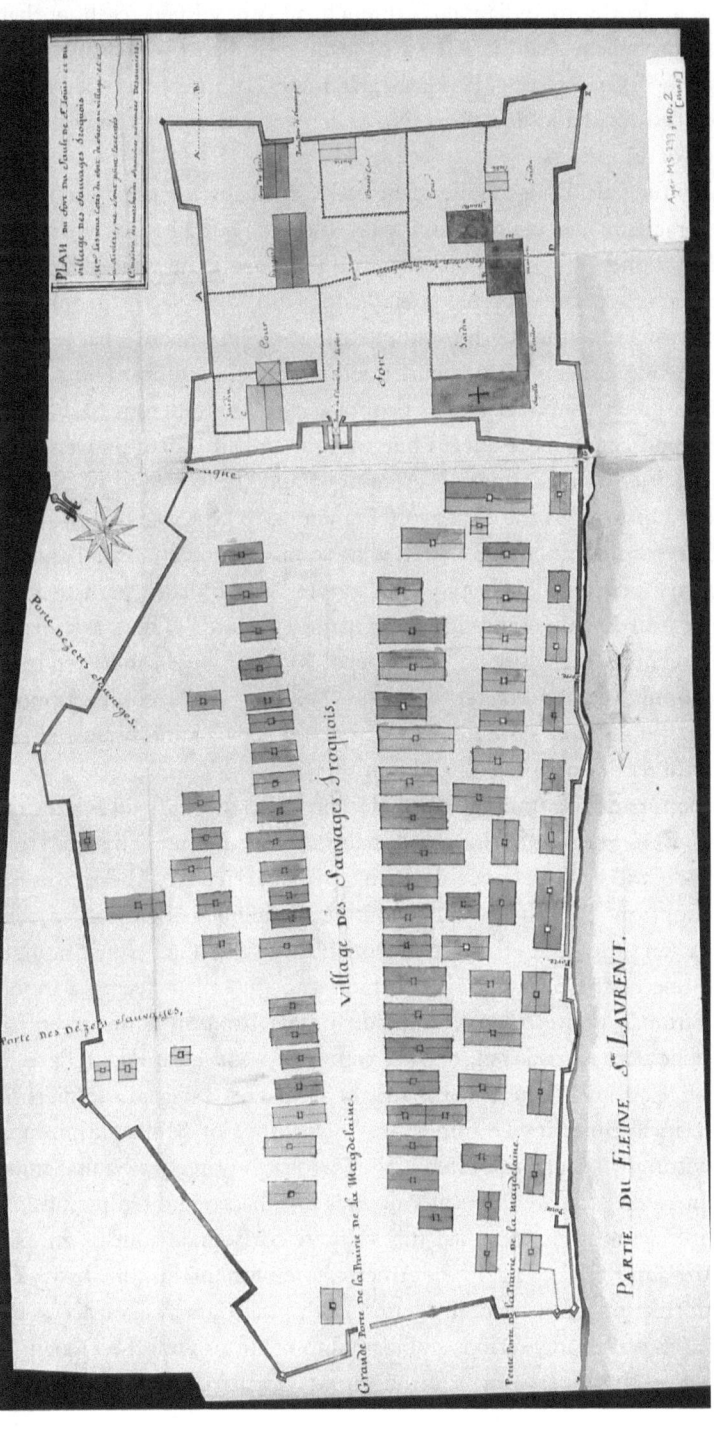

FIGURE 5. *Plan du Fort du Sault de St. Louis et du village des sauvages Iroquois.* In this 1752 survey drawing by marine engineer Louis Francquet, the proximity of French soldiers, Canadians, and Indians from multiple indigenous nations is visible in the quarters shared by the Indian village of Sault-Saint-Louis, also called Kahnawake, southeast of Montreal and the adjacent French fort. Photo courtesy of The Newberry Library, Chicago, Ayer MS 299; Map 2.

Despite an antipathy to Indian allies, French officers wished to show that "one must not believe that the science of leading [Indians] is exclusive only to Canadians."[60] On the other hand, the parameters of interaction had to be carefully constructed and explained. Nowhere was this more complex than in the issue of adoption.

Louis-Antoine de Bougainville criticized Canadians for their immoral, degraded practices and relationships with Indians, but he took pride in being called "father" by the Kahnawake Iroquois during the winter of 1757. Most French officers interpreted their "adoptions" by Native peoples as recognitions of French leadership rather than as polite gestures that also fit into the networks of reciprocity that defined indigenous culture. The Kahnawake name given to Bougainville, Garoniatsigoa (Thunderous Sky), was taken by the officer to represent his fine oratory and an Indian understanding of his refined comportment.[61] Adoptions and the bestowal of Native names served more than the flattery of French egos. Not one but two different Indian communities forged links with young Lieutenant Jean-Baptiste d'Aleyrac. In April 1756 d'Aleyrac was "adopted" by Indians (perhaps Iroquois living near Lachine) and given the name "Renard." Then, as a mark of "their esteem and attachment," the Abenakis of Bécancour inducted him into their community, too, under the name "Soleil."[62] The second adoption explains why indigenous communities claimed d'Aleyrac and bestowed on him powerful names such as Fox and Sun.

As the commander at the village of Bécancour in the difficult winter of 1757–1758, d'Aleyrac controlled the distribution of supplies. The relationships of trade and diplomacy could be happily married, in Abenaki eyes, through adoption: this rite would combine d'Aleyrac's inclusion in the community (and the duties that accompanied this) with a generous attempt to remake one of these strange French men into (in Indian terms) a more civilized, rational, polite Abenaki individual. The Iroquois name given to Pierre Pouchot, Sategariiouaen, or "the center of good business," reflected the type of relationship the Senecas sought with Fort Niagara's soldiers.[63] Even the critical Bougainville fulfilled his obligations of Mohawk kinship, albeit unwittingly, when he visited "his Tortoise brothers at Sault-Saint-Louis [Kahnawake] to give them fifty pounds of tobacco and ten pounds of vermillion."[64] Montcalm presented this vignette to Bourlamaque as an example of the absurdities of life in the Americas, reinforcing his tone by making this information a postscript in a letter. But to the Kahnawakes, access to these materials was deadly serious and central to relations with the French.

Certain French officers affirmed indigenous efforts to reform the French and also confirmed senior French officers' concerns about the deleterious nature of prolonged cross-cultural interaction, contact that was especially close during winter quartering. The sieur de La Milletière, a lieutenant in the Languedoc regiment, apparently got along famously with Indians and easily learned the Iroquois language in his first two years in New France, no doubt through many visits to Iroquois *réserves*. This officer's enthusiasm for cultural adoption surpassed the boundaries of Franco-Indian engagement in language and practice and went far beyond what was expected of metropolitan officers. During the summer of 1757, La Milletière "had the honor of being asked for in full council" of the Kahnawakes, Ottawas, Mississaugas, and Nipissings, showing the respect accorded him by a variety of nations and his willingness to enter Indian urban space.[65] Montcalm heartily seconded Vaudreuil's recommendation that this officer leave the *troupes de terre* to join the *troupes de la colonie* instead, pleased to be rid of such a transgressive individual. "Vaudreuil intends him [La Milletière] to follow in the path of M. de Joncaire," Montcalm wrote in his diary, "whose niece [La Milletière] has married."[66] Multiple generations of Joncaires carried blood ties to the Senecas and had adoptive relatives among this Iroquois nation.[67] Thus, not only did the sieur de La Milletière embrace the Seneca language and customs, but he also allied his very bloodline, his *race*, with Native peoples. To officers like Montcalm or Bougainville, it was more appropriate to view adoption into Indian families comically, as befitted an action initiated by social and cultural inferiors.

For all their detailed observations of Canadians and Indians, few metropolitan officers considered the reasons that marines sought indigenous adoptions and access to trade and gift networks or visited the indigenous allies or communities. At forts and throughout Native villages in Indian country, marine officers performed the exact same type of expensive social dance as the French officers did at Montreal and Quebec—for status—but for a very different audience. Marines serving in the borderlands had to engage in trade as a means of drawing Indians to French outposts, where they were able to cement alliances, supplement their meager martial incomes, and simply pass the time.[68] The ability to provide gifts and goods that interested Indian consumers was the key to prestige and success in negotiations, war, or peace. In early spring 1758, the brothers Chabert de Joncaire reported their failure to prevent Seneca villages from receiving the Chaberts' archrival, William Johnson, whose immense gift-giving ability gave them "little credibility."[69] "Credit" and "credibility" are similar words, deriving from the same root. Even in French court culture, *crédit* played a role as a commodity of nobles. At court, credit took the form of access and opportunities offered by patrons in exchange for continued loyalty and service to them.[70] The Chabert de Joncaires' credit was their access to the material goods in gift and trade needed by their adoptive Native communities. This access bolstered their reputations and gave weight to their words in council. Tobacco honored the sacred bonds of alliance, metal household goods reaffirmed bonds of kinship, and powder and guns promised communal defense against enemies and the growth of warriors' reputation.[71] Laying a good table for visiting Indian embassies enhanced the marines' own status as generous hosts, a point made by a Louisiana commander who complained that, with no news or shipments forthcoming from France, he was ashamed to treat with Indians empty handed.[72]

The sheer volume of merchandise involved in the gift giving and exchanges required thirty thousand *livres* of items for one mission alone. The metropolitans were shocked by the vulgarity of gift giving on this scale. This was either commerce or extortion. It was not gift giving as they practiced it, that is, the giving of one lavender sachet or a Persian fan to an individual in grateful or anticipatory recognition of an obligation. Even the very word used to record the heart of Indian-European councils, the moment of greatest importance, had connotations of mercantile exchange. Indians always came to speak to the French of *bonnes affaires*—good business.[73] Canadian envoys to Native communities almost invariably brought items for their hosts and additional materials as tokens of respect to facilitate talks.[74] French officers sneered at what they considered a Native preference for quantity over quality and assumed the worst intentions on the part of the donors.[75] Moreover, Indians often chose from among the items proffered in a process that, if French officers were present, denied these elite metropolitan men the right to select what they considered to be the appropriate items for each recipient (Indian or French). Viewing "gifts" as "bribes" and "diplomacy" as "appeasement" made French officers unable to reconcile these concepts with French *politesse* and *gentilesse*. To ask for a gift rather than to receive something freely was, from a French perspective, to change the very meaning of the offering. For all the complaints made by French sources about the cost, it was not as if Indians did not also provide some tokens of their own, however. Carefully wrought wampum belts and pelts, tobacco, and slaves undergirded Native-French interactions as Indians gave specific items to respond to specific situations.[76]

The aversion to trade and the deep association of gift giving and Indians with degraded commerce, interest, and manual labor made French officers miss the common ground in their diplomatic and martial traditions. The Duc de Belle-Isle, minister of war by 1758 and Montcalm's own patron, was entirely dependent on the king's financial support as of 1750 because of his standard of living. Belle-Isle's explanation for receiving continuous royal funding rested on the outlay of expenses he incurred while entertaining foreign grandees who visited his Parisian *hôtel particulier*. As a site of public meeting, Belle-Isle's home and hospitality reflected the glory of the king and the success of His Majesty's affairs.[77] The army mimicked its monarch—on a smaller scale. To describe a marine officer like the sieur de Longueuil to the Iroquois Confederacy as "a significant French leader" forced Governor Vaudreuil to ensure that his deputy could materially live up to the designation and status with which he was being endowed.[78] Despite the French court's subsidizing the representational expenses of Belle-Isle and many others, French officers misunderstood that when Canadian seigneurs like the baron and sieurs de Longueuil, the sieurs Chabert de Joncaire, or the Vaudreuils entertained Indians in council, they were executing their official duties by interacting with important foreign (indigenous North American) dignitaries.

To French officers, the gifts, the merchandise, and the Indian councils that continued after 1758 despite bad harvests and the difficulty of resupply from France confirmed their sentiment that "only the Indians escape the reduction [of rations]."[79] Resentment increased with privations. No recourse existed for the poor *habitants* of Canada who participated neither in large-scale Native diplomacy nor in noble grandstanding. This state of affairs poisoned the goodwill of the civilian population, already forced to quarter regulars and serve the army in myriad ways. Militias and marines, especially those married to Canadiennes, genuinely suffered for the defense of the colony or, at minimum, of their own homesteads. But as their deprivations increased, it undermined the king's role as the traditional provider for his people among the colonists.[80]

Domiciled Indians at Kanesatake, Kahnawake, Odanak, and even as far away as Oswegatchie observed the army, marines, and *habitants* closely and interacted with them regularly as well. Indian society required generosity toward the community as a condition of leadership. Insistence on personal displays of magnificence and luxury among the French and Canadian elites in such a time of want could be seen as a crime that hurt every community that was dependent in some way on New France, Native as well as European. Elias Pagan, an Oswegatchie Iroquois captured by the English in June 1759, revealed as much when he was interrogated: "Q: Does [sic] the French intend to attack any of the English Forts during the summer? A: No, they say they have not the Power as they have not the Provisions enough, but at the same time says [sic], the Kings Stores never want plenty—but that the Country People are greatly distress'd."[81] Pagan connected power with provisions: the

French soldiers' ability to support themselves, let alone any Indians to whom they had obligations. Native communities gave weight to leaders who strived to provide for everyone. It was absolutely accurate to say that the "country people are greatly distress'd," but that turn of phrase may have contained Pagan's implicit assessment that if the French failed their own countrymen, the *habitants*, what lay in store for their indigenous friends could only be worse. Montcalm received delicacies and goods of special significance from France destined to be gifts—but gifts only to those whom the general accepted into his social and cultural milieu.

The House Is on Fire

The fall of Louisbourg in September 1758 began the reversal of French fortunes, though the citadel held out just long enough to prevent a direct assault on New France for the remainder of that year. Instead, in order to weaken the perimeters of New France in anticipation of an invasion the following year, Britain's North American forces began trying to uproot the chain of French forts in the Ohio Country one by one and to lay claim to the west, much where they had begun their struggle for domination in 1753 and 1754. The first French loss came at Fort Frontenac, located at the eastern end of Lake Ontario, which surrendered a month after Louisbourg. General John Bradstreet generously offered respectable terms to the sieur de Noyes, sparing the career marine officer further humiliation. But the capture of the fort's supplies raised the cost of the loss to the French Crown; the fort had stockpiled goods worth eight hundred thousand *livres*, which the colony (and the royal treasury) could ill afford to lose.[82] Governor Vaudreuil had sent Paul Joseph Le Moyne, sieur de Longeuil, to travel among the nations of the Iroquois Confederacy only eight days before Frontenac fell to a force that included Onondagas and Oneidas—clearly the envoy had made no inroads among the Iroquois. Worse still, Rigaud de Vaudreuil (the governor's younger brother) and François Marchand, sieur de Ligneris and colonial delegate to the Shawnees in the Ohio Country, reported concerns over the cool treatment the French were receiving from indigenous peoples and noted with alarm the waning of French influence in late 1758. With the conclusion of the Treaty of Easton in October 1758, Britain secured the neutrality of the Delawares, Shawnees, and Mingos in the Ohio Country and robbed New France of a critical tactical advantage. Fort Duquesne, near the site where the war began in 1754, could not be sustained without the help of the Delawares and the Shawnees, nor could the fort count consistently on the presence of Anishinaabeg coming from the *pays d'en haut*.[83] Unable to maintain the position, the retreating French garrison mined the structure in late fall of 1758 before retreating to Fort Machault, all the while desperately continuing to extend diplomatic overtures to the indigenous residents of the Ohio Country in hopes of curbing British advances farther north.[84]

Canadian officials had long explained to the Crown that attracting and retaining Indian allies helped ensure New France's safety. Surely the colony was worth the cost of such alliances even if—by October 1758—the loss of two French forts combined with the independent settlements being made by indigenous peoples with the British undermined the claims of marine officers and the governor to "control" Native peoples for the Crown's purposes.[85] In order to counterbalance the criticism of costly Native alliances being put forward subtly but consistently by the officers of the *troupes de terre*, Vaudreuil forwarded his own negative evaluations of army officers and their criminal negligence against the state:

> It is, therefore, Milord, for the true and most solid interest of the colony that I commit myself to fighting the enemy for our borders foot by foot, unlike M. de Montcalm and the Regulars, who wish only to preserve their reputations and return to France as soon as possible without having experienced a single defeat. They think more seriously about their personal interest than the safety of the colony.[86]

By focusing on the officers' personal ambitions, the statement directly challenged their devotion to the Crown and to the nation by their unwillingness to fight for the very edges of the empire. Vaudreuil recast Montcalm's victorious record so far at Oswego, William Henry, and brilliantly against the odds at Carillon as wanting to quit before the possibility of defeat soiled his and his officers' reputations. Montcalm himself, however, and some of his subordinates might have admitted (as, indeed, Bougainville did privately) that their reputations had already been "sullied." The terms at Louisbourg ensured that the army would not be leaving North America with an unblemished record. But the charge that returning to Europe suited Montcalm's personal interests (or those of Lévis, Bourlamaque, or Désandrouins) and that they were putting these personal interests first was serious. As Vaudreuil saw it, disputing every inch of New France would require the types of sacrifices made at Fort William Henry: councils, the purchasing of Indian aid by the giving of gifts, and turning a blind eye to "savage atrocity" in war.

In the fall of 1758 special envoys from both factions, the *troupes de terre* and the *compagnies franches de la marine*, rushed back to France to plead their respective cases to their ministries—it was time for the court to weigh in and resolve the disputes between the commanders. Marine major Michel Jean Hugues de Péan, a Canadian officer and an intimate of Intendant Bigot's circle, departed in August for France, arriving in September. Louis-Antoine de Bougainville, Montcalm's aide-de-camp, and army commissary André Doreil left in early October as the general's emissaries to lobby the court for war aid.[87] None of these messengers knew what awaited them at the troubled French court. What they would discover was that the aristocrats surrounding Louis XV cared very deeply about valor being demonstrated in the war and were willing to go to some length to ensure French honor in North America.

Bougainville enjoyed a warm reception at the Ministry of War, which had been under the Duc de Belle-Isle's authority since March. As Montcalm's former commanding officer from the War of Austrian Succession and his patron in Paris circles, Belle-Isle welcomed Bougainville and helped him achieve both a promotion to colonel and the honor of receiving the *croix de Saint Louis* from the king at Versailles. Court politics favored Doreil, and Bougainville especially, over Péan. The new naval minister, Nicolas René Berryer, former Paris chief of police, excelled as a local informant, not an imperial bureaucrat. Péan, Doreil, and Bougainville attempted to convince Berryer of New France's critical situation and its desperate need for supplies and reinforcements; the minister ignored all of their pleas. Bougainville added in his journal that Berryer had no grasp of the strategic value of New France and that Berryer had demonstrated as much when he told the young officer that "one did not try to save the stables [the colonies] when the house [France] was on fire."[88] On the other side, Vaudreuil's proposal to recall Montcalm fell flat; Louis XV refused.[89] Indeed, to make matters worse for the Canadian governor, the king promoted Montcalm to the rank of lieutenant general in January 1759 on the basis of the man's character and victories.[90] Montcalm now outranked Vaudreuil, and Louis XV's intervention indicated a warning to Vaudreuil and the Canadian leadership that they should follow the court's lead and priorities, not those of the colony. Vaudreuil received the honorary *grande croix de Saint-Louis* as a consolation and as a token of his "dedication" to the king. In the memorandum concerning this award, the naval minister hoped to please Vaudreuil as well as the "devoted" colonial militia, marines, *habitants*, and Indians with the honor and favor shown to the governor by the Crown.[91] Among the Canadian elite, Vaudreuil alone received distinction, for no further honors or promotions were provided at this time to officers in the *compagnies franches* or the militia.

Owing to his good relations with Belle-Isle and that minister's favor with the king, Montcalm had secured both a promotion and the authority to conduct battle in North America as he saw fit. The aged maréchal wrote to Montcalm to pass along the good news and added the following:

> I have become responsible for you to the King. I am well assured that you will not dishonor me and that for the good of the State, the glory of the Nation, and your own preservation you will have recourse to the greatest extremities rather than ever submit to conditions so disgraceful as those accepted at Louisbourg, the memory of which you will efface. Such are, Sir, substantially the King's intentions.[92]

Not only had Montcalm's appeals for more Europeanized forms of war been effective, but his patronage at court and his signal victory at Carillon had also succeeded in making honor and legitimate tactics central themes of the war in North America. The epistolary campaign conducted by Montcalm and his closely allied officers to disparage colonial martial actions and to give a place to military authority in running the empire had finally borne fruit.[93] However, the court's inability and unwillingness to send further reinforcements of men and supplies, even as it chose a side in the battle over tactics, dimmed the success of the metropolitan officers at court. How could they, so clearly devoted to the honor of the army, master the situation on the ground without more material support from France?[94]

The ship bearing Bougainville and the official dispatches the regulars were so hoping for left at the end of February, outran the British navy in the north Atlantic throughout April, and arrived at Quebec in mid-May 1759. The correspondence brought across the Atlantic by Bougainville that spring included news that the impending British invasion down the Saint Lawrence River into the heart of New France made possible by the fall of Louisburg would be led by Gen. James Wolfe. He meant to take Quebec City. Power struggles between the architects of New France's defense over how best to counter the new British threat continued. Montcalm argued for a decisive, European-style engagement at Quebec; Vaudreuil preferred limited defense in favor of retreat to Montreal.[95] The arrival of only four hundred French recruits of mediocre quality to strengthen Canada's defense disheartened the entire colony. Ironically, Montcalm's prowess at Carillon had provided an excuse for the court's limited reinforcement, and Berryer told Canada's new defender in chief that "his Majesty's confidence in the depth of your zeal, through which you achieved complete victory with fewer than 4,000 men over such a considerable army at Carillon, allows him to hope that with such brave Troops, along with those of the colony and the militia, you will find a way to block the enemy."[96] The French general should have clearly understood the premise from which Berryer spoke. An aristocrat should rely principally on inexhaustible supplies of devotion and valor to complete assigned tasks in the monarch's service. Berryer sidestepped the practical dilemma, as well as the responsibilities of his ministry; as a result, in spring 1759 the British navy's strength made the commitment to transfer and possibly lose large quantities of military or comestible support to the colonies too great a risk to run. Encouraging sentiments and flattery did little to materially bolster the defense of New France while reinforcing the now inescapable court decisions about "legitimate" strategy and warfare.

Whatever its benefits in securing Indian aid, the pillar of French and Indian diplomacy, gift giving, placed too great a burden on the Crown's resources. Berryer rationalized, on the basis of earlier correspondence, that the affections of powerful groups such as the Iroquois Confederacy were not in jeopardy, ignoring any agency of Native peoples by stating that they were allies to be "led."[97] The need of the naval minister to state this plainly in correspondence to the Canadian governor reflected the Crown's financial crisis after four years of war and the growing file of complaints by army men about fraud and degeneracy in Canada, files that would have spoken to a former policeman. A letter from Vaudreuil to Berryer in March 1759, placed in the context of the French army's criticisms, could easily have been read as an example of French elites fallen away from civility. "I chose what I saw to be the most effective remedy [for desertion]," Vaudreuil wrote, "the necessity of using Indians; our Indians pursued two soldiers of [the] Béarn [regiment] having fallen into this situation, caught up to them, cut the head off one and compelled his companion to carry [the head] himself to the fort, where he was tried . . . it was an example of absolute necessity; I hope it will have made an impression on soldiers who would have followed suit."[98] Desertion plagued European and colonial armies in the eighteenth century, with officers of all nationalities leveling harsh punishments to ensure order and swift execution of commands and to discourage troops from absconding.[99] Vaudreuil's solution for desertion was another case entirely. Berryer had already been presented with evidence by Bougainville and Doreil, prior to the appearance of Vaudreuil's March 1759 letter, that the bulk of royal funds went to the purchasing of English prisoners, rewards for attacks on continental French, as in this case using Indians to deal with deserters as directed by royal officials, and graft. Vaudreuil's "use of the Indians" against soldiers who wore the uniforms of regiments from old France made ever more plausible, perhaps especially to a royal policeman like Berryer, the insinuation by the noble officers that marines partnered with Indians in a terrifying world of barbarous trade and war that effaced French cultures and values.

⚜ La Chute

After seventy years of allowing tactics and practice to be formed by Canadian officers of the colonial regulars, Versailles broke with tradition to promote metropolitan army standards in New France. Military authority had always had a place in empire: the very definition of the governor general's role was as a warrior, a commander in chief. However, aristocratic army officers traded on their *crédit* for winning Carillon to ensure their ascendancy. They believed that how war was conducted and how soldiers behaved should carry as much weight as the defense of France's imperial borders. The king and court agreed. The new standards to be enforced—distinguishing valor from value, honor from trade, zeal from interests—came at the most critical and the worst possible moment for New France.

New France learned of the court's decisions when Bougainville arrived in May 1759, allowing Montcalm to enact his strategy of pulling back the French forces in the spring and summer of 1759 into the core of the Saint Lawrence region in order to defend Quebec from an impending British invasion. After enduring a brutal siege by James Wolfe, lasting from June to September, the defenders of Quebec gambled on their future with a classic European battle and ventured out to attack British forces when they appeared before the city on the Plains of Abraham on September 13, 1759. Montcalm hoped to drive Wolfe's men down into the river before they could solidify their position. His attack failed, however, and cost New France control of Quebec—and Montcalm his life; in addition, it left Montreal and the Saint Lawrence valley completely exposed. Made commander as a result of Montcalm's death, François Gaston de Lévis spent the rest of the fall 1759 campaign season successfully preventing the British from exploiting their victory at Quebec and over the winter pooled the resources of the colonial government and military at Montreal in order to launch what turned out to be an unsuccessful counteroffensive to regain Quebec in April 1760.

French aristocrats serving in the army abroad had been unable to lessen the demands of performance and consumption their nobility conferred on them or to bend the rules nobility imposed. By the fall of 1759, events had rendered irrelevant the old intracommand controversy over the merits of

Indian war, bargaining for allies, and the corruption of elites by their participation in the commerce integral to Indian diplomacy. All that mattered now was territorial defense, but conducting this without Indian eyes and ears, let alone bodies, proved very difficult. Between 1755 and 1759 Native nations repeatedly took stock of their own situation in this war. In the early years of the conflict, many indigenous peoples believed the French to be the lesser of two evils. By 1759, after four years of devastation, epidemics, continuing European claims to their land enforced by violence and by treaty, and finding the French and the British both to make poor allies, most Indians decided that removing themselves from this conflict seemed best. *Réserve* communities in the Laurentian valley, facing the same threat as Quebec in 1759 and then Montreal in 1760, began to conclude their own peace treaties with the British. Predisposed to see Indians as fickle and untrustworthy—views reiterated by many French in both official and private correspondence—metropolitans saw the settlements made by the various Indian confederacies and nations previously allied with New France (especially those domiciled communities that came to be known as the Seven Nations) as the final proof of their long-standing fears. "Just as [Bourlamaque] began to hold a great council [to attract support for a countercampaign]," the chevalier de La Pause recalled, "an Indian of the Five Nations appeared to say their peace was made with the English general, who would, in 4 or 5 days, become the master of Canada and so all the Indians packed up and left M. de Lévis alone."[100]

With no French presence left on the Great Lakes to protect the southern part of the Saint Lawrence, almost no Indian support forthcoming from the *pays d'en haut*, and only a single ship able to arrive from France, the exhausted defenders of New France found themselves restricted to the Villemarie section of Montreal in August 1760, where they faced thousands of British troops under three armies that had surrounded New France over the course of the year.[101] No strategy, no valor could save the beleaguered capital of New France.

When Montreal finally surrendered to Gen. Jeffery Amherst on September 8, 1760, the terms of the capitulation provided for the defending troops to embark for France, and many members of the colonial leadership, along with numerous marines, chose to join their army counterparts for the return to the metropole. Some senior marines no doubt believed that New France's collapse resulted from the court's abandonment of modes of diplomacy and warfare that had been used successfully for more than three hundred years to counter British military and demographic strength while defending the king's immense territorial claims in North America. When Canadian elites and Native peoples refused to acknowledge French officers' natural right to lead, the latter had reacted by clinging more firmly to their core value—honor, as they understood the term—and the sachets, banquet tables, and gracious gestures in war that demonstrated their nobility and right to command. Reflecting as it did the way the court itself wished to be seen, apparently this emphasis had yielded policy value in France. The marine elites should have paid more attention to this result. In France during the winter of 1760–1761, the Canadian martial elite would similarly reveal their accustomed attributes of status, but in the metropole, they would discover that they had no means with which either to trade for status or to invoke gratitude for their service in defense of France's Atlantic empire.

⚜ Chapter 5

The Losing Face of France

Buffeted by strong winds portending winter and barred from serving in North America by the terms of New France's capitulation, the troops of France's armies embarked for home in autumn 1760, leaving behind a Canada ravaged by the last six years of war. The desperate spring campaign of 1760 had not saved the colony—by September, three British armies had encircled Montreal, the last free city of New France, and offered the choice of capitulation or annihilation. Canada's leaders chose the former and acquiesced to Gen. Jeffery Amherst's terms because he promised a generous treatment of the *habitants*, including the right to Roman Catholic worship. Despite anxieties about living under British occupation, about 95 percent of New France's colonial population chose Canada as their home and opted to remain in North America rather than migrate to France. The Canadian militia, a handful of regular soldiers, and even some marine officers, especially those who still served at posts deep in the North American interior or who, like Charles Mouet de Langlade, had family ties to Native communities, also chose to cast their lots with the new British regime as well.

Those individuals who did leave the colony belonged disproportionately to the administrative, military, and mercantile elites of New France. They were those who had strong contacts with France or desired to continue in royal service. After Montreal fell, many marine officers hurriedly left for

France, thinking that the large amounts of paper money—bills of exchange, promissory notes, colonial currency—they brought back with them to the metropole would ensure some financial security for their families in France. Barred from continued service in the ongoing war by the terms of the Montreal capitulation, these men in the *compagnies franches de la marine* and in the regulars, the *troupes de terre*, all had to find new ways of living—and new sources of income.

France had been scarred by notable losses and global setbacks in its war effort for two years before the ships bringing the refugees from New France arrived in November 1760. The previous year, Louis XV's troops had lost Guadeloupe and Martinique in the Caribbean, Pondicherry in India, and the battle of Minden in Germany. Gorée Island in West Africa and Louisbourg on Cape Breton had been captured in 1758; now New France had surrendered. The capitulation of Montreal especially stung because here the British commanding general, Jeffery Amherst, continued the policy of denying the honors of war to the surrendering French army, a policy he had first forced on the French at the fall of Louisbourg. Shortly after his arrival in France in December, former governor Vaudreuil received a letter from Louis XV, who was angry and demanded explanations for both the surrender of Montreal without the honors of war and for the loss of Canada.[1] There was also the matter of years of war expenses that continued to grow exponentially. The paroled and therefore unemployable returning army soldiers, marines, and Canadians now joined the earlier Acadian refugees of the *grand dérangement* (British expulsion), who had arrived in the late 1750s, adding new responsibilities to the Crown's financial load.[2] Interested in stanching the hemorrhaging costs and in restoring France to as strong a position as possible before the anticipated peace talks, Étienne-François de Stainville, Duc de Choiseul, the king's foreign minister (1758–1761) and then chief minister of war beginning in 1761, instituted a series of policies that shaped the lives of the returning Canadian veterans and their world of possible actions.

The setbacks experienced by the marines upon their arrival in France reveal the uncertainty and nervousness royal administrators felt toward this group of immigrants and the legacy they represented. The stunning first blow to the veterans was the suppression of the *compagnies franches de la marine* as a separate military service in November 1761.[3] Then, a commission impaneled on December 18, 1761, one month after the disbanding of *la marine* service, undertook a criminal case to investigate the reasons for the loss of New France, in particular the officers accused of "corrupt practices, embezzlement, and robbery in the fulfillment of their duties in Canada."[4]

The investigation focused public attention on the fur-trading economy and black-market profiteering in metropolitan supplies and led to a sensational corruption trial known as *l'affaire du Canada*. This trial reinforced court-approved ideas of Canada as a colony where only skimming from the royal treasury guaranteed wealth. When the court rendered judgment, it closed the royal book on two hundred years of imperial aspirations in the North Atlantic. Finally, a royal edict, issued in the midst of the trial—the *Ordonnance* of March 24, 1762—ordered the relocation of all of the officers of the returned forty-two *compagnies franches de la marine* to Touraine, a province in east-central France.[5] The *ordonnance* emptied Paris of marine veterans, lessening the carnival-like atmosphere that grew up around the trial, but it also raised new questions about the future of these officers. What happened to the military veterans who returned to France gives depth to the complicated story of why Canada, and indeed French North America, disappeared from national memory.

☙ *L'Affaire du Canada* and Touraine

Of the fifty military and civilian individuals indicted in *l'affaire du Canada*, fifteen were marines, and nine were of elite rank, the most prominent of whom was the former governor general of New France, the Marquis de Vaudreuil. When, with royal approval, Choiseul had issued a directive suppressing the marine service, he also indicated that the officer corps of the navy would absorb the officers of the disbanded *compagnies franches*.[6] Clearly, the men being charged with fraud would not be joining those ranks any time soon. Their shame tainted the reputations of all of their fellow marine officers as well. These elite martial families had extensively intermarried, making almost every officer somehow personally, even if indirectly, linked to those on trial and placed in jeopardy the career prospects of all.[7] Worse still, prosecutors demonstrated a tendency to view the marine veterans as a coherent group, all bent on defrauding the Crown for personal gain. Behind the marines stood their relatives, Canadian and French, a widening circle of interested or affected parties.

Almost all of the accused had commanded or were the final commanders of western frontier outposts: Forts Frontenac, Miramichi, Niagara, Little Niagara, Chambly, St. Jean, Lachine, La Présentation, Toronto, and La Rivière au Boeuf. It is clear that some (if not most) of the men charged with graft deserved such scrutiny, having amassed fortunes in the tens of thousands of *livres* over the previous decade in wartime Canada. When Daniel-

Marie Chabert de Joncaire, commander at the small Fort du Portage (also called Little Niagara) embarked on a mission to the Iroquois Confederacy and the Delawares in April 1758, he oversaw the distribution of trade items valued at eighty thousand *livres*, along with thirty thousand *livres* worth of gifts. Charged to the king's account, these comestibles demonstrated Louis XV's magnanimity to his Indian "children." But Joncaire Chabert (as he called himself) also reaped personal benefit from being the individual in charge of disbursing such riches.[8] Already committed to regaining the king's disappeared revenue or, at least, assigning blame for its loss, prosecutors were further inflamed by the incredible indemnities being claimed by the defendants upon their return to France. Joncaire Chabert alone stated that the Crown owed him more than 1.6 million *livres* for the supplies and trade goods he had covered out of pocket (noting, however, that the records detailing his generosity had unfortunately perished in the fires set around Fort du Portage before the French retreat to Niagara in 1759). Royal prosecutors and finance agents at the Naval Ministry remained skeptical that this wealth came exclusively from Joncaire Chabert's stated interests in the ginseng trade.[9]

Some of the earliest records of how the marines presented their own service in North America to the French court and the public and how these accounts were received come from the individuals involved in the trial. Those caught in the prosecutorial web, as well as the audience following the proceedings, rapidly formed opposing factions to advance their interests. As public curiosity in the trial grew, a torrent of printed pamphlets, especially *mémoires* (depositions) in which each man told his version of events, surged around Paris. These narratives were less about truth than exoneration and functioned primarily as propaganda. Dramatic in tone, they show how the indicted turned on each other in print as they also did in their private letters. Copies of the depositions published by the Imprimerie royale are found in many archives, suggesting a high volume of printing and that an interested reading public followed the trial in the French capital. Together, the letters, depositions, and statements that emerged from the *affaire du Canada* paint a lurid picture of the price of empire in Canada to the delectation of the public, the judges, the court, and the defendants' fellow noble military officers.

François Bigot, New France's last intendant (senior civil administrator) and, next to Vaudreuil, the key figure in the trial, attempted to justify his extensive requests for and use of royal trade goods by asserting in his *mémoire* that his actions had been necessary because exchange was the only way to trade with Indians. They were "insatiable" consumers who would threaten the withdrawal of their support for France if they were not given winter or summer campaign kits, trade goods, and other items.[10] Bigot accurately expressed the reality of Native diplomacy and life in New France in his statement, but the royal judges did not see things that way. They interpreted his rationale for engagement with Indians as weakness on Bigot's part, his caving in to the demands of *les sauvages*. Blaming Indians who could not give either corroborating or contradictory testimony did little to help Bigot's defense. His sworn statements sounded like an excuse. Over and over, the former intendant pointed out that the Naval Ministry well knew the cost of Indian alliance. However, in implying metropolitan understanding (and control) of Indians by these means, Bigot sprang a trap the Crown no doubt wished to avoid, the vital issue of France's complicity in Indian behavior at high cost to its martial honor, most notably demonstrated when the French had presided over the Fort William Henry "massacre."

The subsequent humiliations to French arms that occurred when British commanders had used the "dishonorable" conduct of France's armies to deny the honors of war at the surrenders of both Louisbourg (in 1758) and Montreal (in 1760) stuck in the king's throat. The prosecutors saw that the charges of graft could be made to stick to the Canadian elites, both civilian and military. Bigot's defense of his actions while intendant showed them clearly that the Indian trade was principally an excuse for graft and a temptation to engage in dishonorable conduct. Bigot and his accomplices had corrupted the king's service in Canada. Louis-Joseph de Montcalm, the former army general, had died in 1759, and it was Pierre-François de Vaudreuil who had signed the Montreal capitulation—despite the strenuous objections of Montcalm's army replacement, François Gaston de Lévis. Vaudreuil was not just Louis XV's chief representative in New France but also the highest-ranking marine in the colony. Yet no one was better at claiming ignorance of abuse of the royal purse despite a position of command than Pierre-François de Vaudreuil. His *mémoire* was a rebuttal to Bigot's accusations that the governor general was well aware of private trade at the western posts and had encouraged it by appointing commanders who had the best *crédit* with the Native Americans. In a veiled warning to the French nobility not to hang one of their own out to dry, Vaudreuil stated that his integrity was "as hereditary as his family's honor." Then he revealed aristocratic social capital in France equal to that which he had had in Canada.[11] Louise-Élisabeth, the governor's mother, had been governess to the children of the Duc de Berry, third son of the Grand Dauphin, in 1712. Vaudreuil's kinsman, the young Vicomte de Vaudreuil, resided at Versailles and was a noted etiquette expert.

Vaudreuil's self-defense also played off the prosecutors' and nobles' awareness of the monarchy's bruised reputation. Public faith in "Louis, le Bien Aimé" had declined following his failure to capitalize on France's success in the War of Austrian Succession and continued to drop. The king's deep and visible depression after the Damiens assassination attempt in 1757 had caused the monarch to withdraw further from the public eye, undermining the bond between subjects and king.[12] Moreover, the recent war losses compounded matters by reinforcing a public perception of the monarch and his nobility as weak and decadent. By alluding to his social position and the precariousness of all French nobles, Vaudreuil suggested that this was not the moment to throw in the towel with regard to the military or the nobles who made up the senior officer corps when a more convenient target would do. Bigot's maligning of Canadian officers insulted the honor of all military services, and the marquis did not need to point out that his former intendant was not noble. Playing off this idea, Vaudreuil portrayed himself as the victim; with the North American war absorbing all his efforts, on financial matters he naturally trusted Bigot's own loyalty, zeal, and expertise to guide him.[13] Humanitarian concerns for his fellow officers alone certainly did not drive Vaudreuil to their defense. He, too, belonged to the *compagnies franches*, and he had selected the fort commanders, now on trial, who might turn on him in desperation. Consideration of these facts made Vaudreuil align his interests with those of his fellow officers rather than Bigot's.

Vaudreuil's charity and good image among his cohorts went only so far, however. Frustrated and trapped in his cold Bastille "accommodations," Daniel-Marie Chabert de Joncaire wrote to his sister, explaining that he had been incarcerated and did not know why. But he did have his suspicions, for the letter went on to blame the loss of the war and thus the collapse of Joncaire Chabert's career and private fortune on the Marquis de Vaudreuil. A few days later, a relative, Joncaire d'Autrève, suggested the eighteenth-century version of a public relations campaign in order to clear his cousin's name, one that highlighted Joncaire Chabert's reluctance to follow Vaudreuil's orders.[14] Joncaire Chabert's *mémoire* followed his relative's advice. The essential duties he had performed during the war, the information he had collected in the borderlands, and his continuation of a family specialization in Indian diplomacy, which he had carried out with his brother, Philippe, and son-in-law, La Milletière, disappeared from mention. The *mémoire* was silent regarding Joncaire's Iroquoian language skill and effaced the considerable access to information and trade he was privy to because of his blood ties to the Senecas.[15] Instead, he characterized working with Indians as an irritating task—one he undertook only to prevent Iroquois alliances with the British. In a moment of extreme obfuscation, Joncaire Chabert chose to draw parallels between his time spent with Indians and being a "hostage."[16]

Civilian Bigot hid behind administrative understandings, and high-ranked Vaudreuil behind plausible ignorance, but Joncaire Chabert, the borderlands military and Indian agent, could not do the same. Thus, after distancing himself from his record, Joncaire Chabert concluded his defense with the time-tested tradition of blaming orders from his superiors—a rhetorical tactic not available to Bigot or Vaudreuil but attractive to the other defendants. With no Indians to contradict his testimony, Joncaire Chabert hoped this presentation of his career would fall in line with French expectations for dealings with *les sauvages*. It was important to emphasize his service to the king's goals (frustrating British-Indian alliances) without suggesting that he himself had fallen away from French civility—or possibly preferred another culture to that of France—at least while he remained suspect in the eyes of the Crown.

Dragging on for two years, the trial exhausted and humiliated the proud and formerly elite veterans. Vaudreuil himself experienced the dankness of the Bastille for a couple of months, though with certain privileges befitting his noble rank, including the services of his enslaved manservant, Canon, for his "comfort" and the regular arrival of bottled lavender water from his wife.[17] Incarcerated for three full years, Joncaire Chabert received fewer indulgences from his royal jailers but could at least correspond with his family. When the court finally issued a ruling on December 10, 1763, Joncaire Chabert fared relatively well. The court found him guilty of negligence in regulating the stores at Fort du Portage and warned him not to repeat his actions.[18] The fort was gone, and Joncaire Chabert was in France, so this ruling could only be seen as an acquittal. Distancing himself from the reality of his service perhaps had helped Joncaire Chabert avoid a more severe punishment, a lesson that other marines quickly grasped. Most of Joncaire's accused fellow marines received similar decisions, ranging from the imposition of fines to verbal censure but with no punishments of greater severity, such as banishment. That distinction was reserved for François Bigot alone. Crown prosecutors demanded ruinous restitutions and forced Bigot into exile in Switzerland. But the marine officers who seemingly skated away from *l'affaire du Canada* never escaped the disgrace of the trial, and their implication in scandal still loomed large in the minds of royal administrators years later.

Those marine officers not in the Bastille or implicated in the *affaire* still contended with the effects of the *ordonnance* of 1762, which stated that veterans could put down roots anywhere in the province of Touraine. This decree was intended to indicate the munificence a monarch could display toward his subjects. Like all of the *habitants* of New France, the returned marine officers had suffered severe property damages when British troops under Gen. James Wolfe razed rural homes and seigneuries around Quebec to strike terror into the hearts of colonists in the summer of 1759. Though the *ordonnance* made no reference to the then four-month-old *affaire du Canada*, the trial called into question the worth and credibility of the already-destabilized Canadian paper currency, a strategy employed by the Crown as much to avoid indemnities as to root out corruption.[19] With their Canadian property in ruins or under British occupation and in light of this unexpected monetary destitution, land became the bare minimum these men required to sustain themselves and their families after their return to France—a country where few of these veterans had made any part of their careers or spent any part of their adult lives. Noting the specific needs of this community, particularly that these veterans would need to search for homes in a market of modest prices, the *ordonnance* enabled royal officials to provide them and their families opportunities for both resettlement and a means of securing a successful future. The *ordonnance* also addressed the monetary compensation to which veterans were entitled, outlining the sums at 55 percent (peacetime) pay for officers of each rank: captains (of all services) would receive 600 *livres*, lieutenants 400 *livres*, and ensigns 300 *livres* in four payments per year.[20]

The powerful Duc de Choiseul, who dominated court politics in this period, had strong connections to Touraine. Construction was ongoing in Amboise, close to the city of Tours (the capital of Touraine), for Choiseul's magnificent chateau, Chanteloup. This great home was to serve as the family seat since the duc was also the governor of the province. The influential Voyer d'Argenson family had headed the Ministry of War from the 1730s to the 1750s and had shown an interest in and sympathy for French North America. It is possible that they suggested this region to Choiseul as a relocation area.[21] Versailles and Paris lay within easy traveling distance, and a number of royal and elite noble residences added to the region's local prestige.

Touraine had other benefits as well. In the mid- to late eighteenth century, the cost of living in French urban centers exceeded that in the provinces. Removing cash-strapped veterans to a provincial capital potentially enabled them to enjoy a higher standard of living. Life might never approximate what these families had enjoyed in colonial New France as a result of their seigneurial properties and the close links among the elite of their colonial society, which allowed them to dominate Atlantic trade lines, but the veterans' chances of re-creating some level of domestic comfort would be better in Tours than in Paris. The Crown and Choiseul may even have conceived of Touraine's selection as marking the veterans with a particular favor. Known for its mild weather and calm, flat, landscape, Touraine may have been chosen to provide a soothing environment for the traumatized families coming back to France. Finally, given France's consistent ability to regain territory at treaty tables, it is not inconceivable that some members of the royal council expected there to be a possible return to Canada when the *ordonnance* was issued in 1762. If Canada reverted to French hands during peacetime, as Louisbourg had fourteen years earlier, in 1748, then the New France immigrants would be in a single area, easy to round up and return to their borderlands careers, posts, and homes. In addition, the Canadians themselves may have wanted to be together, much as the Acadian refugees had demonstrated their desire to remain a cohesive community.[22]

Marines settling in Touraine were placed "under the orders of the sieur de Longueuil," a Canadian who had been the last governor of New France's third largest city, Trois-Rivières. He was now created *major de place du Canada*.[23] Descended from an aristocratic family of hereditary barons whose nobility had been granted by Louis XIV in the late seventeenth century, Paul Joseph Le Moyne de Longueuil, *dit* chevalier de Longueuil, was a distinguished marine veteran with a long record of service in diplomacy and administration. Born in the colony, he had spent part of his career at the western post of Detroit in the 1740s before participating in military campaigns in the *pays d'en haut* and the Ohio River region and on the Lake George frontier. Longueuil's skill as a negotiator led him to be repeatedly chosen as an ambassador for diplomatic missions to the Iroquois Confederacy during the Seven Years' War before finally being selected by Vaudreuil as Trois-Rivières' governor in 1758.[24] Longueuil's background, military and civilian, was distinguished enough to ensure the respect of his fellow marines—an important component he needed to wield influence among his peers. His *noblesse*, seniority, bureaucratic experience, and connections made his choice as spokesperson a practical one, suggesting that Longueuil could navigate the French system in order to argue effectively on the veterans' behalf.[25] However, living "under one's orders" sounded a strange note for a peaceful community of veterans. It suggested that the veterans required an overseer to ensure their good behavior and their reintegration into French society. This extra layer of vigilance may have reflected fears that the veterans were unfamiliar with French civilian life and had returned from North America to France with potentially threatening habits. Importantly, Longueuil and the two other men who held this post before it was abolished in 1775 were all Canadians, and, of course, none of them were implicated in *l'affaire du Canada*.[26]

A surprising—and punitive—measure of the *ordonnance* was the directive that if the officers did not accede to these terms of royal resettlement, they would forfeit the king's financial support. Following in the wake of the king's suppression of the *compagnies franches*, this decision doubtless alarmed the veterans. It was bad enough that the decree provided no additional guarantees of income beyond the stipends, which were no more than the regular pensions to which officers on deferred duty were already entitled. Letters from these veterans complaining about the minute pay and the lack of opportunities for them to obtain new sources of revenue indicate that these men greatly feared increasing impoverishment. The strictness of the pension disbursal could have been a demonstration of compliance with the terms of the 1760 capitulation of Montreal, which required New France's defenders to sit out the remainder of the war. By stipulating that the veterans needed to remove to Touraine, the Crown ensured its subjects' adherence to this rule. In any case, the veterans were in no position to decline the offer of royal financial assistance, having been deprived of their livelihoods and their position in society with the loss of New France. Now these men faced the prospect of living on the royal dole in Touraine, with no holdings of their own and none awarded by the Crown and no position to reclaim. The king may have assumed that in time the Touraine refuge would prosper, and, in any case, Choiseul and other ministers may have exhausted what attention they could spare this small Canadian community during the ongoing European war and preliminary peace negotiations.

The resettlement to Touraine, like the *affaire du Canada*, exposes a good deal about how royal officials considered New France's marine veterans. Under the guise of royal generosity, officials segregated the veterans from New France into one province in the Loire River region, keeping them in a single, manageable area away from the rest of the nation. Touraine was not to be merely a temporary stop for Canadian officers, their families, and intimates.[27] It seems that the Crown was responding to its own concerns about the veterans with the *ordonnance*, for Touraine's geographic proximity to the seat of monarchy did more than favor the Canadian refugees with a pleasing setting and climate. With Paris and Versailles and thus the Paris police and the royal guard close by, the grouping of veterans in a controllable region ensured the authorities a higher degree of surveillance over the Canadian population. The service records of the marine officers and the *mémoires* of those on trial spoke clearly to their martial talents; these men specialized in guerrilla warfare under difficult conditions. Whatever their protestations of fidelity, no prudent monarch would permit such a highly skilled, martial population to scatter into the interior of the realm—particularly at a time when the nation roiled with debt and dissent. As one administrative document noted, "we wished to reassure ourselves of the conduct they would have during their time in France."[28] Additionally, French Americans were accustomed to heterogeneous and slave societies, further removing them from metropolitan daily life. By segregating the Canadians, the Crown held them as a group apart, perhaps subliminally suggesting that these North American–born French were products of a different experience and, if not inferior, then perhaps not entirely to be trusted.[29]

"I Find Myself Reduced to Begging"

The marine veterans may have been tired of life on the frontier—they had experienced two official wars in seventeen years. They could have sought a peaceful retirement, quietly returning to the heartland of the nation they had served but little knew. However, the letters of numerous individuals indicate other ambitions. Some wanted recognition for their service in North America; others sought new opportunities. In time, a majority discovered their ambitions would be frustrated, forcing many of them to stare into the widening maw of poverty.

Appeals for favor and financial restitution verging on the pathetic bound the veterans in common as royal petitioners. The letters began as early as 1761 and in some cases continued into the 1770s, taken up by a generation of children who had transferred with their parents to France and were now coming of age. From Paris, from the Bastille, or from Touraine, the former marine officers made their individual cases for restoration, showcasing their service records in North America. During their years of active duty, these marine officers had routinely petitioned their superiors and the Crown for military promotions and honors that carried salary and pension increases. Now these men presented their actions in a manner that contrasted with their earlier letters from the 1740s and 1750s. Prior to 1760, marine correspondence consisted of accounts of successful raids, battles won, and French martial honor upheld. As it became clear that the war was lost, the former officers had nothing to hang on to. As the upper echelon of New France society, they could not have been insensitive to status. Talking about their successful service with Indians would get them nowhere—a conclusion reached early by imprisoned men like Joncaire Chabert and eventually by free veterans as well. Rather, their letters focused on *zèle, patrie*, and loyalty to the Crown. The volume of this correspondence from the 1760s and 1770s suggests that many of these officers felt underappreciated—and undercompensated—for military service performed before and during the Seven Years' War.[30] The response they received showed the Crown felt differently about them as well. The French Crown clearly had a stake in rejecting their indemnities and denying them further service; few marine officers resumed duty in the military even after the Treaty of Paris in 1763 ended the Seven Years' War and released them from the restricted service imposed by Sir Jeffery Amherst through Article I of the 1760 treaty securing Montreal's capitulation.[31]

Descended from a family of military engineers, Gaspard-Joseph Chaussegros de Léry had grown up with education and wealth. In New France, he had been a seigneur, an elite colonial landholder, as well as a marine officer, like many of his fellow *compagnies franches* veterans. Léry aspired to the lifestyle of a royal officer while on campaign, his sword strapped to his hip, his attendants accompanying him in the field as he performed his duty for the glory of the king in a manner befitting Léry's own status.[32] This zeal and panache earned him acclaim after a successful attack on Fort Bull in 1756. Léry also served with distinction at the battle of the Plains of Abraham in 1759 and was awarded a *croix de Saint Louis* for his service. When Léry arrived in France in 1761, he was not among those implicated in *l'affaire du Canada*, and he retained seigneurial property that was recognized by both France and Britain. Landholding provided him security unavailable to others, but Léry still focused intensely on "restoring" his financial situation. In 1762 Léry wrote to the Duc de Choiseul detailing his honorable service record. After explaining that he had left Canada because he could not bear to live under anything but French rule, the letter turned to its key point—as a marine captain, Léry received 600 *livres* of half pay annually, a sum that, he wrote, "cannot suffice to support my family." He inquired after the financial aid being granted to Acadian refugees (about 6 *sols* per day), who benefited from Choiseul's particular concern and featured prominently in Choiseul's planned new colonial settlement in Cayenne. Then Léry asked the minister for a new position. In exchange for such consideration, the former soldier offered his devotion, zeal, and loyalty in the king's service, making no mention of the money a post would of course supply.[33] Though he wrote nothing explicit about where he hoped to serve, a note in Léry's file dating from 1749 showed that at that time he had already requested a posting away from Canada, to Cayenne or Saint Domingue rather than to Detroit. Attuned to the ministry's interest in the tropics and remembering his old request, Léry subtly indicated his willingness to serve somewhere in the Caribbean. Although unspecific in suggesting a location of service, Léry outright solicited continued military opportunities by requesting a promotion to colonel in 1763.[34]

The attention to stipends and reassignment stemmed from financial uncertainty. In order to provide for his family, Léry borrowed 11,000 *livres*—greatly exceeding his pension of 600 *livres*. Like Joncaire Chabert and other officers, Léry also hoped for acknowledgment of and compensation for the severe financial losses he had incurred in the late war. Currency devaluation cost Léry more than 150,000 *livres* worth of bills of exchange.[35] Furthermore, to secure his family's comfort and future, he would have to incur new expenses. Léry arranged to have his elder sons receive a military education in France, an endeavor that could not have been inexpensive. With an unblemished military past and no connection to the disgraceful trial, Léry seemed more likely than scandal-scarred individuals like Joncaire Chabert to be exonerated. Léry was not alone; many fellow veterans made similar appeals, each with a unique spin.

"I find myself reduced to begging," Capt. Joseph Marin de La Malgue wrote of his changed circumstances as he, too, sought a restoration of his financial and social capital.[36] Older and more experienced than Léry and similarly untainted by the trial, Marin had commanded great respect for his skills in North American warfare and his ability to work with Indians in New France. Among his forebears were distinguished military veterans, and he proudly recalled his father's and grandfather's membership in the prestigious chevaliers de Saint Louis.[37] Like many returned veterans, Marin discovered drastic limitations to his connections to patronage and advancement in France. What is more, this soldier could not afford to ignore the *ordonnance* of 1762; because he had suffered major property losses in Canada, the pension the king offered was critical to his family's well-being. From Touraine, Marin produced résumés of his career in New France, showcasing the many successes he had achieved in the king's name. Even if prone to hyperbole, as those seeking advancement sometimes are, Marin claimed some remarkable feats, like defeating the famed English "partisan" Robert Rogers twice, in 1756 and again in 1758. As an envoy to the Indians and as a fighter, Marin was among the best of those who served in New France, a fact he employed to help explain his property losses during the attack on Quebec. Marin wrote that the British visited retributive destruction on him because "[I was] . . . very useful to the [colonial] government . . . attracting Indians, and these skills aroused the hatred of the English and in turn brought about the loss of all [my] titles and goods."[38] He added that his capture at Niagara in 1759 was an event "published in English newspapers," using his notoriety among the enemy to defend Louis XV's North American interests as proof of his great loyalty to France.[39] This impressive colonial record clearly reflected the devoted service of a soldier of France; Marin, like Léry, expected consideration because he had lived up to French military standards. Securing an affidavit for his file from François-Gaston de Lévis, the ranking French army general at the fall of New France, aided him somewhat in achieving this goal. Lévis concurred that Marin had "served with distinction," specifying that Marin's work involved "leading the light troops and Indians numerous times."[40]

Marin sought something far more important than restitution for costly material losses. Somewhere amid the ashes of his Quebec home was the proof of his gracious lineage; a 1745 wedding certificate naming his father as an *écuyer* (gentleman) proved the Marin family's petty nobility.[41] In his quest to have this patent recognized and to obtain damages, Marin sought aid from New France's last governor, the Marquis de Vaudreuil, as well as from Lévis. Vaudreuil and Lévis both verified that Marin's home had suffered heavy damages during the English invasion; the governor also certified that Marin's father and grandfather had been chevaliers de Saint Louis and had provided distinguished service to New France.[42] Marin's claims, even more than Léry's, demonstrate the marine officers' social ambitions and their shock at the inversion of their status when they fled the colony for the metropole.

Even the marine officer with the strongest aristocratic connections spent much of his life after 1760 begging for restitution to replace lost income in Canada. François Pierre de Rigaud de Vaudreuil, younger brother of Canada's last governor, left New France holding the rank of "governor of Montreal." His family enjoyed extensive French Atlantic connections and wealth, and Rigaud's long, distinguished military service earned him a pension of two thousand *livres* "in consideration for his former services" upon his return to France.[43] This sum far exceeded the annuities of other marines, perhaps owing to Rigaud's membership in the military order of Saint Louis (appointments whose pensions varied from eight hundred to two thousand *livres*). Privileged birth appears also to have exempted Rigaud from having to move to Touraine in 1762. Or perhaps he was willing to forgo the smaller sum provided by the *ordonnance* in favor of the larger pension he already had.[44] Despite these advantages, Rigaud persistently applied to Jean-Baptiste Dubuq, *premier commis* at the Naval Ministry, for an increased living allowance. When the French Crown dissolved Canadian paper currency and closed all outstanding colonial debts between 1762 and 1768, Rigaud lamented (in a *mémoire*) the pain of "the enormous loss which has devastated [my] finances," for Canadian currency and notes had been "the only goods [I] and [my] wife brought from that land, where [I] had a fortune and [an] honorable life."[45] Rigaud expected his reader to understand that by "honorable life" he meant social obligations that required certain expenditures and largesse.

The financial restitutions from *l'affaire du Canada* helped the French Crown trim its losses in the midst of an expensive war that doubled royal debts.[46] Those marines implicated in the trial had the added task of defending themselves against corruption charges, explaining that they had not despoiled the king's treasury in the fulfillment of their duties. Rigaud never suffered the indignity of indictment but must have been painfully aware of his brother's incarceration and ordeal. Like the *mémoire* of the trial and the private letters of officers like Léry and Marin, Rigaud's supplications show how military veterans employed similar strategies of recasting and reinterpreting their past service. While asking for greater indemnities in 1768, Rigaud highlighted his zeal for his service, his popularity among Indians, and the essential empire-building nature of his service.[47] By 1774, his letters were accentuating the harshness of Canada's climate, in which Rigaud had performed fifty years of military duty, and a pointed statement that, had it not been for Rigaud's love of France (*ma Patrie*), he could have assumed a post under the new British regime after the cession of the colony, a position that would have brought him an income of sixty thousand *livres*.[48] His approach hinged on emphasizing loyalty and love of country, even to the point of impoverishing himself, while remaining vague about what exactly his frontier exploits had entailed. The one thing Rigaud did not state was how his membership in the *ordre royal et militaire de Saint Louis* might have steadied his unbridled "patriotism." In fact, the order forbade members from becoming British subjects without the approval of the king of France; to disobey this rule usually suggested treason and a shaming of one's family.[49]

In the *mémoires* and in their letters, the veterans all distanced themselves from North American practices of war by saying little about successful campaigns. Rigaud wrote that he would "not speak of the capture of Oswego, of the devastation of English colonies, nor of the numerous successes he attained over France's enemies."[50] This contrasts with pre-1760 applications for advancement. For instance, in 1748 Luc de La Corne (also called La Corne St. Luc) described charging the enemy with "tomahawk in hand," side by side with his "Indian warriors."[51] A soldier's promotions, desired affirmations and awards (like the *croix de Saint Louis*), and merit-related pay increases depended on the critical advantages he claimed to have provided. In light of this long-standing tradition, that Rigaud would remain mute even regarding Oswego, a major victory accomplished by French siege warfare, spoke volumes about the need to leave buried the ministry's bitter memory of the last North American war. He downplayed details and emphasized his loyalty. His omissions anticipated and were meant to assuage lingering discomfort with events that had transpired in New France. His letters wrought a version of his career that preserved his noble martial masculinity, his reputation as a gentleman warrior in the service of his king and who never countenanced savagery, as well as his stature as a man with social obligations but never one driven by venal interests like a *roturier* (a commoner).

Joncaire Chabert made his statements to Crown officials concerning how his thirty years of service in North America should be viewed quite clear. Painting a bleak picture of Canada's environment and of military service in its interior, he queried, "If one wants to understand the work of a Canadian officer like me with the Indians? Interrogate America! . . . [I ask you to] see a lone officer, without escort, defenseless against enemies who have no faith, no pity, no restraint but for the name of his king, the luck of his nation, its arms and valor."[52] By framing his earliest Indian connections in negative terms as a "hostage" experience, Joncaire Chabert hoped his readers would not confuse his many years of service among Native peoples as a rejection of French goals or ideals. Joncaire Chabert, as a well-known and highly visible Indian agent, had to deal more directly with the legacy of his North American service than did Rigaud, Marin, or Léry. Still, Joncaire's published *mémoire* bludgeoned its audience with references to patriotism, French values, and risks taken in the name of the king and of France in almost the same style employed in the private supplications of his fellow veterans.

With the Ministry of War and the Naval Ministry now unified under the control of the Duc de Choiseul and with long-serving *premiers commis* like Dubuq still in place, cadets, ensigns, lieutenants, and captains could hope that their extensive prior service records would remain not only catalogued on file but now might also help qualify them for new opportunities with both the army and the navy. The existence of detailed personnel records partly explains why the veterans like Marin or Rigaud felt it unnecessary to rehash their experiences. However, the extent of the obfuscation of what their service actually entailed, the focus on very specific events that highlighted French martial practices and goals (Fort Bull, Oswego, the battle for Quebec) and the unmistakable language of zealous and loyal service points to another conclusion. The former marines consciously rewrote the older records rather than rely on the bureaucrats to make their decisions based on information already in the ministry's hands.

The Apotheosis of Montcalm

The homecoming experience of the senior French officers in the *armée de terre* who served in New France differed dramatically from that of the elite marine officers and colonial veterans. At the same time that *l'affaire du Canada* was unfolding in courts at Châtelet, colonels François-Charles de Bourlamaque and Louis-Antoine de Bougainville wrote to London along with François-Gaston de Lévis asking for exceptional paroles to release them from the Montreal capitulation. Rank alone did not determine these applications; the Ministry of War recorded a similar petition as well from an infantry captain named Dumas. All of these officers asked that the ministry apply for parole on their behalf from *Sa Majesté britannique*, George III, the sole person who could lift the service restrictions imposed by Amherst's terms at Montreal in 1760. Bourlamaque, Bougainville, and Lévis received their freedom—Dumas likely did as well.[53] In early 1762 Lévis resumed active military duty on the German front, and Bourlamaque followed with an assignment to Ostende a few months later.[54]

Canadian officers appear to have made no requests for parole exemption. During the time that Bourlamaque, Lévis, and Bougainville received their new transfers, the *ordonnance* directed the marines instead to Touraine. Even if the latter had been granted parole, they faced a series of obstacles to renewed active duty. Bound as they were to colonial service, they could not avail themselves of avenues for reassignment available to the army men. By 1761 France had suffered serious reversals in North America, India, the Caribbean, and West Africa, leaving few places to send unemployed colonial troops and officers who might be available in France. Above all else, tainted by Montcalm and his staff's accusations that Canadians lacked discipline, stripped of traditional Indian allies, and having specialized mostly in North American *petite guerre*, the marines did not seem suitable for redeployment in Europe.

The different treatment accorded the army becomes clearest when considering one officer who did not appear on the indictment docket of *l'affaire du Canada*: Pierre Pouchot, final commander of Fort Niagara. An able engineer, Pouchot was the sole officer of the *armée de terre* to serve as a western fort commander between 1755 and 1760. During the period of the trial, rumors circulated that Captain Pouchot, too, was involved in graft, but no formal charges ever materialized. Pouchot successfully fended off a *lettre de cachet* (a royal conviction without trial) by directly appealing to the Ministry of War on the basis of his integrity and good service record.[55] Thus, alone among the frontier post commanders, Pouchot never found his name on the public posters produced by the Crown's prosecutors, a result of Pouchot's access to Versailles and his ability to plead his innocence before the minister. Eager to avoid the Bastille and irreparable damage to his martial reputation, Pouchot clearly took great pains to discredit rumors of corruption. His insulation from the trial—simultaneous with the reinstatement of his superior officers to duty—could not have been accidental. The army had to guard its reputation at all costs. Whatever may have occurred while Pouchot commanded at Niagara, the engineer represented the army and not the marines. He continued to serve.

The urge to protect the servants of the Ministry of War affected the dead as well as the living. Whatever blame could have been laid on the Marquis de Montcalm for the loss of the colony he avoided by expiring in September 1759, a few hours after he was shot in battle on the Plains of Abraham. Dead, Montcalm would bear neither responsibility for the dishonorable capitulation of 1760 nor the cost of the war and the colony. Instead, the general's name almost immediately experienced an apotheosis, one that emphasized his reputation as a devoted leader, loyal subject, and true noble. Canada was conquered, but homage to Montcalm's service exemplified and preserved the honor of the French army. His image was reproduced in an eighteenth-century version of "Dulce et Decorum est / Pro patria mori." He joined a pantheon of French heroes and became, at least until the American Revolution, the sole positive touchstone the French public retained from New France. Along with the marquises de Saint Véran and Montcalm (the general's wife and mother), the senior army officers who stood untainted by the Canada trial endeavored to pay public tribute to their late general's honorable defense of New France.[56] Even a Canadian, albeit one who had been fiercely critical of Vaudreuil, Bigot, and their protégés, André Doreil wrote an elegy to Montcalm that was published in the *Mercure de France*.[57] The Montcalm women wielded to their advantage the social power of the grieving mother and widow of a loyal subject. They worked actively to preserve the name and fame of their fallen "hero." They sued Intendant François Bigot on behalf of their heirs for slandering Montcalm's name during the trial. In their rebuttal to Bigot's charges, the women especially emphasized Montcalm's zeal in serving the king, his disinterestedness, and his noble modesty. Bigot claimed the issues he

CHAPTER 5

had raised at the trial had been necessary in order to controvert fraud charges against him that Montcalm's letters had helped to instigate, but to no avail. The marquises de Montcalm and St. Véran triumphed, obtaining ten thousand *livres* in damages as well as four thousand *livres* in pensions for the general's widow and each of his children.[58] As in the case of fort commander Pouchot, the army's reputation regarding Montcalm's service remained unbesmirched and intact.

Of the many French officers who served in North America and the considerable number who kept diaries, only Pierre Pouchot's journal made it to publication. Unlike the *mémoires* issued by accused officers and administrators during *l'affaire du Canada*, which spoke directly to the circumstances of the trial and defended their authors' actions both before and during the conflict, Pouchot's work, *Mémoires sur la dernière guerre de l'Amérique septentrionale* (Memoirs on the Late War in North America) was a chronicle of his combat in New France in three volumes. By the time the diary came into print, the officer had been dead thirteen years. During the 1770s, tales of sacrifice, whether that of Montcalm at the siege of Quebec or the old, romanticized narrative of Ensign Jumonville, slain by George Washington and Tanaghrisson in 1754, interested the French public more than remembering the disastrous end of New France.[59] The narrative constructed by the court and the trial after the fall of New France was deeply critical of colonial corruption, a sensitive issue in a climate of financial unrest, and the case was closed at the conclusion of *l'affaire du Canada*. Therefore, the commercial prospects for a work such as Pouchot's were limited until imperial war was renewed in North America in 1776. Only then did the Pouchot diary suddenly reemerge as the most up-to-date reference on North America available to readers. The editors of the 1781 edition explicitly cast the posthumous journal as a reference work to give French metropolitan audiences insights into the new American war, where France now fought as an ally of the rebelling British colonies.[60] The narrative of Pouchot's "late war" and the successes and failures of army and naval strategy in New France chronicled therein mattered less to general readers than Pouchot's descriptions of North America, Anglo-Americans, and Indians. The *Mémoires sur la dernière guerre* thus resembled Father Charlevoix's travel narratives, which had been read by French officers in the 1750s to prepare at that time for their deployment to the distant colony.

Despite this framing of the journal, the editors restored certain elements of the war in New France for readers, burnishing Montcalm and the army's legacy in the process. By lauding Montcalm's achievements in almost two full pages of text of the published *Mémoires sur la dernière guerre*, Pouchot's

FIGURE 6. *Mort du Marquis de Montcalm Gozon* (The Death of the Marquis de Montcalm), engraving by G. Chevillet after the François-Louis-Joseph Watteau original, c. 1783. Courtesy of the William L. Clements Library, University of Michigan.

editors went well beyond the Niagara engineer's own respectful half page chronicling the general's demise.[61] The addendum referenced a recent print by the "young Watteau" (François-Louis-Joseph Watteau), who produced *The Death of Montcalm* (figure 6) in 1783 as a pendant to Benjamin West's highly acclaimed 1771 painting titled *The Death of General Wolfe* (figure 7).

Both images capture romantic visions of glorious martial death; Watteau's depiction highlights the bravery and honor of France and depicts Indians who bore little similarity either to West's pensive Native or to any actual indigenous nations of Canada. New France, in Watteau's hands, resembles reality even less, featuring a splendid palm tree on fields allegedly outside the citadel of Quebec.

Montcalm's popularity continued well after the American Revolution and into the 1790s, when portraits of him appeared in French and English works, including one in John Marshall's *Life of George Washington* (figure 8).

The only other actor from Canada who survived a little in public memory, Ensign Joseph Coulon de Villiers de Jumonville, could not compete

FIGURE 7. *The Death of General Wolfe.* Engraving by W. Woolett after Benjamin West's *The Death of General Wolfe*, 1776. Woolett's engraving of West's famous painting circulated widely in Europe and in America and likely served as the inspiration for Watteau's rendering of Montcalm's death. Courtesy of the William L. Clements Library, University of Michigan.

with Montcalm for the same longevity in the commemorative halls of French heroes. He died before the official outbreak of war in 1756. Jumonville's sacrifice, did, however, remind those who cared to remember of a marine who had behaved appropriately.

After 1763 and for the next few decades, many of the army officers enjoyed an unabated ascent of their careers. Pierre-André Gohin, chevalier de Montreuil (shown cradling Montcalm in figure 6) retired as a lieutenant general, as did Anne-Joseph-Hyppolyte de Maurès, Comte de Malartic, who had started his career as a young aide in the Béarn regiment in New France. Bourlamaque, Bougainville, and the engineer Jean-Nicolas Désandrouins all achieved the rank of maréchal de camp; no one did better than François-Gaston de Lévis.[62] Promoted to lieutenant general in 1761, Lévis became a maréchal de France in 1783 and was named a hereditary duke the next year.[63] Clearly, these men had extensive patronage connections in France that their Canadian counterparts did not, save perhaps for the Vau-

FIGURE 8. *Louis-Joseph, Marquis de Montcalm*, engraved portrait by Antoine François Sergent, 1790. Courtesy of the John Carter Brown Library at Brown University.

dreuil family. But another distinguishing element helps clarify the reintegration of these army officers and their upward career trajectories. Montcalm's dramatic and honorable death gave his life in the service of his king a patina that made him deserving of fame and respect. Lévis and his officers, like Vaudreuil and the returning marines, still lived. Unlike Vaudreuil, though, Lévis had clearly stated for the record that he had been willing to lay down his life for his monarch's honor when he objected to Vaudreuil's acceptance of Amherst's peace conditions:

> [W]e have considered it our duty to him [Louis XV], in our name and in that of the principal officers and others of the Regular troops we command, that such Article of the capitulation could not conflict more with the King's service and the honor of his arms, and must be accepted only at the last extremity, since it deprives the State . . . of whatever services [these soldiers] who have acted with courage and distinction, might render it. In consequence, we demand to M. de Vaudreuil to break off at once all negotiation with the English general and to determine on the most vigorous defence [sic] our actual position is capable of.[64]

Protected by the fact that they had been willing to give their lives and risk Montreal's destruction to preserve royal honor although they faced hopeless odds, Lévis and his contemporaries, unlike the marine commanders, had the necessary *crédit* within the army and at court to continue to help their own careers and to dole out military patronage in the form of suggestions for promotions and attestations of good service for others. Lévis, not Vaudreuil, emerged from Montreal with his reputation enhanced. He was a character witness for Canadians whose words mattered to the Crown—while senior marines found themselves devalued and despised by comparison. The army and its last commander, Montcalm's successor, Lévis, not Vaudreuil, final governor of New France, had fought for the king's honor to the end.

⚜ *Je Me Souviens*

At the Treaty of Paris, on September 3, 1763, the French Crown formally ceded Canada to Britain in exchange for Guadeloupe and Martinique. The French Canadian marines, the French army, the domiciled Indians, and the militias had won a majority of the battles but lost their war—and now much more. Going forward, New France's fate was to be France's permanent abandonment of the colony. This terrible reality triggered a new set of actions by the veterans—a sort of *sauve qui peut* that gives us insight into how these men understood the legacy of their service now that their imperial reality had changed and into how they hoped to use their experiences to open up opportunities in a new imperial context.

Joseph Marin de La Malgue eventually managed to continue in the military, something few marines accomplished, no doubt aided in this by an old statement of support from the maréchal de Lévis. But the commission and post that Marin secured was not for service in Europe. Marin left Tours in early 1773 as a lieutenant colonel in Baron Maurice de Benyovski's Madagascar expedition.[65] Given the list of Marin's skills in his file at the Naval Ministry, it appeared he could be very useful in a location understood to be barbarous or savage. The talented and connected Benyovsky was an eastern European noble recently arrived in France, and although his expedition benefited the French Crown, it was neither a crown-directed colonial venture nor an endeavor of the French army. Thus, whatever actions the Polish aristocrat undertook in order to accomplish strategic goals on this island could not reflect directly on Louis XV. In the end, it mattered little, for Marin succumbed to tropical fever almost immediately upon arrival. Even though he had been able to die a soldier, he had not recouped his pre-1760 social status. In 1765 the Crown flatly refused to confirm Marin's nobility, and the old veteran's death left his heirs embroiled in a bitter battle over his few resources.[66]

The majority of Canadian marines who found a way to continue their service in the remaining French Atlantic world were, in the end, those who chose to remain in Canada or, more tellingly, returned from France to North America. Sieur François Coulon de Villiers (a brother of Jumonville, the murdered patriot) never returned to France but chose instead to seamlessly transition into Spanish service in Louisiana. There, Villiers became a success and, like his Canadian friend, La Corne St. Luc, a slaveholder.[67] Giving up their seigneuries and leaving behind generations of memories caused numerous marines like the sieurs Claude-Pierre Pécaudy de Contrecoeur and La Corne St. Luc to decide that taking a chance on a British regime was less risky than the journey to France. For men whose lives were centered in and made by the borderlands, like the *métis* marine Charles de Langlade, a new empire did not necessarily diminish their personal influence in the region because relationships with independent Native peoples remained the same. In fact, as Langlade discovered, British need for his interpretive services could augment his opportunities to advance his own community's interests.[68]

Forging a new type of relationship for themselves between France and Canada became a survival strategy that certain marines eventually adopted. The French Atlantic world in which they had formerly lived and prospered had dramatically shifted, enabling some of them to create new webs of oceanic networks through private family ties on both sides of the Atlantic or by appealing to Canada's British overlords after peace returned. Daniel-Marie Chabert de Joncaire's bitterness over his incarceration may have influenced his decision to leave France. De facto acquittal neither aided Joncaire Chabert's precarious standing with the French Crown nor ensured the possibility of future Crown assignments, and in 1764 he reappeared in Canada. The paper millionaire's connections, experience, knowledge, and skills made the North American borderlands continue to be his best chance to remake his fortune and regain the luster of his former position. Joncaire Chabert's attempts to secure a land grant near the Niagara River, a grant that he insisted had passed from the Iroquois to his father, spoke to his desire for security.[69] If any Seneca relatives remained in the vicinity of the old Fort du Portage, they, too, may have served as a powerful incentive in Joncaire Chabert's desire to return to North America. Nonetheless, just as wealth had made him suspect in the French context, the fact of the Joncaire family's Indian blood and his influence on Native peoples did him no favors with the British.[70] It did not matter whether Joncaire Chabert was *métis*—the mere suggestion placed him outside the ranks of the urban British colonial elite. After appealing to his old rival, Sir William Johnson, one of the few men who could truly appreciate Joncaire's life and skills, the Frenchman regained his access to the borderlands under Johnson's promise of Joncaire's "good conduct."[71] When the former marine ended his career at Detroit in 1771, he left behind what Native trading connections he had recovered and also five printed *mémoires* from *l'affaire du Canada*, including his own, carefully bound in leather—which, alongside his own continuation of French connections to Native America, provide a precious chronicle of his personal loss and remembrance.

Chaussegros de Léry's reinvention of self also spoke to more than a French audience. His redacted service file emphasized his civility in France and minimized any previous actions as a marine officer that might appear distasteful to the new British regime in Canada. Within two years of arriving in France, Chaussegros de Léry explored so many possibilities open to him in British Canada that French authorities began recording his English interactions and contacts in his file at the Naval Ministry. Léry was also on his way back to Canada in 1764, and while passing through England he had the distinction (or disgrace, depending on one's national viewpoint) of being the first Canadian seigneur presented to King George III.[72] While Marin renewed his career in the Indian Ocean, Villiers continued much as before in Louisiana, Joncaire resumed the commercial habits of his old life among the Indians. Instead, Chaussegros de Léry transitioned into a new iteration of empire and made a great political success of his migration to the now British Canada, earning a spot on the legislative council by 1775.[73]

← Dénouement

Of 109 French *compagnies franches de la marine* officers who returned from Canada in 1760, 71 were "sequestered" in a land-locked province rather than probed for advice and recruited for new colonial (or military) ventures.[74] Of those hoping to capitalize on their experiences, only a handful were granted reassignment to distant locales with inhospitable climates and where Crown interest clearly ran toward extractive conquest. The marine with the greatest success in continuing his career, Louis Legardeur de Répentigny, achieved command positions once more, but in Guadeloupe, Martinique, and finally Senegal.[75] The marine veterans threatened the continuing mission of French empire, now being rearticulated after 1763, on two fronts. Even for those acquitted at the trial, the unmistakable implication remained that negotiating with indigenous peoples as equals essentially opened the door to personal wealth through graft. This was, after all, the charge Montcalm and his senior staff had made against Canada's administrators and marines—the charge that inspired and guided *l'affaire du Canada*.[76] To a certain extent, French bureaucrats must have been grateful that marine officers like the French Ottawa Charles de Mouet de Langlade did not return to France, thereby freeing the French Crown from any responsibility to recognize such individuals as its own or to determine how these marines' tactics reflected on national martial culture.

The officers in Touraine and elsewhere all highlighted their extensive service records in an attempt to claim indemnities and higher pensions during their years in France. Those actions in the name of the king consisted of lives spent in near-constant guerrilla warfare, directly engaging in or overseeing violence with or against North American Indians and British colonists. To serve in the borderlands for a lifetime was to experience extreme duress and constant paranoia about the possibility of attack, to fear the slightest rumor on the frontier. As time went by, court bureaucrats remained nervous that veterans might recall things the Crown preferred to forget: that it was France that had given up their homesteads and seigneuries at the treaty table and that racial intermarriage, cultural flexibility, and financial self-interest in the name of colonial growth had flourished among marine officers of the French empire.

These retired *compagnies franches* officers, still demanding all sorts of monies, compensations, honors, and recognitions, after all had cost the Crown too much and had lost the war. Imagining the French bureaucrats' perspective on this community makes the decision to segregate these individuals into a single region, far away from the monarch and the majority of French society, more comprehensible, though not humanitarian. Embittered veterans, possibly driven to desperation, disrupted the peace of the settled elite. The Canadian marine officers were experienced, yes, but had adopted unacceptable patterns of behavior that needed to be stamped out, not spread by entrusting them with the execution of ambitious new colonial and commercial projects. Some marines, like Rigaud de Vaudreuil or the sieurs Michel-Hugues Péan and Charles Deschamps de Boishébert, did find a sort of equilibrium by living out their days in quiet comfort in France. But the majority of the returnees appeared to justify the Crown's concerns by leaving France in frustration for British-held Quebec. A decade after 1762, 60 percent of the Canadians had left Touraine for good.[77]

CHAPTER 6

Paradise

After basking in warm, salty air scented with tiare and coconut and admiring the vibrant fuchsia-colored flowers that would eventually bear his name, Louis-Antoine de Bougainville authored a fantasy account of Tahiti that endures even today. His narrative of his travels to the Pacific, including this "New Cythera," appeared in 1771 as the *Voyage autour du monde fait par la frégate Boudeuse et la flûte Étoile, 1766–1769*. Distanced by thousands of miles from the French Atlantic world, Tahiti soothed Bougainville after the trauma of his experiences in the Seven Years' War and inspired in him an exciting vision for a global French empire. In his depiction of Native Tahitians, Bougainville suggested a new model of interaction that the French Crown and nobility hoped to encourage between themselves and indigenous peoples. Paradise, Bougainville hoped, would distance France from its abysmal record in the Seven Years' War and restore some of the nation's prestige.

More than a decade of travel produced three significant bodies of work by Bougainville: his Canadian diary (1756–1760), the Pacific log of the *Boudeuse* (1766–1768), and the *Voyage autour du monde* (1771). Louis-Antoine's forays into the world of ethnography and exploration began in New France, when he served as a young aide-de-camp to Louis-Joseph de Montcalm. The Canadian diary also set patterns that would continue in all of his future travel writings: every journal richly recorded Bougainville's impressions of these "new worlds," including flora, colonists or Native peoples, and detailed relations of French military or scientific campaigns. Bougainville's personal diary in North America was initially intended for publication but was not published. The edited and revised ship's log he produced during his 1766 world tour, however, appeared in print in 1771 as the *Voyage autour du monde*.[1] The unique continuities in these writings and the fact that the voyages followed one another in very short order invite comparisons of the Atlantic and Pacific material—something that has been little studied beyond biographical accounts of the explorer.[2] Bougainville's experiences in America affected his observations in his Pacific excursions. In particular, the Canadian and Pacific logs and the *Voyage* all describe the indigenous peoples residing in the Americas and in the Pacific, but the presentations of Natives differ dramatically. The "cruel-hearted savages" of New France had nothing in common with the nature-loving, sensual "Cytherans" of Tahiti, a literary fact that suggests that Bougainville's attitudes toward indigenous peoples and their customs had shifted remarkably in the intervening years.

Beyond his transnational voyages, Bougainville's expectations may also have been influenced by the new intellectual currents concerning colonial encounters that circulated in 1760s' France. Physiocrats, *philosophes*, and political theorists all offered views on how to renew France's imperial pursuits. Bougainville was exposed to these ideas after his return from Canada in 1760, during his sojourns in the metropole between his Atlantic and Pacific ventures in 1762 and again in 1766. As the French Crown searched for a reinvigorated model of colonization and empire in the wake of defeat, Bougainville's excellent social connections, desire for position, and solid reputation in military circles coming out of the Seven Years' War in North America made him an excellent candidate to help achieve his nation's goals.

Bougainville's writings also provide a window into the experience of the army officers and illuminate how he, and men like him, understood the legacy of the late war in New France. Through their desire to practice methods of war familiar to them, Montcalm and his officers had demonstrated that metropolitan military standards of conduct should have a place in shaping the empire. The Caribbean sugar islands that France retained after the war had long, well-established imperial habits. Giving up Canada did not mean that France abandoned its interests in the Atlantic; nonetheless, erasing New France from the map allowed the self-consciously enlightened colonial schemes of the postwar Choiseul administration to depart completely from older North American traditions. Thus it was through his participation in new ventures, first to the Îles Malouines (Falkland Islands) and later to the Pacific, that Bougainville developed his own vision of how

French nobles ought to lead colonial ventures and demonstrated both how French elites should interact with Native peoples and the relationship that should exist between colony and metropole. His ideas drew directly from his experiences in North America. When the Crown suppressed the *compagnies franches de la marine* in 1761 and limited the mobility and influence of elite Canadians who had returned to the metropole, their North American colonial experience was silenced. Until peace was established in 1763, almost all of the Canadian notables in France had hoped for the restoration of their colonial homes so that they would not be obliged to undertake new ventures. The sidelining of the marines, along with the undiluted patriotism and loyalty Choiseul's government ascribed to French metropolitan army officers, made it possible for Bougainville to step into the void, alongside the other metropolitan reformers and theoreticians. France used both innovative, "enlightened" colonialism in the Kourou Colony (1763–1765) and the tightly framed voyages of Bougainville's expeditions in order to search for and install a new Atlantic paradigm. Neither strategy referenced New France as an archetype for future colonial encounters, effectively excising it from memory.

⚓ Bougainville, Aspiring *Navigateur*

Born into a wealthy Parisian family of lawyers in 1729, Bougainville was raised in proximity to and educated alongside aristocrats through the patronage and fondness of his *chère maman*, Marie Hélène Hérault de Séchelles, and under the academic supervision of his older brother, Jean-Pierre. He read voraciously, enjoying texts from antiquity from which he sprinkled allusions in his adult journal entries. Contemporary works, such as Leclerc de Buffon's *Histoire naturelle* and the *Encyclopédie* extended his intellectual interests throughout his life. In the early and mid-1750s Bougainville established his reputation as a scientist and an intellectual alongside his developing military career, publishing respected work on calculus in 1755 while serving as a secretary to Charles Pierre Gaston François de Lévis, Duc de Mirepoix, France's ambassador to the court of St. James. The quality of Bougainville's mathematical writings earned him an invitation to become a Fellow of the Royal Society in England in January 1756.[3] The pattern of understanding his overseas service through a lens that merged his knowledge of classical texts with the latest contemporary research would remain a constant in Bougainville's life.[4]

New France provided the aspiring *philosophe* a space in which to observe modern ideas about the state of nature through interaction with France's

Native American allies. Yet both Canada's indigenous and colonial populations disappointed Bougainville's expectations, particularly in their failures to see metropolitan French culture as preferable to their own and to endorse the superiority of French officers by accepting their own subordination. Nor did New France present many opportunities for true career enhancement either through military actions or through erudite discussion and scientific experimentation. Still, when the young colonel returned to France along with the defeated army in 1760, he was in a stronger political position than when he had left, having faithfully served Montcalm's interests, demonstrated valor along French lines during battle, and tended to his French social connections. Bougainville was among the privileged officers to receive parole soon after repatriation, joining Lévis and Bourlamaque on the German front in July 1761 as an aide-de-camp to the Comte de Choiseul-Stainville. Wounded in August, he returned to Paris and after recovery concentrated on joining the elite ranks of natural philosophers and scientists.[5]

Before sailing to Canada in 1756, Bougainville had hoped to enter the French *Académie des sciences*, a goal he continued to pursue despite the war. His brother, Jean-Pierre de Bougainville, was a member of both the *Académie des inscriptions et belle-lettres* and the prestigious *Académie française*. Close to his sickly elder sibling, Louis-Antoine circulated in Jean-Pierre's social circles upon returning to France. This gave him access to the intellectual vanguard of France, an elite group that had begun investigating France's humiliating war experience even before the fighting had ended and sought to reinvigorate the empire. Land, the physiocrats argued, could recover national pride. The *philosophes*' avant-garde embraced social reform and, with it, the belief in antislavery. Still others advocated creating a new empire that would impose modern European society and politics in the Atlantic tropics.[6]

It was among those who acted for imperial reform that Bougainville began to seek a new role for himself. Opportunities for swift promotion on the German front diminished in proportion to expectations of peace in 1761 and 1762. Unlike the returned marines, who anxiously awaited a final resolution to New France's fate, Bougainville had no intention of returning to that "contagious" North Atlantic Thrace. In order to participate in new plans for imperial engagement and to advance his career prospects, Bougainville sought the patronage of the powerful Duc de Choiseul.[7] By 1761 Étienne-François de Stainville, Duc de Choiseul, had ended, or at least contained, the bureaucratic rivalry and divisiveness that had plagued French court politics for most of the 1750s by combining the naval and war ministries into a single superdepartment. Minimizing parochialism favored the restoration of French fortunes, and Louis XV's chief minister formed a broad concept of French imperial goals. Rebuilding the French navy, refining and reasserting French colonial ventures as integral to securing the nation's defense, and frustrating further British Atlantic footholds were among Choiseul's chief aims. Moreover, Choiseul believed that elites supportive of continued oceanic engagement had a responsibility to restore a sense of civility to the thrust of French imperialism.[8] Scientific accuracy in exploration also rose in importance. The anxiety over the cession of Louisiana to Spain in 1762 partly stemmed from fears that French geographers had undervalued Louisiana's potential, an assessment that French explorers had not disproved.[9] It seemed contradictory that France would be willing to forgo the vast territory comprising New France and Louisiana, given France's ambitions to frustrate British Atlantic growth. However, the proven profits to be made from sugar and slavery in Guadeloupe and Martinique were compelling. These colonies more than paid for themselves. As the search for improved and new colonial models became matters of policy, the jettisoning of former French North America allowed the French Crown to reinvent its imperial interactions. Louisiana's border with British North America meant a continuing threat to any French ventures there, whereas the new colony Choiseul hoped to found in Guyana would be geographically more secure.[10] Furthermore, North America had not justified the cost of the Crown's investment; new locations needed to be found.

Bougainville lobbied to be at the forefront of the new French imperialism, and Choiseul granted the young officer an important role in these ventures. Certainly the young colonel excelled at self-promotion. His proven intellectual worth (from the calculus treatise) and strong record as an army officer, moving from captain to colonel in four years, served him in good stead, as did his service in Germany on the staff of Choiseul's kinsman, the Comte de Choiseul-Stainville.[11] Upon his return to France, Bougainville associated himself with leading theorists, reading Charles de Brosse's work on *terra australis incognita* (Antarctica) and pursuing conversations on the subject of discovery with Jean-Pierre de Bougainville, as well as with Jean-Baptiste Thibault de Chanvalon, the former intendant of Martinique who was involved in Choiseul's Guyana project. Well aware of Choiseul's concerns about spending, given France's delicate financial situation, Bougainville and his family shouldered the expense of their proposed outpost on the Îles Malouines.[12] Such an arrangement further dissociated Bougainville from the Canadians, who were accused of defrauding the Crown for decades during their own imperial service. Unlike the marine veterans of New France, Bougainville also benefited from the praise he received from Montcalm, Peyrenc de Moras, and others, which showed that Bougainville was not one to engage with indigenous peoples as equals or neglect the honor of the king's arms. These strategies so successfully convinced Choiseul of Bougainville's "expertise" on Atlantic empire, which was superior to that of any Canadian marine officer, and of his ability to promote French Atlantic ambitions that he even offered Bougainville a governorship in the new colony being planned for Guyana. Bougainville politely declined in favor of his Malouines project and left in September 1763 to scout out and claim French interests in the south Atlantic.[13]

✒ Kourou and the South Atlantic Disasters

As early as 1761, the French Crown had already given its support to the creation of a better and more perfect colonial scheme, a grand and expensive plan for Guyana. The commitment of such funding to Kourou helps to explain the limited resources, apart from two ships and abundant enthusiasm, offered Bougainville by Choiseul for the Falklands project. Preliminary plans for a new colony known as Kourou, situated in Guyana (contemporary French Guiana) had been approved by Choiseul in 1761. Jean-Baptiste Thibault de Chanvalon, chevalier Étienne-François Turgot, and Guyanese planter Brulletout de Préfontaine would work together to make the Kourou project an "ideal" colony to "console the nation for the loss of Canada" and to enact, under the monarch's direct wishes, an enlightened settlement worthy of the new scientific age.[14] Kourou spoke to the new imperial paradigm, possibly drawing its name from the Brahmin priests, *kourous*, on the Malabar Coast, described in Diderot and d'Alembert's *Encyclopédie*.[15] The real innovations in the Kourou project rested in the arrangement of the colony; Choiseul applied colonial improvements that included the rejection of slavery—indigenous or African—except as a last resort, free land distribution to encourage mass immigration, the encouragement of both French and foreign settlers, and religious toleration.[16] Kourou's inspiration came from French nobles' observations of the English Atlantic model, which some considered to be superior to France's efforts. In colonies like Pennsylvania, colonial strength derived from combining free labor in mercantile and agricultural pursuits with religious plurality.[17]

Seventeenth century French expansion into the Atlantic had been small scale, erratic, and often impermanent. Kourou consciously broke this tradition by shipping more than fifteen thousand individuals to South America at one time.[18] When compared to New France's total European and creole population in 1760 of around sixty thousand, the numbers involved in the new project made a dramatic statement. A large European migration discouraged interaction with and dependency on Native peoples in theory and avoided the collaborations, syncretism, and hostility that had shaped the unique cultures of New France and Louisiana. Similarly, enlarging the workforce through sheer numbers of European immigrants addressed the problematic socioeconomic characteristics of the remaining French colonies in Saint Domingue, Guadeloupe, and Martinique. Slave societies demanded unfettered mastery and distasteful extremes of violence and, thanks to the religious and legal innovations issuing from the early French Atlantic, had produced multiple hierarchies of race and communities of interracial, intercultural children. Worse still, on the sugar islands, the Crown doubted the creole elites' fidelity to the metropole since they preferred British slave traders and had surrendered too quickly before the British assault in the Seven Years' War.[19] An instant settler society would resolve this particular problem as it existed in the Antilles and as it had existed in the Canadian borderlands.

Almost none of the elites who had returned from New France and made plain to the Naval Ministry their desire for financial relief or new opportunities found placement in Kourou, though the Duc de Choiseul availed himself of the large Acadian population, encouraging them to migrate after using many of the refugees as an available labor force in France.[20] Lack of status and military training, in addition to their poverty, made Acadians more pliable and trustworthy than the marine veterans. The one Canadian officer involved in Kourou, Charles Deschamps de Boishébert, had significant Acadian connections dating back to the 1750s. Though he helped encourage migration, he was not selected for a leadership role in the Kourou colony, for he had been charged and then cleared in *l'affaire du Canada* and was damaged goods.

The wisdom of experience, the best of intentions, and careful planning did not prevent disaster in the new colony. Taking into account neither the perils of a tropical environment nor the impracticality of imposing a French population wholesale on a new place left settlers and administrators unprepared for reality. The idealistic Kourou mutated into the more descriptive name Courroux, the French word for "elemental, natural rage," and the fearsome climate of the colony came to be known as *l'enfer vert*, or "the green hell."[21] While enlightenment thinkers refused to bow to superstition, bad luck, or worse, *le courroux des dieux*, the "anger of the gods" directed against France seemed to explain the fate of the Kourou colony to a public that evaluated this imperial gamble as devastatingly unsuccessful. Two-thirds of the immigrants died of epidemic disease within the first two years of the colony's existence.[22] With crushing irony, the improved colonial Kourou project had failed far more quickly than the supposedly imperfect imperial endeavors in New France.

Before the full extent of Kourou's public relations nightmare became apparent, Louis-Antoine de Bougainville's Atlantic scheme was well under way. Establishing a French outpost near the South Pole in the Falkland Islands dovetailed with Jean-Pierre de Bougainville's fascination over discovering *terra australis incognita*. With two ships, the *Aigle* and the *Sphinxe*, supplied by Choiseul, the intrepid young officer had sailed off in September 1763 to establish a French presence in the South Atlantic. The chief minister also helped fund the migrants of this new colony, Acadians as in Kourou, albeit in much more modest numbers and in a climate and locale quite the opposite of Guyana's, though vaguely similar to Nova Scotia's windy shores. Bougainville deposited the colonists with supplies and claimed the Îles Malouines for France. When he returned a year later with more supplies, to his great satisfaction Bougainville found the Port Saint Louis settlement to be stable.[23]

In fact, the Port Saint Louis colony lasted only a little longer than Kourou. It, too, failed, although for reasons of diplomacy rather than disease. In 1761 Spain and France had renewed a treaty of mutual support, known as the *Pacte de famille* (Family Pact) in recognition of the dynastic blood shared by France's and Spain's Bourbon monarchs—a treaty that induced Spain's entry into the Seven Years' War, produced the humiliating British conquests of Havana and Manila, and ultimately cost Spain its territory in Florida. Spain's king, Carlos III, was little pleased now to discover French pretensions to Spain's sphere of influence in the South Atlantic—and when Britain also moved to stake a claim to the western Falklands, a diplomatic dispute erupted. Choiseul, unwilling to jeopardize France's position so soon after the Seven Years' War, reluctantly instructed Bougainville to transfer the French colony to Spain—an act the officer made his first task on the global circumnavigation of 1766–1767.[24]

These efforts at reinvigorated colonization in the 1760s demonstrated a shift in France's consideration of its Atlantic world before and after the loss of New France. First, these new colonial ventures drew heavily on privately conducted imaginative theorizing about what constituted an ideal colonial presence. Turgot and Chanvalon shaped Kourou on an enlightenment model, the Bougainvilles framed the Malouines according to the principles of colonization in classical antiquity, and in the late 1760s the Baron de Bessner undertook the Sinnamary settlement in response to the failure of Kourou to prove Europeans' ability to survive the tropics in Cayenne. Encouraging entrepreneurial spirit also allowed the Crown to access private commitments to fund the experiments; the Bougainville family alone raised two hundred thousand *livres* for the Malouines venture. Debt constrained the French Crown, but the Choiseul administration traded royal approval for private cash from colonial founder-investors like Bougainville—an eighteenth-century precursor to modern "public-private" partnerships.[25]

Second, France very selectively plumbed the experience of its former North American colonists. Acadians, rather than Canadian marines, made desirable new colonists, but they always played a subordinate rather than a planning role in these ventures. A few marine veterans managed to find martial roles for themselves in such schemes or helped publicize the undertakings, but the excess of damaged reputations and the limited patronage and financial *crédit* of the veterans meant that almost none of them could reinvent themselves as new colonial entrepreneurs. Those who could were mostly the sons of officers who served in Saint Domingue and Cayenne; one Canadian accompanied Bougainville to the South Atlantic, and one senior Canadian marine, sieur Louis Legardeur de Répentigny, managed to become governor of Gorée Island.[26] Their assignment to Caribbean holdings or to slave trading posts long part of the empire rather than to Kourou or elsewhere helps explain the wariness of French administrators in reassigning elite Canadian colonists. Sending marine officers to unreformed locations—older colonies rather than new projects—could have few adverse effects. If Canadian elites were greedy, self-interested actors (like Intendant François Bigot) or pragmatic accommodators (like the Seneca agent and marine Daniel-Marie Chabert de Joncaire), there was less to be lost by moving such men to small, rich sugar islands. Their desire for profit ensured they would have few scruples about slavery. In New France, some officers, like La Corne St. Luc and Charles de Langlade, had had considerable numbers of both Indian (*panis*) and African slaves. Such men demonstrated the right temperament to survive in difficult colonial backwaters—they did whatever was necessary to thrive. But only a devoted army officer like Bougainville, who put the interests of the Crown and the French nobility first, could be entrusted with the reinvigoration of France's imperial presence and new colonial encounters.

⚜ The Language of Exploration

By 1765 opportunities in the South Atlantic had dwindled, so Bougainville returned to another proposal he had made in 1762 for a mission to the Pacific and presented himself as the perfect choice to conduct this global

162   CHAPTER 6

circumnavigation.[27] Two successful voyages to the Falklands and Bougainville's connections to individuals in the science-oriented Enlightenment gave his proposal weight and the luster of rationality and learning. Approved in 1766, this new venture carried instructions that, like those for the rest of the new 1760s' colonies, distanced this effort from the colonial founding of New France. Seventeenth-century French directives had shaped Atlantic imperial goals around the evangelization of the indigenous population as much as settling the Americas. Bougainville's 1766 orders from César Gabriel de Choiseul, Duc de Praslin, a cousin of Étienne-François de Choiseul and the new naval minister, emphasized reconnaissance and territorial claims in the Pacific—"as no European nation has any establishment or claim on these lands . . . [Bougainville should] take possession of them should they offer items useful to her [France's] trade and her navigation."[28] Choiseul-Praslin also expected Bougainville's journals to be submitted for review upon his return. Thus, although Bougainville's Canadian diary remained private, his Pacific log from the outset was bound to automatically command a wider audience even before its publication as the *Voyage autour du monde*.[29]

Bougainville took this opportunity to reframe the terms of France's imperial encounters post-Canada first for himself (in his ship's log) and then for a broader audience (in the *Voyage*) in his manner of describing territories and peoples in the South Atlantic and Pacific. As with generations of early modern travelers, the observations Bougainville recorded relied on a lexicon familiar to himself and to his French audience when describing the Patagonians (Tehuelches), Tahitians (Maohis), Samoans, Tongans, and others that he encountered between 1767 and 1768.

The publication of the most recent Académie française dictionary in 1762 had defined *sauvage* as "certain people who ordinarily live in the woods more as beasts than as men, without religion, law, or fixed address," an unflattering description but one that intimated individuals in a state of nature.[30] However, Bougainville had had direct experience with so-called *sauvages* in New France, where his diary had categorized neither Indians of the *pays d'en haut* nor Indians of the *réserves*, like the Kahnawakes who adopted him, as redeemable or in a state of nature. Thus, when he deployed the word *sauvage* in 1767, Bougainville placed the South American populations of the Falklands and Patagonia and later the peoples of the Pacific Rim somewhere between the classificatory realm of wild innocents in a state of nature and the consciously barbarous Kahnawake Mohawks or Michilimackinac Ottawas.

A major distinction existed between the *sauvages* of the North American war diary and the Pacific log in this connection between savagery and barbarism. In the officer's North American writings, numerous incidents were described to condemn France's indigenous allies, such as when Bougainville had written that "the cruelty and insolence of these barbarians is horrifying" as he observed Indians lead prisoners away from Oswego in September 1756.[31] The 1768 ship's log and the 1771 *Voyage* contained the word *barbare* only three times: describing the "Barbarian Nation" (Patagonia) becoming civilized by Spanish effort; witnessing a "barbarian remedy" in Tierra del Fuego; and critiquing a Tahitian "barbarian law" pertaining to the social place of servants.[32] At no point did Bougainville refer to Pacific Natives or even Patagonians as barbarians—unlike the North American Indians he had encountered in the 1750s. Usage, as much as word choice, was key. Barbarians were "cruel, inhuman; meaning figuratively a savage who has neither law nor manners," and the central distinction between savages and barbarians lay in manners. Only barbarians could fall away from civility because, unlike savages, they had risen above a state of nature and willfully chosen regression.[33] The 1762 dictionary points to the distinction Bougainville drew between North American Indians and indigenous peoples elsewhere. The dictionary's definition of *barbare* rested on "substantive proof of savagery and cruelty" and then provided the following sample sentence: "The Iroquois are true barbarians."[34] Leaving behind the corrupted world of North America, Bougainville thought he might find savages, he might even find barbaric practices, but he encountered no barbarians. In these untouched regions of the Pacific, Bougainville hoped to show the triumph of the 1760s' French colonial project and incorporate new claims for the empire but, more scientifically, also to demonstrate that no falling away had yet tainted the innocent inhabitants, thereby making them suitable candidates for French interest.

As a cosmopolitan and voracious reader, Bougainville was familiar with contemporary travel literature and had also followed the developmental debates between Montesquieu and Voltaire in the 1740s and 1750s over whether climate or culture had greater influence on the human body.[35] New scientific notions developing by the 1760s, such as the work of Cornelius de Pauw or the climate theory of Bougainville's good friend the Comte de Buffon addressed classification, human development, morality, and observation within these contexts and reshaped the officer's views of human development. The harsh cold of the Americas hindered North American advancement, Buffon proposed; de Pauw suggested that indigenous people and Europeans existed on different developmental levels: the former were able to advance (with European help) but were always behind "on the axis of humanity's continuous progress."[36] Such ideas affirmed Bougainville's own interactions with indigenous North Americans, as when he had deemed Indians "a necessary evil" corrupted by alcohol, their own climate, and barbarism. Native exposure to and trade with commercially oriented, degenerate elite French marines had accelerated Indians' estrangement from civility and the laws that governed "civilized" nations. Moreover, from Bougainville's perspective, reflected in his North American diary, Indians had also corrupted the French in Canada.

The global circumnavigation was to align itself with these scientific inquiries and to add further proof to the climate theory of development. Like many prior explorers, Bougainville placed a premium on his own scientific presentation of his journeys in both the log and the *Voyage*. While visiting windswept and stark Tierra del Fuego, Bougainville reflected his sensitivity to climate and human formation and his concern with the scientific accuracy of his observations. Patagonia had long been considered in European myth to be a land of giants. Bougainville observed instead that the Native population, deemed "savages" like all indigenous Americans, were no giants. Rather, they were "small, ugly, knock-kneed . . . the most wretched of men," attesting to their difficult home landscape and limited civilization.[37] If an Arcadian world existed, one that combined climate theory and optimism about human advancement, it was to be found in the mild and distant southern Pacific, not the tumultuous Atlantic.[38] Bougainville might have been scornful of Jean-Jacques Rousseau's idea of the "noble savage," but this notion likely influenced French readers of the *Voyage* who favorably considered accounts of Tahiti along with Rousseau's ideas on the state of nature.[39]

↙ Creating *La Nouvelle Cythère*

By the time the *Boudeuse* and the *Étoile* sailed away from Tahiti in April 1768, Bougainville and many of his social peers could once more view and present some members of indigenous populations in a favorable light to French audiences and to themselves. Broadly speaking, the technological and physical achievement of reaching the South Pacific and indeed completing a global circumnavigation strongly reinforced the assumption of moral superiority evident in the progression of European reason, science, and civilization. On the island that Bougainville came to name "New Cythera" in particular, Bougainville finally found a place with a Native population who could be used for colonization propaganda in a way that the Indians of his earlier war journal could not. This was a space that contrasted completely with the cultural corruption Bougainville thought he had witnessed in Canada, where French Canadian settlers living in dangerous proximity to Indians had succumbed to the barbarous environment and as a result had lost their compassion and their civility.

Native interactions in Tahiti did not threaten French civility. Instead, they provided numerous opportunities to consciously craft a new model of colonial interactions, a project that Bougainville undertook after completing his journey.

The heavily edited discussion of the navigator's first encounter with a Tahitian woman bears witness to this new vision. The *Voyage* presented to its readers a romantic and positive scene of encounter, proclaiming "The young girl negligently allowed her loincloth to fall to the ground, and appeared to all eyes such as Venus showed herself to the Phrygian shepherd. She had the Goddess's celestial form."[40] It is harder to identify this Tahitian "Venus" with her unvarnished counterpart in the ship's log, a "young and fine-looking woman. . . . almost naked, who showed her vulva in exchange for small nails."[41] Cast as vulgar, uninhibited, and materialistic, the girl in the private journal resembled the American Indians of the Canadian diary. There, indigenous demands for gifts, the backbone of reciprocal alliance in the North American context, had registered as pride, insolence, and laziness. "It is a long job to get them to make up their minds," Bougainville wrote of the Iroquois, Ojibwas, and Ottawas, and "it requires authority, brandy, equipment, food and such. The job never ends and it is very irksome."[42] Despite his private shock at the young Tahitian's corporeal freedom, Bougainville framed his final judgment as one in which "primitive" exchange paired with "charming" naïveté. By separating the young woman's bartering from self-interest, Bougainville personified the innocence and promise of Tahiti and elevated the girl to the status of a delicate Venus. The word *portrait* evoked numerous classical and Renaissance portrayals of a voluptuous and, importantly, modest Venus emerging at her birth. Such a first encounter naturally called for the name Nouvelle Cythère, which Bougainville gave to Tahiti.

Moreover, the rewritten scene of first encounter in the log became a scene of recognition in the *Voyage* and, by doing so, completely reversed the tradition of colonial encounter and experience. Throughout his depictions of Tahiti, Bougainville sharply downplayed any negative aspects of Tahitian culture, particularly the local economies of sexual exchange, pervasive thievery, and warfare.[43] Theft, a frequent complaint in the ship's log, was transformed into an indulged amusement in the 1771 *Voyage*. In New France theft of French items by Abenakis had been attributed to a lack of control exhibited by the corrupt leadership there.[44] Unlike the "proud" American

Indians, whose "self-love is everything, and pride is the only wealth," the Tahitians were reportedly "delighted" to see the French and disheartened to see them leave, a clear sign of their desire for advancement.[45] Bougainville's suggestion that Tahitians "are the best people in the world" and that he "could not leave this fortunate island without praising it once more" contrasted utterly with his thoughts about New France, where "the air one breathes here is contagious of making one accustomed to such callousness."[46]

War had framed the Canadian journal as a principal category of interaction and observation even though Bougainville and indigenous peoples fought on the same side. The Pacific log and then the *Voyage* foregrounded pleasure instead and minimized discussions of conflict. "I do not know whether they [Tahitians] know war with strangers," Bougainville had first noted in his log, attributing peace to the isolation of Tahiti. Eventually the *Voyage* revealed that "[Tahitians] are almost always at war with the inhabitants of neighboring islands" and also noted that in Tahiti "war is conducted in a cruel manner."[47] However, both of these private and public narratives described war only among the indigenous peoples of Oceania—they never described violence directed toward Europeans, unlike the exhaustive examples of such behavior that Bougainville had chronicled in North America. Moreover, in New France the horror of Europeans being forced to deal with issues of war, martial honor, and duty on indigenous terms took precedence over the inter-Indian disputes among France's Native allies. Ten years later in the Pacific, with the French playing the role of self-styled "impartial" observers, warfare and even other forms of "savagery" could receive an appealing gloss. Though Bougainville rarely used the term *sauvage* in Tahiti, he did draw one direct comparison in the *Voyage* to American Indians—in reference to tattooing.[48] Drawing on his knowledge of social relations in the Atlantic, Bougainville, along with his companions, the prince of Nassau-Siegen and Philibert Commerson (the chief scientist), attributed conflict to "the different races [of men] I observed," where poorer, more aggressive, "dark-skinned" Tahitians bore the brunt of the war disputes.[49] Bougainville's log also suggested a Tahitian aversion to Melanesians, an attitude that made the French disdainful of Samoans and Tongans as "blacks," who "were much nastier than the Indians whose color is closer to white."[50] Such language recalled the ugly reality of race-based power hierarchies present in the French Caribbean. The French perspective gave the lighter-skinned Tahitians a leg up on civility and further commended the "Cytherans" for their apparent embrace of racial hierarchies.

Bougainville's turns of phrase also recalled comparisons to North America that the author made, at least for himself. In the winter of 1757, a French Canadian's lack of compassion for starving Acadian refugees led Bougainville to exclaim, "What a country! What morals!" and observe with shock that "[the colonists] let them die of hunger and cold, [and] got all the money they had."[51] Such a callous lack of propriety and charity on the part of a French individual toward another of Louis XV's subjects inverted the categories of "civilized" and "uncivilized." Nine years later, when a Tahitian chief offered his wives to Bougainville as sexual partners, the officer jotted down an almost identical "What a country! What a people!" But while the chief's gesture was an uncivilized act by French standards, the surprising behavior was that of an indigenous person rather than a Frenchman, who knew better. The Tahitian's offer of such precious individuals to a relative stranger marked a vulgar custom but also an excess of generosity, no doubt in tribute to European superiority, Bougainville reasoned.

All of Bougainville's writings drew inspiration from antiquity—Greek and Roman history allowed the Frenchman to find an apt comparison to his own overseas military and ethnographic experiences, a habit of thought that had been encouraged in Louis-Antoine by his equally antiquity-loving brother Jean-Pierre. The classical allusions in the Pacific *Voyage* appeared so frequently that they caused Denis Diderot to dryly note, "Virgil was in the head or the luggage of the navigator."[52] The *Aeneid*, perhaps Bougainville's favorite source, helped the explorer imaginatively translate and make sense of a multitude of events. When he witnessed the alleged massacre of British troops at Fort William Henry in New York in 1757, Bougainville had quoted from the *Aeneid* lines spoken by Polydorus, Priam's envoy to Thrace, killed there by the greed and treachery of its inhabitants. Now in Tahiti, a quite different, more auspicious passage from the *Aeneid* seemed appropriate: "O Venus . . . you who grant rights to those who seek out hospitality . . . make this a happy day."[53] Classical texts like the *Aeneid* helped Bougainville and his readers place global experiences within a context that spoke not only to Enlightenment intellectuals but also to an educated public throughout Europe. Venus, mother of the epic's hero, Aeneas, secretly protects him as he flees the fallen Troy and aids him during his long journey to found a new empire. His goddess mother comes to aid him disguised at one point as a Tyrian maid, her identity, however, revealed through her graceful walk, tumbling perfumed hair, and her perfect shape covered (or uncovered) by her dress.[54] An educated reader would have connected the navigator's analogy between Virgil's divine Venus and the young Tahitian Venus with her

CHAPTER 6

"celestial" form, who similarly "revealed herself" to Bougainville. She served as an allegory of divine providence being bestowed on the French arrival. For Bougainville, this "happy day" in Tahiti marked the transformation from the old colonial experience and empire of the 1750s to the new one of the 1760s. Leaving behind at last "the savage land" of New France, Bougainville presented himself to his readers as a kind of Aeneas. Like his literary model, Bougainville engaged in the dutiful work of creating a new imperial model from the ashes of defeat.

Even visual sources reinforced the empirical nature of the global circumnavigation and the goodwill in interactions Bougainville emphasized. Bougainville produced a lively and functional map of the island of Nouvelle Cythère (figure 9), featuring his two ships and the shape of the land as seen from the water. All the renderings focused on distant and clinical views of the shoreline, reinforcing the observations being made by the French of their objects of inquiry, though they equally suggest the superficial understanding of Tahitian society gleaned by the French. From this safe remove, Bougainville and his crew could evaluate the exotic island without risking their lives by immersing themselves in the particularities of a foreign land, as

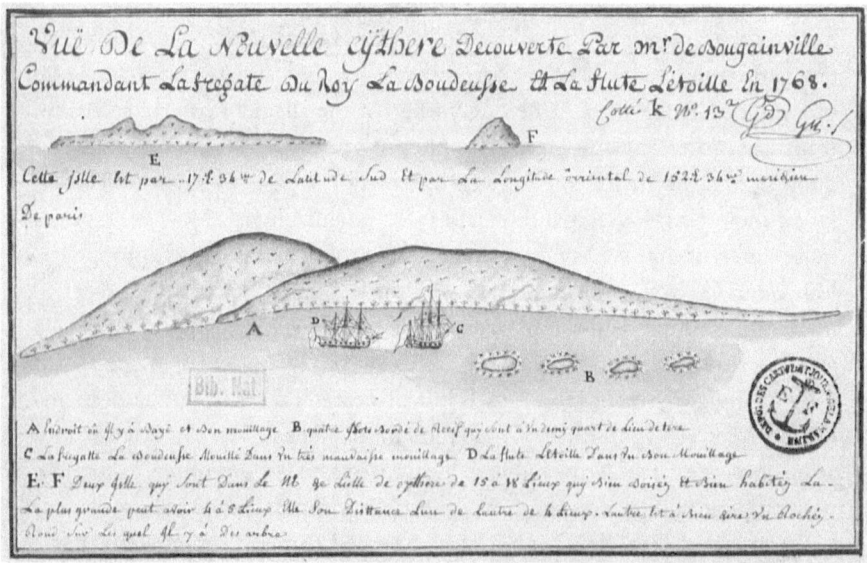

FIGURE 9. *Vüe de la Nouvelle Cÿthere Decouverte par M*^r *de Bougainville*, watercolor map by Louis-Antoine de Bougainville, 1768. The strength and size of French culture are symbolized by the vessels *Boudeuse* and *Étoile*, which loom over four tiny Tahitian canoes. Courtesy of the Bibliothèque nationale de France.

French migrants had in New France or, more recently, in Kourou. No Tahitians appear directly as individuals in any of the map renderings, reflecting Bougainville's and other explorers' lack of interest in accurately recording Native peoples' impressions of Europeans in the Pacific.

The themes of dominant European technology looming over Native space and bodies also graced a map by Alexandre-Joseph Riouffe (figures 10 and 11) and continued into Bougainville's published account. The *Voyage* contained three illustrations, all of Pacific watercraft, from Tahiti, the Navigator Islands, and the Choiseul Islands. Each provided more detail in the representation of Native "canoes" than of their crews, tiny, sticklike figures who appear to be naked.[55] For all their described grace, beauty, and charm, Tahitians remained visually absent. Was it because their skin color was at variance with Bougainville's depiction of paradise? Allowing his readers to conjure up images of Venus as a Mediterranean or Renaissance beauty perhaps seemed preferable. Only a single picture, made by an unknown artist in the French expedition, remains to chronicle the encounters of April 1768 (figure 12).

Bougainville's inattention to Native perspectives also informed his Canadian journal. Indigenous peoples speaking for themselves never made their way onto paper, keeping them from becoming uncomfortable realities. It was not that the French involved with the voyages paid little attention to how others perceived them and their actions, for Bougainville had complained constantly in North America about having to move through life on indigenous terms at ceremonies and with adoption and other events. No images decorated the earlier diary, and, indeed, the renderings made by the various hands of New France that crossed the Atlantic showcased military installations and battles sites or diagrammed the colony's main settlements rather than showing individuals.[56] When Bougainville himself returned to France in late 1758, he had drafted a map of Carillon as a commemoration of Montcalm's great victory for Madame de Pompadour; its only embellishment was a dedication cartouche.[57]

Through revisions and the alteration of pivotal moments, the 1767 expedition log turned into the published *Voyage*, a vision of exchange in Tahiti designed to promote new norms of colonial encounter. The *Voyage* was primarily a literary rather than a scientific achievement, and Bougainville received both accolades and a stinging criticism of his presentation of idyllic primitivism. Given the thematic continuities that underlay the man's writings and the *Voyage*'s success with the public, it is evident that Bougainville chose not to rework and edit his vituperative presentation of Canada's indigenous peoples for publication. Despite the shifts from the Pacific log to

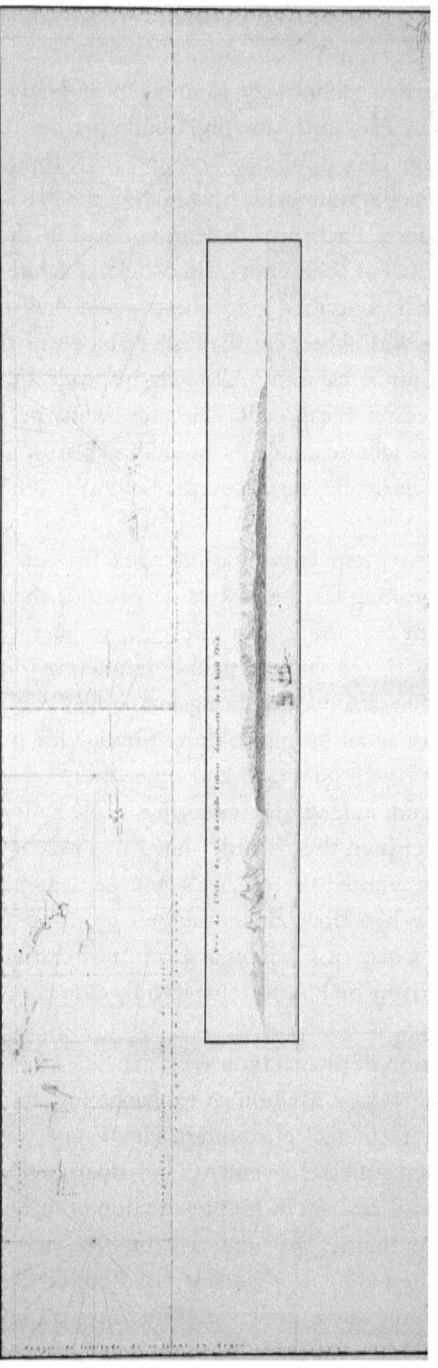

Figure 10. *Itinéraire du voyage de Louis-Antoine de Bougainville, dans le Pacifique, depuis le détroit de Magellan jusqu'à Batavia* [Hydrographic Itinerary of Bougainville's Pacific Voyage from the Straits of Magellan to Indonesia], Alexandre-Joseph Riouffe, 1769. Courtesy of the Bibliothèque nationale de France.

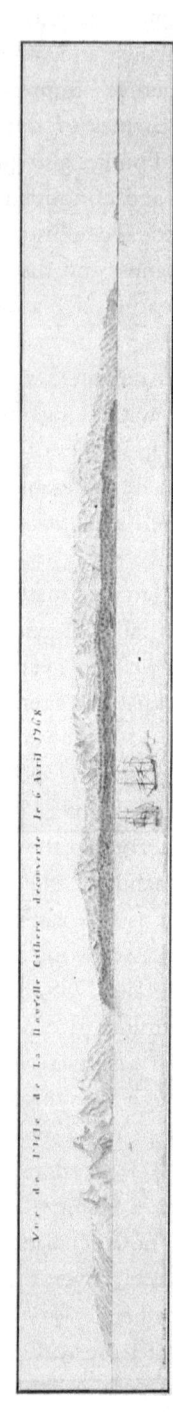

Figure 11. *Vue de l'Isle de la Nouvelle Cithere decouverte le 6 Avril 1768* [View of the Island of Tahiti, discovered April 6, 1768], Alexandre-Joseph Riouffe, 1769. Courtesy of the Bibliothèque nationale de France.

the *Voyage*, which idealized Tahitians, casting Native Americans as living in a state of nature seemed an impossible task. In addition, the North American diary raised too many bad memories about the failure in New France to impose French cultural standards on other peoples. The silencing of that manuscript indicates that Bougainville at the very least found it to be out of step with the latest scientific and political thinking on European and indigenous interactions—theories he embraced and now actively promoted.

With New France fading from French memory, it may also have seemed pointless to recall the North American experience in a publication that might prove controversial or inadvertently jar in any way the memorialization of the fallen French general Montcalm. Even after the American Revolution began, a conflict in which Bougainville participated as a ship's commander in the navy, and at a time when the public showed an interest in material on North America, Bougainville's North American diaries remained private and unpublished. Unlike Pierre Pouchot, who had died more than a decade before his *Mémoires sur la dernière guerre* appeared in print in 1781, Bougainville was very much alive, with a career and a reputation to protect, and he saw nothing to be gained here. In Canada, Bougainville had been a subordinate; in the Pacific, he commanded, and that, too, could have influenced his decision.

The Pacific log, the unvarnished form of the *Voyage*, shows how Bougainville wanted to be seen by the indigenous—in ways that cannot be found in the North American journal. The day after arriving in Tahiti on April 7, 1768, Bougainville wrote, "our white skins delight them, they express their admiration in this regard in the most expressive manner." The Tahitians were "very industrious and would soon reach the level of European nations if we brought them to our crafts," demonstrating a receptivity to European culture that, to Bougainville, in no way resembled the attitudes of Native Americans.[58] The explorer's paradise was not simply one of natural beauty and vigor that rejuvenated the weary traveler. It was also a

---

Alexandre-Joseph Riouffe produced a magnificent, three-meter-long hydrographic map (figure 10) to illustrate the journey of the *Boudeuse* and the *Étoile* from the Straits of Magellan (at far right) to the island of Java (at far left). That Tahiti assumed such prominence for Bougainville is indicated in the detail Riouffe locates at the center of his map. This valorization of "Nouvelle Cithere" minimized the navigator's interactions on Tonga or Samoa or at Praslin Falls and helps to promote Tahiti's centrality to future Pacific imperial schemes. Palm trees rather than dense forests of hickory, maple, and oak line the shore of a clearly delineated island in the distance on the central detail ornamenting Riouffe's 1769 hydrographic map (figure 11). Despite the vastness of the Pacific, Bougainville's state-of-the-art vessels give the appearance of reigning supreme.

FIGURE 12. *Tahitians presenting fruits to Bougainville attended by his officers.* Anonymous pencil and watercolor sketch, circa 1768. Courtesy of the National Library of Australia, Rex Nan Kivell Collection.

restorative destination because it reaffirmed French engagement with a wider world in a manner that valorized the metropole.

⚜ Reaching Back to the Sixteenth Century

In his presentation of contented Tahitians, Bougainville hearkened back to his reading of the earliest years of French Atlantic colonial efforts: Jacques Cartier's search for a route to China and the "discovery" of Tadoussac, the Villegaignon expeditions to Brazil, Jean de Léry's and Jean Mocquet's encounters in the South Atlantic.[59] Most of these sixteenth-century accounts claimed that indigenous Americans welcomed the French arrivals to their shores, entertained amusing relationships with them, and appeared upset by the prospect of these would-be colonists departing for home. The Pacific journal, unlike the North American diary, explicitly drew on this legacy in describing the moment of the Frenchmen's leave-taking. "All the women are weeping over our departure," Bougainville wrote on his last full day in Tahiti, "and the people are very eager for us to return." Bougainville in the same moment recounted the Tahitians' satisfaction that the French had planted "wheat, maize, beans, peas, lentils and the seeds of various vegetables" for them.[60] The departure from Quebec in October 1760 had taken place under the dark cloud of defeat, whereas Bougainville's leave-taking from Tahiti attested to the good relations established by French and Tahitians within two weeks and a positive experience that cast glory on France. The seeds planted represented Euro-Atlantic products, like wheat and corn, and in their acceptance of these foreign fruits, Bougainville demonstrated that Tahitians initiated their transformation from primitive to civilized. The seedling scene did not find a place in the published *Voyage* but attests nevertheless to Bougainville's warmer sentiments toward Tahitians. Heightening the pathos of a wonderful experience drawing to a close, the 1771 edition depicted Tahitian women as piteously crying, "*Tayo, maté,* you were our friends and you are killing us," to show their distress at losing their French visitors.[61]

Ahutoru, a Tahitian chief, eased the pain of French and Tahitian separation by accompanying the French on their return journey and, in doing so, extended to the Pacific another theme from the sixteenth-century Atlantic experience: the travel of an exotic, high-status foreign dignitary eager to visit France. In the insertion of this striking visitor into court society, the Pacific Native's experience was reminiscent of the encounters with Brazilian Tupinambás in the 1500s. On occasions such as the 1550 royal entry of

Henri II into Rouen or the staged dialogue between Jean Mocquet and South American Indians for Henri IV at the turn of the seventeenth century, Brazilian Tupinambás had played an important ceremonial role in the French construction of imperial self. Ahutoru, not Akwesasne or Kahnawake Iroquois, continued this tradition, having been sent by Tahitian chief Ereti as a "friend given to friends" to cement the bond between France and Tahiti.[62] This was not the first visit by an indigenous person to eighteenth-century France. Native Americans had continuously traveled east across the Atlantic. In the 1720s, for instance, a delegation of Illinois led by the Kaskaskia chief Chicagou were received by Louis XV at Versailles, and in the late 1740s or early 1750s at least two Kahnawakes visited Paris.[63] However, these individuals experienced much less pomp and publicity compared to the welcome that had heralded the arrival of their Native predecessors two centuries earlier or that greeted the Tahitian in the late 1760s.[64] Bougainville's decision to bring Ahutoru to Paris with him on the *Boudeuse* and his orchestrating of a media sensation for the Tahitian in Paris suggest that the French navigator consciously sought to invoke the tradition of the French sixteenth century, when France's overseas empire was fresh faced. Though he learned little French, the chief was entertained in court and salon circles, grew fond of the opera, "for he passionately loved to dance," and enjoyed a great friendship with the Duchesse de Choiseul, wife of the great minister. In no account did Ahutoru criticize French culture, as Michel de Montaigne's "cannibals" had, nor did he reject French practices, as American Indians had during the war. After Bougainville's "pains to make his visit to Paris agreeable and productive," the Tahitian exceeded all expectations and thus became the model colonial subject.[65]

Bringing Ahutoru to France laid the groundwork for the final similarity between the sixteenth century and Bougainville's *Voyage*. Like Jean de Léry's *Histoire d'un voyage fait en la terre du Brésil* (1578) or even Jean Mocquet's *Voyages en Afrique, Asie, et Indes orientales et occidentales* (1617), Bougainville's *Voyage autour du monde* drew its authority from its recording of the author's firsthand experience, his personal interaction with new lands and new individuals. Léry's work influenced writers besides Bougainville, inspiring the explorer's contemporaries Abbé Raynal, Denis Diderot, and Jean-Jacques Rousseau with the "breviary of the ethnologist." The format, which combined the elements of the "adventure novel" with the affirmations that the story designed by Léry was true, worked to great effect in Bougainville's *Voyage*.[66] Portraying himself as a man of science and buoyed by his successful global circumnavigation, Bougainville earned his readers' trust and convincingly conveyed the existence of South Pacific marvels.

Underpinned by the testimony of an actual ship's log, the navigational passages of the *Voyage* helped "validate the empirical origins" of both Bougainville's travel and experiences.[67] These credentials enabled him to supply a modern update of the older tradition, but one that still relied on the audience's impulse for "the truth," for an eye-witness report, for proof and physical evidence in the form of foreign visitors, just like the sixteenth-century works.

Valorizing the sixteenth-century model of exploration and colonization meant the possibility of continuing to refine and innovate models of empire while simultaneously retaining the most economically productive older colonies. The French Crown needed more options to reinvigorate its overseas ambitions. Kourou, for all its innovation and enlightenment reforms, had proven a disaster and was unable to refresh French colonial schemes. The abject failure of cultural fidelity in settlement colonies like New France still threatened the remaining Atlantic holdings. Saint Domingue, Guadeloupe, and Martinique generated immense wealth, but the well-established slave societies and colonial cultures unique to those islands could not be easily modernized. Supporting intrepid entrepreneurs, like Cartier in the sixteenth century or Bougainville in the eighteenth, cost the Crown comparatively little except in patronage, and at least France could in this way still acquire territories and establish trade beneficial to the metropole. Bougainville's designs on the Spanish-claimed Îles Malouines in the early 1760s had sparked international drama by endangering the stability of the "Family Pact" between France and Spain and ending with France's formal cession of the Falklands on April 1, 1767. No such problems arose from Bougainville's *Voyage*. Instead, this journey provided the war-weary intellectual audience of France with something new and fascinating and garnered support for more overseas missions.

The *Voyage* famously inspired Denis Diderot's *Supplement to Bougainville's Voyage* in 1772, which used imagined Tahitian primitive innocence to critique Europe's artifice and indicted Bougainville's colonial gaze through a dialogue between "the Almoner" and the Tahitian chief, "Orou."[68] In the idealized and culturally superior tone that Bougainville adopted vis-à-vis Tahitian culture, Diderot saw a lack of French self-criticism. However, could an indigenous individual like the fictional "Orou" in Diderot's *Supplement* or Rousseau's un-self-reflexive "noble savage" be literal, not only literary possibilities, when American Indians clearly rejected French superiority? Bougainville himself had noted that even Catholicized, domiciled Native Americans "are always savages just as much as those who have been the least tamed" and that "one is a slave to Indians in this country."[69] The navigator and his patrons may have been unwilling to revisit the critique of French civility from the disastrous Seven Years' War that a *supplement* to his Canadian journals might inspire—and the audience that avidly consumed the *Voyage* would not have accepted it.

Bougainville's circumnavigation reset the clock on French American experiences and, in doing so, excised New France almost completely from the national memory of imperial encounter. The colonies that France did retain (Saint Domingue, Martinique, Guadeloupe, Cayenne, and Gorée) were so far removed from the experience of New France, by virtue of their small French or French creole populations and by being overt slave societies, that they fell into a different category of being. Of course, violence flourished in these locations, but these colonies had never been designed to be more perfect versions of France overseas. Kourou was both a tragedy and a political disaster, but the very attempt to come up with a new model of colonization suggested that French imperialists felt profound discomfort with the old model. Of the loyal colonists who had defended New France, only the marine and civilian elites had returned to France after the war, and by 1764 some of these individuals were going back to British Canada in order to seek better opportunities. In fact, the only colonists who by French terms displayed their consistent fidelity as a group to the French Crown were the Acadians, those individuals who fared poorly in the new French Atlantic.

The instructions given to Bougainville by the Crown permitted him to claim land in the name of France, and his enthusiasm for naming across the Pacific and Indian Oceans (the Choiseul Islands, Praslin Island, Bougainville Island) attested to his willingness to excel in this task. Beyond providing France with a major scientific achievement, the circumnavigation also connected the remaining French holdings at Île Bourbon (Réunion) and Île de France (Mauritius) with the remnants of the French Atlantic. Tracing a route through the east renewed France's ties and commitments to this region and looked to future endeavors between the sugar islands of the Caribbean and the vanilla and spice lands of the Indian Ocean and Pacific Rim.

As Bougainville's presentation of his interactions with indigenous peoples hearkened back to the sixteenth century, so his goals, the search for extractive resources, mirrored that past as well. But his contemporary experience completely informed his actions and those of the French Crown. *La Nouvelle France* was lost, but new ventures awaited. In the 1770s France would assert colonial interests in Madagascar, and it would continue its commercial schemes at Saint Louis in Gorée and in the Antilles. As a dedicated naval officer of the *ancien régime* and then a respected scientific figure in the Directory, Bougainville would also remain committed to his imperial vision. The year 1798 would see Bougainville serving on the commission preparing the French expedition to Egypt, for which Napoleon gained great fame.[70] However, in 1768 he was homeward bound from the Pacific, sailing aboard the *Boudeuse*, a ship named for a mood, sulkiness (and, when used as a noun, for a flirtatious courting chair), returning from the landfall at Tahiti that he took to be *la nouvelle Cythère*, which is Venus's birthplace reincarnated. In some part of his mind Bougainville was on an expedition that emulated the aristocratic *fêtes galantes* depicted by Antoine Watteau—traveling a world away metaphorically and literally from the disasters of New France.[71]

Epilogue: *Mon Frère Sauvage*

> She sings the fates, and in her frantic fits
> The notes and names, inscribed to leaves, commits.
> What she commits to leaves, in order laid
> Before the cavern's entrance are displayed;
> Unmoved they lie; but if a blast of wind
> Without, or vaporous issue from behind,
> The leaves are borne aloft in liquid air,
> And she resumes no more her museful care;
> Nor gathers from the rocks her scattered verse,
> Nor sets in order what the winds disperse.
> Thus, many not succeeding, most upbraid
> The madness of this visionary maid,
> And with loud curses leave the mystic shade.
>
> (Virgil, *The Aeneid*)

The journey from Kahnawake, Kanesatake, or Akwesasne to Philadelphia entailed dangerous risks for an Iroquois in the early autumn of 1778, the third year of the North American colonies' rebellion against Britain. The hostility of the white Anglo-American colonists toward the indigenous peoples, focused on Mohawks, led by the pro-British chief, Joseph Brant, had increased since the failed invasion of New York colony by Gen. John Burgoyne in 1777. The sensational murder at that time of Jane McRae (fiancée of one of Burgoyne's own officers) by a Native American and tales of "depredations" by British and British-allied Native troops in the Wyoming and Cherry valleys had exacerbated Anglo-Americans' fears. Paranoia exploded into ethnic-based violence early in October 1778, when Lt. Col. William Butler led the 4th Pennsylvania Regiment on a scorched-earth retaliatory mission against the Six Nation Iroquois towns of Unadilla and Oquaga.[1] Yet, despite the perils, an unknown number of Canadian Indian chiefs, most likely Iroquois from Kahnawake near

Montreal, undertook the 450-mile voyage to the Pennsylvania capital. The goal of this extraordinary mission was to meet with France's emissary to the Continental Congress, Conrad Alexandre Gérard de Rayneval, who had arrived in North America in the spring.[2]

No archival traces tell us what the Indian travelers experienced on their journey south, but they indeed reached Philadelphia and achieved their goal of being introduced to Rayneval. Recording the details of his conference with these Canadian notables in an internal report dated October 21, 1778, the French minister plenipotentiary expressed amazement that a member of the Indian delegation spoke French. The visiting Iroquois planned their voyage and their appearance carefully. At least one man, Rayneval pointed out, wore a medal given to him by Pierre de Rigaud, Marquis de Vaudreuil, the last governor of New France. The point of recalling old bonds of alliance and of the French empire's engagement with indigenous communities through this physical manifestation of reciprocal obligation would have been obvious to the Indian men. Even Rayneval appeared struck by this proof that French influence continued in North America almost two decades after the surrender of Montreal.

From Philadelphia, the Indians traveled to Boston, where the French expeditionary fleet sent by King Louis XVI to aid the North American rebels rode at anchor in the harbor, under the command of Admiral Jean Baptiste Charles-Henri Hector, Comte d'Estaing. Aboard his flagship, the *Languedoc*, the admiral wrote in greater depth than his Philadelphia colleague about the diplomatic conversation he had entertained with his Native visitors, "who had come from a very great distance." D'Estaing delineated for his superior, Naval Minister Antoine de Sartine, the intentions of their visit, which the Indians had clearly expressed to him:

> To see for themselves whether we were truly French, to ask to see the white banner, whose appearance still makes them dance, to hear the Mass, which they have been deprived of for seventeen years, to receive the accolades of the reverend recollect father, who is our confessor, not to mention the several guns, powder, shot, and brandy, which they took in moderation but received with great pleasure.[3]

Twenty years had passed since a golden fleur-de-lys blooming on a snowy field had flown over North American soil. Nevertheless, these Native ambassadors retained sharp memories as to who could claim the name of "French" and what that might mean in terms of alliance and exchange. D'Estaing, like Rayneval, must have noticed the royal medal worn on the chest of one of the men, and it likely symbolized to the admiral both the triumph of French culture over indigenous forms and the yearning of these *sauvages* to return to its protective embrace.

Nonetheless, this bronze or silver disk said less about French authority than it did about indigenous interpretation and repurposing of the legacy of French America, which had shaped interactions between Native peoples and Europeans in Canada since 1760. Rayneval's recognition of the medal showed, in Indian eyes, that he understood its power. By recollecting and accepting the object, the admiral indeed proved to them that he was French. D'Estaing's report unquestioningly accepted the Indians' desire "to see for themselves whether we were truly French." He reported this as fact, with no disdain. His own willingness to affirm Native expectations both acknowledged indigenous agency in defining "Frenchness" in North America and laid the groundwork for a renewal of Franco-Indian alliances, should the opportunity arise amid the uncertainty of war. After all, in Iroquoian and Algonquian America, white, the emblematic color of the French Bourbons, symbolized the restoration of a middle ground and the return to a mutually beneficial alliance. The white standard that "still makes them dance" reinforced the intertwining of alliance and trade—a space designated for ritual exchange and display. While the Montreal capitulation and the Murray Treaty with the Seven Nations dictated by Montreal's conquerors, British generals James Murray and Jeffery Amherst, both signed in 1760, had protected French and Native Roman Catholic freedom of worship, d'Estaing's reference to their having "been deprived of" celebrating Mass unmistakably signaled the changes wrought by twenty years of British rule over Canada. *Habitants* and Indians from the *réserves* could remain Roman Catholic, but their access to priests and to the distinctive material culture of a Roman Catholic French Atlantic world had declined following the imposition of a British regime.

For these Indian ambassadors, it was an individual who provided proof of the veracity of the French return to North America more than any material product. Late in October, while aboard the frigate *Languedoc*, the Indians experienced an unexpected and, to them, welcome meeting. Eighteen years had passed since Louis-Antoine de Bougainville had last served in Canada or sighted the eastern coastline of North America; now he did so as the commander of the ship *Guerrière*. In the 1760s in France, Bougainville had styled himself an expert on North America; now he was a literary celebrity thanks to his *Voyage autour du monde*. And on October 28, 1778, the explorer directly confronted the legacy of his youthful past in America in Boston harbor. Meeting with the visiting Native delegation that day, Bougainville wrote in his journal that one among them was the grandson of Onoraguete, the Kahnawake chief who had adopted him, then a twenty-nine-year-old army officer, into the Mohawk Turtle clan back in 1757.[4] D'Estaing made no mention of this encounter, perhaps because he could not grasp its significance or was not present at the reunion. Bougainville's diary tells us nothing of how Onoraguete's grandson received him, but the fact that the two met suggests that the Kahnawakes may have heard rumors of Bougainville's return and that this in part inspired the journey. Or perhaps, given the frequency with which Canadian high officials and veteran marines had returned to New France during the seventeenth and eighteenth centuries, the Iroquois might have assumed that they would indeed see familiar faces among the French forces at Philadelphia and Boston.

Gérard de Rayneval's writings provide more clues about what transpired at this exchange, adding details omitted by Bougainville and d'Estaing. His material suggests the Kahnawakes and this grandson of Onoraguete specifically sought a cousin among the French men serving in the fleet: Bougainville.[5] Less interested in the possibility of renewing a past Franco-Indian alliance, as d'Estaing appeared to be, Rayneval instead focused on something he found to be a salacious detail about a famous man: the grandson's claim to be Bougainville's nephew. Although Rayneval failed to describe other elements of the meeting, we can perhaps imagine how this encounter took place. Given the Indians' declarations of positive memories of France, it is possible that Onoraguete's grandson embraced a startled Bougainville, drew him close to his breast, respectfully called him "Uncle," and then engaged in a modified ceremony of arrival complete with gifts and speeches. In diplomacy and even when at war with the French in North America, Iroquoians (among many Native peoples) routinely referred to French interlocutors as "fathers" or "brothers." To call someone "Uncle" carried more weight. In this matrilineal society, where clan affiliation rested on mothers, a sister's brother (an uncle) constituted an important male figure in a child's life, and the term connoted genuine rather than fictive or diplomatic kinship. That Rayneval heard enough about what was discussed at Bougainville's meeting with the Iroquois to be able to record it suggests that the dialogue aboard the *Languedoc* took place in French, mediated by the Iroquois who had served as translator in Philadelphia. It is tempting to consider whether this bilingual individual was Onoraguete's grandson and whether his conscious use of French at this moment attested further, at least in Iroquois minds, to the bonds of affection and obligation they were demonstrating between themselves and Bougainville.

Bougainville's reaction, like the other details of this exchange, remains lost to us, but his discussion with the Kahnawakes thrust previously private elements of his Canadian war experience into the open, at least briefly. Rayneval wrote that Onoraguete's grandson claimed to be related to Bougainville by marriage as well as by adoption, as the son of Bougainville's wife's sister. If Bougainville had any fears about what this familiarity with indigenous Americans could do to his career or his reputation, he gave no sign of it. But Louis-Antoine's silence on this topic in his own memoirs speaks volumes about the French officer's attitude toward his North American experiences as opposed to that shown by his Kahnawake kin. His relationship with Indians had ended in 1760. Whatever memories and concerns this meeting and its implications for his reputation stirred up, the famed explorer's period of anxiety was brief; Canada failed to return to French hands in 1783 at the conclusion of the Treaty of Paris, thus voiding any fears Bougainville might have had of his Indian connections returning to light in a meaningful way. The October 28, 1778, meeting disappeared in France for the most part from memory and historical record.

In North America, however, the complex narrative continued its meandering path. Monsieur de Meux, secretary in the French embassy to Brazil, was traveling from Pittsburgh to Saint Louis as part of a tour of the western United States in 1811, when he heard word of a Shawnee war chief who claimed a connection to the famous navigator, Louis-Antoine de Bougainville. "I met at Cape Girardeau on the river of the same name," Meux wrote, "an Indian chief named Lorimier, who claimed to be the son of Monsieur de Bougainville, which was confirmed by most respectable actors." Lorimier had "acquired such a reputation for oratory and courage" by the time that Meux met him "that he became one of their leading war chiefs." In every facet of his description, Meux confirmed that this "son of Bougainville in an Indian chief" lived up to his own French idealization of a *métis*. Though "a man of modest height, with no education," Lorimier nevertheless was "endowed with great courage, great vitality, splendid ingenuity, and able to develop and realize many things...." Meux spent no time speculating about Lorimier's mother but did reinforce Lorimier's Native blood by noting that the chief had "married thrice to women of mixed Shawnee descent." At some point, Meux's chance meeting in the North American borderlands passed into the hands of one of Bougainville's sons. There Meux's record joined the explorer's papers under the heading "*Notice sur mon frère sauvage*" [Note on my Indian Brother].[6]

Distanced by a new century, an ocean, and the landmass of the United States republic, the tale of Lorimier, unlike the immediate encounter between Bougainville and his Kahnawake nephew in 1778, added color and flair to the Bougainville family history as seen from France. Though Meux traveled through the region in 1811, his story did not appear until 1838: no flesh and blood Indians had arrived in France in the intervening years claiming familiarity and kinship, giving Bougainville's family little to fear in terms of actual inheritance implications stemming from such a connection. Rather, the Bougainvilles, like Meux before them, clearly interpreted the splendor and leadership reputed to Lorimier, their *frère sauvage*, as evidence of the excellence of Louis-Antoine's blood. Lorimier's existence proved to his French brothers their father's virility and the importance of their family's imprint on the great world by word, deed, and now kinship. The "discovery" of an exotic sibling did not turn into an effort to make contact with Lorimier, and the story drifted back into the silence of the archive. And here a typical French Atlantic story would end.

Yet the fleeting encounter in Boston harbor and the Lorimier mystery demands that we engage with the French legacy in North America as more than an anecdote. By the time that d'Estaing and his fleet arrived in North America, France had reevaluated its Atlantic imperial experiences and utilized them to create new possibilities for its empire. The veteran marines and New France itself had been put aside, made obsolete, largely to be erased from the national memory, while the experience of the Seven Years' War was used to propel new and different imperial models forward, however unsuccessfully. The 1778 travels of the Iroquois through the battle lines of the American Revolution to reconnect with their French kin and the public reappearance of the Bougainville name in the Missouri region a generation after that both serve as reminders that processes of reevaluating the experience of New France were also taking place in North America independently of the metropole.

Native peoples nurtured their own memories of the Seven Years' War and engaged with the war's legacy in the same way that they interpreted, rejected, or adapted to changing environments, politics, and people—on their own terms. Their perspectives, as well as the continued presence of former French colonists, open up a different way of looking at French engagements in North America after the Seven Years' War.[7] Native peoples did more than act as cameo players in a larger, Eurocentric narrative about the struggle for North America. Nor did France live exclusively in the hearts and minds of the *habitants* who were left behind, as the Kahnawake delegation's testing of French arrivals in 1778 demonstrates. The French empire had intimately engaged with indigenous peoples. This relationship invites ending not on a desiccated page in the Bibliothèque nationale but in

North America. And so we return to Lorimier, lost son of Bougainville and scion of France's North American empire in order to reconfigure spatial and temporal boundaries to reflect the Indian-French prism and resolve the legacy of French North America and France's Seven Years' War in a Native perspective.

After the fall of New France in North America in 1760, the Bougainville family history unfolded rather differently and in a manner that would have surprised Louis-Antoine's three surviving French sons. Pierre-Louis de Lorimier (*dit* Louis Lorimier) without question represented all of the qualities of a "noble savage" in French eyes: adept at survival in a wild environment, courageous, intelligent, and formidable as an adversary in war and trade. But Lorimier was not their brother. And he may not even have been of Indian descent.[8] Born as the second son of marine captain Claude-Nicolas-Guillaume Lorimier in 1748, in the final years of French North America, Louis transitioned into frontier trade after New France's 1760 transfer to British control. Family connections prepared him well for a borderlands career. Louis's father, like many marine peers, spent years conducting business alongside military operations while commanding at Oswegatchie/La Présentation (a fact that led to Captain Lorimier *père*'s indictment in absentia during *l'affaire du Canada*). In 1769 Louis took over the family's interests at "Laramie Station" (a corruption of Lorimier Station), a trading post located between the Maumee and Great Miami Rivers; the young entrepreneur operated on soil cleared by another French Canadian marine, Charles de Langlade, in the 1752 raid on Pickawillany.[9] For the next sixty-four years, Lorimier made himself indispensible to no less than three empires and one imperially inclined republic (France, Britain, Spain, and the United States), crossing swords with Anglo-American folk heroes Daniel Boone and George Rogers Clark, only later to welcome others, like Meriwether Lewis. Lorimier settled in Cape Girardeau in 1793 while still a Spanish agent and encouraged displaced Indians from Ohio and Indiana to relocate to his region, with about one thousand Shawnees alone eventually settling in Missouri, securing a grant for the land from Spanish governor general Francisco Luis Héctor de Carondelet in October 1795. Lorimier's success in creating a thriving, mixed community and gaining access to Shawnee trade networks at Saline Creek (on Big Shawnee Spring) was due to the family connections brought by his marriage in 1788 to a Shawnee-French woman.[10]

In the world of the borderlands, where reputation meant everything, Lorimier established himself as a man of valor and intelligence. Don Manuel de Salcedo praised Lorimier in 1803 as much for his military skills as for his finesse in Indian affairs. Meriwether Lewis, traveling west that same year and staying as a guest in Lorimier's house, described him much as Meux would eight years later, as "a man about 5 F 8 I high." Lewis's more detailed physical account of the man's "dark skin hair and [e]yes" helps to explain Meux's unquestioning acceptance of Lorimier's Indian and French parentage, reinforced further by the American's "remarkable suit of hair; ... he informed me that it was on[c]e so long that it touched the ground when he stood errect [sic]—nor was it much less remarkable for its thickness; this I could readily believe from its present appearance." Admiring his host, who was still vigorous at "about 60 years of age, and yet scarcely a grey hair in his head," Lewis also had an opportunity to meet Lorimier's spouse at the Cape Girardeau homestead. Madame Lorimier was a "Shawnee woman, from her complexion is half blooded only," who garnered favorable approval from Lewis as "a very desent [sic] woman and if we may judge from her present appearance has been very handsome when young." It stood to reason that this businesswoman in the borderlands dressed "after the Shawnee manner with a stroud leggings and mackinsons, differing however from them in her linin [sic] which seemed to be drawn beneath her girdle of her stroud." And yet, attesting to the hybrid nature of her community, Lorimier's wife also sported "a short Jacket with long sleeves over her linin with long sleeves more in the stile [sic] of the French Canadian women." Lewis said nothing of a Bougainville connection, preferring to lavish his diary's attentions on one of the "remarkably handsome" Lorimier daughters, who was "much the most descent [sic] looking female I hae [sic] seen since I left the settlement in Kentuckey [sic]."[11]

Despite these clarifications about Lorimier's background, Louis Lorimier did not entirely fabricate his connections to Bougainville. When his "very handsome" Shawnee wife died in 1808, the grieving widower erected a marble gravestone in her honor, inscribing it to "Charlotte P. B. Lorimier." A simple slip between the French words for son (*fils*) and son-in-law (*beau-fils*) likely turned Lorimier into Bougainville's child when the true heir was in fact the individual described on her eternal resting place as the "noblest matron of the Shawnee race": Charlotte Pemanpieh Bougainville Lorimier. She entered the world at the very height of the war for French North America, in 1758, the result of a sexual interaction—liaison, common-law marriage (*marriage à la façon du pays*), or other arrangement—between Louis-Antoine and a Shawnee refugee woman living among the Kahnawakes and known perhaps as Ceuta or as Pemanich Pemanpieh. Only two European archival fragments reference this relationship. The first, a letter from Bougainville to his *chère maman*, Madame de Séchelles, and dated September 22, 1759, states, "Adieu, my dear mother, your child has broken off the relationship which displeased you and caused you to complain."[12] Nearly two decades later in Boston Harbor, the second mention appears in the gossip of Rayneval, describing the meeting between Bougainville and his self-proclaimed Kahnawake nephew.

If Charlotte Bougainville's mother indeed was a Shawnee refugee and adoptee at Kahnawake, she would likely have followed Mohawk matrilineal custom, where men bound themselves to their wives' clan and house. The Kahnawake nephew of Bougainville could have been a blood relative or bound by fictive kinship, but either way, the bond would have been given weight. Lorimier's embrace of indigenous trade, life, and marriage partners (as well as French ideas of *race*) easily included a perspective that enabled him to see himself as being as much a part of his wife's heritage and clan as of his own. His own brother married a Mohawk woman, a family connection that reinforced Louis's perspective. After a lifetime in the borderlands and an entangled history with Native communities, Lorimier may well have told Meux that he was Bougainville's son—or at least part of the Bougainville family—because he had no trouble believing himself to be so by virtue of association with his wife's kinship networks.

Charlotte's gravestone provides further clues to the intertwining of French and Indian traditions:

> She lived the noblest matron of the Shawnee race
> And native dignity covered her as does this slab.
> She chose nature as her guide and virtue,
> and with nature as her leader spontaneously followed good,
> As the olive, the pride of the grove, without the planter's care
> Yearly brings its fruits to perfection.[13]

Olives and olive groves, common to the Mediterranean rather than the Mississippi region, seem an unusual choice to reference natural perfection as opposed to a native American plant. The inscription rather spoke to European customs, adorning heroes with olive and juniper (symbols of peace and virtue). But in this intermingling of Native and French conventions lay a reality that would have been less palatable to the Bougainville family. Louis-Antoine had had sons in France, but in this North American inversion, here lay a Shawnee-French daughter, a merchant and negotiator rather than the heroic "noble savage" warrior carrying on the family legacy. Furthermore, she had achieved renown and love through her own actions and the world of Native and transimperial connections she built, not through reliance on a disappeared father's interest.

Where French custom was supposed to dominate, Charlotte and Louis stand as evidence of the continued reappropriation and reinterpretation of New France for indigenous ends. One example lies in Louis Lorimier's silence on his Bougainville connection while hosting Meriwether Lewis in 1803, a strange absence considering that Lewis and William Clark would surely have been familiar with the earlier, and celebrated, explorer's work. Faced with the prospect of having to negotiate a future in a new North American empire after the Louisiana Purchase, neither Charlotte nor Lorimier sought to foreground their old roots in New France or British Canada. William Clark was the younger brother of George Rogers Clark—Lorimier's old antagonist in the days when Lorimier, as a French subject-turned-British-agent sought to block North American expansion to the west and enlisted Shawnee aid in these endeavors.[14] In a seamless continuation of French marine pragmatism Lorimier, and his wife in particular, suppressed some information until the lie of the land became clearer and until they had secured ties (through Lewis, notably, not Clark) to the new regime.

Governor Salcedo's respect for Lorimier derived from this man's ability to engage the Shawnee community connected to Cape Girardeau in Spanish interests. But Lorimier's access rested heavily on his personal ties to Charlotte. Shawnees maintained connections over great distances, and individuals drew on one another as sources of strength while moving between far-flung communities. Shawnee men and women, especially individuals of both indigenous and European descent, showed a willingness to adapt and adopt European customs to add ever more strategies for survival.[15] Regardless of whether Bougainville recognized or acknowledged his child, Charlotte's death monument, erected by her husband, ascribes to her a quality greatly sought by the French and Canadian officers who clashed with her maternal world. "Native dignity" is her innate quality, along with a nobility rooted in the olive-growing soil of classical antiquity, transforming her into a Roman matron in North America. The celebration of Charlotte's choice to follow "nature as her leader" did not necessarily place her in opposition to the morals and gender roles laid out by Roman Catholicism or thrust her into the orbit of "Indian as part of natural history." Her expensive burial marker was one of the foundational interments in the Cape Girardeau cemetery and demonstrated that Charlotte had some connection to the church, an institution that long endured in the Illinois Country and Louisiana Territory and was manipulated by Native peoples to suit their own interests.[16] Charlotte commanded a leader's affection and respect, marking her autonomy from European princes and attesting to her remarkable character. This was a woman who lived life on her own terms, not those set out for her by the

EPILOGUE

Montcalms or Bougainvilles of the world, and commanded the affection and respect of their French Canadian peers. Charlotte Bougainville very consciously lived in a Native America as well, as her decisions were guided first and foremost by the realities of Indian Country rather than those of European empires.

These slight, almost teasing references in the archives raise ever more questions. What did it mean for Shawnees in Missouri to claim the Bougainville name in 1811? Or for Kahnawakes and other Iroquois to publicly assert a relationship between a long-absent French officer and Onoraguete's grandson in Boston harbor in 1778? The numerous accounts that trace Bougainville's life and mention the meetings in Boston Harbor or in Missouri do not consider how these interactions change the narrative of France's Seven Years' War. In many ways, it matters little that the identity and name of Bougainville's Indian lover or spouse remains unknown and that the entire affair is alleged, for we have Bougainville's own writings, which indicate both close contact with indigenous communities and a calculated presentation of his past. When Bougainville wrote of his Iroquoian adoption in his memoirs from both the 1750s and the 1770s, he made sure to do so in an unflattering manner, such as his comment "I am an ugly Iroquois," which punctuated a letter he sent to Madame de Séchelles in 1757. Comparing that with a mocking note in one of Montcalm's letters describing Bougainville "visiting his Tortoise brothers to give them tobacco and vermillion" suggests he had perhaps more sustained relationships.[17] Desiring to settle the past, Bougainville did note his renewed North American acquaintance in 1778, but not in terms of "my cousin" or "my nephew" or even "my adopted kin" but rather of "the grandson of Onoraguete," thereby placing a barrier between him and the past, between him and his bonds of kinship.

How the war is named, whether it should be the politically incorrect "French and Indian War" or the blandly nondescript "Seven Years' War," continues to obfuscate and limit the possibilities seen by historians in this period. Tracing individuals' lives and thinking carefully about their experiences beyond the boundaries of the war years help to uncover more complete narratives that in turn frame new questions for familiar material. From the perspective of this nameless Kahnawake nephew, Charlotte P. B. Lorimier, or Louis Lorimier it mattered little that Bougainville no longer resided in a French-claimed Saint Lawrence valley. To these people, it was the idea of Bougainville and of the French imperial past and the space these legacies opened to them in the borderlands that was valuable.

The experiences of Charlotte Lorimier and of the Kahnawake delegation visiting the French fleet in 1778 demonstrate that Native peoples of North America and Canadians or French metropolitans reacted differently to the formal closure of the French empire. Near the end of Charlotte's life in 1808, she and Louis Lorimier lived and operated in a thriving Native space and borderland used by indigenous peoples and French North Americans. Colonists of French descent and their increasingly creole descendants also resolved to live in a world of their own creation and memory and in this showed a similarity to Charlotte's Shawnee community. Most the *habitants* of *la Louisiane, le Canada*, the *pays d'en haut*, and the *pays des Illinois* who had not left in 1760 with the military removal tended to remain in the old strongholds of New France, nurturing and extending their interconnected lives as if still part of a French empire.[18] For many indigenous communities in particular, what mattered most was guaranteeing the continuance of the informal trading networks formerly championed by France. The reach of formal French power in the interior of North America had been tenuous at best. It had always depended on prestige among Native peoples to sustain itself. In fact, New France in the North American interior had always been more a "shadow empire" that reflected metropolitan and Laurentian aspirations rather than any reality of control or territorial claims on the ground.[19] Thus, until 1803 and even afterward, these individuals' daily reality continued much as it had before the great global war ended New France. It had not uprooted the *habitants* or the old colony's Native allies, neighbors, and enemies, nor had it changed their habits of interaction. The imperial borderlands of contested space even remained, though now they lay between British and Spanish and then later U.S. claims. But as Native peoples moved in a space whose contours were still only roughed out by European imperial contests, the center spaces remained firmly indigenous. The metropole, from this perspective, continued to be experienced as a peripheral place, as it always had been.

To use the name "Bougainville" for Charlotte or for Louis Lorimier may have been an indicator of their intimate connections to the gift-giving, Atlantic trade networks that comprised New Orleans, Detroit, Montreal, and Quebec. Rather than identifying the military prowess or great intellect of a French officer, the name "Bougainville" might have functioned as a kind of currency in the very borderlands transactions between Native peoples and Euro-Americans that French officers—and Bougainville himself—had abhorred and rejected between 1756 and 1760. Although Onoraguete's grandson did claim a positive relationship of kinship, the other Iroquois' desire "to see for themselves whether we were truly French" may have spoken to the distinctions Iroquoians and Algonquians had learned to make during the war years—that, in their eyes, not all French acted the way the French father should. Their voyage was a test to determine exactly which French had returned.

The circulation of "Bougainville" in the borderlands relied heavily on a Native America continuing to find a utility in the expectations and obligations evoked by this officer's name and his former position. Whether he served as living proof of the expeditionary squadron's "Frenchness" twenty years after New France's demise or his name signified access to gifts and to imperial trade, Bougainville's continued relevance in North America rested on the French officer's symbolic absorption into indigenous networks. Thus, Bougainville's postwar encounters with indigenous America and the French Atlantic world mirrored the ordeal undergone by Memeskia (La Demoiselle/Old Briton), the Miami chief who had rebelled against New France in the late 1740s. In 1752 it was Memeskia who was physically and ritually absorbed back into the French network of trading alliances by Native Americans through cannibalism. By 1811 Bougainville (through his name) was, too. And so, the Indian alliances formed by New France to ensure its survival accomplished that because, after 1760, there was manifestly a New France still in existence, albeit the interpretation of the New France that had always suited indigenous peoples, not European defenders of empire. Charlotte Lorimier, for one, left a gravestone and numerous descendants to imbed her interpretation of this history into the fabric of old empires and new republics and in doing so maintained a space of particular possibilities and negotiation.[20] This resilient New France took the form of well-traveled trading networks between indigenous and French Canadian actors whose reserve cultural currency consisted of their common ties to the old French North American empire.

The marine veterans in metropolitan France, ironically, were less successful legatees of New France than the Native peoples whom they had been charged to either convert and change or force into a world allegedly defined along French lines. French policy guaranteed the disappearance of their branch of military service, the disgrace of some, and the lack of new opportunities for most others. These policies—and the new colonial ventures and explorations that followed—ensured the loss of New France from general memory in the metropole. No markers today exist in Tours, now in the *département* d'Indre-et-Loire, in tribute to the establishment of the community of veterans and their families there after their evacuation from French North America.

NOTES

Introduction. Glory beyond the Water

Epigraph: Homer, *The Iliad*, trans. Robert Fagles (New York: Penguin, Viking, 1996), 77.

1. Entry for June 18, 1756, *Journal du Marquis de Montcalm durant ses campagnes en Canada de 1756 à 1759*, in *Collection des manuscrits du maréchal de Lévis*, published under the direction of Abbé H. R. Casgrain (Quebec: Imprimerie de L.-J. Demers et Frère, 1895), vol. 7, 71.

2. Montreal, June 16, 1756, Montcalm to the Marquise de Saint Véran (his mother), *Report for the Public Archives of Canada* (Ottawa: F. Acland, 1929), 44–45; Montreal, June 12, 1756, Montcalm to Minister of War d'Argenson, Service Historique de la Défense, Armée de Terre, Paris, France, A^{1}3417, f. 137/3.

3. Entry for June 28, 1756, *Le journal du chevalier de Lévis*, édition originale et augmentée, ed. Roger Léger (Montreal: Les Éditions Michel Brûlé, 2008), 39.

4. On the wide variety of modes of Native diplomacy and decision making in eighteenth-century North America, see Francis Jennings et al., eds., *The History and Culture of Iroquois Diplomacy: An Interdisciplinary Guide to the Treaties of the Six Nations and Their League* (Syracuse, NY: Syracuse University Press, 1985); Richard White, *The Middle Ground: Indians, Empires, and Republics in the Great Lakes Region, 1608–1815* (Cambridge: Cambridge University Press, 1991); Daniel K. Richter and James H. Merrell, eds., *Beyond the Covenant Chain: The Iroquois and Their Neighbors in North America* (University Park: Pennsylvania State University Press, 2003); James Merrell, *Into the American Woods: Negotiators on the Pennsylvania Frontier* (New York: W. W. Norton, 2000); Michael Witgen, *An Infinity of Nations: How the Native Nations Shaped Early North America* (Philadelphia: University of Pennsylvania Press, 2012); Jon Parmenter, "L'arbre de Paix: Eighteenth-Century Franco-Iroquois Relations," *French Colonial History* 4 (2003): 63–80; Timothy J. Shannon, *Indians and Colonists at the Crossroads of Empire: The Albany Congress of 1754* (Ithaca, NY: Cornell University Press, 2000). Other studies of ritual diplomatic exchanges include Tracy Neal Leavelle, *The Catholic Calumet: Colonial Conversions in French and Indian North America* (Philadelphia: University of Pennsylvania Press, 2012); Gilles Havard, *Empires et métissages: Indiens et Français dans le pays d'en haut, 1660–1715* (Paris: Septentrion, 2003) and *The Great Peace of Montreal of 1701: French-Native Diplomacy in the Seventeenth Century*, trans. Phyllis Aronoff and Howard Scott (Montreal: Septentrion, 2001); and Brett Rushforth, "A Little Flesh We Offer You: The Origins of Indian Slavery in New France," *William and Mary Quarterly* (hereafter cited as *WMQ*), 3rd ser., 60,

no. 4 (October 2003): 777–808. For French importance in fostering Native American diplomatic spaces, see, for instance, Gregory Evans Dowd, "The French King Wakes Up in Detroit: 'Pontiac's War' in Rumor and History," *Ethnohistory* 37, no. 3 (Summer 1990): 254–78, and Catherine Desbarats, "The Cost of Early Canada's Native Alliances: Reality and Scarcity's Rhetoric," *WMQ* 52, no. 4 (October 1995): 609–30.

5. For examples of profound changes wrought by the Seven Years' War on France alone, see James C. Riley, *The Seven Years' War and the Old Regime in France: The Economic and Financial Toll* (Princeton, NJ: Princeton University Press, 1986), and Rafe Blaufarb, "Noble Privilege and Absolutist State Building: French Military Administration after the Seven Years' War," *French Historical Studies* 24, no. 2 (2001): 223–46.

6. The use of the standard French term, *la guerre de Sept Ans*, in France and Canada demonstrates how the Americas are seen as an integral part of the European conflict. See, for instance, *La guerre de Sept Ans en Nouvelle France*, ed. Laurent Vessyières (Quebec: Septentrion, 2012), and Gordon M. Sayre, *Les Sauvages Américains: Representations of Native Americans in French and English Colonial Literature* (Chapel Hill: University of North Carolina Press, 1997), 254.

7. The inability to access indigenous names is not simply the result of current historians' neglect. For some Native peoples, the desire to exert control over their own history, so long the target of colonial appropriation, is reflected in an unwillingness to make these terms public. In addition, historians have begun attending to Native perspectives on the conflict regardless of terminology. See, for instance, Ian K. Steele, "The Shawnee Origins of Their Seven Years' War," *Ethnohistory* 53, no. 4 (2006): 657–87.

8. Louise Dechêne, *Le peuple, l'état et la guerre au Canada sous le régime français* (Montreal: Les Éditions du Boréal, 2008), 287; François Furstenberg, "The Significance of the Trans-Appalachian Frontier in Atlantic History," *Journal of American History* (hereafter cited as *JAH*) 89, no. 2 (March 2003): 647–77. A broader timeline is also found in *The Sixty Years' War for the Great Lakes*, ed. David Curtis Skaggs and Larry L. Nelson (East Lansing: Michigan State University Press, 2001).

9. Pekka Hämäläinen and Samuel Truett, "On Borderlands," *JAH* 98, no. 2 (September 2011): 357.

10. Ibid., 358–59. Scholars critical of borderlands studies point out that the idea of "borderlands" is troubling in its negation of Native residence and agency—the Great Lakes, for instance, were not borderlands but the "center of the earth" for the Anishinaabeg. (On the Great Lakes as the "center of the earth," see Eric Hemenway, historian and repatriation representative, Little Traverse Bay Bands of Odawa Indians, "Presenting Pontiac at Michilimackinac: Interpreting the Anglo-Indian War of 1763," paper presented at "The War Called Pontiac's, 1763–2013" [conference, McNeil Center for Early American Studies, Philadelphia, Apr. 4, 2013]). My work maintains that the invitation to reconsider turning points derived from borderlands studies is not in opposition to this important alternate view.

11. Susan Juster, "What's 'Sacred' about Violence in Early America? Killing, and Dying, in the Name of God in the New World," *Common-Place* 6, no. 1 (October 2005), http://www.common-place.org/vol-06/no-01/juster/.

12. For some considerations of the restorative power of war and its expression of Native sovereignty in Iroquoian and Algonquian cultures, see Francis Jennings, *The*

Invasion of America: Indians, Colonialism, and the Cant of Conquest (Chapel Hill: University of North Carolina Press, 1975); Daniel K. Richter, "War and Culture: The Iroquois Experience," *WMQ* 40, no. 4 (October 1983): 528–59; Merrell, *Into the American Woods*; White, *Middle Ground*; Witgen, *Infinity of Nations*; Gregory Evans Dowd, *War under Heaven: Pontiac, the Indian Nations, and the British Empire* (Baltimore: Johns Hopkins University Press, 2001); Colin Calloway, *The Abenaki* (New York: Chelsea House, 1989); Wayne Lee, "Peace Chiefs and Blood Revenge: Patterns of Restraint in Native American Warfare, 1500–1800," *Journal of Military History* 71 (2007): 701–41.

13. On questions of a French Atlantic empire, see James Pritchard, *In Search of Empire: The French in the Americas, 1670–1730* (Cambridge: Cambridge University Press, 2004); Sylvia Marzagalli, "The French Atlantic," *Itinerario* 23, no. 2 (1999): 70–83; and Kenneth J. Banks, *Chasing Empire across the Sea: Communications and the State in the French Atlantic, 1713–1763* (Montreal: McGill-Queens University Press, 2002). This field continues to expand with a work in progress on the topic by Brett Rushforth and Christopher Hodson. A novel, pan–French Atlantic perspective is offered by Brett Rushforth's exploration of the slave trade's links between New France, the *pays d'en haut*, and Martinique in *Bonds of Alliance: Indigenous & Atlantic Slaveries in New France* (Chapel Hill: University of North Carolina Press, 2012). An evaluation of a national French historiographic tradition by Cécile Vidal offers interesting reflections on the stakes of these approaches. See "The Reluctance of French Historians to Address Atlantic History," *Southern Quarterly* 43, no. 4 (Summer 2006): 153–89. Vidal's coauthored work with Gilles Havard, *Histoire de l'Amérique française* (Paris: Fayard, 2003), inaugurates the first cohesive history of French North America and shows the growing popularity of this field among scholars in both the United States and Europe. Regardless of their position on the question of an empire, all of these authors demonstrate the fruition of a vibrant field in French Atlantic history. After Havard and Vidal, studies of Acadian history have yielded the most global or North Atlantic approaches to date. See, for instance, John Mack Faragher, *A Great and Noble Scheme: The Tragic Story of the Expulsion of the French Acadians from Their American Homelands* (New York: W. W. Norton, 2006), and Christopher Hodson, *The Acadian Diaspora: An Eighteenth-Century History* (Oxford: Oxford University Press, 2012).

14. The Haitian Revolution lends itself especially well to studies of reappropriated and reinterpreted French ideology, starting with C. L. R. James's classic, *The Black Jacobins: Toussaint L'Ouverture and the Santo Domingo Revolution* (New York: Vintage, 1989). Among many fine works see also Laurent Dubois, *Avengers of the New World: The Story of the Haitian Revolution* (Cambridge, MA: Harvard University Press, 2005), and Carolyn Fick, *Making Haiti: Saint Domingue Revolution from Below* (Chattanooga: University of Tennessee Press, 1990). Newer scholarship has broadened comparative French–French Caribbean interests beyond Haiti. For studies of the ill-fated Kourou colony see Emma Rothschild, "A Horrible Tragedy in the French Atlantic," *Past and Present* 192, no. 1 (2006): 67–108, or Marion Tayart Godfroy de Bormes, *Kourou, 1763: Dernier rêve d'une Amérique française* (Paris: Flammarion, 2011). Rebecca Hartkopf Schloss's study of Martinique, *Sweet Liberty: The Final Days of Slavery in Martinique* (Philadelphia: University of Pennsylvania Press,

2009), and Miranda Spieler's work on Guyana in *Empire and Underworld: Captivity in French Guiana* (Cambridge, MA: Harvard University Press, 2012) argue for the importance of both a careful historical consideration of other French colonies and the new insights to be gained by bridging the eighteenth and nineteenth centuries. On the North American side, see Havard, *Great Peace of Montreal of 1701*, which follows the extension of metropolitan authority into the Saint Lawrence Valley and the Great Lakes by comparing North American and European diplomatic forms at the groundbreaking peace treaty between the colony of New France and the Iroquois League. Although comparative within French America as opposed to Atlantic France, Arnaud Balvay shows how much depth is gained by a broadly colonial approach within one institution (in this case, *la marine*); see his *L'epée et la plume: Amérindiens et soldats des troupes de la marine en Louisiane et au Pays d'en Haut (1683–1763)* (Quebec: Presses Universitaires Laval, 2006). Cécile Vidal's work on violence, the state, and society in colonial French Louisiana sets a new standard for demonstrating the cohesion and coherence of the French empire in the eighteenth century. For more on this see her "Private and State Violence against African Slaves in Lower Louisiana during the French Period, 1699–1769," in *New World Orders: Sanction and Authority in the Colonial Americas*, ed. John Smolenski and Thomas J. Humphreys (Philadelphia: University of Pennsylvania Press, 2006), 92–110. Also focused on Louisiana, Sophie White's investigations of dress and culture similarly take seriously norms on both sides of the Atlantic; see her *Wild Frenchmen and Frenchified Indians: Material Culture and Race in Colonial Louisiana* (Philadelphia: University of Pennsylvania Press, 2012).

15. The most complete work in the British Atlantic field is Fred Anderson's magisterial epic, *Crucible of War: The Seven Years' War and the Fate of Empire in British North America, 1754–1766* (New York: Alfred A. Knopf, 2000), and *The War That Made America: A Short History of the French and Indian War* (New York: Viking, 2005). Comparative French works have been more limited in scope, focusing on single services or Atlantic episodes. See Jonathan Dull, *The French Navy and the Seven Years' War* (Lincoln: University of Nebraska Press, 2005), or David Bell, "Jumonville's Death: War Propaganda and National Identity in Eighteenth-Century France," in *The Age of Cultural Revolutions: Britain and France, 1750–1820*, ed. Colin Jones and Dror Wahrman (Berkeley: University of California Press, 2002), 33–61.

16. Ian K. Steele's *Betrayals: Fort William Henry and the Massacre* (Oxford: Oxford University Press, 1992) constitutes the most complete and thorough account of an event of the North American Seven Years' War from the perspective of all of its actors—British, French, and Indian. Karl Jacoby's work on the 1868 Camp Grant massacre suggests new methodological approaches to writing about such overwhelming episodes of violence. See his *Shadows at Dawn: A Borderlands Massacre and the Violence of History* (New York: Penguin, 2008). Both works, importantly, trace the lingering aftereffects of these spectacular outbursts.

17. Numerous works describe the straightforward military narratives of the French Seven Years' War. Some classic treatments include Guy Frégault, *Canada: The War of Conquest* (Toronto: Oxford University Press, 1969); Colloque international d'histoire militaire, *Conflit de sociétés au Canada français pendant la guerre de Sept Ans* (Vincennes: Ministère de la Défense État-Major y Commission Française d'Histoire Militaire, 1978); and W. J. Eccles, "The Military Establishment," in *Essays*

on *New France* (Oxford: Oxford University Press, 1987), and *The Canadian Frontier: 1534–1760* (Albuquerque: University of New Mexico Press, 1983). See also Dêchene, *Le peuple, l'état, et la guerre sous le régime français*; René Chartrand, *Ticonderoga, 1758: Montcalm's Victory against All Odds* (Oxford: Osprey, 2001), and *Louisbourg, 1758: Wolfe's First Siege* (Oxford: Osprey, 2005); Stephen Brumwell, *Redcoats: The British Soldier and War in the Americas, 1755–1763* (Cambridge: Cambridge University Press, 2002); D. Peter MacLeod, *Northern Armageddon: The Battle of the Plains of Abraham* (Montreal: Douglas y McIntyre, 2010); Martin Fournier, "L'art de la guerre sous le régime français: Adaptation réciproque des Français et des Amérindiens," *Recherches amérindiennes au Québec* 32, no. 1 (2002): 3–11; Laurent Vessyières, ed., *La guerre de Sept Ans en Nouvelle France* (Quebec: Septentrion, 2012); and John Shy, "Armed Forces in Colonial North America: New Spain, New France, and Anglo-America," in *Against All Enemies: Interpretations of American Military History from Colonial Times to the Present*, ed. Kenneth J. Hagan and William R. Roberts (New York: Greenwood, 1986), 3–20. Wars in Europe and North America are well covered by John Lynn, *Battle: A History of Combat and Cultures* (Boulder, CO: Westview, 2003); Wayne Lee, *Warfare and Culture in World History* (New York: New York University Press, 2011); Wayne Lee, ed., *Empires and Indigenes: Intercultural Alliance, Imperial Expansion, and Warfare in the Early Modern World* (New York: New York University Press, 2011); Armstrong Starkey, *European and Native American Warfare, 1675–1815* (Norman: University of Oklahoma Press, 1998); and Guy Chet, *Conquering the American Wilderness: The Triumph of European Warfare in the Colonial Northeast* (Amherst: University of Massachusetts Press, 2003).

18. Among the works that have centered indigenous perspectives in this period are the following: White, *Middle Ground*; Rushforth, *Bonds of Alliance*; Michael McConnell, *A Country Between: The Upper Ohio Valley and Its Peoples, 1724–1774* (Lincoln: University of Nebraska Press, 1992); Gail MacLeitch, *Imperial Entanglements: Iroquois Change and Persistence on the Frontiers of Empire* (Philadelphia: University of Pennsylvania Press, 2010); Steele, "Shawnee Origins of Their Seven Years' War"; Jon Parmenter, "After the Mourning Wars: The Iroquois as Allies in Colonial North American Campaigns, 1676–1760," *WMQ* 64, no. 1 (January 2007): 39–76; Timothy J. Shannon, "War, Diplomacy, and Culture: The Iroquois Experience in the Seven Years' War," in *Cultures in Conflict: The Seven Years' War in North America*, ed. Warren R. Hofstra (New York: Rowman and Littlefield, 2007), 79–104; Eric Hinderaker, *The Two Hendricks: Unraveling a Mohawk Mystery* (Cambridge, MA: Harvard University Press, 2010) and "Declaring Independence: The Ohio Indians and the Seven Years' War," in *Cultures in Conflict*, 105–26; Kathleen DuVal, *The Native Ground: Indians and Colonists in the Heart of the Continent* (Philadelphia: University of Pennsylvania Press, 2006).

19. The experience of interior Indian nations can be found in McConnell, *Country Between*; Dowd, *War under Heaven*; White, *Middle Ground*; Witgen, *Infinity of Nations*; Steele, "Shawnee Origins of Their Seven Years' War" and *Betrayals*; Colin Calloway, *The Scratch of a Pen: 1763 and the Transformation of North America* (Oxford: Oxford University Press, 2006); David R. M. Beck, *Siege and Survival: History of the Menominee Indians, 1634–1856* (Lincoln: University of Nebraska Press, 2002); Jan Grabowski, "French Criminal Justice and Indians in Montreal, 1670–1760,"

Ethnohistory 63 (1996): 405–29; Jacqueline Peterson, "Many Roads to Red River: Métis Genesis in the Great Lakes Region, 1680–1815," in *The New Peoples: Being and Becoming Métis in North America*, ed. Jacqueline Peterson and Jennifer S. H. Brown (Lincoln: University of Nebraska Press, 1985), 185–93. For the experiences of the Canadian *habitants*, see Dêchene, *Le peuple, l'état, et la guerre sous le régime français*.

20. On "wild," see White, *Wild Frenchmen and Frenchified Indians*.

Chapter 1. Onontio's War, Louis XV's Peace

1. Archives nationales d'Outre Mer (hereafter cited as ANOM), Marin Personnel File, E 302, f. 12v.

2. Rising prices demanded by French merchants and a reduction of trade goods due to naval conflict in the Atlantic also primed the Indians in the Great Lakes region to be discontent with their French interlocutors and with the vanishing "middle ground." See Richard White, *The Middle Ground: Indians, Empires, and Republics in the Great Lakes Region, 1650–1815* (Cambridge: Cambridge University Press, 1991), 202, 204–6. Despite his errors in policy, La Galissonière correctly assessed the necessity to reform the fur trade and to mitigate some of the other damage he had caused in his two years as governor (ibid., 210–11).

3. Frédéric Guelton, "La guerre de Sept Ans: Le contexte français," in *La guerre de Sept Ans en Nouvelle-France*, ed. Laurent Veyssière et Bertrand Fonck (Montreal: Septentrion, 2012), 62; Robert Darnton, "An Early Information Society: News and the Media in Eighteenth-Century Paris," *American Historical Review* 105, no. 1 (February 2000): 26.

4. Louise Dechêne coins the term "sixteen-year war" to describe this period in *Le people, l'état, et la guerre au Canada sous le régime français* (Montreal: Boréal, 2008), 287.

5. Theodore K. Rabb, *The Struggle for Stability in Early Modern Europe* (Oxford: Oxford University Press, 1975), 121; Julius Ruff, *Violence in Early Modern Europe, 1500–1800* (Cambridge: Cambridge University Press, 2001), 53, 64.

6. Rabb, *Struggle for Stability*, 121–22. I am grateful to Wayne Lee for raising the importance of intention in conversation in June 2007. On Jacobites, see Geoffrey Plank, *Rebellion and Savagery: The Jacobite Uprising of 1745 and the British Empire* (Philadelphia: University of Pennsylvania Press, 2005). See also Wayne Lee, "From Gentility to Atrocity: The Continental Army's Way of War," *Army History* 62 (Winter 2006): 4–19.

7. Cases of brutality included Louis XIV's ordering of the destruction of most towns in the Palatinate in 1688 and 1689 to prevent them from becoming a base of operations against France (Ruff, *Violence in Early Modern Europe*, 56). Comparisons of Bergen-op-zoom to violence during the Thirty Years' War are in M. S. Anderson, *War and Society of the Old Regime, 1618–1789* (Avon: Leicester University Press, 1988), 194–95.

8. J. R. Hale, *War and Society in Renaissance Europe: 1450–1620* (Montreal: McGill-Queens University Press, 1998), 99. Geoffrey Parker describes the development of long-term military technology and its effects on changing cultural perceptions of war in *The Military Revolution: Military Innovation and the Rise of the West, 1500–1800* (Cambridge: Cambridge University Press, 1988).

9. John A. Lynn ties eighteenth-century military practice to three interwoven phenomena: early modern aesthetics, the "military enlightenment" (which produced academies and war texts), and international law developments that contained conflict. See Lynn, *Battle: A History of Combat and Cultures* (Boulder: Westview, 2003), 115–16. The French royal engineering school, the École du génie de Mézières, preceded the École militaire by three years. England's Royal Military College at Woolwich, in southeast London (1741), and Spain's Real Academia de los Guardias Estandartes de las Galeras (1735) predated these French institutions. Only in 1810 did Berlin receive the Prussian Kriegsakademie. In 1808 France added another academy (which remains an officers' school even today) at Saint Cyr by transforming a girls' convent school founded by Madame de Maintenon into an academy of war. Professional soldiers and aristocrats had been publishing treatises on the art of war, sieges, and artillery since the 1680s. See, for example, Sieur la Fontaine, *The Military Duties of the Officers of Cavalry* (1648); Jacques Ozanam, *The Treatise of Fortification* (1711); André Tacquet, Thomas Venn, and Francis Vere, *Military and Maritime Discipline in Three Books* (1672); Sir James Turner, *Pallas Armata* (1671); John Darker, *A Breviary of Military Discipline* (1692); Louis de Gaya, *L'art de la guerre et la manière dont on la fait à present* (1678); and Capt. J. S., *Fortification and Military Discipline* (1688).

10. Rafe Blaufarb, *The French Army, 1750–1820* (Manchester: Manchester University Press, 2002), 20–22.

11. John Childs, *Armies and Warfare in Europe, 1648–1789*, (Manchester: Manchester University Press, 1982), 22; Lynn, *Battle*, 123, 133.

12. Barbara Donagan, "Atrocity, War Crime, and Treason in the English Civil War," *American Historical Review* 99, no. 4 (October 1994): 1142.

13. Anderson, *War and Society (Old Regime)*, 190; Donagan, "Atrocity, War Crime, and Treason," 1154–55.

14. Gail Bossenga, "A Divided Nobility: Status, Markets, and the Patrimonial State in the Old Regime," in *The French Nobility in the Eighteenth Century: Reassessments and New Approaches*, ed. Jay M. Smith (College Park: Pennsylvania University State Press, 2006), 51.

15. Sevigné, quoted in Lynn, *Battle*, 140.

16. For a discussion of tensions between the *noblesse commerçante* and the *noblesse militaire*, see John Shovlin, *The Political Economy of Virtue: Luxury, Patriotism, and the Origins of the French Revolution* (Ithaca, NY: Cornell University Press, 2006), 62–65. On traditional criteria for nobility, see Ellery Schalk, *From Valor to Pedigree: Ideas of Nobility in France in the Sixteenth and Seventeenth Centuries* (Princeton, NJ: Princeton University Press, 1986).

17. Blaufarb, *French Army*, 14–15.

18. Lynn, *Battle*, 124.

19. Élisabeth Bégon, *Lettres au cher fils: Correspondance d'Elisabeth Bégon avec son gendre (1748–1753)*, préface de Nicole Deschamps (Montreal: Éditions Hurtubise HMH, Ltée, 1972), 154, letter/entry of Jan. 20, 1750. (Unless otherwise noted, all translations are my own). Olive Patricia Dickason has suggested that Madame Bégon's in-laws stated fact—that Élisabeth may have been an Iroquois girl adopted by the Morandières in Montreal. See Dickason, "From 'One Nation' in the Northeast to 'New Nation' in the Northwest: A Look at the Emergence of the Métis," in *The*

New Peoples: Being and Becoming Métis in North America, ed. Jacqueline Peterson and Jennifer S. H. Brown (Minneapolis: Minnesota Historical Society Press, 2001), 28n54.

20. Bégon, *Lettres au cher fils*, 168, letter/entry of May 3, 1750. For the term "middling nobles" see Shovlin, *Political Economy of Virtue*, 42.

21. Robert Nye, *Masculinity and Male Codes of Honor in Modern France* (Oxford: Oxford University Press, 1993), 20–21. See also Kristen Neuschel on violence and honor as "the building blocks of political life" in *Word of Honor: Interpreting Noble Culture in Sixteenth-Century France* (Ithaca, NY: Cornell University Press, 1989), 18.

22. Bossenga, "Divided Nobility," 52. On categories of nobility, see Elie Haddad, "The Question of the Imprescriptibility of Nobility in Early Modern France," in *Contested Spaces of Nobility in Early Modern Europe*, ed. Matthew P. Romaniello and Charles Lipp (London: Ashgate, 2011), 148.

23. Sophie White, "A Baser Commerce: Retailing, Class, and Gender in French Colonial New Orleans," *William and Mary Quarterly* (hereafter cited as *WMQ*) 63, no. 3 (July 2006): 521–22.

24. Nye, *Masculinity*, 28. Jonathan Dewald notes that the manners and practices of the court increasingly appeared in military camp life after 1660 and that one was as likely to learn dancing as marksmanship despite the increased mortality and scale of war of the eighteenth century. See Dewald, *The Aristocratic Experience and the Origins of Modern Culture* (Berkeley: University of California Press, 1993), 58, 206.

25. While initial critiques of decadence appeared during the War of Austrian Succession, the French public's concern with royal debauchery and its corruption of glories in war dated back to the 1730s. See Tabetha Leigh Ewing, "Rumor and Foreign Politics in Louis XV's Paris during the War of Austrian Succession" (PhD diss., Princeton University, 2005), 199. The reevaluation of luxury and a widespread participation in the culture of excess, as John Shovlin notes, led to fears that the social order would be unhinged by "immoderate consumption." See Shovlin, "The Cultural Politics of Luxury in Eighteenth-Century France," *French Historical Studies* 23, no. 4 (2000): 587. On the royal body and its symbolism see Thomas E. Kaiser, "Louis le Bien-Aimé and the Rhetoric of the Royal Body," in *From the Royal to the Republican Body: Incorporating the Political in Seventeenth- and Eighteenth-Century France*, ed. Sara Melzer and Kathryn Norberg (Berkeley: University of California Press, 1998), 131–61.

26. On sisters and their role at court, see Michel Antoine, *Louis XV* (Paris: Hachette, 1989), 484–92. On the "affair of the three sisters" see Darnton, "Early Information Society," 14.

27. On nobility being governed by custom, see Haddad, "Question of the Imprescriptability of Nobility in Early Modern France," 150, 163, 166.

28. Robert Darnton, *The Forbidden Best-Sellers of Pre-Revolutionary France* (New York: W. W. Norton, 1996), 235.

29. On the sacred, see Darnton, "Early Information Society," 15–16. Poisson, formerly madame d'Étiolles, was invested as Marquise de Pompadour in June 1745 to make her liaison with the king possible according to protocol. Pompadour both came from and married into financier families based in Paris, the center of the ultrawealthy nonnobility. On the metaphor of the royal bed as connector between finance and the court, see Shovlin, *Political Economy of Virtue*, 31.

30. Ewing, "Rumor and Foreign Politics," 404–7.

31. The salience of religious difference, particularly with the rise of conservative Catholic reformers (Jansenists) in the 1740s and 1750s, cannot be understated. Saxe's Protestantism limited even his honors in death. A contemporary record noted the following (entry for Nov. 30, 1750): "King and subjects mourn equally . . . the King, unable to accord [Saxe] the funerary honors given to M de Turenne [maréchal de France under Louis XIV] due to the general's religion, ordered the royal treasury to [instead] shoulder the cost of his transport. . . ." See *Journal historique, ou fastes du règne de Louis XV, surnommé Le Bien-Aimé*, première partie (Paris: Chez Prault; Chez Saillant, 1766), 70–71.

32. Ewing, "Rumor and Foreign Politics," 460–65.

33. *A New and General Biographical Dictionary: containing an Historical and Critical Account of the Lives and Writings of the Most Eminent Persons in Every Nation* . . . (London: G. G. and J. Robinson et. al., 1798), vol. 6, 245–46.

34. Rafe Blaufarb, "Noble Privilege and Absolutist State Building: French Military Administration after the Seven Years' War," *French Historical Studies* 24, no. 2 (Spring 2001): 228. On the army as refuge, see Lee Kennett, *The French Armies in the Seven Years' War* (Durham, NC: Duke University Press, 1967), 56. The *noblesse de cour* (such as the Broglie, Rohan, Ségur, and Noailles families) dominated the military hierarchy.

35. Kennett, *French Armies in the Seven Years' War*, 60.

36. Luc Lépine, "Les stratégies militaires françaises et britanniques lors de la guerre de Sept Ans en Nouvelle-France," in *La guerre de Sept Ans en Nouvelle-France*, 136–37; Arnaud Balvay, *L'épée et la plume: Amérindiens et soldats des troupes de la marine en Louisiane et au Pays d'en Haut (1683–1763)* (Quebec: Les Presses de l'Université Laval, 2006), 38; Jay Cassel, "The *Troupes de la Marine* in Canada, 1683–1760: Men and Materiel" (PhD diss., University of Toronto, 1987), 46–51; James B. Collins, *The State in Early Modern France*, 2nd ed. (Cambridge: Cambridge University Press, 2009), 200; *Les ministres de la Guerre, 1570–1792*, ed. Thierry Sarmant (Paris: Éditions Belin, 2007), 139; Jonathan Dull, *The French Navy and the Seven Years' War* (Lincoln: University of Nebraska Press, 2005), 9.

37. John Shy, "Armed Forces in Colonial North America: New Spain, New France, and Anglo-America," in *Against All Enemies: Interpretations of American Military History from Colonial Times to the Present*, ed. Kenneth J. Hagan and William R. Roberts (New York: Greenwood, 1986), 6.

38. James Pritchard, *In Search of Empire: The French in the Americas, 1670–1730* (Cambridge: Cambridge University Press, 2004), 82. Land *en roture* was offered to peasants, and larger tracts of seigneur-owned land were available to increase the settlements and greater agricultural output while providing for the colonists' subsistence. See W. J. Eccles, *Essays on New France* (Oxford: Oxford University Press, 1987), 40, 136. On nobles in Canada, see White, "Baser Commerce," 521n7, and Lorraine Gadoury, *La noblesse de Nouvelle France: Familles et alliances* (Quebec: Hurtubise, 1992).

39. Francis Parkman papers (hereafter cited as Parkman), Massachusetts Historical Society, 33 XT: Quebec, Jan. 24, 1667, Projet de Réglement fait par Mrs. De Tracy et Talon, pour la justice et la distribution des terres du Canada du Janvier 24, 1667, 168–70.

40. An example of French re-creation of a hierarchical society was in the provision of French wives for Canadians. Common female orphans, *filles du roy*, were potential brides for average men; dowered ladies of good convent breeding, *demoiselles*, were socially acceptable wives for military officers whom the Crown intended to form New France's upper caste. See Parkman 61: Quebec, Oct. 27, 1667, Talon to Colbert, 177.

41. Eccles, *Essays on New France*, 56; Thierry Berthet, *Seigneurs et colons de Nouvelle France: L'émergence d'une société distincte au XVIIIème siècle* (Cachan: Éditions de l'École Normale Supérieure, 1992), 77; François-Joseph Ruggiu, "Extraction, Wealth, and Industry: The Idea of Noblesse and of Gentility in the English and French Atlantics (17th–18th Centuries)," *History of European Ideas* 34 (2008): 454.

42. Eccles, "The Social, Economic and Political Importance of the Military Establishment in New France," in *Essays on New France*, 121.

43. Balvay, *L'épée et la plume*, 41.

44. Evan Haefeli and Kevin Sweeney, *Captors and Captives: The 1704 Raid on Deerfield* (Amherst: University of Massachusetts Press, 2004), 50–54.

45. ANOM E290, f.5–7; Andrew Rodger, "Le Moyne de Longueuil, Paul Joseph," in *Dictionary of Canadian Biography Online* (hereafter cited as *DCBO*), http://www.biographi.ca/en/bio/le_moyne_de_longueuil_paul_joseph_4E.html, accessed Mar. 27, 2007.

46. ANOM E243, f.6–7v, Ensign La Corne St. Luc.

47. ANOM E243, Montreal, Sept. 29, 1747, f.1–2, Capt. Louis La Corne to La Galissonière requesting a *croix de Saint Louis* for service rendered on Grand Pré in Nova Scotia. See C. J. Russ, "La Corne, Louis," *DCBO*, http://www.biographi.ca/en/bio/la_corne_louis_de_3E.html, accessed Jul. 31, 2013.

48. ANOM E243, Quebec, Oct. 9, 1749, letter to La Corne announcing receipt of the *croix de Saint Louis* (award issued May 1749). Portraits of individuals wearing the decoration can be seen in the painting titled *Marquis de Boishébert—Charles Deschamps de Boishébert et de Raffetot*, McCord Museum of Canadian History in Quebec, and in the portrait titled *Pierre de Rigaud de Vaudreuil, Marquis de Vaudreuil*, Library and Archives of Canada in Ottawa.

49. Balvay, *L'épée et la plume*, 252–23; "A Court of Enquiry held at Detroit, April 6th, 1765" (appended to John Campbell's letter to Sir Thomas Gage, Detroit, Apr. 28, 1765), Thomas Gage papers, American Series, William L. Clements Library, The University of Michigan, vol. 35, Apr. 23–May 11, 1765, f.2.

50. Not all of the soldiers excelled in the borderlands. Mactigue de Macarty, commander in the Illinois region in 1751, for instance, mismanaged the diplomacy placed in his care initially, failing to provide the resources necessary to sustain alliance chiefs in his region. White, *Middle Ground*, 199, 202 (on time and experience), 206 (on Macarty), 215. In 1753 a Seneca council recalled a visit by Niverville.

51. "Personnel File," ANOM E 302, f.12v; Donald Chaput, "Marin de La Malgue, Joseph," *DCBO*, http://www.biographi.ca/en/bio/marin_de_la_malgue_joseph_4E.html, accessed Jul. 31, 2013.

52. ANOM E322, f.5–5v.

53. White, *Middle Ground*, 210–11.

54. *On the Eve of Conquest: The Chevalier de Raymond's Critique of New France in 1754*, ed. and trans. Joseph L. Peyser (East Lansing: Michigan State University Press, 1997), 28; Versailles, May 31, 1754, Rouillé to Duquesne, ANOM B 99: 199–200; Parkman 14: Versailles, Apr. 9, 1753, Rouillé to Duquesne and Bigot, 286–87. For an excellent study of cost complaints in New France and colonial responses, see Catherine Desbarats, "The Cost of Early Canada's Native Alliances: Reality and Scarcity's Rhetoric," *WMQ* 52, no. 4 (October 1995): 609–30.

55. Cassel, *"Troupes de la Marine* in Canada," 39; Kennet, *French Armies in the Seven Years' War*, 89.

56. Ewing, "Rumor and Politics," 407. Ewing argues that *gazettes, on-dits,* and manuscript news (*nouvelles à la main*) circulated extensively through Paris, providing insight into the formation of contemporary public opinion.

57. On Raymond's biography and career, see Peyser, *On the Eve of Conquest*, 1–8.

58. Ibid., 6–8.

59. On Raymond, see ibid., 77, 99. Céloron de Blainville famously buried lead plaques—stating Louis XV's claim to American soil in their Latin inscriptions—along the Ohio River in 1749; Daniel Liénard de Beaujeu would lead the attack on Gen. Edward Braddock in 1755 and be one of the few French casualties of that battle, and the Chevalier de Ramezay would, in 1759, cede Quebec to the English after panicking in the French retreat from the Plains of Abraham.

60. Blaufarb, "French Military Administration," 227.

61. *Mémoire du maréchal de Noailles sur les colonies d'Amérique*, July 1749, annexed to an Aug. 1, 1749, letter of Maréchal de Noailles to Louis XV, in *Correspondance de Louis XV et du Maréchal de Noailles publié par ordre de son excellence le maréchal comte Ramdon* (Paris: P. Dupont, 1865), vol. 2, 290–93.

62. *Correspondance*, Compiègne, Aug. 1, 1749, Maréchal de Noailles to Louis XV, 286. In 1754 the Duc de Noailles personally invested in a French Atlantic world by ceding the islet of Massacre in Saint Domingue to his son, who retained the property until 1778. See ANOM E322.

63. National Archives of Canada (NAC), Roland Michel Barrin, Marquis de La Galissonière, *Mémoire sur les colonies de la France dans l'Amérique septentrionale*, folio 255v, 270. http://collectionscanada.gc.ca/pam_archives/index.php?fuseaction=genitem .displayEcopies&lang=eng&rec_nbr=3072107&rec_nbr_list=3072108,3068780 ,3072107,3055946,4133598&title=%5BMémoire+de+La+Galissonière +%28et+Silhouette%29+sur+les+%26%2334%3Bcolonies+de+ . . . %5D .+&ecopy=e000869595&back_url=(), accessed Mar. 27, 2007.

La Galissonière's work is notable for its use of the term "empire" to describe both British holdings and thinking of the same category applying to New France (ibid., 255). See also *Memoir of La Galissonière* at "France in America," Library of Congress, http://memory.loc.gov/cgi-bin/ampage?collId=gcfr&fileName=0007 /gcfr0007.db&recNum=204&itemLink=r?intldl/ascfr:@field(DOCID +@lit(gcfr0007_0183))%230007187&linkText=1, 119, accessed Mar. 26, 2007.

64. NAC, *Mémoire sur les colonies*, 251v.

65. Ibid., 254–54v.

66. Blaufarb, *French Army*, 15.

67. Jay M. Smith, *Nobility Reimagined: The Patriotic Nation in Eighteenth-Century France* (Ithaca, NY: Cornell University Press, 2005), and Shovlin, *Political Economy of Virtue*, provide excellent overviews of "nobility" and inequality debates.

68. Bossenga, "Divided Nobility," 51–54.

69. Mita Choudhury, "Women, Gender, and the Image of the Eighteenth-Century Aristocracy," in Smith, *French Nobility in the Eighteenth Century*, 182, 185–86.

70. Blaufarb, "French Military Administration," 228–29; Kennett, *French Armies in the Seven Years' War*, 56.

Chapter 2. Interpreting Landscapes of Violence

1. Eric Hinderaker, *Elusive Empires: Constructing Colonialism in the Ohio Valley, 1673–1800* (Cambridge: Cambridge University Press, 1999), 41–42. Accounts of how mercantile shortages sent the Illinois and Great Lakes regions into revolt are in Richard White, *The Middle Ground: Indians, Empires, and Republics in the Great Lakes Region, 1650–1815* (Cambridge: Cambridge University Press, 1991), 199–200; Fred Anderson, *Crucible of War: The Seven Years' War and the Fate of Empire in British North America, 1754–1766* (New York: Knopf, 2000), 25.

2. Marly, May 4, 1749, Minister to Jonquière, in *Collections of the State Historical Society of Wisconsin* (hereafter cited as *WHS*), ed. Reuben Gold Thwaites (Madison: Published by the Society, 1908), vol. 18, 20. Rouillé's letters responded to reports from Jonquière's predecessor, the Marquis de La Galissonière, regarding Indian attacks on French posts at Detroit and Scioto in the Ohio Country and throughout the Illinois region. Michael N. McConnell, *A Country Between: The Upper Ohio Valley and Its People, 1724–1774* (Lincoln: University of Nebraska Press, 1992), 83–88.

3. Céloron de Blainville, *Journal de la campagne que moi, Céloron, Chevalier de l'ordre Royal et Militaire de Saint-Louis, Capitaine Commandant d'un détachement envoyé dans la Belle-Rivière par les orders de M. le Marquis de La Galissonière, Commandant Général de toute la Nouvelle France et Pays de Louisiane*, Francis Parkman papers (hereafter cited as Parkman), Massachusetts Historical Society, 15: 54–55; White, *Middle Ground*, 208; Hinderaker, *Elusive Empires*, 44; (on geographies broadly) Tracy Neal Leavelle, *The Catholic Calumet: Colonial Conversions in French and Indian North America* (Philadelphia: University of Pennsylvania Press, 2011), chap. 3.

4. Mémoire du Roy pour servir d'instruction au Sieur Marquis de Duquesne, Marly, May 15, 1752, Parkman 14: *New France VI Canada, 1751–1754*, 151, 160, 166. The forts included Presque Isle, on the southern shore of Lake Erie; Machault, at Venango (a Delaware town); Le Boeuf; and, most famously, Duquesne, at the confluence of the Ohio and Monongahela Rivers.

5. On "colonial" and Indian woods, see James Merrell, *Into the American Woods: Negotiators on the Pennsylvania Frontier* (New York: W. W. Norton, 1999), 141.

6. Mémoire du Roy, May 15, 1752, Parkman 14: 143; Mémoire du Roy and Minister to Duquesne, May 15, 1752, Parkman 14: 141–43; Naval Minister to Duquesne, June 3, 1753, Parkman 14: 322–23. On bureaucratic connections and appeasement, see Catherine Desbarats, "The Cost of Early Canada's Native Alliances: Reality and Scarcity's Rhetoric," *William and Mary Quarterly* (hereafter cited as *WMQ*) 52, no. 4 (October 1995), especially 615.

7. Merrell, *Into the American Woods*, 145; Leavelle, *The Catholic Calumet*, 48; Julianna Barr, "Geographies of Power: Mapping Indian Borders in the "Borderlands" of the Early Southwest," *WMQ* 68, no. 1 (January 2011): 5–46. For a broad interpretation of geography, power, and meaning, see Christine DeLucia, "The Memory Frontier: Uncommon Pursuits of Past and Place in the Northeast after King Philip's War," *Journal of American History* 98, no. 4 (March 2012): 975–97.

8. McConnell, *Country Between*, 86–88, 99–100.

9. Ian K. Steele, *Warpaths: Invasions of North America* (Oxford: Oxford University Press, 1994), 183; White, *Middle Ground*, 231; Longueuil to Rouillé (which notes twenty-six killed), Aug. 18, 1752, *Collections of the Illinois State Historical Library* (hereafter cited as *IHC*) (Springfield: Trustees of the Illinois State Historical Library, 1940), vol. 29, 652–53; Macarty to Vaudreuil (noting thirty-two killed and six prisoners taken and adding that Macarty's Indian informants said two Piankshaws, one Wea, one Delaware, two Iroquois, and two Shawnees were among the dead), Sept. 2, 1752, *IHC*, vol. 29, 680–81; De Ligneris to Vaudreuil, Oct. 3, 1752, *IHC*, vol. 29, 733. The numbers de Ligneris presents are quite different, five to six dead, and he stated, "this blow . . . not of great account" but "what was better was their killing three English and taking six prisoners after seizing their merchandise." De Ligneris makes no mention of Memeskia; letter from Robert Callendar to the Pennsylvania governor, Aug. 30, 1752, in William Trent, *Journal of Captain William Trent from Logstown to Pickawillany A.D. 1752*, ed. Alfred T. Goodman (Cincinnati: Robert Clarke for William Dodge, 1871), 47. Trent's account, from eyewitness Thomas Burney, lists "one white man" and fourteen Indians killed, along with five "white men" taken prisoner. On the physical importance of Pickawillany, see Anderson, *Crucible of War*, 29.

10. Trent, *Journal of Captain William Trent*, 49, 87–88, 89.

11. White, *Middle Ground*, 231. White also shows that the conflict centered on the actions not of "old alliance chiefs" but of the *métis* and those deemed "rebels" by the French for challenging France. Almost every recent history of the Ohio frontier contains some account of Pickawillany; see, for instance, Hinderaker, *Elusive Empires*, 44–45; McConnell, *Country Between*, 98–99; Anderson, *Crucible of War*, 29; William M. Fowler, *Empires at War: The French and Indian War and the Struggle for North America, 1754–1763* (New York: Walker, 2005), 28.

12. Minister to Duquesne, Versailles, June 16, 1752; Secretary of Louis XV to Baron de Longueuil, Compiègne, July 9, 1752; Duquesne to Minister, Quebec, Oct. 25, 1752; Minister to Duquesne and Intendant Bigot, Versailles, Apr. 9, 1753, Parkman 14 (Dépêches et Ordres du Roy): 189, 198, 259, 289. The official reports by Governor Duquesne concerning "La Demoiselle" and his followers' annihilation received replies addressing decreases in the expense of Indian diplomacy and the court's delight that the frontier had been "pacified."

Though cannibalism was unusually brutal, the capture of English (and Indian) civilians for sale in New France as slaves and the acceptance of ritual torture of indigenous captives (and English enemies) by France's Indian allies was not. On the indigenous slave trade, see Brett Rushforth, "A Little Flesh We Offer You: The Origins of Indian Slavery in New France," *WMQ* 60, no. 4 (October 2003): 777–808; for examples of English slavery in New France, see William H. Foster, *The*

Captor's Narrative: Catholic Women and Their Puritan Men on the Early American Frontier (Ithaca, NY: Cornell University Press, 2003), and John Demos, *The Unreedemed Captive: A Family Story from Early America* (New York: Vintage, 1995).

13. Duquesne to the Naval Minister, Quebec, Oct. 25, 1752, Parkman 14: 259.

14. Duquesne to Minister Rouillé, Oct. 28, 1753, Parkman 14: 357.

15. Duquesne to Minister Machault, Oct. 10, 1754, *IHC*, vol. 29, 904.

16. The half commission and early status as a cadet (rank equivalent to senior soldier) most likely reflected Langlade's primary assignment in Indian service. It is unclear when Langlade was commissioned as an ensign, a post traditionally filled by the ranks of Canada's elite—and denoting Langlade's expectation of becoming an officer: *ancien régime* Ministère de la Marine archives date his commission as full ensign to 1755 (ensign *en second* in 1754), yet the records in Mackinac, Michigan (formerly his home post of Michilimackinac), suggest an earlier military commission date. On military status at Mackinac, see *WHS*, vol. 18, 131. On the 1755 commission, see Archives nationales d'Outre Mer (hereafter cited as ANOM), "Langlade," $D^{2c}61$, *Canada: Officiers civils et militaires, 1736–1758*, 166. On marine rank, see Andrew Gallup and Donald F. Shaffer, *La Marine: The French Colonial Soldier in Canada, 1745–1761* (Bowie, MD: Heritage Books, 1992), 240.

17. Michael A. McDonnell, "Worlds of Warfare: Indians, French, and Métis and the Sixty Years' War for Empire" (paper presented at the Conference on Warfare and Society in Colonial North America and the Caribbean, Knoxville, TN, Oct. 7–8, 2006). McDonnell argues that Charles Langlade was "groomed from birth" for a role as an intercultural mediator facilitating Indian, rather than French, interests.

18. On Langlade and his prominent Ottawa uncle, see David A. Armour, "Nissowaquet," and Paul Trap, "Mouet de Langlade, Charles-Michel," in *Dictionary of Canadian Biography Online* (hereafter cited as *DCBO*), http://www.biographi.ca/EN/ShowBio.asp?BioId=36202&query=nissowaquet, accessed Mar. 27, 2007.

19. In August 1754 Langlade wed Charlotte Enbroise Bourassa, a merchant's daughter in a ceremony witnessed by both families and marine officer friends. Prior to this, Langlade had had a relationship and a child with an Ottawa woman. The actual and future earnings of the Bourassa-Langlade alliance is alluded to in the complex property inheritance clause of the marriage contract. Langlade had great wealth in slaves; in November 1754, shortly after his own wedding, he oversaw the marriage of his servant, Marie. See *WHS*, vol. 28, 135–39; for Langlade's and Marie's marriages, 428. For Langlade's Ottawa union and child, see Parkman 14: 259 (Duquesne to the Minister, Quebec, Oct. 25, 1752); *WHS*, vol. 28, 415.

20. Interim Canadian governor Longueuil to Minister Rouillé, explaining the reluctance of the nations of the *pays d'en haut* to campaign until late spring and the inability of the French to force them to do so, Apr. 21, 1752, *Documents Relative to the Colonial History of the State of New York* (hereafter cited as *NYDC*), ed. and trans. E. B. O'Callaghan (Albany: Weed Parsons, 1858), X: 246; McConnell, *Country Between*, 100. Although the Naval Ministry did outline imperial goals to the leadership of New France, the ministry and the French Crown did not dictate the exact forms that influence seeking should take.

21. Langlade's reputation dovetails with a rapid career ascent—second ensign in 1754, ensign in 1755, and captain by 1759. On Canadian attention to racial purity

see Guillaume Aubert, "The Blood of France: Race and Purity in the French Atlantic World," *WMQ* 3, no. 61 (July 2004), 439–78.

22. St. Pierre to Virginia governor Dinwiddie, Dec. 16, 1753, in *Papiers Contrecoeur et autres documents*, ed. Fernand Grenier (Quebec: Laval, 1952), 84.

23. Philippe Chabert de Joncaire's background, including his Seneca name, Nitachinon, and his Seneca family appear in Sieur Louis de Courville, *Mémoires sur le Canada depuis 1749 jusqu'à 1760: en trois parties; avec cartes et plans lithographiés* (Quebec: Imprimerie de T. Cary, 1838), 18–19, and Malcom MacLeod, "Chabert de Joncaire, Philippe-Thomas," in *DCBO*, http://www.biographi.ca/009004-119.01-e.php?&id_nbr=1246&&PHPSESSID=ychzfqkvzape, accessed Mar. 28, 2011. Seneca wives bolstered French- and Englishmen's influence within communities. See William B. Hart, "Black 'Go Betweens' and the Mutability of 'Race': Status and Identity on New York's Pre-Revolutionary Frontier," in *Contact Points: American Frontiers from the Mohawk Valley to the Mississippi, 1750–1830*, ed. Andrew Cayton and Fredericka Teute (Chapel Hill: University of North Carolina Press, 1997), 88–114.

24. Michael Witgen, *An Infinity of Nations: How the Native New World Shaped Early North America* (Philadelphia: University of Pennsylvania Press, 2011), 218, 313.

25. On absorption see Anderson, *Crucible of War*, 751n12; White, *Middle Ground*, 231. Robert Rogers noted that the ability to speak Ottawa-Ojibwa (Central Algonquian) and one Iroquoian language would enable an individual to trade with "upwards of 100 tribes of Indians." See Robert Rogers, *A Concise Account of North America* (London: J. Millan, 1765), 245–46. In Algonquian, the word "Odawa," which inspired the French term "Ouatouas" and the English "Ottawa," referenced a position, not a nationality. Ottawas (and the Ojibwas and Potowatomis) referred to themselves as Anishinaabe, "the people."

26. Quotation from Rogers, *Concise History of North America*, 227. On "tree writing" as a means of recording battles and laying claim to territory, see Garrick Mallery, *Picture-Writing of the American Indians* (New York: Dover, 1972), vol. 2, 554, 558. Pictography as Indian literacy is discussed in Birgit Brander Rasmussen, *Queequeg's Coffin: Indigenous Literacies and Early American Literature* (Durham, NC: Duke University Press, 2012), chap. 3. Merrell, *Into the American Woods*, 145, 148; Ottawas and Ojibwas taunted the Miamis at Pickawillany by telling them that, in their surrender of British captives, the Miamis made *themselves* responsible to the British for the traders' fates. See White, *Middle Ground*, 233–34.

27. McConnell points out the Ohioan Indians' distress at the composition of Marin's army and their land "overrun with Caughnawagas, Ottawas, Potowatomis, and Ojibwas—including, perhaps, warriors who had destroyed Pickawillany" (*Country Between*, 103). Marin's mobility rested on the skills and personal connections of his chief translator, Philippe de Chabert, who was the son and husband of Seneca women and used this relationship to advantage in this Iroquoian community. On Iroquoian decisions, see ibid., 106. In 1754 Ohioans' fears flared up when a Delaware man and woman were murdered by French-allied Indians. July 7, 1754, "Journal de Chaussegros de Léry," in *Rapport de L'Archiviste de la Province de Québec pour 1927–1928* (hereafter cited as *RAPQ* plus applicable date) (Quebec: L.-Amable Proulx, 1928), 374.

28. "Journal de Léry," June 20, 1754, *RAPQ 1927–1928*, 367. Léry repeated the story of Jumonville again on July 7, when Contrecoeur forwarded the deposition of

English deserter Denis Kaninguen (likely a Catholic Iroquois partisan of Tanaghrisson) (ibid., 373). This famous quote is notable for its use of the familiar "tu" rather than "vous" (the more respectful address to a "father"). Tanaghrisson had used "tu" in councils with the French in 1752 and 1753, indicating his disdain for and perhaps claiming the authority of the French (Marin in 1753 also referred to Tanaghrisson as "tu"). See *Papiers Contrecoeur*, 48–58.

29. "Journal . . . de Villiers," in *Papiers Contrecoeur*, 196, 202.

30. Ibid.

31. Anderson, *Crucible of War*, 64–65; Fred Anderson, *The War That Made America: A Short History of the French and Indian War* (New York: Viking, 2005), 51–52.

32. David Bell, *The Cult of the Nation in France: Inventing Nationalism, 1680–1800* (Cambridge, MA: Harvard University Press, 2001), 80, 88, 103. Bell notes that the war propaganda around Jumonville defined this conflict as one of "irreconcilable nations" rather than using the older model of dynastic or religious rivalries. Accounts of Jumonville appeared in the widely circulated *L'Observateur hollandois* and *Le Moniteur françois*. The attention to Jumonville importantly reinserts the Americas into French historical narratives, and the use of the marine by a variety of newspapers serving different political factions suggested a universal affront to French honor. Popular poetry, like Antoine Léonard Thomas, *Jumonville. Poëme.* par M. Thomas, P. E. L'U. D. P. (n.p.: 1759), also discussed Jumonville and Villiers, suggesting the widespread political utility of a martyr.

33. "Journal de la Campagne de M. de Villiers au Fort Nécessité," in *Papiers Contrecoeur*, 196.

34. *Mémoire contenant le précis des faits, avec leur pièces justificatives, pour servir de réponse aux observations envoyées par les ministres d'Angleterre, dans les cours de l'Europe* (Paris: L'Imprimerie Royale, 1756); "Journal de la Campagne de M. de Villiers," *Papiers Contrecoeurs*, 197–99.

35. "Journal de Campagne," *Papiers Contrecoeur*, 201; Duquesne to the Minister, Oct. 12, 1754, regarding Villiers restraining the "fury" of his Indians, Parkman 14: 459. Duquesne requested the *croix de Saint Louis*, a coveted military honor, for both Contrecoeur (commander of Fort Duquesne) and Villiers on the basis of "brilliant service . . . that all soldiers can hardly believe in a land that only knows surprise war." He went on to lavish praise on Villiers's self-restraint, a critical element in holding back the Canadians and Indians; otherwise, "not a sole Englishman would have escaped their blows."

36. "Journal de Campagne," in *Papiers Contrecoeur*, 201; emphasis added.

37. Anderson, *War That Made America*, 52.

38. When the Shamokin resident Mushemeelin killed English trader Jack Armstrong in 1744 over debts, the Delawares of the town took this affair very seriously because they recognized the right of Jack's brother, Alexander, to seek revenge on the individuals who had caused him grief. See Merrell, *Into the American Woods*, 52. On Iroquoian rites of revenge see Daniel K. Richter, "War and Culture: The Iroquois Experience," *WMQ* 40, no. 4 (October 1983): 528–59.

39. *Journal de Coulon de Villiers*, MS Can 9, Houghton Library, Harvard University, f.1, 2, 6v–7. Contrecoeur's statement does not appear in either the *Précis des faits*, published in Europe, or in the account in the Quebec archives. The *Papiers*

Contrecoeur fused these Paris and Quebec editions, enabling the reader to follow the editorial process. The Harvard manuscript appears to be the original journal, complete with its manuscript map.

40. Jon Parmenter suggests that Ohio Iroquois withdrew from aiding Washington at Fort Necessity in order to avoid bloodshed with their own northern kin and that they visited the Laurentians in the French camp and allowed them to take four Virginians back to Kahnawake (their home at Sault-Saint-Louis, near Montreal) despite the terms of Washington's capitulation disallowing this. Individual actions that threatened the overall Iroquois League could be punished through violence. See "After the Mourning Wars: The Iroquois as Allies in Colonial North American Campaigns, 1676–1760," *WMQ* 64, no. 1 (January 2007): 63–66.

41. Robert Callendar, quoted in Anderson, *Crucible of War*, 65; emphasis in the original.

42. Anderson, *Crucible of War*, 94–95. Braddock adopted certain colonial conventions as well, such as bounties for indigenous scalps. See "Halkett's Orderly Book" (June 26 entry), in Charles P. Hamilton, ed., *Braddock's Defeat: The Journal of Captain Robert Cholmley's Batman, the Journal of a British Officer, Halkett's Orderly Book* (Norman: University of Oklahoma Press, 1959), 133.

43. *Relation de ce qui s'est passé cette année en Canada, 1755* (Paris: Bureau d'Addresse aux Galeries du Louvre, 1755), 2–4. The account also described the discovery of Braddock's strategy, detailing the British government's four-pronged assault plan on French American holdings.

44. Contrecoeur to Vaudreuil, July 14, 1755, Parkman 15: 221–22; Anderson, *Crucible of War*, 97, 99, 103.

45. Vaudreuil to the Minister, Montreal, Aug. 5, 1755, Parkman 15: 234; Anderson, *Crucible of War*, 97, 104.

46. Entry for July 9, 1755, "The Journal of a British Officer," in *Braddock's Defeat*, 50–52. Private French letters also indicated disorder. Contrecoeur to Vaudreuil, July 14, 1755, forwarded by Intendant Bigot to the minister on Aug. 6, 1755, Parkman 15: 221; Journal entry for July 14, 1755, "Journal of Captain Robert Cholmley's Batman," in *Braddock's Defeat*, 32.

47. Jill Lepore notes instances of "uncontrolled" behavior during King Philip's War, in which Wampanoags specifically targeted familiar domestic sites such as houses or graves to destroy an English sense of control over their environment, their bodies and afterlife, or the war itself. She points out also that the English responded in kind. See Lepore, *The Name of War: King Philip's War and the Origins of American Identity* (New York: Knopf, 1998), particularly chap. 4. In the Seven Years' War, with sweeping North American battlegrounds and multinational belligerents, it would be difficult to state that these excesses were so specific and conscious.

48. *Relations de ce qui s'est passé* (1755), 5–6.

49. Bigot to the Minister, Quebec, Oct. 4, 1755, Parkman 15: 245.

50. The "amateurish," hasty scalping of Hendrick's body, Ian Steele notes, disturbed the relations between English-allied and French-allied Mohawks. See Steele, *Betrayals: Fort William Henry and the Massacre* (Oxford: Oxford University Press, 1990), 53–54. The Kahnawake women, armed with bayonets, had been left to defend the baggage train; Hendrick had been repeatedly warned before the ambush to withdraw in

order to avoid injury. For more on this see Parmenter, "After the Mourning Wars," 66; regarding Mohawk women being those who killed Hendrick, assumed by the small size of the scalplock, and on the distress and grief of Hendrick's son, Paulus, see Eric Hinderaker, *The Two Hendricks: Unraveling a Mohawk Mystery* (Cambridge, MA: Harvard University Press, 2010), 261, 266.

51. Bigot wrote to the minister that Dieskau expected the Canadians and Indians to behave like regular troops, without knowing that neither group would fight out in the open, suggesting that Dieskau had yet to acclimate to war cultures in North America. See Parkman 15: 244, 252–53.

52. Anderson, *Crucible of War*, 106.

53. A major innovation of the 1670s' Franco-Dutch Wars was Louis XIV's combination of partisan war with standard war (*la petite guerre* with *la grande guerre*). See George Satterfield, *Princes, Posts, and Partisans: The Army of Louis XIV and Partisan Warfare in the Netherlands (1673–1678)* (Leiden: Brill, 2003), 179–80, 193, 201. Military treatises such as Turpin de Crissé, *Essaie sur l'art de la guerre*, 2 vols. (1754); Hector de Grandmaison, *La Petite Guerre* (1756); and Capitaine de Jeney, *Le partisan ou l'art de faire la petite guerre* (1759), show the rise of irregular combat in the eighteenth century. On *la petite guerre* in Europe and its role in shaping mentalités among army elites, see Sandrine Picaud-Monnerat, *La petite guerre au XVIIIe siècle* (Paris: Economica, 2010).

54. *Relations diverses sur la bataille du Malangueulé gagné le 9 juillet, 1755, par les François sous M. de Beaujeu, Commandant du Fort du Quesne sur les Anglois sous M. Braddock, Général en Chef des troupes Angloises*, comp. John Marie Shea (New York: Cramoisy, 1860), 19.

55. Parkman 15: Vaudreuil to the Minister, Montreal, Aug. 5, 1755, 235.

56. A similar case is made for Pennsylvania negotiators. See Merrell, *Into the American Woods*, 149.

57. Entry for July 6, 1755, "The Journal of a British Officer," in *Braddock's Defeat*, 47; Steele, *Betrayals*, 49, 53–54.

58. Hinderaker, *Two Hendricks*, 186. In 1747 French-allied Menominees claimed to have killed Hendrick (a French target), arguing that the especially distinctive white hair of the scalp taken proved it was the man. This example suggests that Hendrick was highly recognizable and thus known to his assailants in multiple ways on the day of the "Bloody Morning Scout."

59. The pro-British Mohawk leader Gingengo led a failed expedition in 1748 against the Kahnawake settlement, resulting in his beheading and the placing of his body by the defenders of that community to be found in the snow. Jon Parmenter argues that Hendrick, like Gingengo, suffered the consequence of placing individual interest above those of the Iroquois as a whole. See Parmenter, "After the Mourning Wars," 62, 66.

60. Courville, *Mémoires sur le Canada depuis 1749 jusqu'à 1760*, 72; "Relation de la prise de Fort Bull, in Journal d'une campagne au Canada à bord de la sauvage (Mars–Juillet 1756) par Louis-Guillaume de Parscau du Plessix, Enseigne de Vaisseau," in *RAPQ 1928–1929* (Rédempti Paradis, 1929), 218–19; *Journal de ce qui s'est passé au Canada depuis le mois d'Octobre 1755 jusqu'au mois de Juin 1756*, in Parkman 15: 290–91.

61. Bigot to the Minister, Apr. 12, 1756, ANOM F^{3}14: 238.

62. "Relation de la prise de Fort Bull," *RAPQ 1928–1929*, 219.

63. Both British and French colonial régimes ran afoul of the Iroquois Confederacy when they erected installations without permission in Iroquoia. In 1756 the confederacy failed to warn British Fort Oswego of an impending threat from New France, and the garrison lost to Montcalm's army. Three years later Niagara surrendered to William Johnson, again through Iroquois "inaction."

64. "Journal de Campagne," *Papiers Contrecoeurs*, 197–99; entry for June 25, 1755, "Journal of a British Officer," in *Braddock's Defeat*, 45.

65. Entry for June 26, 1755, "Journal of a British Officer," in *Braddocks' Defeat*, 45. English captain Orme also notes similar "tree-taunts" in his own journal: "They had stripped and painted some trees, upon which they and the French had written many threats and bravados with all kinds of scurrilous language."

66. "A Court of Enquiry held at Detroit, April 6th, 1765" (appended to John Campbell's letter to Sir Thomas Gage, Detroit, Apr. 28, 1765), Thomas Gage papers, American Series, William L. Clements Library, The University of Michigan, vol. 35, Apr. 23–May 11, 1765, f.1v–2.

67. Laurent Nerich, "Le système de défense de la Nouvelle-France face à la Guerre de la Conquête," in *La guerre de Sept Ans en Nouvelle-France*, ed. Laurent Veyssière et Bertrand Fonck (Montreal: Septentrion, 2012), 280.

68. Bigot to the Minister, Quebec, Oct. 4, 1755, Parkman 15: 245.

69. White, *Middle Ground*, 241.

70. McConnell, *Country Between*, 119; Anderson, *Crucible of War*, 95.

71. Abstracts of Vaudreuil's letters to the Ministry of Marine between Feb. 2 and 8, 1756, *NYDC*, X: 408.

72. Native peoples needed to negotiate the changing boundaries of a serious imperial war involving regulars for the first time, and, as Gregory Evans Dowd has shown, it is unsurprising that it was at this same moment that Indians began to contest and define what being "Indian" meant. See Dowd, *A Spirited Resistance: The North American Indian Struggle for Unity, 1745–1815* (Baltimore: Johns Hopkins University Press, 1992).

Chapter 3. Culture Wars in the Woods

1. W. J. Eccles, "Rigaud de Vaudreuil de Cavagnial, Pierre de, Marquis de Vaudreuil," in *Dictionary of Canadian Biography Online*,
http://www.biographi.ca/en/bio/rigaud_de_vaudreuil_de_cavagnial_pierre_de_4E.html, accessed Jul. 31, 2013.

2. Lee Kennett, *The French Armies and the Seven Years' War* (Durham: Duke University Press, 1967), 56, 65.

3. Francis Parkman papers (hereafter cited as Parkman), Massachusetts Historical Society, 18: *New France X Canada, 1756–1758*: Montreal, June 8, 1756, Vaudreuil to Naval Minister Machault, 7–8; Parkman 16: *New France VIII, Canada 1756–1759*: Vaudreuil to Machault; Montreal, June 12, 1756, Vaudreuil to Machault, 16, 17. See also Montreal, June 12, 1756, Montcalm to Minister of War d'Argenson, Service Historique de la Défense, Armée de Terre (hereafter cited as SHD), Paris, France, A^{1}3417: Versailles, Mar. 11, 1756, "De par le Roy; d'Argenson" (orders for assignment).

4. Entry for June 3, 1756, *Journal du Marquis de Montcalm durant ses campagnes en Canada de 1756 à 1759*, in *Collection des manuscrits du maréchal de Lévis*, published under the direction of Abbé H. R. Casgrain (Quebec: Imprimerie de L.-J. Demers et Frère, 1895), vol. 7, 69.

5. Montreal, June 16, 1756, Montcalm to the Marquise de Saint Véran (his mother), *Report of the Public Archives of Canada for the Year 1929* (hereafter cited as *RPAC*) (Ottawa: F. A. Acland, 1929), 44. The documents in this volume are available in English translation, with no accompanying original French text and no translator given.

6. Machault d'Arnouville was comptroller general of finances before moving to the French navy in 1754. See Michel Antoine, ed., *Le gouvernement et l'administration sous Louis XV: Dictionnaire biographique* (Paris: Éditions du Centre National de la Recherche Scientifique, 1978), 174. See also Parkman 18: Versailles, Jan. 17, 1756, Machault to Vaudreuil (coded letter), warning of potential English attempts on Canada in the upcoming year (1); Versailles, Jan. 17, 1756, Machault to Vaudreuil and Bigot noting supplies and troops being sent and suggesting vigilance (3–4); Versailles, Feb. 20, 1756, Machault to Vaudreuil, informing him that Loudon was replacing Braddock and naming Montcalm as Dieskau's replacement (7–8).

7. Parkman 18: Versailles, Feb. 20, 1756, Machault to Vaudreuil, 4–6; Andrew Gallup and Donald F. Shaffer, *La Marine: The French Colonial Soldier in Canada, 1745–1761* (Bowie, MD: Heritage Books, 1992), 221.

8. Parkman 18: Feb. 20, 1756, Machault to Vaudreuil, 4–6.

9. Ibid., Versailles, Mar. 14, 1756, Machault to Montcalm, 13–14.

10. Ibid., Versailles, Mar. 15, 1756, Machault to Vaudreuil and Montcalm, 13–14.

11. James B. Collins, *The State in Early Modern France*, 2nd ed. (Cambridge: Cambridge University Press, 2009), 200; Thierry Sarmant, ed., *Les ministres de la Guerre, 1570–1792* (Paris: Éditions Belin, 2007), 139; Jonathan Dull, *The French Navy and the Seven Years' War* (Lincoln: University of Nebraska Press, 2005), 9.

12. Antoine, *Le gouvernement et l'administration sous Louis XV*, 250. On bureaucratic rivalry see SHD A^{1}3417, no. 71, Versailles, Mar. 15, 1756—Garde des Sceaux/Naval Minister Machault to Commissary General Doreil, noting distinctions in duties being outlined for army officers going to New France in contrast with those mandated for the "officiers de la colonie." On Naval Ministry clerks, see Jay Cassel, "The *Troupes de la Marine* in Canada, 1683–1760" (PhD diss., University of Toronto, 1987), 37–38. Cassel points out that these individuals undertook an extraordinarily heavy workload. On comparative finance, see Kennett, *French Armies in the Seven Years' War*, 89–90.

13. Parkman 16: June 16, 1756, Vaudreuil to Machault, 3; Parkman 19: *New France XI, Canada, 1756–1759*: June 19, 1756, letter from Montcalm to Minister of the Army Argenson, 83.

14. The expectations of Native American hairiness referred to European myths and traditions of forest-dwelling "naturals" or "wild men" who were initially compared to indigenous populations for sharing similar habitats and characteristics. On ideas of wild men, see Olive Patricia Dickason, *The Myth of the Savage and the Beginnings of French Colonialism in the Americas* (Edmonton: University of Calgary Press, 1984), 64–68. See also Karen Ordahl Kupperman, *Settling with the Indians: The Meet-*

ing of English and Indian Cultures in America, 1580–1640 (New York: Rowman and Littlefield, 1980), and Karen Ordahl Kupperman, ed., *America in European Consciousness, 1493–1750* (Chapel Hill: University of North Carolina Press, 1995).

15. Montreal, June 16, 1756, Montcalm to the Marquise de Saint Véran, RPAC, 44. Montcalm had also stated in a March letter to his mother that he had read Charlevoix while he was still in France. Lyons, Mar. 8, 1756, Montcalm to the Marquise de Saint Véran, RPAC, 35.

16. Brett Rushforth, *Bonds of Alliance: Indigenous and Atlantic Slaveries in New France* (Chapel Hill: University of North Carolina Press, 2012), 309. About four thousand French lived in the Montreal district, with about two thousand settled Indians nearby (at least half of whom were at Kahnawake).

17. Jean Baptiste D'Aleyrac, *Aventures militaires au XVIIIe siècle d'après les mémoires de Jean-Baptiste d'Aleyrac*, ed. Charles Coste (Paris: Éditions Berger-Levrault, 1935), 36.

18. Parkman 19: July 15, 1756, letter of Le Duchat to Lamy de Chatel (his father?), 105. Le Duchat observed Indians in close quarters on campaigns in 1756 and 1757 and in French garrisons like Fort Saint-Frédéric and Fort Carillon on Lake Champlain.

19. D'Aleyrac, *Aventures militaires*, 36; Parkman 19: Le Duchat to Lamy, July 15, 1756, 105.

20. Entry for July 6, 1755, Anne-Joseph-Hippolyte de Maurès, Comte de Malartic, *Journal des mouvements et campagnes qu'a fait le Second Bataillon du Régiment de Béarn reformé depuis le 8 Avril 1755 qu'il s'embarqua à Brest pour le Canada jusqu'au 25 Novembre 1760 qu'il debarqua à Larochelle fait par Malartic, capitaine aide major chargé du detail de ce bataillon aujourd'hui maréchal de camp* (manuscript), 12.

21. Parkman 19: Le Duchat to Lamy, 105; d'Aleyrac, *Aventures militaires*, 29.

22. D'Aleyrac, *Aventures militaires*, 36.

23. Parkman 19: Le Duchat to Lamy, 102.

24. Every French account contains examples of indigenous practices such as scalping, described almost from the moment of arrival in the Americas. See, for example, diary of July 10, 1756, Louis-Antoine de Bougainville, *Écrits sur le Canada: Mémoires, journal, lettres* (Sillery, Quebec: Septentrion, 2003), 107; Malartic, *Journal des mouvements et campagnes*, 22–23; d'Aleyrac, "Campagnes 1755," in *Aventures militaires*, 53–55; *Le journal du chevalier de Lévis*, édition originale et augmentée, ed. Roger Léger (Montreal: Les Éditions Michel Brûlé, 2008), 32–38; Montcalm to the Marquise de Saint-Véran, July 20, 1756, RPAC, 46. For public transcripts, see "Detail de ce qu'il est passé en Canada depuis le débarquement des troupes de terre de juin 1755 jusqu'au 1er mai 1756," SHD A¹3417, no. 122(v).

25. Montreal, June 16, 1756, Montcalm to the Marquise de Saint-Véran, RPAC, 44.

26. July 20, 1756, Montcalm to the Marquise de Saint-Véran, RPAC, 46.

27. Journal entry for July 28, 1756, *Journal du chevalier de Lévis*, 39.

28. Montreal, June 16, 1756, Montcalm to Marquise de Saint Véran, RPAC, 44; Pierre Pouchot, *Mémoires sur la dernière guerre de l'Amérique septentrionale entre la France et l'Angleterre: suivis des observations, dont plusieurs sont relatives au théâtre actuel de la guerre, & de nouveaux détails sur les mœurs & les usages des sauvages, avec des cartes topographiques. Par M. Pouchot, chevalier de l'Ordre Royal & Militaire de St. Louis, ancien*

capitaine au Régiment de Béarn, commandant des forts de Niagara & de Lévis, en Canada (Yverdon: 1781), vol. 1, 98. Pouchot also notes the presence of Native women at a 1759 council that involved Kaendaé, Onondaga, and Cayuga envoys, William Johnson, and Pouchot himself (ibid., vol. 2, 68).

29. Summer officer kits given to Native families in exchange for war aid in *Mémoire pour Messire François Bigot, ci-devant intendant de justice, police, finance & marine en Canada, accusé: Contre Monsieur le Procureur-Général du Roi en la Commission, accusateur,* première partie, *Contenant l'histoire de l'administration du sieur Bigot dans la colonie, & des réflexions générales sur cette administration* (Paris: de l'imprimerie de P. Al. Le Prieur, Imprimeur du Roi, rue Saint Jacques, 1763), 32.

30. On the interactions between Canadian women and men, particularly those ensnared in the brisk trade in captives, see William Henry Foster, *The Captor's Narrative: Catholic Women and Their Puritan Men on the Early American Frontier* (Ithaca, NY: Cornell University Press, 2003), and on *panis*, see Rushforth, *Bonds of Alliance*, chaps. 5 and 6. See also Per Kalm, *Travels into North America: Containing Its Natural History . . . Translated into English by John Reinhold Forster, F.A.S.*, 2nd ed. (London: T. Lowndes, 1774), vol. 2, 224. Kalm reported that French and Québécois ladies considered their Montreal counterparts, like the unfortunate *Iroquoise* Élisabeth Bégon, to be overly Indianized (401–2).

31. Entry for Aug. 26, 1759, *Journal du chevalier de Lévis*, 148. Sibyls, associated with the cult of Apollo in antiquity, played a role in counseling Aeneas in Virgil's epic, *The Aeneid*, which circulated widely among the French officers in North America.

32. Parkman 19: Montreal, June 12, 1756, Montcalm to Argenson, 71.

33. Louise Dechêne offers an in-depth look at the radically different war experience of average *habitants* serving in the militia or drafted as extramilitary personnel during this period. See *Le peuple, l'état, et la guerre au Canada sous le régime français* (Montreal: Éditions Boréal, 2008), chaps. 8, 10. See also Ian K. Steele, *Betrayals: Fort William Henry and the "Massacre"* (Oxford: Oxford University Press, 1990), 93, and René Chartrand, "La milicie Canadienne et la guerre de Sept Ans," in *La guerre de Sept Ans en Nouvelle-France*, ed. Laurent Veyssière et Bertrand Fonck (Montreal: Septentrion, 2012), 291–301. On distinctions of "woods," see James Merrell, *Into the American Woods: Negotiators on the Pennsylvania Frontier* (New York: W. W. Norton, 1999).

34. Entry for Aug. 7, 1755, Malartic, *Journal des mouvements*, 24. English sources also record the exchange, trade, or sale of useful commodities between Indians and Europeans during wartime. For examples, see entry for Oct. 5–6, the Seth Tinkham Diary, William L. Clements Library (hereafter cited as WLCL), The University of Michigan, 32–33.

35. Michel Foucault, *Discipline and Punish: The Birth of the Prison*, trans. Alan Sheridan (New York: Vintage, 1995), 171. On discipline as a means of state control in early modern France, see Robert Muchembled, *Popular Culture and Elite Culture in France, 1400–1750*, trans. Lydia Cochrane (Baton Rouge: Louisiana State University Press, 1985), chap. 4.

36. John Keegan, *The Face of Battle: A Study of Agincourt, Waterloo, and the Somme* (New York: Penguin Books, 1976), 114–15, 184. For a discussion of metropolitan versus indigenous attitudes toward alcohol in colonial Mexico (a similar case) see

William Taylor, *Drinking, Homicide, and Rebellion in Colonial Mexican Villages* (Stanford, CA: Stanford University Press, 1979). Poor foot soldiers were not the only ones who sought alcoholic beverages. Montcalm repeatedly asked for and received cases of fine wines from his wife and mother explicitly for use on his campaign table. See, for instance, Montreal, July 6, 1757, Montcalm to Marquise de Montcalm (his wife), *RPAC*, 57–58, requesting two hundred bottles of muscatel and Montcalm to Bourlamaque regarding officers' wine stores, July 14, 1756, *Collection des manuscrits*, vol. 5, 131.

37. Robert Nye, *Masculinity and Male Codes of Honor in Modern France* (Oxford: Oxford University Press, 1993), 30. For a discussion of common drinking in urban France, see Thomas Brennan, *Public Drinking and Popular Culture in Eighteenth-Century Paris* (Princeton, NJ: Princeton University Press, 1988). Peter Mancall describes social fears about the effects of lower-class drinking both in London and in the English colonies, which parallels the French case; see Mancall, *Deadly Medicine: Indians and Alcohol in Early America* (Ithaca, NY: Cornell University Press, 1995), 19–20.

38. Sept. 21, 1756, Malartic, *Journal des mouvements*, 107.

39. On the Pennsylvania frontier, inebriated individuals wrought havoc on delicate treaty negotiations. See Merrell, *Into the American Woods*, 264, 268, 279–80. On alcohol and Indian communities, see Mancall, *Deadly Medicine*, 4–7, 26–28, 149–54. On debt slavery through alcohol and trade, see Richard White, *The Roots of Dependency: Subsistence, Environment, and Social Change among the Choctaws, Pawnees, and Navajos* (Lincoln: University of Nebraska Press, 1983). On alcohol as motivation for Nativist critiques, see Gregory Evans Dowd, *A Spirited Resistance: The North American Indian Struggle for Unity, 1745–1815* (Baltimore: Johns Hopkins University Press, 1996). See also Claudio Saunt, *A New Order of Things: Property, Power, and Transformation of the Creek Indians, 1733–1816* (Cambridge: Cambridge University Press, 1999), and Nathaniel Sheidley, "Hunting and the Politics of Masculinity in Cherokee Treaty-Making, 1763–75," in Martin J. Daunton and Rick Halpern, eds., *Empire and Others: British Encounters with Indigenous Peoples, 1600–1850* (Philadelphia: University of Pennsylvania Press, 1999), for southeastern Indian perspectives.

40. Parkman 19: July 15, 1756, Le Duchat to Lamy, 105.

41. Steele, *Betrayals*, 86.

42. D'Aleyrac, *Aventures militaires*, 37.

43. Montreal, Aug. 30, 1756, Montcalm to the Marquise de Boulay (his sister-in-law), *RPAC*, 47 (identical letter sent to the Marquise de Montcalm); Parkman 29: Montreal, Aug. 28, 1756, Desandrouins to Argenson, 143. See Pierre Pouchot, *Mémoires sur la dernière guerre de l'Amérique septentrionale entre la France et l'Angleterre*, vol. 1, 88.

44. Parkman 19: Montreal, Aug. 28, 1756, Désandrouins to Argenson, 143.

45. *Journal du chevalier de Lévis*, 48.

46. Entry for June 29, 1757, Malartic, *Journal des mouvements*, 177–78.

47. Kennett, *French Armies in the Seven Years' War*, 75–77; entry for Oct. 14, 1756, Bougainville, *Écrits sur le Canada*, 146.

48. John Childs, *Armies and Warfare in Europe, 1648–1789* (New York: Holmes and Meier, 1982), 69–70; D'Aleyrac, *Aventures militaires*, 25, 37.

49. Montreal, June 12, 1756, Montcalm to Argenson, SHD A^{1}3417, no. 139.

50. Parkman 19: Montreal, Aug. 28, 1756, Montcalm to Argenson, claiming the ability to turn Canadians into grenadiers in six months, 135–36.

51. Montcalm to Bourlamaque, Montreal, June 13, 1757; Fort Saint Jean, Aug. 30, 1757, *Lettres de M de Bourlamaque au chevalier de Lévis*, vol. 5, 164, 191.

52. Parkman 18: Montreal, Aug. 10, 1756, Vaudreuil to Machault, 296. Canada, too, had a long relationship of violence and alcohol. At the end of the seventeenth century, French governors complained of an excessive number of "cabarets" in New France—as many as twenty out of twenty-five houses in one town had such a tavern license (Paris, Apr. 28, 1677, Colbert to Intendant Duchesneau, Parkman 7 XT: *Canada lettres du roy, 1675–1689, etc.*, 30–31; Quebec, Nov. 13, 1685, Denonville to Naval Minister Seignelay; Parkman 34 XT: *Correspondance officielle des gouverneurs du Canada, 1680–1686*, 365). Royal and colonial administrators linked alcohol abuse with colonists' laziness and implied that drink exacerbated the colonists' independence from authority. One solution to this was the reorientation of the Canadian elite's men and boys into marine service, proposed by Jacques Brisay de Denonville, governor, 1685–1689.

53. Chaussegros de Léry, "Journal de la campagne d'hiver, du 13 février au neuf Avril 1756 que Gaspard-Joseph Chaussegros de Léry, lieutenant dans les troupes détachées de la marine et à present Capt. et Ch-er de St. Louis, a faite en consequence des ordres de Pierre de Rigaud, Marquis de Vaudreuil, gouverneur et lieutenant-général pour le roi en toute la Nouvelle France, terres et pays de la Louisiane (à présent commandeur de l'ordre roial et militaire de St Louis) aux entrepôts que les Anglais avaient formés pour se faciliter la conquête du Canada, au grand portage entre la Rivière Chouéguen dite des Onnontagués qui se décharge dans le Lac Ontario et la Rivière Schenectady qui tombe dans la Rivière d'Hudson," in *Rapport de L'Archiviste de la Province de Québec pour 1926–1927* (hereafter cited as *RAPQ* plus applicable date) (Quebec: L.-Amable Proulx, 1927), 386.

54. Bougainville noted the marine officers Luc de La Corne (La Corne St. Luc) and Joseph Marin de La Malgue participating actively in councils with Abenakis, Algonquins, Kahnawakes, and Menominees in July 1756. Diary entry for July 13–15, 1756, *Écrits sur le Canada*, 109–11.

55. Chevalier de La Pause, "Mémoire et observations sur mon voyage en Canada," *RAPQ 1931–1932*, 74.

56. Parkman 19: Montreal, Aug. 28, 1756, Montcalm to Argenson, 135–36.

57. Louis-Joseph de Montcalm de Saint-Veran, *Relation de la prise des forts de Choueguen, ou Oswego; & de ce qui s'est passé cette année en Canada* (avec permission, 1756) (n.p.), 3, 5; Parkman 19: Montreal, Aug. 28, 1756, Montcalm to Argenson, 135–36.

58. *Relation de la prise des forts de Choueguen*, 8.

59. Montreal, Aug. 30, 1756, Montcalm to the Marquise de Montcalm; to the Marquise de Boulay, *RPAC*, 47.

60. Parkman 18: Fontainebleau, Nov. 7, 1756, Machault to Vaudreuil and Bigot, 56.

61. Ibid., Montreal, Aug. 10, 1756, Vaudreuil to Machault, 314–16.

62. Stephen Cross, a New Hampshire carpenter, surrendered at Oswego and endured transport first to Quebec and then to France as a prisoner of war. Oct. 4, 1756; Nov. 16, 1756, the Stephen Cross Journal, WLCL, 28, 33.

63. Aug. 14, 1756, Malartic, *Journal des mouvements*, 106; Steele, *Betrayals*, 79; Fred Anderson, *The War That Made America: A Short History of the French and Indian War* (New York: Viking, 2005), 95. Steele points out that "embellished" tales of spoils from Oswego greatly aided French recruiting efforts among the Anishinaabeg (Ottawas, Ojibwas, and Potawatomis) of the *pays d'en haut*.

64. Parkman 18: Montreal, Sept. 1, 1756, Vaudreuil to Machault, 325–29; Parkman 19: Montreal, Oct. 23, 1756, Vaudreuil to Machault, 355.

65. Montreal, Sept. 1, 1756, Vaudreuil to Machault, Archives nationales d'Outre Mer (hereafter cited as ANOM), Marin Personnel File, $F^{3}14$: 302.

66. Entry for June 18, 1756, *Journal du Marquis de Montcalm durant ses campagnes en Canada*, vol. 7, 71.

67. On Canadian and Indian zeal for "pillage" see the entry for Aug. 13, 1756, chevalier de La Pause, "Mémoire et observations sur mon voyage en Canada," *RAPQ 1931–1932*, 33. On the idea of betrayals after the battle of Fort William Henry, see Steele, *Betrayals*, 132–33, and for campaign numbers, ibid., 79.

68. Parkman 16: Montreal, Feb. 15, 1758, Vaudreuil to Naval Minister Moras, 431–32.

69. Journal entry for Mar. 27, 1756, Chaussegros de Léry, "Journal de la campagne d'hiver, du 13 février au neuf Avril 1756," *RAPQ 1926–1927*, 386–87.

70. Journal entry for Sept. 20, 1756, Louis-Antoine de Bougainville, *Adventure in the Wilderness: The American Journals of Louis-Antoine de Bougainville, 1756–1760*, trans. and ed. Edward P. Hamilton (Norman: University of Oklahoma Press, 1990), 41.

71. Entry for Aug. 13, 1756, chevalier de La Pause, "Mémoires et observations," *RAPQ 1931–1932*, 34.

72. Much literature on early New England posits similar connections on the deleterious effect of the wilderness on Europeans. See, for instance, Martha L. Finch, "'Civilized' Bodies and the 'Savage' Environment of Early New Plymouth," in *A Centre of Wonders: The Body in Early America*, ed. Janet Moore Lindman and Michele Lise Tarter (Ithaca, NY: Cornell University Press, 2001), 43–61.

73. Entry for Aug. 14, 1756, Stephen Cross Journal, WLCL, f. 25.

74. British officers, like the French, expressed concern at the environment of North America. Henry Fletcher's wartime journal described a North American ranger, Lieutenant Hazzen, in Nova Scotia, who "on his return through the woods . . . chanc'd to fall in with one poor [Acadian] family, 6 he made Prisoners & after the cruel custom of the Savages, whom the Americans copy, scalped 2 women & 2 children." See Henry Fletcher, *Manuscript Diary of an Officer of the 35th Foot in America, 1757–1756*, John Carter Brown Library, 25–26. On the famous captivities and redemptions after Fort William Henry, see Steele, *Betrayals*, 162–65.

75. Sixty percent of Britain's forces had fewer than two years of service, in comparison to the French. See *Combattre pour la France en Amérique: Les soldats de la guerre de Sept Ans en Nouvelle-France 1755–1760*, sous la direction de Marcel Fournier (Montreal: Société généaologique canadienne-française, 2009), 25; Sandrine Picaud-Monnerat, *La petite guerre au XVIIIe siècle* (Paris: Éditions Economica, 2010), 95–98.

76. Parkman 19: Montreal, Nov. 1, 1756, Montcalm to Argenson noting Colonel de Bourlamaque's desire to return to France for his health and other reasons, 181; Parkman 16: Montreal, Oct. 30, 1756, Chevalier Lemercier to Machault, 79–80. In

April of the following year, Montcalm made much clearer statements, pointing out that Lévis, Bourlamaque, and of course Montcalm himself looked forward to their continental homecoming as soon as peace could be established. Parkman 19: Montreal, Apr. 24, 1756, Montcalm to Argenson, 272.

77. Parkman 19: Montreal, Apr. 24, 1757, Montcalm to Argenson, 270; (on climate) 295–96.

78. Quebec, May 29, 1756, Montcalm to Argenson, SHD A^{1}3417, no. 129; Bougainville also drew parallels to Flanders. See Bertrand Fonck, "'Joindre au système de tactique d'Europe l'usage à faire des sauvages': Le commandement des armées françaises en Nouvelle-France," in Veyssière et Fonck, *La guerre de Septs Ans en Nouvelle-France*, 158.

79. Parkman 19: Montreal, Apr. 24, 1757, Lévis reporting officers' dissatisfaction to Argenson, 278. On the exclusion of the Comte de Malartic (who had eighteen months of experience in North America and a great willingness to undertake irregular warfare), entry for Feb. 16, 1757, *Journal du Marquis de Montcalm durant ses campagnes en Canada*, vol. 7, 160.

80. François Marie Peyrenc de Moras, born in 1718, rose at court through the graces of his father-in-law, Moreau de Séchelles, and became comptroller general of finances in 1756. By February 1757, he was a minister of state and a naval minister—positions he held until June of the following year. See Antoine, *Le gouvernement et l'administration sous Louis XV*, 201.

81. Parkman 18: Versailles, May 27, 1757, Moras to Vaudreuil, 86–87. On volumes of correspondence (at least a thousand pages arriving from the American colonies in one month and requiring response in no more than five), see Cassel, "*Troupes de la Marine* in Canada," 35.

82. Parkman 18: Versailles, May 27, 1757, Moras to Montcalm, 93.

83. Ibid., 94.

84. Ibid., Mar. 3, 1757, Moras to Montcalm, 140.

85. Quebec, Nov. 1, 1757, Montcalm to Moras, SHD A^{1}3457. Montcalm noted that Bougainville had become his aide-de-camp through the indirect work of young Moras, who had been recommended by Madame de Séchelles and her sister, Madame Hérault.

86. The French insisted in private and in public that the terms had been explained to and accepted by Native leaders. For an example of an official version see "Canada, historique des campagnes de 1755 à 1758," SHD A^{1}3417, no. 12.

87. Steele, *Betrayals*, 139–41.

88. Parkman 18: Montreal, Aug. 18, 1757, Vaudreuil to Moras, 374; entry for Aug. 10, 1757, Lévis, *Journal de Lévis*, 78; entries of Aug. 12–31, Bougainville, *Écrits sur le Canada*, 233.

89. Parkman 18: Montreal, Sept. 15, 1757, Vaudreuil to Moras, 401–9; Bougainville, *Adventure in the Wilderness*, 172. The English translation in *Documents Relative to the Colonial History of the State of New York* (ed. and trans. E. B. O'Callaghan [Albany: Weed Parsons, 1858], X: 631) omits the Abenaki narrative in the original French text. Indigenous, French, British, and Canadian reactions to Fort William Henry are best described in Steele, *Betrayals*, chap. 7.

90. D'Aleyrac, *Aventures militaires*, 70–71.

91. Translation courtesy of Carolyn Dewald, Bard College. Journal entry for Aug. 15, 1757, Bougainville, *Adventure in the Wilderness*, 175. Edward Hamilton identifies the quotation from *The Aeneid* (book 3, lines 17–44) and translates it as "Ah! Flee the cruel lands, flee the cruel shore!" A Robert Fitzgerald translation of the same Virgil passage, however, encompasses a much greater depth of meaning: "Ah, Put the savage land behind you! Leave / this shore of greed! / [For I am Polydorus.]" This is suggestive of a direct correlation between Indians (*sauvages*) and the bloodthirsty soil of Thrace, land of Mars. See *The Aeneid*, trans. Robert Fitzgerald (New York: Vintage, 1984), 66.

92. Steele points out that several Indians carefully selected prisoners of African descent for the specific purpose of selling them and points out that Jeffery Amherst demanded the return of all black and Indian servants and slaves as much as military prisoners. See *Betrayals*, 140.

93. Quebec, Sept. 20, 1757, Bougainville to Madame de Séchelles, *Écrits sur le Canada*, 383–85. This letter is almost identical as well to the passage in Bougainville's journal.

94. D'Aleyrac, *Aventures militaires*, 44.

95. Entry for Aug. 9, 1757, chevalier de La Pause, "Mémoires et observations," *RAPQ 1931–1932*, 62.

96. Quoted in Steele, *Betrayals*, 99.

97. *The Jesuit Relations and Allied Documents*, ed. Reuben Gold Thwaites (Albany: Burroughs Brothers, 1900), vol. 70, *1747–1764*, Saint François, Oct. 21, 1757, letter from Father XXX [now known to be Pierre Roubaud], missionary to the Abenakis, 129, 133, 181–83, 197. Father Roubaud rescued an English baby by trading a scalp borrowed from an Abenaki to exchange with the baby's Huron captor. Good deeds did not go unpunished—English fears of Jesuit collusion with demons were reinforced by the sight of a Jesuit running between Indians bearing bloody scalps and an infant. See Steele, *Betrayals*, 120. On the cost of redemption, see ibid., 131.

98. Parkman 19: *Au camp sous les ruines du fort William Henry, appelé par les Français le fort George*, Aug. 15, 1757, Montcalm to the Minister of War, the Marquis de Paulmy, 314.

99. *Relation de la prise du Fort Georges, ou Guillaume-Henry, situé sur le Lac Saint-Sacrement, & de ce qui s'est passé cette année en Canada* (Paris: Bureau d'adresse avec privilège du roi, 1757), 11.

100. Parkman 18: Montreal, Aug. 18, 1757, Vaudreuil to Moras, 374.

101. Parkman 19: Québec, Nov. 4, 1757, Montcalm to Paulmy, 359; camp at Carillon, Aug. 8, 1758, Montcalm to Minister of War Belle-Isle, SHD A¹3499, no. 1, 1v.

102. Quebec, Aug. 31, 1758, Doreil to Belle-Isle, SHD A¹3499, no. 45/15.

103. Sieur Louis de Courville, *Mémoires sur le Canada depuis 1749 jusqu'à 1760: en trois parties; avec cartes et plans lithographiés* (Quebec: Imprimerie de T. Cary, 1838), 97.

104. French correspondence, whether from the army, the marine service, or New France's government tended to differentiate between the domiciled communities, the Cinq Nations (Iroquois Confederacy), and the Indians of the *pays d'en haut*. In the end, though, French officers seemed to assume that all these peoples

shared the undesirable elements of being Indians. Bougainville noted, "The nations of the *pays d'en haut* are easier to lead than our domiciled [Indians]. They have greater respect for the French, whom they see less frequently; moreover, because of the distance of their homes, they are less likely to disappear after every *coup* they make." Oct. 2, 1756, *Écrits sur le Canada*, 140. Bougainville's reference to "respect for the French" is not limited to army officers—I believe he includes all Europeans in this term and helps to explain how Canadians and metropolitans were viewed the same way.

105. Montreal, Sept. 1, 1756, Vaudreuil to Machault, ANOM F^{3}14: 303.

106. Steele, *Betrayals*, 110; Timothy J. Shannon, "War, Diplomacy, and Culture: The Iroquois Experience in the Seven Years' War," in *Cultures in Conflict: The Seven Years' War in North America*, ed. Warren R. Hofstra (New York: Rowman and Littlefield, 2007), 84.

107. Chevalier de La Pause, "Mémoires et observations," *RAPQ 1931–1932*, 61.

108. Quebec, Sept. 20, 1757, Bougainville to Madame de Séchelles, *Écrits sur le Canada*, 385. On French associations with honor, see Fonck, "Joindre au système de tactique," in Veyssière et Fonck, *La guerre de Sept Ans en Nouvelle-France*, 166.

109. Bougainville, *Adventure in the Wilderness*, 172, 174–75, and Quebec, Sept. 17, 1757, Bougainville to Jean-Pierre de Bougainville, *Écrits sur le Canada*, 379.

110. Ewing, "Rumor and Foreign Politics in Louis XV's Paris," 451–72; Wayne E. Lee, "From Gentility to Atrocity: The Continental Army's Ways of War," *Army History* 62 (Winter 2006): 1–19.

111. Sept. 8, 1757, Capt. John Knox, *An historical journal of the campaigns in North America for the years 1757, 1758, 1759, and 1760: containing the most remarkable occurrences of that period, particularly the two sieges of Québec &c. &c.*, . . . *as also several manifestos, a mandate of the late bishop of Canada, the French orders and disposition for the defence of the colony &c. &c. &c.* (London: Printed for the author and sold by W. Johnston in Ludgate Street, 1769), vol. 1, 142.

112. Carillon, Aug. 19, 1757, chevalier de La Pause, captain in the Guienne Regiment, to Paulmy, SHD A^{1}3457, no. 120. Graces in this context could be anything from recommendation for a *croix de Saint Louis* to a meritorious pay increase or a promotion in rank.

Chapter 4. Assigning a Value to Valor

1. Dale K. Van Kley details the interconnections between Jansenism, rising *parlémentaire* authority, and the Crown during and after the Damiens affair in *The Damiens Affair and the Unraveling of the Ancien Régime, 1750–1770* (Princeton, NJ: Princeton University Press, 1984). Michel Foucault also investigates the social constructions surrounding Damiens's execution in *Discipline and Punish: The Birth of the Prison* (New York: Vintage, 1995), 3–5, 47–48, 54.

2. Jonathan Dull, *The French Navy and the Seven Years' War* (Lincoln: University of Nebraska Press, 2005), 76.

3. *Les ministres de la guerre, 1570–1792*, ed. Thierry Sarmant (Paris: Éditions Belin, 2007), 371, 373. Argenson also relied on a close circle of aides, including his eventual successors, the Marquis de Paulmy and the Duc de Belle-Isle.

4. Jonathan Dull, "Great Power Confrontation or Clash of Cultures?" in *Cultures in Conflict: The Seven Years' War in North America*, ed. Warren R. Hofstra (New York: Rowman and Littlefield, 2007), 69–70.

5. David Bell, *The Cult of the Nation in France: Inventing Nationalism, 1680–1800* (Cambridge, MA: Harvard University Press, 2001), 91. France, as it came to see itself as a nation, had to justify and defend its actions in print. "[T]he war [was] one in which every individual citizen had a stake." But in this new formula, if the monarchy made a public misstep, then it was viewed as being out of touch with the nation's desires.

6. Robert Darnton, *Poetry and the Police: Communication Networks in Eighteenth-Century Paris* (Cambridge, MA: Belknap Press of Harvard University Press), 119. For the quote in context in Paris, see Tabetha Leigh Ewing, "Rumor and Foreign Politics in Louis XV's Paris during the War of Austrian Succession" (PhD diss., Princeton University, 2005), 475.

7. See, for instance, *Relaçaõ de huma batalha, succedida no campo de Lake George* (Lisbon 1756) and *Noticia verdadeira da guerra da America entra os francezes e inglezes com a tomade do forte de Sam Jorze* (Lisbon 1757). On the question of French interest in British news and newspapers, see the Archives nationales de France (hereafter cited as AN), B^{4}91, f.4–5.

8. Other notable victories and losses outside Europe included Fort Saint David in India (a stunning upset over Britain by the Comte de Lally) and the capture of Gorée Island. Historians have tended to assume that, as European concerns expanded, France was little interested in events in North America during the Seven Years' War. Published accounts of battles by printers in Paris and in important provincial centers suggest otherwise. See *Relations de la prise de forts de Choueguen ou Oswego* (Grenoble 1756), *Relations des avantages remportés par les armes du roy sur les Anglois* (Paris 1757), or *Journal de l'affaire du Canada passée le 8 juillet 1758* (Rouen 1758). See also the John Carter Brown Library, *Annual Report*, vol. 2 (1934), 25.

9. Kenneth J. Banks, *Chasing Empire across the Sea: Communication and the State in the French Atlantic, 1713–1763* (Montreal: McGill University Press, 2003), 48–54. At the birth of the Comte d'Artois, Louis XV ordered a *Te Deum* to be sung throughout the empire. "Order from the King to Commanders and Intendents of the Navy," Versailles, Oct. 20, 1757, AN, B^{2}356, f.487.

10. Battle accounts from French officers circulated privately among friends and family. See, for instance, Montcalm's letter to the Marquise de Montcalm, Feb. 19, 1758, concerning winter campaigns in *Report of the Public Archives of Canada for the Year 1929* (hereafter cited as *RPAC*) (Ottawa: F. A. Acland, 1929), 63, and Louis-Antoine de Bougainville to Madame de Séchelles, June 30, 1757, in Louis-Antoine de Bougainville, *Écrits sur le Canada: Mémoires, journal, lettres* (Sillery, Quebec: Septentrion, 2003), 370–71. For official celebrations, see "Ordres du Roi" (to commanders and intendants of the navy to sing a *Te Deum* to honor the Carillon battle), Versailles, Sept. 18, 1758, AN, B^{2}359, f. 449. Carillon is the only battle I found listed in the rolls to have this distinction.

11. Camp at Carillon, Aug. 8, 1758, Montcalm to the Marquise de Boulay (his sister-in-law), *RPAC*, 75.

12. Dull argues that the French public did not become patriotic until the 1759 battle of Quiberon Bay, preferring to focus on disputes between the archbishop of

Paris and the Jansenists in the Parlement de Paris. See Dull, "Great Power Confrontation or Clash of Cultures?" 70, 72–73.

13. James B. Collins, *The State in Early Modern France* (Cambridge: Cambridge University Press, 2009), 277–79. Aristocrats cared less about the king's carnal weaknesses than the Parisian public did. By the mid-1750s, Parisian tastes rather than the court set public opinion, and Parisians viewed the ever-lower class of royal mistresses with distaste.

14. July 11, 1757, Montreal, Montcalm to Fumeron, *Report for the Public Archives of Canada* (Ottawa: F. A. Acland, 1929), 44–45; Montreal, June 12, 1756, Montcalm to Minister of War d'Argenson, Service Historique de la Défense, Armée de Terre (hereafter cited as SHD), Paris, France, A^{1}3457, 81/f. 4.

15. On "clandestinity," see Ewing, "Rumor and Foreign Politics." On reputation and the unspeakable in France, see Robert Darnton, "An Early Information Society: News and the Media in Eighteenth-Century Paris," *American Historical Review* 105, no. 1 (February 2000): 1–35.

16. Montcalm to Bourlamaque, Montreal, June 9, 1757, *Collection des manuscrits du maréchal de Lévis: Lettres de M de Bourlamaque au chevalier de Lévis* (Quebec: Imprimerie de L.-J. Demers et Frère, 1891), 5: 158–59.

17. Ibid., June 10, 1757 (noted as a supplemental letter), 5: 159.

18. Foucault, *Discipline and Punish*, 35, 47.

19. Daniel K. Richter, "War and Culture: The Iroquois Experience," *William and Mary Quarterly* (hereafter cited as *WMQ*) 40, no. 4 (October 1983): 532–34, 543, 559.

20. Francis Parkman papers (hereafter cited as Parkman), Massachusetts Historical Society, 18: Versailles, Feb. 14, 1757, Moras to Vaudreuil, 132.

21. Complaints regarding Canadians and Indians at Oswego from Montreal, Sept. 1, 1756, Vaudreuil to Machault, Archives nationales d'Outre Mer, F^{3}14: 299–302. On Montcalm's secondary (though still important) role in embassies, see Montcalm, diary entry for Dec. 6, 1756, *Le journal du Marquis de Montcalm durant ses campagnes en Canada de 1756 à 1759*, in *Collection des manuscrits du maréchal de Lévis*, published under the direction of Abbé H. R. Casgrain (Quebec: L.-J. Demers et Frère, 1895), vol. 7, 130.

22. Parkman 18: Versailles, Mar. 3, 1758, Moras to Montcalm, 138–39.

23. Foucault describes a shift in paradigm from individuality to a compartmentalization and an interchangeability of positions in service to the state. See *Discipline and Punish*, 151–53. The appeal to duty above the self, dating back to medieval-era fealty, manifested loyalty among the *noblesse militaire*—noble soldiers—to their commander-king.

24. Parkman 18: Carillon, Aug. 2, 1758, Montcalm to Vaudreuil, 445–47. Montcalm's letter does not reveal the name of the New York newspaper. However, during the summer 1758 campaign, the French general and his opponent, British general Abercromby, maintained a correspondence, and Abercromby passed the Anglophone materials concerning international affairs to Montcalm, which were duly translated by Bougainville.

25. Many thanks to James Merrell for suggesting this point.

26. *Documents Relative to the Colonial History of the State of New York* (hereafter cited as *NYDC*), ed. and trans. E. B. O'Callaghan (Albany: Weed Parsons, 1858), X: July 1758, Abercromby to Montcalm, 774.

27. Loudon, quoted in Ian K. Steele, *Betrayals: Fort William Henry and the Massacre* (Oxford: Oxford University Press, 1990), 145.

28. Parkman 18: *New France X, Canada, 1756–1758*: Versailles, Sept. 23, 1758, Naval Minister Massiac to Montcalm, 171–72.

29. Ibid.

30. On *gloire* and *zèle* as central themes of Carillon, see Julia Osman, "The Citizen Army of Old Regime France" (PhD diss., University of North Carolina–Chapel Hill, 2010), 84–86.

31. On the Montreal council, see Parkman 19: Montreal, Apr. 24, 1757, Montcalm to Argenson, 280; June 14, 1757, Bougainville, *Écrits sur le Canada*, 189. Bougainville also used the phrase *conseil à l'ordinaire* in September 1756, suggesting a near-daily formalized interaction with Indians (133). On the Ottawas' appropriation of all animals, June 28, 1757; June 29, 1757 (council and fight), see Anne-Joseph-Hyppolite de Maurès, Comte de Malartic, *Journal des mouvements et campagnes qu'a fait le Second Bataillon du Regiment de Béarn reformé depuis le 8 Avril 1755 qu'il s'embarqua à Brest pour le Canada jusqu'au 25 Novembre 1760 qu'il debarqua à Larochelle fait par Malartic [Anne Joseph Hippolyte de Maurès, comte de] capitaine aide major chargé du detail de ce Bataillon aujourd'hui maréchal de camp*, John Carter Brown Library, 176–78. Malartic notes that some Iroquois declined Montcalm's request that they help to retrieve wounded French officers after a scouting party and on another occasion demanded an escort of one hundred French or Canadian soldiers. See June 12–13, 1757, *Journal des mouvements*, 165, 167.

32. On the tensions between Europeans and Indians over the issue of gifts and "enforced gift giving," see Evan Haefeli, "On First Contact and Apotheosis: Manitou and Men in North America," *Ethnohistory* 54, no. 3 (October 2007): 432.

33. *Journal de l'affaire du Canada passée le 8 Juillet 1758 entre les troupes du roi, commandés par M. le Marquis de Montcalm, & celles d'Angleterre, qui, ou nombre de vingt mille hommes, ont été mises en fuites par trois mille deux cent cinquante François* (Rouen: Borel, Sept. 23, 1758), 4.

34. Parkman 18: Versailles, Aug. 26, 1758, Massiac to Montcalm, 166.

35. Parkman 16: Montreal, Sept. 16, 1758, Montcalm to Vaudreuil, 263.

36. Extract from a letter from Vaudreuil to Montcalm, attached to Carillon, Aug. 8, 1758, Montcalm to Belle-Isle, SHD A^{1}3499, no. 2.

37. Lee Kennett, *The French Armies in the Seven Years' War* (Durham, NC: Duke University Press, 1967), 59.

38. On the antipathy between nobles and *roturiers*, see Gilles Havard and Cécile Vidal, *Histoire de l'Amérique française* (Paris: Éditions Flammarion, 2008), 543. An excellent analysis of gift giving and finance appears in Catherine Desbarats, "The Cost of Canada's Early Alliances: Reality and Scarcity's Rhetoric," *WMQ* 52, no. 4 (October 1995): 609–30. On competition between *troupes de terre* and Native allies, see Osman, "The Citizen Army of Old Regime France," chap. 2.

39. Diary entries for Dec. 12, 1757–Mar. 1, 1758, Louis-Antoine de Bougainville, *Adventure in the Wilderness: The American Journals of Louis-Antoine de Bougainville, 1756–1760*, trans. and ed. Edward P. Hamilton (Norman: University of Oklahoma Press, 1990), 196.

40. Parkman 20: *New France XII, Canada, 1757–1761*: Quebec, Feb. 25, 1758, Doreil to the Minister of War, the Marquis de Paulmy, 29–30.

41. Parkman 19: Montreal, Apr. 24, 1757, Montcalm to Argenson, 269, 272. Argenson left office by Feb. 1, 1757, a fact that reached New France much later. Thus the intended recipient was the Comte d'Argenson, though the *premier commis* Fumeron and the new minister of war, the Marquis de Paulmy, acquired the note.

42. Oct. 14, 1757, Bougainville, *Adventure in the Wilderness*, 187–88.

43. Entry for May 13, 1756. Montcalm notes Intendant Bigot's grand, forty-person reception in honor of the general's arrival and Longueuil's offering to host a gathering as well. *Journal du Marquis de Montcalm durant ses campagnes en Canada*, vol. 7, 62. Lévis allegedly took up a relationship, thanks to the scintillating society of Montreal, with the beautiful—and married—Madame Pennisseault. As reported in Sieur Louis de Courville (Louis Léonard Aumasson de Courville), *Mémoires sur le Canada depuis 1749 jusqu'à 1760: en trois parties; avec cartes et plans lithographiés* (Quebec: Imprimerie de T. Cary, 1838), 86.

44. Montreal, July 6, 1757, Montcalm to the Marquise de Montcalm, *RPAC*, 57–58.

45. Mar. 6, 1757, "Sumptuary Law for the Reduction of Baggage Trains and Tables for Officers during War Campaigns," *Journal historique ou fastes du règne de Louis XV, surnommé le Bien Aimé*, première partie (Paris: Chez Prault; Chez Saillant, 1766), 129. See also Kennett, *French Armies in the Seven Years' War*, 67.

46. July 6, 1757, Montcalm to the Marquise de Saint Véran, *RPAC*, 57–58.

47. On exotic goods: Aug. 24, 1758, Montcalm to the Marquise de Saint Véran, *RPAC*, 74. Luxury goods circulated throughout North America from Montreal and New York to Oswego and Quebec. See, for instance, Detroit, May 29, 1765: James Sterling to Ensign Magill Wallace at Michilimackinac, James Sterling Letterbook, William L. Clements Library (hereafter cited as WLCL Gage Papers AS), The University of Michigan, f. 141, and Brian Leigh Dunnigan, *A Picturesque Situation: Mackinac before Photography, 1615–1860* (Detroit: Wayne State University Press, 2008).

48. Feb. 19, 1758, Montcalm to the Marquise de Montcalm, *RPAC*, 63; Jean-Baptiste d'Aleyrac, *Aventures militaires au XVIIIe siècle*, 53, 76; François-Gaston de Lévis, *Journal du chevalier de Lévis*, édition originale et augmentée, ed. Roger Léger (Montreal: Les Éditions Michel Brûlé, 2008), 85, 92.

49. Montreal, July 6, 1757, Montcalm to the Marquise de Montcalm, *RPAC*, 57–58. Requests for multiple items may have been intended to offset the odds against loss during naval transport.

50. Quebec, Sept. 9, 1756, Bougainville to his brother, Jean-Pierre de Bougainville regarding personal items, as well as gifts for Monsieur de Vienne, *Écrits sur le Canada*, 365.

51. Montreal, June 4, 1756, Bougainville to his brother, Jean-Pierre de Bougainville, *Écrits sur le Canada*, 359.

52. D'Aleyrac, *Aventures militaires au XVIIIe siècle*, 29–30.

53. May 13, 1756, *Journal du Marquis de Montcalm durant ses campagnes en Canada*, vol. 7, 62.

54. Nov. 1, 1757, *Journal du chevalier de Lévis*, 86 (marine threats to riot); December 1757, 91–92 (women's riots). See also Quebec, Feb. 20, 1758, Bougainville to

Chevert on soldiers trying to reject horsemeat and Lévis having to suppress another riot. SHD A¹3498, no. 16.

55. The commissary general, closely tied to the distribution of supplies, pointedly said that elite army officers set the tone by eating horsemeat and boosted public morale by this choice. Parkman 20: Quebec, Feb. 25, 1758, Doreil to Paulmy, 29–30.

56. Camp at Carillon, Sept. 21, 1758, Montcalm to Crémille, *NYDC* X: 857; complaints by Vaudreuil to Massiac on being compelled by Montcalm to provide additional funds for officers of the regulars, Montreal, Nov. 4, 1758, *NYDC* X: 885–86.

57. Parkman 16: Quebec, Dec. 1, 1758, Pontleroy to Massiac, 339.

58. Frontier commanders stole with impunity, Courville wrote, forging bills of exchange to be redeemed from the Montreal treasury by their wives, and named the sieurs Bellestre (at Detroit), Vergor and Duverger de Saint Blin (at Machault), and Vaudreuil's own stepson, Verryer (at Michilimackinac). *Mémoires sur le Canada*, 104–5.

59. March 1759, *Examination of Three French Prisoners*. These men claimed that while the troops and inhabitants suffered deprivations, Vaudreuil ordered the *habitants* to fill the supply stations in order to keep the army stocked, but this drove up the price of all of the provisions. WLCL Gage Papers AS, vol. 2, March–July 1759, 1–1v. Courville noted that in 1758 Governor Vaudreuil attracted too many Indians who ate food that could have been used to feed Quebec, *Mémoires sur le Canada*, 105.

60. *Journal du Marquis de Montcalm durant ses campagnes en Canada*, vol. 7, 169.

61. Bougainville, *Adventure in the Wilderness*, 197; Aug. 19, 1757, Bougainville to Madame de Séchelles, *Écrits sur le Canada*, 377.

62. d'Aleyrac, *Aventures militaires au XVIIIe siècle*, 53, 76; Lévis, *Journal du chevalier de Lévis*, 48 (Iroquois?), 77 (Abenakis).

63. Montcalm recorded Pouchot's naming as an adoption, though Pouchot's text does not state that explicitly. *Mémoires sur la dernière guerre de l'Amérique septentrionale entre la France et l'Angleterre: suivis des observations, dont plusieurs sont relatives au théâtre actuel de la guerre, & de nouveaux détails sur les mœurs & les usages des sauvages, avec des cartes topographiques. Par M. Pouchot, chevalier de l'Ordre Royal & Militaire de St. Louis, ancien capitaine au Régiment de Béarn, commandant des forts de Niagara & de Lévis, en Canada*. (Yverdon: 1781), vol. 2, 10; *Journal du Marquis de Montcalm durant ses campagnes en Canada*, vol. 7, 64. Timothy J. Shannon argues that William Johnson's Mohawk name, Warraghiyagey, or "doer of great things," may be more "accurately rendered as 'keeper of deep pockets.'" "War, Diplomacy, and Culture: The Iroquois Experience in the Seven Years' War," in *Cultures in Conflict*, 92.

64. Montreal, Mar. 3, 1758, Montcalm to Bourlamaque, *Collection des manuscrits du maréchal de Lévis—Lettres de M. de Bourlamaque au chevalier de Lévis* (Quebec: L.-J. Demers et Frère, 1891), vol. 5, 204.

65. Montcalm to Bourlamaque, Montreal, May 23, 1757, *Lettres de M de Bourlamaque au chevalier de Lévis*, vol. 5, 152.

66. Montreal, Apr. 18, 1758, Montcalm to Paulmy, SHD A¹3498, no. 61/5; entry for Aug. 24–31, 1758, *Journal de Montcalm durant ses campagnes en Canada*, vol. 7, 436. Pierre Pouchot at Niagara reported to Montcalm in 1759 that Millitière was captured by the English along with Chabert de Joncaire near Niagara. Entry for July 16, 1759, *Journal de Montcalm durant ses campagnes en Canada*, vol. 7, 574.

67. Sieur Louis de Courville reported Chabert *père*'s alleged Seneca family in *Mémoires sur le Canada* , 18–19. Richard White, *The Middle Ground: Indians, Empires, and Republics in the Great Lakes Region, 1650–1815* (Cambridge: Cambridge University Press, 1991), 215.

68. Havard and Vidal, *Histoire de l'Amérique française*, 544–45.

69. Parkman 16: Montreal, July 28, 1758, Vaudreuil to Massiac, 235.

70. Sharon Kettering, *Patrons, Brokers, and Clients in Seventeenth-Century France* (Oxford: Oxford University Press, 1985), 3–4. The Marquis de Paulmy, nephew of the disgraced Comte d'Argenson, lacked the *crédit* needed at court to remain minister of war. Sarmant, *Les ministres de la guerre*, 398.

71. Michael Witgen, *An Infinity of Nations: How the Native Nations Shaped Early North America* (Philadelphia: University of Pennsylvania Press, 2012), 263.

72. May 6, 1758, Malartic, *Journal des mouvements et campagnes qu'a fait le Second Bataillon du Regiment de Béarn reformé depuis le 8 Avril 1755 qu'il s'embarqua*, 249.

73. One example is in Bougainville's diary entry for Sept. 30, 1756, during a council with Potawatomis, *Écrits sur le Canada*, 139. On the explicit cost of *bonnes affaires*, Bibliothèque nationale de France, Mélanges sur l'Amérique, MF 1041, f. 45. On the translation of *travailler aux bonnes affaires* as "maintaining good relations," see D. Peter MacLeod, *The Canadian Iroquois and the Seven Years' War* (Toronto: Dundurn, 1996), 15.

74. Parkman 16: Montreal, Aug. 4, 1758, Vaudreuil to Massiac, noting that the Indians of La Présentation accompanied Baron de Longueuil's mission to the Five Nations; Malartic noted that during this same diplomatic venture, Cayugas came to Montreal, complaining to Vaudreuil that Longueuil had not brought them gifts (or they had not had access to what had been distributed at La Présentation). In exchange for their offer to aid the French militarily, Vaudreuil "gave them many gifts" along with his thanks. Sept. 1, 1758, Malartic, *Journal des mouvements*, 294. Courville describes the "laying out of gifts along the lakeshore" during Longueuil's mission to the Onondagas on Aug. 6, 1758. *Mémoires sur le Canada*, 113.

75. Bougainville, *Écrits sur le Canada*, 254. Arnaud Balvay argues that the marines' bilateral gifts to Indians can be viewed as the same practice in European diplomacy. Interpretations suggest other conclusions are possible. See Arnaud Balvay, *L'épée et la plume: Amérindiens et soldats de troupes de la marine en Lousiane et au Pays d'en Haut (1683–1763)* (Quebec: Les Presses de l'Université Laval, 2006), 148–49.

76. A Kanesatake Iroquois or Nipissing contingent, for instance, gave the commander of Fort Duquesne, Contrecoeur, a wampum belt to console the marine on his son's death. July 26, 1756, *Journal du Marquis de Montcalm durant ses campagnes en Canada*, vol. 7, 74. On slaves and diplomacy, see Brett Rushforth, *Bonds of Alliance: Indigenous and Atlantic Slaveries in New France* (Chapel Hill: University of North Carolina Press, 2012), esp. 156–57.

77. François Bluche, *La noblesse française au XVIIIe Siècle* (Paris: Hachette, 1973), 92–93. For more on the nobles' dependence on royal funds, see Pierre-Marc de Voyer de Paulmy, Comte d'Argenson, *Correspondance: Lettres des maréchaux de France*, (Paris: Messein, 1924), 8 vols.

78. Courville, *Mémoires sur le Canada*, 111–12.

79. Montreal, May 14, 1757, Montcalm to Bourlamaque, *Collection des manuscrits*, vol. 7, 146.

80. The king's waning popularity among the population appears in satirical songs from 1759 expressing the people's faith in the Virgin Mary (rather than the king) to preserve Canada. See Thierry Berthet, *Seigneurs et colons en Nouvelle France: L'émergence d'une société distincte au 18e siècle* (Quebec: Cachan, 1992). On "Notre Dame de Victoire/Notre Dame des Victoires," see Catherine Desbarats and Allan Greer, "The Seven Years' War in Canadian History and Memory," in *Cultures in Conflict: The Seven Years' War in North America*, ed. Warren R. Hofstra (New York: Rowman and Littlefield 2007), 169–70.

81. *June 27, 1759—Interrogation [they say "The Examination"] of Elias Pagan, an Indian taken at Fort Harkeman as a Spy on 26th June, taken before and certified by Archibald Montague Brown, commander, Fort Haskeman*, WLCL Gage Papers AS, vol. 2, f.2v.

82. Fred Anderson, *Crucible of War: The Seven Years' War and the Fate of Empire in British North America, 1754–1766* (New York: Vintage, 2000), 262–63. The destruction or capture of forts and supplies, disturbing commanders' access to gifts, could lead to the loss of allies. Ohio Delawares would not go to war on behalf of the French at Fort Duquesne in January 1758 because they received fewer presents, the result of heavily depleted stores. Malartic, *Journal des mouvements*, 240. See also Ian Steele, *Warpaths: Invasions of North America* (Oxford: Oxford University Press, 1994), 214–15.

83. Witgen, *Infinity of Nations*, 313.

84. White, *Middle Ground*, 252, 255. Parkman 16: Montreal, Feb. 15, 1759, Vaudreuil to the Naval Minister, 430–32, including transcriptions of Ligneris's report.

85. Parkman 16: Montreal, Aug. 4, 1758, Vaudreuil to Massiac.

86. Ibid., Nov. 1, 1758, Vaudreuil to Massiac, 303–4.

87. Parkman 20: *New France XII, Canada, 1757–1761*: Camp at Carillon, Oct. 14, 1758, Montcalm to the minister of war, the Duc de Belle-Isle, 109–10. Bougainville and Montcalm openly called Péan a "liar" and emphasized that only men of birth, rank, and character (i.e., French officers) truly understood the affairs of the colony and what New France needed.

88. Bougainville, *Adventure in the Wilderness*, 322–23, and *Écrits sur le Canada*, 349. "This minister loved parables and told me aptly that one did not save the stables when the fire was in the house. I was thus able to obtain for these poor stables only 400 recruits and a few war munitions." This quotation is almost as famous as Voltaire's quip in the context of explaining the loss of New France.

89. Eccles, "Vaudreuil de Cavagnal," in in *Dictionary of Canadian Biography Online*, http://www.biographi.ca/en/bio/rigaud_de_vaudreuil_de_cavagnial_pierre_de_4E.html, accessed Jul. 31, 2013; *NYDC* X: Abstract of and Ministerial Minute on the Dispatches from Canada, 907.

90. Parkman 18: Versailles, Jan. 29, 1759, Belle-Isle to Montcalm, 518. The prestigious *croix de Saint Louis* did not bestow the right to plan strategy.

91. Parkman 19: Feb. 23, 1759, memorandum titled "Canada," 62.

92. *NYDC* X: Minister of War to Montcalm, Versailles, Feb. 19, 1759, 944; on Belle-Isle securing Montcalm's promotion, see Parkman 18: Versailles, Feb. 16, 1759, Berryer to Vaudreuil, 221.

93. Parkman 16: Montreal, Sept. 16, 1758, Montcalm to Vaudreuil, 263; *NYDC* X: Montreal, Mar. 12, 1759, Montcalm to Crémille, 959; *NYDC* X: Montreal, Apr. 12, 1759, Montcalm to M. le Normand, 966; Parkman 20: Quebec, Sept. 1, 1758, Doreil to the minister of war, 89.

94. Madame de Pompadour offered to help raise the two million *livres* needed for a plan Bougainville proposed and brought this project to the ministers' council but was ultimately unsuccessful. See "Mémoire depuis le 15 novembre 1758," in Bougainville, *Écrits sur le Canada*, 350; Bougainville, *Adventure in the Wilderness*, 324.

95. Parkman 18: Versailles, Feb. 16, 1759, Berryer to Vaudreuil, 218.

96. Ibid., Feb. 3, 1759, Berryer to Montcalm, 239.

97. Ibid., Jan. 20, 1759, Berryer to Vaudreuil, 200–1; Steele, *Warpaths*, 215.

98. National Archives of Canada, Montreal, Mar. 23, 1759, Vaudreuil to Naval Minister Berryer, MG1-C^{11}A, folio 35v–36.

99. John Childs, *Armies and Warfare in Europe, 1648–1789* (New York: Holmes and Meier, 1982), 69–70. The death penalty was a frequent punishment for court martial, but other responses to disobedience, such as the perennial British army favorite, whipping, rarely found use in the French army. Childs suggests that the "individualism" of the French army's more humane discipline ultimately helped create the modern army of the French Revolution.

100. Entry for Sept. 1, 1760, chevalier de La Pause, "Mémoires et observations," *Rapport de L'Archiviste de la Province de Québec pour 1931–1932* (Montreal: L.-Amable Proulx, 1932), 122.

101. Steele, *Warpaths*, 220–21. The frigate *Machault* departed from Bordeaux in April 1760 with supplies for New France, albeit in far smaller numbers than Lévis requested. The fall of Fort Niagara in July 1759 ended French control of the western waterways (216–17).

Chapter 5. The Losing Face of France

1. Versailles, Dec. 5, 1760, Louis XV via Naval Minister Choiseul to Vaudreuil, Francis Parkman papers, Massachusetts Historical Society, 20: 299–300.

2. Christopher Hodson, *The Acadian Diaspora: An Eighteenth-Century History* (Oxford: Oxford University Press, 2012), 85–86.

3. D. Neuville, *État sommaire des archives de la Marine antérieures à la Révolution* (Paris: Baudoin, 1898), 434–35; note for Nov. 5, 1761, in *Journal historique ou fastes du règne de Louis XV, surnommé le Bien Aimé* (Paris: Chez Prault, Chez Saillant, 1766), 172.

4. Note for Dec. 18, 1761, *Journal historique*, 174–75.

5. Claude Bonnault, "Le Canada perdu et abandonné," in *Revue de l'histoire de l'Amérique française* 2, no. 3 (1948): 332; Robert Larin, *L'exode de Canadiens à la conquête, le Petit-Canada de la Touraine* (Montreal: Société généalogique canadienne-française, 2008), 8.

6. Neuville, *État sommaire*, 434–35; note for Nov. 5, 1761, *Journal historique*, 172.

7. For an example of this kinship by marriage, consider that Capt. Michel-Hugues Péan was not only the nephew of Capt. Claude Pecaudy de Contrecoeur but also the brother-in-law of Nicolas Desméloizes. Louis Legardeur de Répentigny (officer in the colonial regulars and future governor of Senegal) married the daughter of Quebec's most prominent family of military engineers, Marie Madeleine Régis Chaussegros de Léry. Her sister married another marine, Jean Marie Baptiste Landrièvre des Bordes, suggesting the extensive nature of these families and their ties.

8. Journal entry of Apr. 25, 1758, *Le journal du Marquis de Montcalm durant ses campagnes en Canada de 1756 à 1759*, in *Collection des manuscrits du maréchal de Lévis*, published under the direction of Abbé H. R. Casgrain (Quebec: L.-J. Demers et Frère, 1895), vol. 7, 344.

9. Dunn Jr., "Chabert de Joncaire de Clausonne," in *Dictionary of Canadian Biography Online* (hereafter cited as *DCBO*),
http://www.biographi.ca/en/bio/chabert_de_joncaire_de_clausonne_daniel_marie_4E.html, accessed Jul. 31, 2013; Sieur Courville's account notes that in 1752 the ginseng trade brought a high of twenty-four francs per pound—and also wrote later that frontier fort commanders profited by creating false bills of inventory for fort expenses, for which their wives were reimbursed at the royal treasury in Montreal. Sieur Louis de Courville, *Mémoires sur le Canada depuis 1749 jusqu'à 1760: en trois parties; avec cartes et plans lithographiés* (Quebec: Imprimerie de T. Cary, 1838), 11, 104–5. William Johnson, Britain's superintendant for Indian affairs in the northern colonies and a great rival of Joncaire's for Iroquois influence, also accumulated wealth from the ginseng trade.

10. *Mémoire pour Messire François Bigot, ci-devant intendant de justice, police, finance & marine en Canada, accusé: Contre Monsieur le procureur-général du roi en la commission, accusateur, première partie, contenant l'histoire de l'administration du sieur Bigot dans la colonie, & des réflexions générales sur cette administration* (Paris: de l'imprimerie de P. Al. Le Prieur, Imprimeur du Roi, rue Saint Jacques 1763), 21, 155.

11. *Mémoire pour le Marquis de Vaudreuil, grand-croix de l'ordre royal et militaire de Saint-Louis, ci-devant gouverneur et lieutenant général de la Nouvelle-France* (Paris: de l'imprimerie de Moreau, rue Galande, 1763), 4. On "social capital," see Catherine Desbarats and Allan Greer, "The Seven Years' War in Canadian History and Memory," in *Cultures in Conflict: The Seven Years' War in North America*, ed. Warren Hofstra (New York: Rowman and Littlefield, 2007), 168.

12. Jonathan Dull, *The French Navy and the Seven Years' War* (Lincoln: University of Nebraska Press, 2006), 76–77; Hodson, *Acadian Diaspora*, 79.

13. *Mémoire pour le Marquis de Vaudreuil*, 28.

14. Archives de la Bastille, Bibliothèque de l'Arsenal (hereafter cited as AB), Manuscripts 12143: Bastille, Feb. 2, 1762, Joncaire Chabert to his sister, f. 122v; Paris, Feb. 7, 1762, Joncaire d'Autrève to Joncaire Chabert, f. 159v–160v.

15. Courville, *Mémoires sur le Canada depuis 1749 jusqu'à 1760*, 19. The accomplished gossip Courville wrote that Joncaire Chabert's father lived a "good" life, moving between his French wife and his Seneca spouse and children. Sporadic records list Phillipe Chabert de Joncaire as *métis*, which seems plausible considering the dual French and Seneca families; no evidence suggests whether Daniel-Marie was Seneca by birth as well as by adoption.

16. *Mémoire pour Daniel de Joncaire-Chabert, ci-devant commandant au petit Fort de Niagara contre M. le Procureur-Général de la Commission établie pour l'affaire du Canada* (Paris: Châtelet, 1763), 3.

17. Paris, Mar. 30, 1762, police commissioner Sartine to Jumilhac regarding Vaudreuil's incarceration in the Bastille; Paris, Apr. 8, 1762, letter of Muval *père* regarding items Vaudreuil was permitted to receive. AB, MS 12501, vol. 27, 110, 128.

18. *Jugement rendu souverainement et en dernier ressort dans l'affaire du Canada par messieurs les lieutenants général de police* (Paris: de l'Imprimerie d'Antoine Boudet, Imprimeur du Roi et Du Châtelet, 1763), 204.

19. J. F. Bosher, "The French Government's Motives in the Affaire du Canada, 1761–1763," *English Historical Review* 96, no. 378 (January 1981): 70.

20. Regular pay was 1,080 *livres*, 720 *livres*, and 360/340 *livres*, respectively; even at reduced sums the cost of living in Touraine, according to François José de La Corne in a letter to his brother-in-law in 1785, was not excessive. Life in the city of Loches was "[a]ffordable, even for those with little income," as quoted in Larin, *L'exode*, 9. Although this was true in the 1780s, it would not have been so between 1763 and 1770, when the cost of living rose throughout France. The daily wage of a laborer in France around this period was roughly five *sols* a day (twenty *sols* made a *livre*). For more see Gilles Pacquet and Jean Pierre Wallot, "Some Price Indexes for Quebec and Montreal 1760–1913," in *Histoire Sociale/Social History* 21, nos. 61 and 62 (1998): 314.

21. Jean-François Mouhot, "Les 'pieds blancs' venus du froid? Les refugiés canadiens à Loches et en Touraine à la fin du 18e siècle," in *Les amis du pays Lochois/ Société des amis du pays Lochois,* (n.p., 2003), 132n19.

22. Ibid., 131–32.

23. Archives nationales d'Outre Mer (hereafter cited as ANOM), $F^3$16:160, "Ordonnance."

24. ANOM E 290: Le Moyne de Longueuil, f. 6, 6v.

25. Andrew Rodger, "Le Moyne de Longueuil," *DCBO*, http://www.biographi.ca/en/bio/le_moyne_de_longueuil_paul_joseph_4E.html, accessed Jul. 31, 2013.

26. Larin, *L'exode*, 9.

27. Mouhot, "Les 'pieds blancs' venus du froid?" 134. A paper trail following the veterans when the Crown turned to the thorny issue of Canadian paper money and indemnities led all the way to Tours, where all acts of the royal council were dutifully forwarded for public proclamation. Dozens of *arrêts, ordonnances,* and *edits* in the regional archives of Indre-et-Loire, copies to be made public and posted around Touraine, went from Paris to the intendant of Touraine. The volume suggests a compact community that stayed in the region for at least a decade.

28. ANOM B 115, f. 84–84v.

29. Archives départementales Indre-et-Loire, Archives Civiles C 360.

30. Larin, *L'exode*, 16.

31. W. J. Eccles, "The French Forces in America during the Seven Years' War," in *Dictionary of Canadian Biography*, ed. Frances G. Halpenny (Toronto: University of Toronto Press, 1974), vol. 3, xvii.

32. "Journal de Chaussegros de Léry, 1754–1755," *Rapport de L'Archiviste de la Province de Québec pour 1927–1928* (hereafter cited as *RAPQ* plus applicable date) (Quebec: L-Amable Proulx, 1928), 364.

33. Chaussegros de Léry (Ch.er) Joseph Gaspard, ANOM E 77: f. 13–13v. Léry could not have known that the generous sum being given to the Acadians was to maintain the pride of the French Crown. Although the Acadians had been in Britain, the Duc de Nivernais, the French ambassador, reported that they had received sixpence daily. See Hodson, *Acadian Diaspora*, 96. On Choiseul's Atlantic plans, see Marion Godfroy-Tayart de Bormes, "La guerre de Sept Ans et ses conséquences

atlantiques: Kourou ou l'apparition d'un nouveau système colonial," *French Historical Studies* 32 (2): 167–91. Robert Larin's *Canadiens en Guyane, 1754–1805* (Quebec: Éditions du Septentrion, 2006) looks at the Canadian *habitants* (not marine officers) who participated in France's schemes in the Kourou and the Caribbean.

34. Léry to the Naval Minister, Quebec Oct. 15, 1749, ANOM E 77: f. 4–4v. Saint Domingue, Cayenne, and even Louisiana carried the lure of great riches and the threat of tropical fever. Léry's commitment to Atlantic service is evident in his request for assignment to more prosperous colonies rather than to a position in France. Perhaps he believed he had the skills necessary for this assignment (and ready connections to his remaining Canadian family), or he may have understood that he had limited choices because his commission was in the *troupes de la marine*, a colonial service. On promotion see Léry, note given to M. Rodier, July 7, 1763, ANOM E 77: f. 14.

35. ANOM E 77: f. 14.

36. Lévis affidavit, Paris, Dec. 3, 1764, and Marin personnel file, ANOM E 302: f. 2, 13.

37. De Marin, Joseph La Malgue File, ANOM E 302: f. 12. Marin's son noted his father's excellent record, including the *croix de Saint Louis*, and his family's century of history in Canada, when making his own appeal for promotion in the 1780s. See Marin to Naval Minister Castries, Paris, Sept. 15, 1783, and Marin, *lieutenant colonel au corps des volontaires de Benowsky* File, ANOM E 302: f. 24.

38. Marin file, ANOM E 302: f. 3.

39. Marin file, ANOM E 302: f. 13.

40. Lévis affidavit, Paris, Dec. 3, 1764, and Marin personnel file, ANOM E 302: f. 2, 13.

41. *Mémoire*, Mar. 10, 1765, ANOM E 302: f. 5.

42. Lévis affidavit; *Mémoire*, ANOM E 302: f. 2–3, 5v.

43. "Versailles 31 Dec 1764," ANOM E 384: Vaudreuil, f. 49.

44. Vaudreuil's family interests in Saint Domingue and elsewhere in the Atlantic after 1760 provided Rigaud potential sources of funds. His complaints may also have distinguished between the treatment of soldiers and administrators. Jacques Prevost de la Croix, civil administrator at Louisbourg, managed to become the intendant at Toulon in 1776. When de la Croix retired in 1781, he earned a pension of sixteen thousand *livres* in addition to the income of two thousand *livres* from his *croix de Saint Louis*.

45. Vaudreuil file, ANOM E 384: f. 50–50v.

46. Bosher, "French Government's Motives in the Affaire du Canada," 59–78. Prior to 1756, the French treasury spent 30 percent of its budget on debt. After 1763, interest payments on debt alone consumed 60 percent of the budget. See James C. Riley, *The Seven Years War and the Old Regime in France: The Economic and Financial Toll* (Princeton, NJ: Princeton University Press, 1987), 161, 231.

47. Vaudreuil file, ANOM E 384: f. 50–50v.

48. Vaudreuil file, ANOM E 384: f. 67–67v.

49. Eccles, "French Forces in America during the Seven Years' War," in *Dictionary of Canadian Biography*, vol. 3, xxii.

50. Vaudreuil file, ANOM E 384: f. 67.

51. La Corne St. Luc file, ANOM E 243: f. 6, 6v, 7. In the 1747 application La Corne St. Luc uses the term *guerriers* to describe the Abenakis, with whom he has gone to war, rather than the more common term, *sauvages*. Additionally, the weapon used is indeed a tomahawk (a *casse-tête*) rather than the generic hatchet (*hâche*).

52. *Mémoire pour Daniel de Joncaire-Chabert*, 20–21.

53. Bibliothèque nationale de France (hereafter cited as BN), Nouvelles Acquisitions Françaises, 9408, f. 20 (for Bougainville); Service Historique de la Défense, Armée de Terre (hereafter cited as SHD), Vincennes: A^{1}3624, Marine, Amérique, 1761–1762, f. 13 (Mar. 24, 1761, parole for Lévis from Whitehall); f. 207 (Aug. 26, 1762, letter from M. Egremont to Bourlamaque confirming his parole). Dumas: SHD A^{1}3628, f. 11.

54. SHD A^{1}3624, f. 206.

55. Pierre Pouchot, *Mémoires sur la dernière guerre de l'Amérique septentrionale entre la France et l'Angleterre: suivis des observations, dont plusieurs sont relatives au théâtre actuel de la guerre, & de nouveaux détails sur les mœurs & les usages des sauvages, avec des cartes topographiques. Par M. Pouchot, Chevalier de l'Ordre Royal & Militaire de St. Louis, ancien capitaine au Régiment de Béarn, commandant des forts de Niagara & de Lévis, en Canada* (Yverdon: 1781), vol. 1, xxi–xxiii; Peter Moogk, "Pouchot, Pierre," *DCBO*, http://www.biographi.ca/009004-119.01-e.php?BioId=35723, accessed Nov. 12, 2010.

56. BN, Nouvelles Acquisitions Françaises, 9408, p. 14, correspondence between William Pitt and Bougainville to erect a monument to Montcalm in Canada, Paris, Mar. 24, 1761; *Report of the Public Archives of Canada for the Year 1929* (Ottawa: F. A. Acland, 1929), 90, Paris, Dec. 3, 1760, Bougainville to the Marquise de St. Véran, asking for Montcalm's biographical information for said monument.

57. Charles de Bonnechose, *Montcalm et le Canada français* (Paris: Hachette, 1882), 605.

58. *Mémoire pour Messire François Bigot*, 731, 734; *Jugement rendu souverainement*, 57; Bonnechose, *Montcalm et le Canada français*, 153.

59. Antoine Léonard Thomas's romantic epic, *Jumonville*, appeared in 1759 and went through repeated printings in 1763, 1767, and 1771—a testament to the poem and the subject's popularity. John Carter Brown Library, *Annual Reports*, vol. 2 (Providence, RI: John Carter Brown Library, 1935), 1935, 17–18.

60. Editorial notes run throughout the volumes. The explicit American Revolution context is noted in the preface and also later in the text, such as in the editors' notes to Pouchot's account of the Jumonville incident. The editorial "corrective" sought to exonerate Washington, now France's ally, by claiming that Villiers did not intend to call Washington a murderer in his capitulation terms. See editors' notes in Pouchot, *Mémoires*, vol. 1, 15, 17. The publication history of Pouchot is thoroughly discussed in Brian Leigh Dunnigan's "Introduction" to Pierre Pouchot, *Memoirs on the Late War in North America between France and England*, rev. ed., trans. Michael Cardy, ed. and annotated by Brian Leigh Dunnigan (Youngstown, NY: Old Fort Niagara Association, 2004). See especially 10–11.

61. Pouchot, *Mémoires*, vol. 2, 145–46.

62. SHD Y^{2}D: Dossiers personnels des lieutenants-generaux, 1153 (Montreuil); Y^{3}D: Dossiers personnels des maréchaux de camp, 2393 (Boulamaque); 2759 (Bougainville); Desandrouins (3251).

63. William J. Eccles, "François Gaston de Lévis, duc de," *DCBO*, http://www.biographi.ca/en/bio/levis_francois_de_4E.html, accessed Jul. 31, 2013.

64. Montreal, Sept. 8, 1760, "Protest of Chevalier de Lévis against obliging the troops to lay down their arms," *Documents Relative to the Colonial History of the State of New York*, ed. and trans. E. B. O'Callaghan (Albany: Weed Parsons, 1858), X: 1106; on Lévis speaking on behalf of his officers to protest a "dishonorable capitulation" see entry of Sept. 7, 1760, Jean-Guillaume-Charles de Pantavit de Margon, *dit* chevalier de La Pause, "*Mémoire et observations sur mon voyage en Canada*," *RAPQ 1931–1932*, 123.

65. Marin commission, Versailles, Dec. 30, 1772, ANOM E 302: f. 1.

66. Naval Minister Choiseul to Marin de La Malgue, June 28, 1765 (copy in file), ANOM E 302: f. 8; Marin (son) to the Minister, Versailles, July 6, 1775, and Blois, Aug. 10, 1775; Benyovsky to Marin (son), Cap, Sept. 20, 1782, ANOM E 302: f.7, 10v, 18–18v. One of the Marin sons accompanied his father to Madagascar and succumbed to the same fever.

67. For more on this, see William J. Eccles, "Coulon de Villiers, François," *DCBO*, http://www.biographi.ca/en/bio/coulon_de_villiers_francois_4E.html, accessed Jul. 31, 2013.

68. Michael A. McDonnnell, "Worlds of Warfare: Indians, French, and Métis and the Sixty Years' War for Empire," paper presented at the Warfare and Society in Colonial North America and Caribbean conference, Oct. 7–8, 2006, Knoxville, TN.

69. Dunn Jr., "Chabert de Joncaire," *DCBO*.

70. Joncaire Chabert's return to British Canada in 1764 caused consternation among British administrators, who feared his intention to resume trade and reclaim his influence. William Johnson to Thomas Gage, Nov. 24, 1767, Thomas Gage papers, American Series, William L. Clements Library, The University of Michigan, vol. 72, 3.

71. Dunn Jr., "Chabert de Joncaire," *DCBO*.

72. F. J. Thorpe, "Chaussegros de Léry," *DCBO*, http://www.biographi.ca/en/bio/chaussegros_de_lery_gaspard_joseph_1721_97_4E.html, accessed Jul. 31, 2013; Léry file, ANOM E 77: f. 14v.

73. Ibid.

74. For demographic statistics, see Larin, *L'exode*, 10.

75. Étienne Taillemitte, "Legardeur de Repentigny, Louis," *DCBO*, http://www.biographi.ca/en/bio.php?id_nbr=2008, accessed Jul. 31, 2013.

76. Pouchot wrote his memoirs partially in self-defense against charges of fraud and in his introduction stated that it was Naval Minister Berryer who set into motion the corruption raids, with this theme picked up by Choiseul upon his accession to this position. See Pouchot, *Mémoires*, xix.

77. See Robert Larin, "L'exode de Canadiens à la Conquete—De la mémoire selective à la mémoire retrouvé . . . en Guyane," in *Bulletin Mémoire Vives*, Bulletin 22 (October 2007), and Robert Larin and Yves Drolet, "Les listes de Carleton et de Haldimand. États de la noblesse canadienne en 1767 et 1778," *Histoire Sociale/Social History* 41, no. 82 (November 2008): 563–603. Larin painstakingly follows the lives of the Canadian exiles but also categorizes anyone who married in Canada, married

a Canadian, or had children in Canada as "Canadian." Such a broad definition has provided excellent archival work for other historians to follow, but, in this instance, my considerations are the narrower band of officers of the *troupes franches de la marine* who served in Canada until the capitulation of 1760. For contrasting views, see Bonnault, "Le Canada perdu et abandonné," 339, 346.

Chapter 6. Paradise

1. Edward P. Hamilton, "The Seven Years' War in America," in Louis-Antoine de Bougainville, *Adventure in the Wilderness: The American Journals of Louis-Antoine de Bougainville, 1756–1760*, trans. and ed. Edward P. Hamilton (Norman: University of Oklahoma Press, 1990), xx. The journal remained in manuscript form despite Bougainville's initial intention to publish it and remained so until the twentieth century.

2. The most recent biography is John Dunmore, *Storms and Dreams: The Life of Louis de Bougainville* (Fairbanks: University of Alaska Press, 2007), first published as *Storms and Dreams: Louis de Bougainville: Soldier, Explorer, Statesman* (Auckland, NZ: Exisle, 2005). Dunmore points out that the seeds of Bougainville's Pacific ethnography are evident in the North American journals but focuses on the placement of both American Indians and Pacific Islanders in an ancient Greek framework. See especially the 2005 edition, pages 53–56 on this point. Bougainville's most thorough biographer was René de Kerallain, *Les français au Canada: La jeunesse de Bougainville et la guerre de Sept Ans* (Paris: Thion, 1896), who had the distinct advantage of accessing the Bougainville family papers before their dispersal in a 1950s auction. Mary Kimbrough's *Louis-Antoine de Bougainville, 1729–1811: A Study in French Naval History and Politics* (Lewiston, NY: E. Mellen Press, 1990), contains more North American material than Dunmore, drawing heavily on Kerallain to fill in archival gaps. Jean-Étienne Martin-Allanic's *Bougainville: Navigateur et les découvertes de son temps* (Paris: Presses Universitaires de Paris, 1964) skips over the Seven Years' War years. Literary criticism of Bougainville's *Voyage*, beginning with Denis Diderot's *Supplement to Bougainville's Voyage* (1772), continues today. See, for instance, *Journal de la Société des océanistes* 24, no. 24 (1968), and *Strangers in the South Seas: The Idea of the Pacific in Western Thought*, ed. Richard Lansdown (Honolulu: University of Hawai'i Press, 2006).

3. Dunmore, *Storms and Dreams*, 12, 15, 22.

4. See chap. 4 for examples of Bougainville's pursuit of the latest academic texts. Quebec, Sept. 9, 1756, Bougainville to Jean-Pierre de Bougainville, Louis-Antoine de Bougainville, *Écrits sur le Canada: Mémoires, journal, lettres* (Sillery, Quebec: Septentrion, 2003), 365.

5. John Dunmore, Introduction, in Louis-Antoine de Bougainville, *The Pacific Journal of Louis-Antoine de Bougainville, 1767–1768*, trans. and ed. John Dunmore (London: Hakluyt Society, 2002), xix. Martin-Allanic, *Bougainville: Navigateur*, vol. 1, x–xi.

6. Christopher Hodson, *The Acadian Diaspora* (Oxford: Oxford University Press, 2012), 90, 104–5; Marion Godfroy Tayart de Bormes, "La guerre de Sept Ans et ses conséquences atlantiques: Kourou ou l'apparation d'un nouveau système colonial," *French Historical Studies* 32, no. 2 (Spring 2009): 167–69.

7. Bougainville, *Écrits sur le Canada*, 379.

8. As a protégé of Adrien-Maurice, Duc de Noailles, Choiseul continued his patron's insistence that overseas colonies and maritime strength were key to limiting British hegemony. See Marion F. Godfroy, *Kourou, 1763: Le dernier rêve de l'Amérique française* (Paris: Vendémiaire, 2011), 28–29. On the navy's importance to 1760s' French policy, see Paul Mapp, *The Elusive West and the Contest for Empire, 1713–1763* (Chapel Hill: University of North Carolina Press, 2011), 375. On responsibility see Dunmore, Introduction, in Bougainville, *Pacific Journal of Louis-Antoine de Bougainville*, lxxiii–lxxiv.

9. Mapp, *Elusive West*, 361, 368. On the inaccuracy of French maps, see 371–72. The reality of having to interact with the indigenous inhabitants of those lands contributed as much to this diminished interest in Louisiana as the revelation of inaccurate geographic trends.

10. Godfroy, *Kourou, 1763*, 45.

11. Martin-Allanic, *Bougainville: Navigateur*, 64.

12. On readings and associations, see ibid., 72–73, and Hodson, *Acadian Diaspora*, 135. John Dunmore, Introduction, in Bougainville, *Pacific Journal of Louis-Antoine de Bougainville*, xx. Major funding for the expedition came from the Bougainville family, especially his uncle Pierre d'Arboulin, a former postmaster general and great friend of the Marquise de Pompadour, his relative Bougainville de Nerville, and Monsieur de Marville, member of the royal council and son-in-law to Madame de Séchelles. See Martin-Allanic, *Bougainville: Navigateur*, 83, 179.

13. Godfroy, *Kourou, 1763*, 42.

14. Emma Rothschild, "A Horrible Tragedy in the French Atlantic," *Past & Present* 192 (August 2006): 71, 73. Godfroy-Tayart de Borms, "La guerre de Septs Ans," 167–91; Robert Larin, *Canadiens en Guyane, 1754–1805* (Paris: Septentrion, 2006); Hodson, *Acadia Diaspora*, 92–93, 104.

15. *Encyclopédie, ou dictionnaire raisonné des sciences, des arts et des métiers*, ed. Denis Diderot and Jean le Rond D'Alembert. University of Chicago: ARTFL Encyclopédie Project (Spring 2010), ed. Robert Morrissey, http://encyclopedie.uchicago.edu/, 9: 137; Rothschild, "Horrible Tragedy," 71.

16. Rothschild, "Horrible Tragedy," 73; Godfroy-Tayart de Bormes, "La guerre de Sept Ans," 168.

17. John Shovlin, "Political Economy and the French Nobility, 1750–1789," in *The French Nobility in the Eighteenth Century: Reassessment and New Approaches*, ed. Jay M. Smith (University Park: Pennsylvania State University Press, 2006), 116. For an early example of the strategic benefit of colonies see "Mémoire du maréchal de Noailles sur les colonies d'Amérique, July 1749," annexed to a letter of Aug. 1, 1749, from Noailles to Louis XV, *Correspondance de Louis XV et du maréchal de Noailles publié par ordre de son excellence le maréchal comte Ramdon* (Paris: P. Dupont, 1865), vol. 2, 290–93.

18. Peter Moogk, "Reluctant Exiles: The Problem of Colonization in French North America," *William and Mary Quarterly* 46, no. 3 (July 1989): 463–505.

19. Hodson, *Acadian Diaspora*, 105.

20. Hodson, "Bondage So Harsh," 98. "Integrated empire" that disavowed slavery is discussed on 99. See also Hodson, *Acadia Diaspora*. Jean-François Mouhot studies

Acadian migration to and reintegration in Europe through continental colonial settlement plans in *Les réfugiés acadiens en France, 1758–1785: L'impossible réintégration?* (Sillery, Quebec: Septentrion, 2009).

21. Rothschild, "Horrible Tragedy," 71. On *courroux*'s elemental association see *Dictionaire de l'Académie française*, 1694 ed., http://artflx.uchicago.edu/cgi-bin/dicos/pubdico1look.pl?strippedhw=courroux, accessed Feb. 3, 2012.

22. Godfroy argues that the embarrassed Choiseul administration blamed the disaster on Guyana's climate and disease (factors beyond ministerial control) rather than accept that the devastating epidemics had begun in Europe, then spread to the embarkation ports and to the migrants. See *Kourou, 1763*, 228–29.

23. Hodson, *Acadian Diaspora*, 135–38. Choiseul agreed to continue funding the 150 Acadians' stipend of 6 *sols* a day while in the Falklands. Martin-Allanic, *Bougainville: Navigateur*, 83–84.

24. Hodson, *Acadian Diaspora*, 142; Bougainville, *Pacific Journal of Louis-Antoine de Bougainville*, xx.

25. Sinnamary, which was designed to prove that whites could indeed survive, work, and thrive in the tropics, was conceived as a physiocratic settlement. See Barbara Traver, "After Kourou: Settlement Schemes in French Guiana in the Age of Enlightenment" (PhD diss., University of Washington, 2011). In 1772 Baron de Benyovsky led an expedition to Madagascar on behalf of France but funded by himself. For Bougainville, see Martin-Allanic, *Bougainville: Navigateur*, 118–20. Bougainville's uncle, Arboulin, anticipated that funds would be the stumbling block for the Îles Malouines proposal. Arboulin and Bougainville asked only for royal approval to aid them in raising private capital.

26. Antoine-Charles de Saint Simon, the Canadian who accompanied Bougainville to the Falklands, stands as the exception to the rule. Saint Simon had been a marine but was so young that he had barely served in New France; Bougainville hoped to mold him according to French, not Canadian, tradition. By 1767 Saint Simon was a commander in Saint-Domingue. See *Collections of the State Historical Society of Wisconsin*, ed. Reuben Gold Thwaites (Madison: Published by the Society, 1908,) vol. 17, 36.

27. Dunmore, Introduction, in Bougainville, *Pacific Journal of Louis-Antoine de Bougainville*, xxiii.

28. Bibliothèque nationale de France (hereafter cited as BN), Nouvelles Acquisitions Françaises, 9407, f.53–54. Translation of instructions from Bougainville, *Pacific Journal of Louis-Antoine de Bougainville*, xliv–xlv. "Instructions" did not mean with a royally mandated mission, for the king's *mémoire* drafted by the Naval Ministry was little more than a rewording of Bougainville's original proposal. The financial burden of the voyage remained on Bougainville's shoulders, not the Crown's.

29. Bougainville, *Pacific Journal of Louis-Antoine de Bougainville*, xlvi. An example of seventeenth-century royal instructions to governors in New France is the following: "Mémoire pour servir d'instruction au sieur Marquis de Denonville, gouverneur et lieutenant général de la Nouvelle France sur les éclaircissements à donner au sujet des contestations qui sont entre les Français es les Anglais touchant la propriété des pays de l'Amérique septentrionale," Mar. 8, 1688, in Francis Parkman papers, Massachusetts Historical Society, 7: *XT Canada, Lettres du Roy, etc., 1675–1689*.

30. Dictionnaires d'Autrefois, the ARTFL Project, http://artflx.uchicago.edu/cgi-bin/dicos/pubdico1look.pl?strippedhw=sauvage, accessed Dec. 30, 2011.

31. Entry for Sept. 20, 1756, Bougainville, "Lettres et journaux de Bougainville," BN, Nouvelles Acquisitions Françaises, 9405, f.121. In the summer of 1759 Bougainville reported that Gen. James Wolfe had asked the Marquis de Vaudreuil to refrain from using "barbarians"—Indians—in the defense of Quebec. See BN, Nouvelles Acquisitions Française,s 9405, f.269v.

32. Bougainville, *Voyage* (1771), 96, 160, 229.

33. David Bell, *The Cult of the Nation in France: Inventing Nationalism, 1680–1800* (Cambridge, MA: Harvard University Press, 2001), 84–86.

34. Dictionnaire de l'Académie française, 1762. Dictionnaires d'Autrefois, the ARTFL Project, http://artflx.uchicago.edu/cgi-bin/dicos/pubdico1look.pl?strippedhw=barbare, accessed Dec. 30, 2011. A comparison of the 1694 and 1762 editions' definition of "barbarian" attests to a transition in meaning. In 1694 one definition of *barbare* adhered to the Greek roots of the word: an unintelligible language with "no relation to our language" and which sounded "shocking to our ears, [for example,] *Les Yroquois parlent une langue fort barbare* [the Iroquois speak a very barbaric language]."

35. *The Dictionary of the History of Ideas: Studies of Selected Pivotal Ideas*, ed. Philip P. Wiener (New York: Charles Scribner's Sons, 1973–1974), vol. 2, 129. Montesquieu and Voltaire wrangled over older traditions of the relationship between environment and government, hearkening back to the tradition of sixteenth-century French theoretician Jean Bodin. The rational classification and categorization of the natural world began in earnest in the 1750s, with the works of Diderot and d'Alembert, as well as Linnaeus, Buffon, and Blumenbach. Thus, Bougainville's service in New France was contemporaneous with the development of the newest climatic theories rather than such ideas circulating before his army service. For more on this see Roxann Wheeler, *The Complexion of Race: Categories of Difference in Eighteenth-Century British Culture* (Philadelphia: University of Pennsylvania Press, 2000), 28–29.

36. Réal Ouellet and Mylène Tremblay, "From the Good Savage to the Degenerate Indian: The Amerindian in the Accounts of Travel to America," in *Decentring the Renaissance: Canada and Europe in Multidisciplinary Perspective, 1500–1700*, ed. Germaine Warkentin and Carolyn Podruchny (Toronto: University of Toronto Press, 2001), 168–69. In 1768 de Pauw changed the language of colonial "degeneration" away from the destructive lure of civilization by maintaining that it was the result of major biological, geographical, and historical determinism. With this theory, degeneration could not stem from or affect Europeans who lived in the "perfect" climate and showed clear signs of a "civilized" progression. For implications of Buffon's ideas in North America, see Thomas Jefferson, *Notes on the State of Virginia* (1787). For a discussion of the racial implications, particularly during and after Thomas Jefferson's presidency, see Reginald Horsman, *Race and Manifest Destiny:The Origins of American Racial Anglo-Saxonism* (Cambridge, MA: Harvard University Press, 1981).

37. Bougainville, *Pacific Journal of Louis-Antoine de Bougainville*, 28. The survivors of the Narváez expedition repeatedly referred to "Christian" rather than "Indian" as the marker of difference. See *The Narrative of Cabeza de Vaca: Álvar Núñez Cabeza*

NOTES TO PAGES 164–166

de Vaca, ed. Rolena Adorno and Patrick Charles Pautz (Lincoln: University of Nebraska Press, 2003), 41–177. Francisco de Coronado named a Pawnee guide who led him deep into the North American grasslands "the Turk." See Patricia Nelson Limerick, *The Legacy of Conquest: The Unbroken Past of the American West* (New York: W. W. Norton, 1987), 225.

38. Dunmore, Introduction, in Bougainville, *Pacific Journal of Louis-Antoine de Bougainville*, lvii–lviii; Bougainville, *Adventure in the Wilderness*, entries for Sept. 19, 1756; Oct. 8, 1756; Oct. 14, 1756, 40, 41, 51, 55 (noting that Canada is "dangerous for discipline"); entries for Oct. 20, 1756; Dec. 27, 1756, 59–60, 75–76 (on Catholic Hurons, "for they are always savages just as much as those who have been the least tamed"); entries for Aug. 9, 1757, Aug. 15–19, 1757, 170, 174.

39. Bougainville, *Pacific Journal of Louis-Antoine de Bougainville*, 12, 25. Bougainville's log, though not the *Voyage*, contains a snide remark about Patagonians and Rousseau's "natural man."

40. Louis-Antoine de Bougainville, *Voyage autour du monde*, édition critique par Michel Bideaux et Sonia Faessel (Paris: Presses de l'Université de Paris-Sorbonne, 2001), 204.

41. Bougainville, *Pacific Journal of Louis-Antoine de Bougainville*, 60.

42. Entry for Sept. 12–13, 1756, Bougainville, *Adventure in the Wilderness*, 36.

43. Bougainville and his crew did not realize that an English expedition had "discovered" Tahiti a year prior to the French voyage. Captain Samuel Wallis, a veteran of the Seven Years' War who had spent some time in North American waters, commanded the HMS *Dolphin* and arrived in Tahiti on June 18, 1767. In this initial encounter between English and Tahitian cultures, the indigenous population learned quickly that European projectile weapons were deadlier than their own (Wallis's canons destroyed a number of canoes) and that the most effective and safest interactions depended on welcoming Europeans, supplying them with food and women, giving them supplies, and then sending them swiftly on their way. Dunmore, Introduction, in Bougainville, *Pacific Journal of Louis-Antoine de Bougainville*, lvi–lvii. For more on the Wallis voyage see Samuel Wallis, "The Discovery of Tahiti," in *Exploration and Exchange: A South Seas Anthology, 1680–1900*, ed. Jonathan Lamb, Vanessa Smith, and Nicholas Thomas (Chicago: University of Chicago Press, 2000), 57–72.

44. Bideaux and Faessel, Introduction, in *Voyage*, 37; ibid., 226. Compare the references to theft in Tahiti to the constant complaints about this subject in North America. In a 1758 entry, Bougainville goes so far as to suggest that the unchecked theft and robberies by the Abenakis and the lack of hierarchy to control this thievery stemmed from from corrupted French leadership, where common interpreters (rather than officers) serve as intermediaries in Indian and official French affairs. Entry for July 13, 1758, Bougainville, *Adventure in the Wilderness*, 242–43.

45. Entry for Oct. 20, 1756, Bougainville, *Adventure in the Wilderness*, 60; Apr. 6, 1768; Bougainville, *Pacific Journal of Louis-Antoine de Bougainville*, 61, 70.

46. Apr. 15, 1768, Bougainville, *Pacific Journal of Louis-Antoine de Bougainville*, 70, 72; entry for Sept. 20, 1756, Bougainville, *Adventure in the Wilderness*, 41.

47. Bougainville, *Pacific Journal of Louis-Antoine de Bougainville*, 60; Bougainville, *Voyage*, 227.

48. Bougainville, *Voyage*, 226. Note that Bougainville refers to Native Americans in the *Voyage* as the *indigènes du Canada*, not as the *sauvages*, as he had in his earlier North American journals.

49. Bougainville, *Voyage*, 227, 227n37.

50. Bougainville, *Voyage*, 115.

51. Entries for Dec. 12, 1757–Mar. 1, 1758, Bougainville, *Adventure in the Wilderness*, 196, in reference to Canadians ignoring the suffering of refugee Acadians; Apr. 10, 1766, Bougainville, *Pacific Journal of Louis-Antoine de Bougainville*, 66.

52. Denis Diderot, quoted in Bideaux and Faessel, Introduction, in *Voyage*, 40.

53. Bougainville, *Pacific Journal of Louis-Antoine de Bougainville*, 63. "O Venus, hospitibus nam te dare jura loquuntur, hunc loetum Tyrisque diem Trojaque profectis esse veils nostrosque hujus meminisse minores" [O Venus, for they say it is you who grant rights to those who seek hospitality, may it be your pleasure to make this a happy day for those who set out from Troy and one our descendants will remember], from Virgil, *The Aeneid* 1, trans. Robert Fitzgerald (New York: Vintage, 1984), 731–33]. Compare this to Bougainville's journal entry on Aug. 15, 1757: "Ah, Put the savage land behind you! Leave / this shore of greed! / [For I am Polydorus]," from Virgil, *Aeneid* 3, 17–44). *Adventure in the Wilderness*, 175. For analysis in original context, see chap. 3, note 91, this volume.

54. Virgil, *Aeneid* 1, 328–425 [378–428]. Although all translators agree on Virgil's intentions to reference Venus's dress, various editions interpret this as one where Venus reveals herself either by her distinctive, delicate garment or by her nudity. Compare the following: "the length of her shimmering gown," *Aeneid*; "in the length of train descends her sweeping gown," 1, 560; Virgil, *The Aeneid*, trans. John Dryden (Hertfordshire, UK: Wordsworth Editions, 1997), 18–19; "down to her feet fell her raiment," Virgil, *Eclogues. Georgics. Aeneid* 1–6, trans. H. R. Fairclough (Cambridge: Loeb Classics, 1999), ln. 403).

55. Louis-Antoine de Bougainville, *Voyage autour du monde par la frégate du roi la Boudeuse et la flûte l'Étoile* (Paris: Chez Saillant et Nyons, 1771), 220–21 (Tahiti); 238 (Navigator Islands); 268 (Choiseul Islands). The only one of the images to give a hint of opinion is the *"canot sauvage"* of the Choiseul Islands.

56. Charlevoix's *Histoire et description de la nouvelle France* (1744) did not have the same number of lush illustrations as Bacqueville de la Potherie's earlier work. The trend in French narratives of the eighteenth century appeared to be for topographical images, schema, and maps (which Charlevoix and Pouchot both contained). One 1758 work that does not follow this trend is Le Page du Pratz's *Histoire de la Louisiane*. By comparison, British sources provide a relative wealth of material for the same period in both private journals and published engravings. This material includes the small drawings of Ottawas by Gen. George Townshend, sketches made at Fort Ligonier by Henry Hamilton, and the famous engraved portrait of Thayanoguin/King Hendrick. *Adventure in the Wilderness* reproduces no images; *Écrits sur le Canada* includes a series of linear drawings reminiscent of eighteenth-century diary images in its diary reproduction.

57. BN, Nouvelles Acquisitions Françaises, 9406, f.49–50.

58. Log entry, Apr. 7, 1768, Bougainville, *Pacific Journal of Louis-Antoine de Bougainville*, 63; Apr. 10, 1768, ibid., 67.

59. For a good overview of the sixteenth-century French Atlantic, see Philip Boucher, "'Revisioning the French Atlantic': or, How to Think about the French Presence in the Atlantic, 1550–1625," in *The Atlantic World and Virginia, 1550–1624*, ed. Peter Mancall (Chapel Hill: University of North Carolina Press, 2007), 274–307.

60. Apr. 14, 1768, Bougainville, *Pacific Journal of Louis-Antoine de Bougainville*, 70.

61. Bougainville, *Voyage*, 217.

62. Ibid., 219.

63. Tracy Neal Leavelle, *The Catholic Calumet: Colonial Conversions in French and Indian North America* (Philadelphia: University of Pennsylvania Press, 2012), 68; Sophie White, *Wild Frenchmen and Frenchified Indians: Material Culture and Race in Colonial Louisiana* (Philadelphia: University of Pennsylvania Press, 2012), 42, 55, 110.

64. The identity and the travel dates of the two Kahnawake Mohawks remain unclear. Favored with special outfits to mark the occasion of their travels, including one sent by the Dauphin, they might have gone to court and at least met officials from the Naval Ministry. Entry for Apr. 26, 1757, *Le journal du Marquis de Montcalm durant ses campagnes en Canada de 1756 à 1759*, in *Collection des manuscrits du maréchal de Lévis*, published under the direction of Abbé H. R. Casgrain (Quebec: Imprimerie de L.-J. Demers et Frère, 1895), vol. 7, 187.

65. Bougainville, *Voyage*, 234–35.

66. Frank Lestringant, "The Philosopher's Breviary: Jean de Léry in the Enlightenment," in *New World Encounters*, ed. Stephen Greenblatt (Los Angeles: University of California Press, 1993), 129, 131.

67. Gordon Sayre, *Les Sauvages Américains: Representations of Native Americans in French and English Colonial Literature* (Chapel Hill: University of North Carolina Press, 1997), 85.

68. Ralph Bowen, Introduction and Preface, in Denis Diderot, *Rameau's Nephew and Other Works*, trans. Jacques Barzun and Ralph H. Bowen (Cambridge, MA: Hackett, 2001), xii; Diderot, *Rameau's Nephew and Other Works*, 178.

69. Entries for Dec. 27, 1756, and Aug. 9, 1757, Bougainville, *Adventure in the Wilderness*, 75–76, 170.

70. Étienne Taillemite, Preface, in *Écrits sur le Canada*, 15–16.

71. *HarperCollins Robert French Unabridged Dictionary*, 7th ed. (New York: Harper Collins, 2005), 117. One of Watteau's most celebrated and widely reproduced images was his 1717 *L'embarquement pour Cythère* [Voyage to Cythera], where gorgeously arrayed aristocrats and cherubs frolicked in the beauty and mild climate of the island of Venus's birth.

Epilogue: *Mon Frère Sauvage*

Epigraph: from John Dryden's translation of Virgil's *Aeneid* (London: Wordsworth Classics of World Literature, 1997), III: 564–77.

1. Colin G. Calloway, *The American Revolution in Indian Country: Crisis and Diversity in Native American Communities* (Cambridge: Cambridge University Press, 1995), 124–26.

2. Henri Doniol, *Histoire de la participation de la France à l'établissement des États Unis: Correspondance diplomatique et documents* (Paris: Imprimerie Nationale, 1886),

vol. 3, 423, 425. Gerard de Rayneval, first official minister of France to the North American colonies had previously been involved in the negotiations over the Treaty of Alliance and the Treaty of Amity and Commerce. On the likelihood that these ambassadors hailed from Kahnawake, see Calloway, *American Revolution in Indian Country*, 35–36.

3. Doniol, *Histoire de la participation de la France*, vol. 3, 423n2. Doniol's footnote quotes d'Estaing's *mémoire* dated Nov. 5, 1778, "Rapport du 5 Novembre 1778," Archives nationales de France (hereafter cited as AN), B⁴141, f. 246–47.

4. Réné de Kerallain, "Bougainville à l'escadre du Cte d'Estaing, guerre d'Amérique, 1778–1779," *Journal de la Société des Américanistes* 19, no. 19 (1927): 173.

5. Doniol, *Histoire de la participation de la France*, vol. 3, 423. Doniol's sources come from Gérard, "Rapport du 21 Octobre 1778," and d'Estaing's own testimony on Nov. 5, 1778, AN, B⁴141, f. 246–47. The actual visit appears to have been on Oct. 28, 1778. D'Estaing drew on this for his proclamation to French Canadians, made on the same date, reminding the former residents of New France of past glory, while taking great care to avoid upsetting Anglo-American patriots by referencing any events that smacked of Burgoyne's "manifesto" of June 24, 1777. See Doniol, *Histoire de la participation de la France*, vol. 3, 424.

6. Bibliothèque nationale de Paris (hereafter cited as BN), Nouvelles Acquisitions Françaises, 9406, 369–70. Kerallain relates this narrative in his biography of Bougainville but describes the French visitor as an émigré named the Chevalier de Mun. Moreover, Kerallain skirts the question of consanguinity, writing instead that refugee Shawnees in Louisiana "joined with the family of a true Canadian, Louis de Lorimier, governing in Spain's name the Cape Girardeau district, without forgetting the memory of Bougainville." Bougainville's son noted the results of his father's indigenous affair in the 1830s, prior to France's serious engagement with rapacious and heavily racialized colonialism in West Africa and southeast Asia, which shaped society's views on interracial unions at the time Kerallain was writing. See *Bougainville à l'escadre du Cte d'Estaing*, 173n1. Of Bougainville's three sons who lived to adulthood (Hyacinthe, Jean-Baptiste, and Adolphe), it is unclear which one added the text on Lorimier from an 1838 letter from Meux to their father's papers before giving them to the Bibliothèque nationale.

7. Many transformative works served to reorient colonial and imperial history to foreground Indian perspectives and have indigenous peoples carry the narrative rather than European dates and actors. Richard White, *The Middle Ground: Indians, Empires, and Republics in the Great Lakes Region, 1650–1815* (Cambridge: Cambridge University Press, 1991); Gregory Evans Dowd, *War under Heaven: Pontiac, the Indian Nations, and the British Empire* (Baltimore: Johns Hopkins University Press, 2004); Colin Calloway, *The Scratch of a Pen: 1763 and the Transformation of North America* (Oxford: Oxford University Press, 2006); Ian K. Steele, "The Shawnee Origins of Their Seven Years' War," *Ethnohistory* 53, no. 4 (October 2006): 657–87; Gail MacLeitch's *Imperial Entaglements: Iroquois Change and Persistence on the Frontiers of Empire* (Philadelphia: University of Pennsylvania Press, 2011); and Michael Witgen, *An Infinity of Nations: How the Native New World Shaped Early North America* (Philadelphia: University of Pennsylvania Press, 2011) all consider the Seven Years' War and its aftermath through Indian eyes in the northeast and Great Lakes region. Kathleen

DuVal, *The Native Ground: Indians and Colonists in the Heart of the Continent* (Philadelphia: University of Pennsylvania Press, 2007), probes Indian experiences within a changing French orbit in the Missouri River region. On reframed French colonial experiences in nineteenth-century North America, see Jay Gitlin, *The Bourgeois Frontier: French Towns, French Traders, and American Expansion* (New Haven, CT: Yale University Press, 2010).

8. Robert Englebert posits that Lorimier may have been of indigenous and French descent, based on the fact that he is the sole member of his family to be missing a baptismal record from La Présentation. A conclusive statement on Lorimier's heritage remains undecided at present, though. Conversation with Englebert, May 31, 2012, French Colonial Historical Society Annual Meeting, New Orleans, LA.

9. Margaret Beggs, "Lorimier, Louis 1748–1812," in *Dictionary of Missouri Biography*, ed. Lawrence O. Christensen, William E. Foley, Gary R. Kremer, and Kenneth H. Winn (Columbia: University of Missouri Press, 1999), 501–2; Louis Houck, *A History of Missouri from the Earliest Explorations and Settlements until the Admission of the State into the Union* (Chicago: R. R. Donnelly and Sons, 1908), vol. 2, 171–72; Louis Lorimier, *Louis Lorimier in the American Revolution, 1777–1782: A Mémoire by an Ohio Indian Trader and British Partisan*, trans. and with an introduction by Paul L. Stevens (Naperville, IL: Center for French Colonial Studies Extended Publications Series, no. 2, 1997), 3.

10. *Dictionary of Missouri Biography*, 501–2. Lorimier's earlier trading post was irreparably damaged during the American Revolution, making his westward movement necessary. See Lorimier, *Louis Lorimier in the American Revolution*, 4, 6; John Mack Faragher, "More Motley than Mackinaw: From Ethnic Mixing to Ethnic Cleansing on the Frontier of the Lower Missouri, 1783–1833," in *Contact Points: American Frontiers from the Mohawk Valley to the Mississippi, 1750–1830*, ed. Andrew R. L. Cayton and Fredericka J. Teute (Chapel Hill: University of North Carolina Press, 1996), 306–7; Colin Calloway, *The Shawnees and the War for America* (New York: Viking, 2007), 116.

11. Houck, *History of Missouri*, vol. 2, 180; entry for Nov. 23, 1803, Meriwether Lewis, *Journals of the Lewis and Clark Expedition*, http://lewisandclarkjournals.unl.edu/read/?_xmlsrc=1803-11-23.xml&_xslsrc=LCstyles.xsl, accessed Jan. 3, 2012.

12. Sept. 22, 1759, Camp de Lorette, Bougainville to Madame de Séchelles, BN, Nouvelles Acquisitions Françaises, 9406, 294; Louis-Antoine de Bougainville, *Écrits sur le Canada: Mémoires, journal, lettres* (Sillery, Quebec: Les Éditions du Septentrion, 2003), 404. Not all historians agree on the identity of the lady in question in this illicit Canadian relationship. At least one speculation has suggested the paramour was perhaps Madame Delafortelle; see *Écrits*, 404. Bougainville's affair with this woman, the wife of a nobleman, took place in France in 1755, and although it is possible he resumed the acquaintance upon his return in winter 1758, it seems unlikely he would wait until September 1759 to inform Madame de Séchelles of a rupture. John Dunmore takes note of Bougainville's adoption by the Kahnawakes, reported in the letter to Madame de Séchelles, and muses "whether this ceremony was then consummated in the arms of a young Indian girl." While Dunmore agrees that a French traveler met an "Indian chief" named Lorimier claiming to be Bougainville's son, he argues that the evidence is slim and unlikely. See *Storms and*

Dreams: Louis de Bougainville: Soldier, Explorer, Statesman (Auckland: Exile, 2005), 77. Tracing the name of Charlotte's mother is difficult. Houck and Beggs identify Lorimier's wife as "Charlotte Pemanpieh Bougainville Lorimier," suggesting that Pemanpieh was Charlotte's maiden and/or Shawnee name. Houck, *History of Missouri*, vol. 2, 170; Beggs, *Dictionary of Missouri Biography*, 501. Victor Suthren, relying on Mary Kimbrough as a source, nominates a displaced Shawnee woman from Ohio, "Ceuta," adopted by the "Christian Iroquois," as the likely candidate for Charlotte's mother. See *The Sea Has No End: The Life of Louis-Antoine de Bougainville* (Toronto: Dundurn, 2004), 54, 97–98. Stevens notes only that Charlotte Pemanpieh Bougainville's "surname implies blood ties to Louis de Bougainville." See Lorimier, *Louis Lorimier in the American Revolution*, 4.

13. Robert Sidney Douglass, *A History of Southeast Missouri: A Narrative Account of Its Historical Progress, Its People, and Its Principal Interests* (Chicago: Lewis, 1912), vol. 1, 73; Houck, *History of Missouri*, vol. 2, 179n2. Both Douglass and Houck provide the original Latin text as well as the translation used here. "To the memory of Charlotte P. B. Lorimier, consort of Maj. L. Lorimier, who departed this life on the 23d day of March, 1808, aged 50 years and two months, leaving four sons and two daughters; *Vixit, Chaoniae praeses dignissima gentis; / Et decus indigenum quam lapis iste tegit; / Illa bonum dedicit natura—magistra. / Et, duce natura, sponte secuta bonum est. / Talis honos memorium, nullo eultore, quotannis Maturat frustus mitis oliva suos.*" In contrast to Charlotte's epitaph, Louis Lorimier's Latin inscription is far simpler: *Ossa Habeant pacem tumulo cineresque sepulti: / Immortali animae luceat alma dies* ("Peace go his bones and ashes interred in this grave; may the eternal day illumine his immortal soul.")

14. After George Rogers Clark and the Kentucky militia burned Lorimier's storehouses in November 1782 (a retaliation for raids led by Louis Lorimier and Charles Beaubien into Kentucky), the aggrieved merchant attempted to gain restitution from Britain, asking for his friend Lieutenant Governor Hamilton to intercede on his behalf for damages. Lorimier, *Louis Lorimier in the American Revolution*, 6–7, 15; Faragher, "More Motley than Mackinaw," 308–9. In the *mémoire* seeking financial compensation, Lorimier notably emphasized to Hamilton his status among Shawnees rather than his status among English or French individuals.

15. Various works focus on Shawnee movements and interconnections. See Sami Lakomakis, *Singing the King's Song: Constructing and Resisting Power in Shawnee Communities, 1600–1860* (Oulu, Finland: Oulu University Press, 2009), Stephen Warren, *The Shawnees and Their Neighbors, 1795–1870* (Urbana-Champaign: University of Illinois, 2009), and Calloway, *The Shawnees and the War for America*, esp. chaps. 1, 5, 6. Laura Keenan Spero's work makes the point that historians have overdetermined Shawnee patrilineality, arguing instead that this was one of many adaptations to facilitate movement and cross-cultural encounters, and traces the experiences of Shawnees in this period. See "Stout, Bold, Cunning and the Greatest Travellers in America: The Colonial Shawnee Diaspora" (PhD diss., University of Pennsylvania, 2010).

16. Tracy Neale Leavelle notes that Indian fidelity to Catholicism in the Illinois Country and the *pays d'en haut* should be neither underestimated nor interpreted exclusively as the imposition of an institution serving European colonial interests. *The Catholic Calumet: Colonial Conversions in French and Indian North America* (Philadelphia: University of Pennsylvania Press, 2012), 13, 15.

17. Montreal, Mar. 3, 1758, Montcalm to Bourlamaque, *Collection des manuscrits du Maréchal de Lévis—Lettres de M. de Bourlamaque au chevalier de Lévis* (Quebec: L.-J. Demers et Frère, 1891), vol. 5, 204.

18. Recent interest in these regions demonstrates the longevity of the French regime as a result of legal institutions, trade networks, and continued settlements. See, for instance, Gitlin, *Bourgeois Frontier*, looks at French trade dynasties in Saint Louis and the importance of French Canadian *habitants* to the Louisiana territory. Following institutions, Robert Englebert traces much commonality between New France and the Illinois Country in the last quarter of the eighteenth century. See "Beyond Borders: French Mental Mapping and the French River World in North America, 1763–1803" (PhD diss., University of Ottawa, 2010). The remarkably resilient nature of the French communities in Detroit is seen in Catherine Cangany, "Fashioning Moccasins: Detroit, the Manufacturing Frontier, and the Empire of Consumption, 1701–1835," *William and Mary Quarterly* 69, no. 2 (April 2012): 265–305.

19. Witgen, *Infinity of Nations*, 277.

20. From among her children, Charlotte boasted of at least two sons, Louis Lorimier Jr. and Augustus Bougainville Lorimier, who eventually attended the U.S. Military Academy at West Point, one with the recommendation of Meriwether Lewis himself.

INDEX

Acadia, 16, 67–68, 97
Acadians
  as colonists, 159, 160, 176
  as refugees in New France, 107, 127, 134, 137, 167
Aeneid (Virgil), 15, 88, 167–68
Ahutoru, 173–74
Aleyrac, Jean-Baptiste d', 71, 76, 87–88, 89, 110, 114
Algonquins, 59, 67, 72
  See also Native Americans
alliances, British-Indian, 52, 55, 57, 61, 106
alliances, Franco-Indian
  "adoption" and, 114–17
  British invasion, 122–25
  Dieskau, Baron de, and, 53–54, 55
  La Galissonière on, 35
  Langlade, Charles-Michel Mouet de, and, 43
  legacy of, 179–90
  Ohio Country, 46
  Oswego campaign and, 79–81
  overview, 62, 63, 64
  Pickawillany and, 46, 205n27
  Treaty of Aix-la-Chapelle and, 16–18, 39
  Vaudreuil and, 106, 119
  waning of, 118–19, 124
American Revolution, 14, 143, 145, 171, 178–79, 183
Amherst, Jeffery, 93, 105–6, 124–25, 126, 127, 137, 180
Argenson, Marc-Pierre Voyer de Paulmy, Comte de, 19, 69, 83, 96, 107, 133
armée de terre. See troupes de terre (line infantry)
armies. *See* British forces; *compagnies franches de la marine*; Native Americans; *troupes de terre* (line infantry)
author's approach, 10–15

Beaujeu, Daniel-Hyacinthe-Marie Liénard de, 33, 55
Bégon family, 22
Belle-Isle, Charles-Louis-Auguste Fouquet, Duc de, 26, 106, 116–17, 120, 121
Berryer, Nicolas René, 96, 120, 121–22
Bigot, François, 53, 107, 110–11, 129–30, 131, 132, 143–44, 161
Bougainville, Louis-Antoine de
  "adoption" and, 92, 114, 115, 181, 188
  assignment to New France, 66
  Atlantic missions, 160–61, 175
  classical allusions of, 167
  discipline and, 87–88
  envoy to the French court, 120, 121, 122
  honorable conduct and, 107
  imperial reforms and, 155–56, 157–58, 162, 168, 176–77
  Kahnawake delegation and, 180–82, 188
  legacy of, 189–90
  lifestyle of, 108, 110
  Lorimier family and, 181–83, 184, 185–86, 187
  Madame de Séchelles and, 73, 86, 90, 96
  Native Americans and, 77, 81–82, 89, 104, 162–66, 169, 171
  new standards and, 123
  Pacific missions, 161–62, 164–74, 176
  parole request, 142
  promotion of, 146
  writings of, 153–55, 169, 171, 174–75
Boulay, Marquise de, 79
Bourlamaque, François-Charles de
  arrival of, 66, 67
  New France career, 77, 83, 84, 93, 106, 107, 124
  parole of, 142, 156
  promotion of, 146
Braddock, Edward, 43, 51–53, 55, 57

243

INDEX

British forces
  alliances, British-Indian, 52, 55, 57, 106
  conquest of New France, 5–6, 122–25, 133
  Fort Carillon battle, 102–6
  Fort William Henry, 86–94
  French forts and, 118–19
  naval blockade, 38
  Ohio Country and, 51–53
  Oswego supply station, 74–81
  Pickawillany assault, 41–44

Campbell, John (Earl of Loudoun), 67, 103
Canada. *See* New France (Canada)
cannibalism, ritual, 42, 44, 45, 190, 203n12
Cape Breton. *See* Louisbourg fortress
Cayugas, 12
  See also Native Americans
Céloron de Blainville, Pierre-Joseph de, 31, 33, 39, 40, 41, 49, 201n59
Chabert de Joncaire family, 44, 63, 81, 111, 115–16, 117, 131–32
  See also Joncaire Chabert (Daniel-Marie Chabert de Joncaire)
Chaussegros de Léry, Gaspard-Joseph, 59–60, 81, 83, 108, 137–39, 140, 150–51
Choiseul, Étienne François, Comte de Stainville, Duc de, 128, 133–34, 135, 137, 141, 154–55, 156–61
compagnies franches de la marine, 126–52
  "adoption" and, 114–16
  advancement opportunities for, 28, 29–30, 32–34
  background of, 13, 27–31
  battles, 51–53, 59–60, 74–80, 81, 84, 86–92
  corruption and, 32–34, 111, 127–32
  diplomatic expertise of, 29–31, 34, 36
  dissension within the, 32–34
  as distinct service, 68–69, 127
  envoys to the French court, 119–23
  honorable conduct and, 36–37, 63
  legacy of, 190
  military goals of, 50–51
  Treaty of Aix-la-Chapelle and, 17–18
  veterans, 126–27, 132–42, 149–52, 159, 161
  winter quarters and, 112–14, 113f5
  See also alliances, Franco-Indian; Bougainville, Louis-Antoine de; British forces; Native Americans; *troupes de terre* (line infantry); violence, legitimate

conduct, honorable. *See* honorable conduct
corruption, 5, 32–34, 111, 127–32, 133, 151
Coulon de Villiers, Louis, 47, 48, 50, 61
Coulon de Villiers de Jumonville, Joseph, 47–49, 145–46
croix de Saint Louis, 29–30, 36, 120, 137, 139, 140
cultural norms. *See* gift exchanges; honorable conduct; violence, legitimate

Deschamps de Boishébert et de Raffetot, Charles, 152, 159
d'Estaing, Jean Baptiste Charles-Henri Hector, Comte, 179, 180, 181, 183
Diderot, Denis, 70, 158, 167, 174, 175
Dieskau, Jean Erdman, Baron de, 41, 51, 53–55, 61, 63, 68
diplomacy. *See* alliances, British-Indian; alliances, Franco-Indian; France, imperial; gift exchanges
drunkenness, 75–79, 82, 87, 104–5, 212–13n36, 214n52
Duquesne de Menneville, Ange, Marquis de, 32, 35–36, 40, 42, 43, 46

Fort Beauséjour, 67–68
Fort Bull, 59–60, 137
Fort Carillon, 72, 98, 102–6, 121, 123, 169
Fort Duquesne, 40, 47, 51–52, 61, 118–19
Fort Frontenac, 118, 128
forts, French, 39–40, 118–19
Fort William Henry, 84, 86–92, 98–99, 104–6, 167
France, imperial
  Atlantic missions, 160–61, 175
  goals of, 34–36
  Kourou, 158–61
  overview, 7
  Pacific missions, 161–62, 164–74, 176
  reforms to, 154–58, 162, 168, 176–77
  veterans serving in, 149
  See also Bougainville, Louis-Antoine de; Louis XV; New France (Canada)
French public opinion, 20, 52, 77, 97–98
  See also Louis XV

gift exchanges
  "adoption" and, 114, 115–17
  austerity measures and, 32
  Bougainville, Louis-Antoine de, 188
  Fort Duquesne, 47
  Fort William Henry, 104–5

within French elite, 109–10
goods for loyalty, 31, 32, 111
importance of, 72, 73, 106
La Corne Saint Luc, 28–29
l'affaire du Canada and, 129–32
prisoners, 2–3, 29, 72, 81
Tahitian, 165
Vaudreuil and, 224n74
welcoming celebrations, 1, 2–3
See also diplomacy

Hendrick, King (Theyanoguin), 54, 59, 61, 207–8n50, 208n58, 208n59
honorable conduct
aristocratic values and, 19–23, 63, 68, 92–94, 123–24
compagnies franches de la marine and, 36–37, 63
conflicting views of, 36–37
court politics and, 120–23
Franco-Indian alliances and, 92–94, 100, 101, 122–24
imperial reforms and, 155–57
luxuries and, 107–10
honors of war, 93, 127, 130
Hotchig (Ochick), 76

Iliad (Homer), 3, 15
Indians, American. *See* Native Americans; *specific names of nations*
Iroquois
adoptions and, 92, 114–15, 188
Bougainville and, 163, 165
Braddock's army and, 52, 57
diplomacy and, 40, 65, 72, 104, 117–18, 122, 129
discipline and, 76, 104
Fort Duquesne and, 47–48, 49
Fort William Henry and, 80–81, 87, 91
Kahnawake delegation, 178–82, 183, 188–90
La Corne and, 29, 30
l'affaire du Canada, 132
Lake George battle and, 54
Niverville and, 31
Onoraguete, 181–82, 188, 189
Oswego campaign and, 74
Pickawillany, 41
political concerns of, 57, 59–60
Tanaghrisson, 47, 49, 50, 144
use of term, 12–13
winter quarters and, 112, 113f5
See also Native Americans

Johnson, William, Sir, 53–54, 81, 115, 150
Joncaire Chabert (Daniel-Marie Chabert de Joncaire)
alliances, Franco-Indian, 44, 63, 81, 111, 115–16
diplomacy and, 117
l'affaire du Canada, 128–29, 131–32, 136, 138, 141
return to Canada, 150–51
See also Chabert de Joncaire family
Jouy, Antoine Louis Rouillé, comte de, 32, 40, 43
Jumonville, Joseph Coulon de. *See* Coulon de Villiers de Jumonville, Joseph

Kahnawake (Sault Saint-Louis), 2, 3, 112, 112f4
Kinsenik, 71
Kourou, 158–61, 175

La Corne, Louis de, Chevalier de la Corne, 29–30
La Corne, Luc de (La Corne St. Luc), 28–29, 33, 88–89, 140, 149, 161
l'affaire du Canada, 5, 127–32, 133, 136, 138, 141, 151
La Galissonière, Roland-Michel Barrin, Marquis de, 16, 17, 30, 34, 35–36, 196n2
La Jonquière, Jacques-Pierre de Taffanel, Marquis de, 31, 35–36, 40, 41
Lake George, battle of, 53–55, 56f1, 56f2, 57, 59, 62, 81
La Milletière, sieur de, 115, 131
landscape, relationships to, 55, 56f1, 56f2, 57, 58f3
Langlade, Charles-Michel Mouet de
alliances and, 55, 63, 90, 91
assignment of, 204n16
Braddock's army and, 52
family of, 204n19
later life of, 126, 149
Pickawillany, 42–44, 45, 46, 184
slavery and, 161
violence, legitimate, and, 50–51
See also Ottawas
Legardeur de Saint Pierre, Jacques, 44, 46, 54
Léry, Jean de, 173, 174
Lévis, François Gaston de
arrival of, 66
diplomatic efforts by, 3
Fort William Henry and, 84, 87

Lévis, François Gaston de (*continued*)
  gift exchanges, 72
  l'affaire du Canada and, 130
  later life of, 142, 146, 148
  Marin de La Malgue and, 139, 149
  Native women and, 73–74
  surrender of Montreal, 10
Longueuil, Paul-Joseph Le Moyne,
    Chevalier de, 28, 90, 117, 118, 133–34
Lorimier, Charlotte Pemanpieh Bougainville, 185–90
Lorimier, Louis, 182–83, 184–89
Louisbourg fortress
  compagnies franches at, 27
  importance of, 32, 121
  return to Britain, 25, 97, 105–6
  return to Quebec, 16, 17, 38
Louisiana
  cession to Spain, 157
  fort building and, 40
  gift exchanges, 116
  Lorimier, Charlotte, 187, 189
  overview, 9, 13
  political value of, 35
Louis XV
  assassination attempt on, 95–96, 98–101, 131
  loss of Canada and, 127
  political concerns of, 66, 97–98, 131, 135–36, 151–52
  promotions by, 120–21
  scandalous behavior of, 23–26
  Treaty of Aix-la-Chapelle and, 17–18
  See also Onontio

Machault d'Arnouville, Jean-Baptiste de, 43, 67–68, 80, 84, 96
Machiqua, 2–3, 81
Malartic, Anne-Joseph-Hyppolyte de Maurès, Comte de
  New France experiences, 71, 75–76, 84, 87, 89, 100, 104, 224n74
  promotion of, 146
Marin de La Malgue, Joseph
  appeals for restitution, 138–39
  corruption and, 33, 111
  diplomatic expertise of, 30–31, 91
  later life of, 149, 151
  Ohio Country and, 46, 62–64
Massiac, Claude-Louis d'Espinchal, Marquis de, 96, 103–4
Maurepas, Jean-Frédéric Phélypeaux, Comte de, 31–32

medals, 29–30, 120, 137, 139, 140, 179–80
Memeskia (Old Briton, La Demoiselle), 39, 41–42, 44, 45, 47, 49, 190
Menominees, 2, 12
  See also Native Americans
Meux, Monsieur de, 182–83, 185, 186
Miamis
  alliances with French, 14, 63
  Memeskia (Old Britain, La Demoiselle), 39, 41–42, 44, 45, 47, 49, 190
  Pickawillany, 41–46, 49–50, 62, 184, 205n27
  trade and, 39
  See also Native Americans
Michilimackinac, 42, 43, 45, 52, 91, 104
Ministry of War
  appeals to, 120, 142–43
  assignments by, 66, 68
  Bougainville and, 120
  discipline and, 76
  finances of, 111
  management of, 69, 96
  unification with Naval Ministry, 141
  See also Naval Ministry (Ministry of the Marine)
Mississaugas, 3, 72–73, 115
  See also Native Americans
Mohawks
  alliances with French, 30, 46
  Hendrick, King (Theyanoguin), 54, 59, 61, 207–8n50, 208n58, 208n59
  Iroquois Confederacy, 12
  overview, 11
  political concerns of, 54, 59–60
  as prisoners, 31
  réserves (mission communities), 12–13
  violence, legitimate, 61, 71, 99, 162, 178
  See also Native Americans
Monongahela, battle of, 43, 51–53, 55, 60
Montaigne, Michel de, 174
Montcalm, Louis-Joseph de Saint Véran, Marquis de
  "adoption" and, 115
  arrival of, 2–3, 66–69
  assassination attempt and, 99–101
  British invasion, 121–23
  death of, 123, 145, 145f6
  diplomacy and, 2–3, 67, 68, 72, 81, 106
  discipline and, 77, 79–80, 111
  education of, 15
  extravagance of, 108–10, 111, 212–13n36
  Fort Carillon battle, 102–6

Fort William Henry, 84, 86–92, 104–5
  legacy of, 142–48
  Moras's relationship with, 85–86
  Oswego campaign, 74–80, 82
  portrait, 147f8
  son's career, 98
  Vaudreuil and, 68–69, 101–2, 106, 119, 120–23
  winter raids and, 83–84
Montcalm, Marquise de, 79, 108, 143–44
Montreal
  discipline in, 77, 90
  elites of, 22, 27
  Fort Carillon and, 103, 105
  slavery in, 82, 89
  surrender of, 5, 9–10, 93, 123–27, 130, 135
  welcoming celebrations, 1–4, 15, 67, 70–73. *See also* Vaudreuil de Cavagnal, Pierre de Rigaud, Marquis de
  See also gift exchanges; New France (Canada)
Moras, François-Marie Peyrenc de, 84–88, 90, 96, 101–2

Native Americans
  "adoption" and, 92, 114–17, 181, 188
  American Revolution and, 178–79
  assassination attempt and, 99–101
  colonial wars and, 7–8, 57, 59
  as couriers, 62
  delegations to Europe, 174
  discipline and, 75–79, 87–88, 90–94, 104–6
  distinctions between groups, 91, 217–18n104
  drunkenness, 75–79, 82, 87, 104–5
  Fort Bull attack, 59–60
  Fort Duquesne and, 118–19
  Fort William Henry, 86–92, 93–94
  French elites and, 64, 71, 75–81, 175–76
  Jumonville assassination and, 47, 49, 50
  l'affaire du Canada and, 129–32
  Lake George, battle of, 53–55, 59, 81
  lead plaques and, 39
  Lorimier, Louis, 181–82
  military goals of, 29, 45, 47, 49–51, 53, 207n40
  Monongahela, battle of, 51–53
  Montcalm and, 79–81, 87
  New France legacy among, 178–84, 189–90

Ohio Country, 1, 40, 46, 205n27
  Oswego campaign, 74–81
  prisoners and, 92
  relationship to the land, 55, 57–58, 58f3
  slavery among, 87–88, 92
  spoils of war and, 87
  terms used in text for, 12–13, 192n7
  trade, 39, 40, 41–44, 45, 72, 74, 189
  Treaty of Aix-la-Chapelle and, 16–17
  tree writings by, 45–46, 61
  view of French behavior, 102, 117–18
  waning of French influence with, 91, 94, 124
  at welcoming celebrations (1756), 67
  winter quarters and, 113f5
  See also alliances, British-Indian; alliances, Franco-Indian; race; violence, legitimate; *specific battles*; *specific names of nations*
Naval Ministry (Ministry of the Marine)
  appeals to, 120
  compagnies franches and, 13
  finances of, 32, 63, 122, 129–30, 139
  honorable conduct and, 34
  imperial expansion and, 50
  importance of, 35
  leadership problems of, 69, 84–86, 96, 102
  management of, 69
  reassignments, 149, 150, 159
  unification with Ministry of War, 141
  See also Ministry of War
New France (Canada)
  corruption in, 32–33
  cultural fidelity in, 175
  envoys to the French court, 120–23
  expense of maintaining, 31–32, 39, 63
  exports of, 32
  fort building by, 62
  forts, losses of, 118–19
  French impressions of, 69–74
  hierarchical society of, 27, 200n40
  influence on imperial France, 9
  legacy of, 178, 182–84, 189–90
  loss of, 5–6, 121–26
  military goals of, 35–36
  Native couriers, 62
  trade, 39, 40, 41–44, 45, 72, 74
  transition to transatlantic conflict, 4
  use of term, 13
  wealth disparities in, 110–11, 117–18
  See also Louisbourg fortress; Montreal; Ohio Country

Nipissings
  battles and, 47, 54, 59, 87–88, 104
  diplomacy and, 2–3, 67, 72, 81, 115
  See also Native Americans
Nissowaquet (La Fourche), 43
Niverville, Joseph Boucher de, 30, 31
Niverville Montizambert, Pierre-Louis Boucher de, 31
Noailles, Adrien Maurice, Maréchal-Duc de, 34–35
nobles, French, 18–23, 25–26, 35, 36
  See also troupes de terre (line infantry)

Odyssey (Homer), 15
Ohio Country
  1753–1756 war, 1, 38–41, 62, 63
  British armies in, 51–54
  Fort Bull attack, 59–60
  Fort Duquesne, 52
  forts, losses of, 118–19
  Jumonville assassination and, 47, 49, 50
  Monongahela, 43, 51–53, 55, 60
  Pickawillany, 41–44, 46, 49–50, 62, 184, 205n27
  See also Braddock, Edward; Dieskau, Jean Erdman, Baron de
Ojibwas, 2, 42, 44, 45–46, 91, 165
  See also Native Americans
Oneidas, 12, 39, 44, 49, 59, 70–71, 118
  See also Native Americans
Onondagas, 12, 30, 40, 73, 81, 91, 118
  See also Native Americans
Onontio, 18, 30, 39, 67, 91
  See also Louis XV; Vaudreuil de Cavagnal, Pierre de Rigaud, Marquis de
Onoraguete, 181–82, 188, 189
order of Saint Louis, 29–30, 36, 120, 137, 139, 140
Oswego campaign, 74–75
Ottawas
  Bougainville and, 162, 165
  Braddock's army and, 52
  diplomacy and, 2, 115
  discipline and, 76, 77, 92, 104
  Pickawillany, 42, 43–46, 47, 62, 63
  political concerns of, 11, 14, 49–51, 91
  See also Langlade, Charles-Michel Mouet de; Native Americans

Péan, Michel-Jean-Hugues de, 111, 120, 152
Pennahouel, 71

Pickawillany, 41–44, 46, 49–51, 53, 62–63, 184, 205n27
Pompadour, Marquise de, 19, 21, 23–26, 73, 96, 98
Potowatomis, 45, 52, 205n231
  See also Native Americans
Pouchot, Pierre, 108, 114, 142–44, 171
Praslin, César Gabriel de Choiseul, Duc de, 161–62
prisoners
  Fort William Henry, 87–89
  in gift exchanges, 2–3, 29, 72
  Oswego campaign, 80, 81
  redeeming of, 89, 104, 217n97
  slavery and, 80, 82, 89, 92, 104
public opinion, 20–21, 48, 144–46

race
  "adoption" and, 115
  commoner status and, 22
  distinctions between groups, 91
  hierarchies of, 166, 169
  intermarriages, 181–83, 184, 185–86
  mixed, 22, 43, 44, 115
  slavery and, 88, 217n92
Raymond, Charles de, 32–34
Rayneval, Conrad Alexandre Gérard de, 179, 181–82
Rigaud de Vaudreuil, François Pierre de, 66–67, 84, 91, 118, 139–40, 152
Rouillé. See Jouy, Antoine Louis Rouillé, comte de
Rousseau, Jean-Jacques, 174, 175

Saint Véran, Marquise de, 108, 109, 143–44
Sault Saint-Louis (Kahnawake), 2, 112f4, 113f5
Saxe, Maurice de, 19, 25, 26, 55, 93, 96
scalping, 29, 71, 82, 93, 217n97
  See also violence, legitimate
Scarouady (Monacatothé), 39, 57
Séchelles, Marie-Hélène Hérault de, 73, 86, 90, 185–86
Senecas, 12, 44, 63, 114, 115, 131–32
  See also Native Americans
Seven Years' War, 4–15, 41
  See also specific names; specific topics
Sevigné, Madame de, 21
Shawnees, 184–87, 188, 189
  See also Native Americans
Shingas, 52
slavery, 73, 80, 82, 88–89, 92, 104, 159

Tahiti, 164–74, 168f9, 170f10, 170f11, 172f12
Tahitians, 165, 166, 167–69, 171–74, 172f12, 236n43
Tanaghrisson, 47, 49, 50, 144
Ticonderoga. *See* Fort Carillon
trade, 39, 40, 41–44, 45, 72, 74, 189
trading posts, 32, 40, 184
Treaty of Aix-la-Chapelle, 13, 16–18, 38
Treaty of Paris (1763), 4, 137, 148, 182
troupes de terre (line infantry)
"adoption" and, 116–17
advancement opportunites for, 20, 26, 36, 66
arrival of, 2–3
background of, 18–23
commitment to New France, 119
defined, 13
discipline and, 74–80
as distinct service, 68–69
envoys to the French court, 119–23
first impressions of North Americans, 69–74
Fort Carillon battle, 102–6
Fort William Henry, 84, 86–94
gift exchanges and, 116–17
ignorance of, 68
lifestyle of, 107–11, 117
military goals of, 68
opinions of North Americans, 85–86, 116–17
Oswego campaign, 74–80, 81–83
public opinion and, 19–20
return to France, 126–27
Treaty of Aix-la-Chapelle and, 17–18
valor and, 36–37
veterans, 142–48
wealth anxieties of, 36
winter quarters and, 106–8, 112–14, 113f5
winter raids and, 83–84
See also alliances, Franco-Indian; *compagnies franches de la marine*; honorable conduct; nobles, French; violence, legitimate
troupes franches de la marine (colonial regulars), 2–3
Tuscaroras, 12
See also Native Americans

valor. *See* honorable conduct; violence, legitimate
Vaudreuil de Cavagnal, Pierre de Rigaud, Marquis de
1756 preparations, 65–66
"adoption" and, 115

discipline and, 77–78
extravagance of, 108, 110, 111
Fort William Henry and, 84, 87, 90–91
Franco-Indian alliances and, 62, 119
l'affaire du Canada (1761–1763), 127–32
Louisbourg fortress, 105–6
Marin de La Malgue and, 139
Monongahela, battle of, 53–54, 55
Montcalm and, 68–69, 79–80, 101–2, 119, 120–23
Montreal, surrender of, 9–10
veterans, 126–27, 132–52, 159, 161
violence, legitimate, 38–64
brutalities, minimizing of, 19–20
cannibalism, ritual, 42, 44, 45
colonial violence and, 20
deflecting of blame, 93
discipline and, 78
executions, 96, 100–101
Fort Bull attack, 59–60
Fort Carillon battle, 104–6
Fort William Henry, 86–94
French military reforms and, 18–19
honorable conduct and, 92–94, 100, 101
Indian expectations and, 29
internal uses of, 20
irregular warfare, 42, 55, 82–83, 92–94
Jumonville assassination and, 47–49
Lake George, battle of, 53–55
land claims and, 39–40
legitimate war, 19
massacres, 59–60, 87–88, 89, 92
Monongahela, battle of, 51–53, 60
Native perspectives, 55, 57, 59, 208n59
Pickawillany, 41–46
prisoners and, 82
revenge, 47, 48, 49, 76, 87, 206n38
ruins as markers, 45–46, 60
scalping and, 29, 71, 82, 93, 217n97
tactical brutality, 19, 196n2, 207n47
technologies and, 19
trade and, 41
tree writings, 45–46, 61
varied interpretations of, 50–51, 60–61, 63–64
War of Austrian Succession (1744–1748), 93
See also cultural norms
Voltaire, 4, 9, 163

warfare. *See compagnies franches de la marine*; honorable conduct; Native Americans; *troupes de terre* (line infantry); violence, legitimate; *specific battles*
War of Austrian Succession (1744–1748), 6, 16, 17–19, 36, 43, 82–84, 93
  See also Treaty of Aix-la-Chapelle
Washington, George, 41, 44, 47–49, 50, 54, 145
Wolfe, James, 121, 123, 133, 145, 146f7

women
  Canadian, 72–73
  French elite, 21
  French wives, 200n40
  Native Americans, 39, 46, 59, 72–74, 91, 165, 184
  Tahitian, 165, 166, 167–68, 173
  See also specific names
Wyandots, 39, 52
  See also Native Americans

www.ingramcontent.com/pod-product-compliance
Lightning Source LLC
Chambersburg PA
CBHW021348230426
43666CB00006B/445